# A DICTIONARY OF INDONESIAN ISLAM

Howard M. Federspiel teaches political science at the Ohio State University, Newark, Ohio 43055.

# A DICTIONARY OF INDONESIAN ISLAM

by

**Howard M. Federspiel**

Ohio University Center for International Studies
Monographs in International Studies

Southeast Asia Series Number 94
Athens, Ohio 1995

Center for International Studies
Ohio University
Athens, OH 45701

Printed in the United States of America


02 01 00 99 98 97 96 5 4 3 2

The Monographs in International Studies Series is printed on recycled acid-free paper ∞

LIBRARY OF CONGRESS CATALOGING-IN-PUBLICATION DATA

Federspiel, Howard M.
A dictionary of Indonesian Islam / by Howard M. Federspiel.
p. cm. – (Monographs in International Studies. Southeast Asia series; no 94)
Includes bibliographical references.
ISBN 0-89680-182-9
1. Islam–Indonesia–Dictionaries. 2. Indonesian language–Dictionaries–English. 3. Islam–Dictionaries. I. Title. II. Series.
BP63.I5F43 1995
297'.09598–dc20 94–40777
CIP

# CONTENTS

# PREFACE

Between 1985 and 1990 I reviewed over 300 Indonesian-language books, magazines and manuscripts concerning Indonesian Islam. The work was rewarding; I found it enjoyable to study several aspects of Indonesian Islam which previously I had not investigated fully. I came away with a new appreciation of the strength of Islam and of Islam's particular historical and cultural manifestations in Southeast Asia.

The intensive reading made me acutely aware of some deficiencies in the general research materials concerning Indonesian Islam. Perhaps the most pressing need is for standard reference works to provide scholars with basic information. Certainly there are Indonesian and European language dictionaries, encyclopedias, and other reference works on Islam which can be tapped for some information. However, most researchers working on Indonesian subjects are untrained in Middle Eastern research sources and are unaware of all but a few, such as the *Encyclopedia of Islam*. This is particularly true of many scholars in the social sciences, where Islamic manifestations in society and political life are especially germane. In fact, only a few scholars would know the reference materials in jurisprudence, Tradition study, Qur'an, and mysticism which offer real perspectives into Islamic dynamics. Of course, even such sources do not cover the special cases where Indonesian Islam has its own terms and concepts that are not found in standard sources; the Islamicists who prepared them usually describe the central Islamic world and often ignore peripheral areas such as Indonesia.

Still, despite the foregoing remarks, the record is not devoid of accomplishment and promise. Western scholars know more about Indonesian Islam today than they did twenty years ago. In particular, one can cite the work of Australians (Johns and Brakel), the Dutch (Breunissen and Steenbrink), Indonesians (Abdullah and Kuntowijoyo), and Americans (Woodward and

Hefner). Published works together with student papers, theses, and dissertations from Indonesia, Europe, and North America have produced a great deal of meaningful research, a trove of modern knowledge on Islam.

In contrast to general studies of Indonesian Islam, preparation of reference works is less well advanced, although some progress has been made, especially by Indonesian writers. One can point to *Al- Quraan dan Terjemahnya* (The Qur'an and Its Translation), the *Ensiklopedi Islam di Indonesia* (The Encyclopedia of Islam in Indonesia), and *Leksikon Islam* (Islamic Lexicon). These three works represent the heart of an effort that is helping to define the data base and to set the standards needed for an Indonesian national understanding of Islam. All of these works are in the national language, Bahasa Indonesia, and addressed to the general Indonesian Muslim public rather than international scholars.

This volume seeks to address this situation in part. It is a dictionary designed for researchers using Indonesian Muslim materials. Some will read works in the Indonesian language; others will read works in European languages. Accordingly this dictionary is intended to provide the references necessary for understanding the technical terms in Indonesian Islam. It does not assume any great understanding of Islam on the part of the reader, even though some of the entries do deal with complex matters of doctrine and practice. Still, there is an effort to provide basic information and clarity that nonspecialists on Islam should find useful. In short, this work will serve as a general reference work explaining words, terms, and expressions used in Indonesian Islam.

This dictionary is the work of some thirty-five years of study. It would be difficult to acknowledge all of the people and institutions with whom I worked over the years. People and institutions in Asia, Europe, and North America were involved. I can give only a general blanket acknowledgement of their assistance; fortunately most have been thanked in other writings for more specific assistance.

The major part of the assembly of the dictionary was done at the Institute of Islamic Studies, McGill University, Montreal, while I was a visiting scholar during the 1991-92 academic year. The library director, Adam Gacek, and his staff assisted me in locating materials. I extend them my thanks. The Indonesian students under a joint project of the Canadian International Development Agency and the Institut Agama Islam Nasional (the CIDA-IAIN project) at McGill provided me with numerous ideas in their papers and class discussion; they have my good wishes in becoming the next generation of scholars in the national Islamic Studies institutions. I extend thanks to Nurcholis Madjied, who also was a visiting scholar at McGill and who gave me new insights and perceptions about Indonesian Islam through his lectures, writings and discussions. Further I would like to express my appreciation to Uner Turgay and Charles Adams, along with all the faculty and staff members of the Institute of Islamic Studies, who made my year at McGill such a rewarding experience. Finally, I would like to express my appreciation to James L. Cobban, Gillian Berchowitz, Kent Mulliner, and Lian The at Ohio University who arranged the publication of this document.

# INTRODUCTION

The purpose of this dictionary is twofold: first, to provide basic material useful in reading Indonesian texts dealing with Islam and to provide a general source about Indonesian Islam for students and scholars doing research on Indonesia where reference to Islam appears. It does not explain terms in detail, but gives basic information so that the reader can quickly identify terms, phrases, concepts, and personalities. A review of approximately fifty texts and three major journals dealing with contemporary Islam and with the current Muslim views of historical development of Islam is provided in Indonesian. The result is some 1800 entries and 450 cross references which provide basic information to explain references made in most books and articles written about Indonesian Islam, in both Indonesian and Western languages.

The dictionary does not attempt to replace the standard Indonesian-English dictionaries in common use, such as Echols and Shadily or Wojowasito and Poerwadarminta. Those dictionaries refer to the general use of language; material in them is not ordinarily repeated in *A Dictionary of Indonesian Islam* unless it deals specifically with Islam in Indonesia. By the same token the dictionary does not seek to show common language usage, since other sources cover such usage quite well. This work may be considered a supplement to other dictionaries, or a special tool for dealing with Islamic terminology.

## Format

The following format is used in the presentation of entries in this dictionary.

1 2 3 4
Term (Language derivation) Field of Knowledge Definition

5
Indonesian Usage

*Illustration*

1 2 3 4

**Berhala** (In.) Relig. Idols; idolatry.
5 Usage: *menjembah* ___, the worship of idols.

In the illustration *berhala* is the term being described. The parenthetical reference (In.) indicates that the term is an Indonesian word, while the citation "Relig." indicates the term is concerned with religious subject matter. The term is defined in English as meaning "idols; idolatry." In Indonesian usage the term is combined with *menjembah*, i.e., "to worship," to show its ordinary use in Indonesian. All abbreviations and references are explained further in the explanation below.

**Terms**

The terms identified in this dictionary were gleaned from a wide reading of Indonesian Muslims writings on history, Qur'an, Traditions, jurisprudence, Islamic belief and practice, development studies, and contemporary affairs. Writings since 1970 constituted the major source of entries. A selected group of source materials is included at the end of this introduction.

1. Terms included in this dictionary reflect the spelling in which they are found in the Indonesian sources. Many times that spelling may differ from the common spellings of words in the language from which particular words are derived, especially English, Javanese, and Arabic.

*Illustration*
**Kromo** (In.); krama (Jav)....

In the illustration the word *kromo* is used in Indonesian to indicate the high form of Javanese in which an inferior addresses a superior. In Javanese the term is spelled differently and pronounced somewhat differently. In this dictionary the emphasis is on Indonesian, so the Indonesian spelling indicates the term being defined.

2. Names of Indonesian personalities are considered correct in their Indonesian spelling, even when derived from Arabic names; no Arabic transliteration is provided since the name is correct by definition. On the other hand, genuine Arabic names are given in their Indonesian spelling, but an Arabic transliteration follows for clarity.

*Illustration*
**Soorkati, Ahmad** (In.) ....
**Al Sayuthi, Jalaluddin** (Ar: jalalūddīn as-sayūṭī)....

Titles used with personal names are enclosed with a set of brackets to indicate that they are not a part of the name itself. This is done only where the name is fully identified, but is not done on cross references.

*Illustrations*
**Gresik, (Sunan)** (In.) Biog. ....
**Malik Ibrahim**. *See* **Gresik, Sunan.**

3. Terms are placed in alphabetical order. In words where a long vowel is indicated with double letters (aa, ii, uu), the word is placed as if the vowel were single (which, in reality, it is). Words containing either an Arabic "alif" or "‘ayn" are placed in context by ignoring their markers (‘ and ’) and using the following vowel only. This follows the Indonesian and English practice for listing such words.

*Illustration*
I‘tiqad is the same as Itiqad for placement.

4. Terms sometimes have different spellings in various sources because different transliteration systems were used in

rendering terms from foreign languages; this is particularly true in the transliteration of Arabic. In Arabic the use of symbols is markedly different from the Latin characters used in Indonesian. Grammatical structure is based on different principles. In this dictionary the general principle is to present the variations generally used and to list the term according to the following hierarchy of options: (1) Indonesian spelling in the official Indonesian dictionary *(Kamus Besar Bahasa Indonesia)*; (2) Indonesian spelling according to Department of Religion's dictionaries and handbooks; (3) rendition according to common transliteration systems; (4) other variations.

*Illustration*
**Ramadan**; Ramadhan (In.); Ramalan (Ar: ramaḍān)

In the illustration "Ramadan" is the accepted Indonesian dictionary spelling, while "Ramadhan" is found in Department of Religion documents and "Ramalan" is a local variation of the transliterated term from Arabic. All three terms appear in Indonesian Muslim writing, with the preference given to "Ramadan." Elsewhere in this dictionary only the term "Ramadan" is used, to prevent confusion.

5. The first term of an entry is given in bold print. Other terms following are in regular print. See last illustration. Book and Journal titles are given in italics.

*Illustration*
*Jami'ul Bayan* (Ar: jāmi' al-bayān). Lit. title.

6. Terms usually are defined only once. Where several versions of a term exist, only the preferred spelling receives a full description. Secondary spellings are cross-referenced.

*Illustration*
**Karamah** Spelling variant. *See* **Keramat**.

Here the term is defined under Keramat, so the entry at Karamah refers to that definition.

7. Word particles are indicated when it helps clarify a term's meaning, as in the case of language articles, special modifiers and titles.

*Illustrations*
**Al.** Arabic prefix. See following word.
**Izzuddin.** ... Honorific for princes and prestigious scholars of Islam. See following word.

8. Abbreviations and acronyms are listed but not immediately defined. Instead they are cross-referenced to their full phrases and names.

*Illustration*
**Persis.** *See* **Persatuan Islam.**

9. The placement of terms is by alphabetical order as would occur in an English-language dictionary. Terms are not presented by root words as in Indonesian or by radicals as in Arabic. Placements usual to Indonesian and Arabic styles would be difficult and confusing, particularly since only a few users of this dictionary could be expected to have enough knowledge of both languages to use it effectively. Straight alphabetical style seemed the best approach.

*Illustration*
Menghisab, not hisab (In.)
Tarāwiḥ, not r-u-ḥ (Ar.)

**Language derivation**

Terms originate in a number of different languages and knowledge of that information is often useful or even important to the dictionary user. This information is the second element in the entry and is found in the parenthesis ( ) immediately following the term. Abbreviations are used in accordance with the following key:

| | | | |
|---|---|---|---|
| Aceh. | Acehnese | Batak | Batak |
| Ar. | Arabic | Bugi. | Buginese |

| | | | |
|---|---|---|---|
| Chin. | Chinese | Eng. | English |
| Dutch | Dutch | Ger. | German |
| In. | Indonesian | San. | Sanskrit |
| Jap. | Japanese | Sun. | Sundanese |
| Jav. | Javanese | Urdu | Urdu |
| Min. | Minangkabaui | | |

1. Terms from Arabic constitute a complex problem, primarily because of the passage of Arabic words into Bahasa Indonesia. The problem involves three different sets of terms originating from Arabic. First, a large number of words fully accepted into general Indonesian vocabulary are derived from or adopted from Arabic. Examples are *kabar*, (news) and *hayat* (life). These words have a daily Indonesian use which clearly transcends any particular Islamic usage. In preparing the dictionary these words are considered to be Indonesian words. Of these terms only those with specific Islamic usage are included in this dictionary and are labeled as Indonesian. In some cases the Arabic root word is included for clarity, if relevant. Second, another large number of terms from Arabic exist which deal with Islamic matters—worship, belief and practice—but they have not yet been considered by compilers of Indonesian dictionaries. For this dictionary these terms are acknowledged as Arabic and labeled as such. The third set of Arabic works are those brought into Indonesian texts by writers for literary and religious reference. These are also indicated as Arabic and so labeled.

I have attempted to differentiate among the three categories. Terms include the spelling of government sources where available, but other spellings are included as well. The following illustration shows a case where an official Indonesian spelling and several other variations exist that were derived from Arabic.

*Illustration*
**Berkat** (In.); barkat, barakat, barakah (Ar: barakah)

Here *berkat* is the spelling in the official dictionary, while the other three forms seem to be derived from general transliterations of Arabic into Indonesian. As such the standard Arabic transliteration in English is shown for clarity.

2. Transliteration from Arabic to Indonesian follows several different schemes. That commonly used in Indonesian is found in *Quran dan Terjemahnya*, included here for general reference, which covers well over half of the cases. There have been some attempts to standardize transliteration, but scholars have not yet abandoned the several competing systems. Letters whose values do not change between languages are not included in the following chart. The common Anglo-American transliteration values from Arabic to English are given as well.

| Arabic symbol | Arabic name | Indo. Trans. | Engl. Trans. |
|---|---|---|---|
| خ | khā' | kh | kh |
| ض | ḍād | dh | ḍ |
| ط | thā' | th | ṭ |
| ص | ṣad | sh | ṣ |
| ظ | ẓa | zh | ẓ |
| غ | ghayn | gh | gh |
| ذ | dhal | dz | dh |
| ش | shīn | sy | sh |
| ث | tha' | ts | th |
| ز | zāy | z | z |
| ق | qāf | q | q |
| ه | hā' | h | h |
| ح | ḥā' | h | ḥ |
| ا | hamzah | / | ' |

| | | | |
|---|---|---|---|
| ع | ‘ayn | ‘ | ‘ |
| آ | alif | aa | ā |
| ي | yā’ | ii | ī |
| و | wāw | uu | ū |

The modifier of the noun is added to the previous word.

*Illustration*
**Tafsirul Manar** (In.) (Ar: tafsīr al-manār)

In this case the Arabic *al-* is added to the preceding word as *ul.*

The Arabic ending on names indicating "from" is transliterated into Indonesian both as "y" and as "i," so that Ibnu Arabi and Ibnu Araby are both common. For consistency the "i" is used in this dictionary, unless the "y" has clear preference in a particular case of usage. Sometimes a dash (-) is placed between two syllables to indicate an important division of the word into syllables. Often the consonants are difficult to understand without it.

*Illustration*
**Al Kas-syaf** (Ar: kashshaf)

In this dictionary when defining Arabic words the English transliteration system indicated above is used in parenthesis.

*Illustration*
**Ilmu Tasawwuf** (In.) (Ar: ‘ilm at-tasawwuf)

The most common difficulty in transliterating Arabic into Indonesian centers on the following:

a. Confusion between the Arabic *kaf* and *qaf.* Indonesian language specialists have moved nearly everything to Indonesian "k" leaving very few words with "q." Muslim writers tend to differentiate, using the *qaf* as "q" when they transliterate from Arabic. It is particularly confusing when an Arabic word has been accepted into Indonesian with a "k" but a transliteration of the same word shows up with a "q."

*Illustration*
**Taklid** (In.) taqlid (Ar: taqlīd)

b. Confusion with the Arabic *alif/hamza* and *ayn*. Indonesian language specialists tend to eliminate the symbol for *hamza*, (') altogether. They eliminate the *ayn* at the beginning of the word and substitute a "k" when it appears in the middle or end of the word. Indonesian Muslim writers generally use no symbol to indicate *alif* at the beginning of a word and a (') to indicate an *ayn* at the beginning of a word and both an *hamza* and an *ayn* in the middle of the word and an *ayn* at the end of a word.

*Illustration*
(*alif* at the beginning of a word)
Allah (In.) (Ar: Allah) ....
(*ain* at the beginning of a word)
Adat (In.); 'adat (Ar: 'ādah) ....
(*alif* in the middle of a word)
Makmum (In.) (Ar: ma'mūm)
(*ain* in the middle of a word)
Iktikad (In.); i'tiqad (Ar: i'tiqād) ....
(*ain* at the end of a word)
Ijmak (In.) ijma' (Ar: ijmā')

3. Confusion with the Arabic letters *za*, ẓ and *dha*. Indonesian language specialists make them all "z" Indonesian Muslim writers differentiate rendering the "za" as a "z," the ẓ as *zh* and the *dh* as *dz*.

*Illustration*
zina (In.) zinah (Ar: zinā) ....
zalim (In.) zhalim (Ar: ẓālim) ....
zimmi (In.) dzimmi (Ar: dhimmī) ....

3. Indonesian Muslims use a wide number of Arabic terms to express Islamic concepts, but they are not exclusive in

using Arabic for that purpose. They also use many Indonesian terms derived from Sanskrit as alternates, or sometimes, as preferred terms. This is especially noticeable in theological terms where the Hundred Beautiful Names (asmaul husna) are usually given in their Arabic forms, although many of those names have Indonesian equivalents in words derived from Sanskrit.

*Illustrations*
Al 'Ali (Ar: al-'alī)
Yang Maha Tinggi (In.)

Both terms mean "God, the Most High." Indonesian Muslim writers draw on both languages here. Further, apparently as part of the learning process, there is some tendency to explain some matters in a non-Arabic vocabulary as a means of increasing comprehension among learners. Still Arabic terms express Islamic identification and I have made a conscientious attempt to use them. The use of the Arabic term *Musabaqah Tilawatil Qur'an* for the "Qur'an Recitation Competition" shows this tendency.

Indonesian national efforts are moving away from the use of Arabic and toward greater Indonesianization of Arabic terms as well as showing a preference for Western terms and phrases. The Indonesianization of terms, in spelling in particular, runs counter to the use of Arabic, particularly by substituting "o" for "u" and making the "q" and "k" indistinguishable (see above). The trend away from Arabic also can be seen in the emphasis on Sanskrit, as in the emphasis on *Tuhan*, rather than "Allah," for the word "God."

**Field of Knowledge**

The third element of an entry concerns the field of knowledge to which the term relates. This is found immediately after the listing of the term and its language derivation. This is also an abbreviation of one of twenty-three different subject areas. The abbreviations, the full name of the field of knowledge, and a general description of the field of knowledge follows:

Anthro. Anthropology. Terms, names, and concepts which are characteristic of a particular culture, mostly in the Muslim world. Terms common to Indonesian culture or one of the Indonesian subcultures, including customary law (adat).

Arch. Architecture. Names of prominent structures in Islam, such as mosques, and prominent buildings in Indonesia.

Assn. Associations. Names of Indonesian Muslim organizations of the twentieth century.

Biog. Biographical name. Prominent Muslim scholars past and present; prominent religious activists past and present; key Muslims from Islamic history; prominent Indonesian Muslim scholars, past and present; prominent Indonesian Muslim activists; prominent rulers from Islamic history; prominent Dutch personalities of the colonial era relating to Islam; prominent figures from Indonesian history with reference to Islam; and prominent Western scholars writing on Islam.

Cal. Calendar. Dates, terms, names, and concepts relating to Muslim concepts of time and the significance of certain days and months. Includes holidays and feast days.

Doct. Doctrine. Terms, names, and concepts describing the major points of Islamic belief and practice, especially eschatology, philosophy and philosophic movements, non-human creatures, concepts of revelation and prophetship; names of sects reflecting doctrinal differences in Islam.

Econ. Economics. Financial institutions and concepts in Muslim culture.

Educ. Education. Terms, names, and concepts in Muslim education, including names of educational institutions common in the Muslim world; classifications of knowledge.

| | |
|---|---|
| Expres. | Religious expression. Phrases and epithets in common or special use by Muslims as a means of expressing religious meaning. |
| Gen. Vocab. | General Vocabulary. Terms of importance enjoying general usage in Arabic or Indonesian, but without specific meaning in any of the other subject areas. |
| Geog. | Geography. Place names of importance in Islamic and Indonesian history. |
| Hist. | History. Terms of importance, concepts, and keys to periods of Islamic history; names of kingdoms, empires, and other important political jurisdictions in the Muslim past; documents used for the telling of history to new generations; terms and concepts from the Dutch colonial era; and common designations of historical eras and epochs. |
| Juris. | Jurisprudence. Terms common in Muslim jurisprudence (fikih), particularly relating to marriage, divorce, separation and inheritance; matters concerning prayer, its preparation, its undertaking and its proper observance; concepts of sin and sinful behavior; alms, poor tax and gifts to the poor; financial matters countenanced or not acceptable; punishment; matters relating to the pilgrimage; women's behavior and clothing; burial matters; law sects and schools. |
| Lang. | Language. Names of important languages carrying Islamic significance; concepts and terms connected with literature and literary forms; and concepts of language usage, especially in Indonesian and Arabic. |
| Lit. title. | Literary Title. Prominent books used in Muslim history; journals, newspapers and magazines carry- |

ing an Islamic theme in twentieth-century Indonesia; and special titles related to Indonesian Islam.

Myst. Mysticism. Concepts, words and practices used in the study and understanding of mysticism by Muslims; expressions used in mystical literature serving as code words for mystical expression; the names of key Islamic mystical orders of importance in Indonesia.

Pol. Politics. Political symbols, special Muslim terms used in a political sense in Indonesia; political movements related to Indonesian Islam; and the political offices of the Indonesian government.

Pop. Islam. Popular Islam. Terms describing beliefs and practices among Muslims in general, usually undertaken without regard to scriptural or doctrinal support; special celebrations and rites undertaken among Muslims, often in addition or in place of prescribed religious practices; and concepts calling for the use of supernatural power for the use of the petitioner.

Qur. Qur'an, the primary scripture of Islam. Names and content of the chapters (surah) of the Qur'an; special terms used in the assembly and description of the Qur'an; names of prophets and prominent people mentioned in the Qur'an; and usage of the Qur'an.

Relig. Religion. Terms describing various religious traditions, generally including Islam.

Theo. Theology. Names of God; and concepts relating to the nature of God.

Title. Titles of Personal Respect; and titles of office in Islam and in Southeast Asia.

Trad. Traditions (hadith) or record of the Prophet (sunnah). Terms relating to the collection and analysis of the reports in early Islam concerning the words and actions of the Prophet Muhammad; classifications of Traditions; and classifications of the Way of the Prophet.

**Definitions**

The fourth element of an entry is the definition itself.

1. Some entries list dates, particularly those dealing with biography and history. Where the Muslim system of dating is used, an "H" is listed after the date to indicate "Hijrah," which is the common Arabic designator. When the Western system of dating is used, which is most often, the date stands by itself, which it normally would in an English-language publication, which this is. The practice also follows the general Indonesian style, except among Indonesian Muslim writers writing about Islamic subjects.

*Illustration*
**Maturidi** ... Biog. (d. 944). Major Sunni theologian, who ... determined Sunni standards ... in the tenth century.

2. In the definitions references are made to particular periods of time and eras both in Islamic history and in Indonesian history. While an attempt is made to include actual time references, the general time references for the various eras are listed below.

(a) Islamic history

Classical age of Islam (612 to 1250)
Middle period of Islam (1250 to 1850)
Modern period of Islam (1850 to the present)

(b) Indonesian History

Nationalist era (1908 to 1945)

Independence period (1945 to present)
Japanese period (1942 to 1945)
Period of the revolution (1945 to 1949)
Liberal democracy era (1950 to 1957)
Guided democracy era (1957 to 1966)
Old Order era (1945 to 1966)
New Order Era (1966 to present)

3. Some terms have more than one relevant definition. In such cases, each meaning is given and is indicated by the appropriate numbers, i.e., 1., 2., ....

*Illustration*
**Khalwat** ... 1. Myst. Removing oneself from external distractions to center on worship of God ... 2. Juris. For people to go into private ... often to undertake unauthorized sexual relations.

4. Some terms are introductory to a group of specific items or people and are followed by a list of proper names.

*Illustration*
**Masjid**. .... The Islamic house of worship and local center of religious activity. ....
___ Masjid Al Aksa. A famous mosque in Jerusalem ....
___ Masjid Agung. An eighteenth century mosque at Yogyakarta ....
___ Masjidil Haram. The Great Mosque in Makkah which contains the Kabah.

5. When explaining terms, names and words used for the explanations are rendered in their Indonesian spelling rather than in the spelling of the original language.

*Illustration*
**Shiffin** .... The site of a battle in 657 between the forces of Ali and Mu'awiyah, wherein the latter defeated the former and consolidated the Umawi kingdom over the early Muslim community.

The names "Ali," "Mu'awiyah" and "Umawi," are all spelled as they are in Indonesian, rather than the transliteration into English from Arabic. See guidelines for language usage above.

6. Finally, in some cases, antonyms and synonyms are provided as assistance to the reader.

*Illustration*
**Akaid**, akidah ... Correct belief. Syn: arkanul Islam.

**Indonesian language usage**

The fifth element of some entries is listed separately below the definition and is clearly marked with the word "usage."

1. In this section actual usage of the term in its Indonesian language context is shown. In particular noun markers and verb selection, which are common features of Indonesian language structure, are given. Such presentation is common in Indonesian language dictionaries.

*Illustration*
**Percaya**. ... Faith, belief in God.
*Usage*: *ke___an*, belief(s).

**Pahala**. ... Merit for certain pious actions, usually seen in religious terms. ....
*Usage*: *ber___*, to be involved in activities that gain religious merit.

In the first illustration the noun construction is shown for the term *percaya*, in which the word "faith" is transformed into "belief." In the second case the term *pahala* is shown in one of its verb forms indicating that a person is actually undertaking that action. These illustrations show general Indonesian grammar at work.

2. Further, common patterns for comprehension and colloquial patterns are shown. This becomes important because some of the terms are Arabic forms being brought into

Indonesian, so that occasionally mixing of the language forms is done.

*Illustration*
**Wudu** .... The lesser ablution ....
*Usage*: *rukun* ___, the rite of ritual washing; *menbatalkan* ___ to negate purification [by some unclean act].

3. The presentation of terms is listed according to a three-fold category. Verbal forms of the term (e.g., ber___, men___, meng___) and noun forms (e.g., ke___an, peng___) are listed first. Phrases and idiomatic expressions beginning with the term itself are listed second. Other phrases and expressions in which the term appears are listed third. Alphabetical order is used in all three cases.

*Illustration*
**Tafsir** (In.) (Ar: tafsīr) Qur. A genre of religious literature that provides commentary on the structure, language and usage of the Qur'an.
*Usage*: *men___kan ayat-ayat suci*, to undertake commentary on the verses of the Qur'an. ___ menafsirkan, to undertake commentary; ___-___ *khalaf*, commentaries by the later scholars of the Classical Era; ___-___ salaf, commentaries by the early scholars.
*Ahli* ___, Classical and Middle Period Muslim scholars who made commentaries on the Qur'an; *kitab-kitab* ___, the major commentaries on the Qur'an.

## BIBLIOGRAPHY


'Abbas, Siradjuddin. *40 Masalah Agama* (40 Religious Questions). 4 vols. Jakarta: Pustaka Tarbiyah, 1985.

Abubakar Aceh. *Sejarah Al Qur-an* (History of the Qur'an). Solo: Ramadhani, 1986.

Ali, Abdul Mukti. *Beberapa Persoalan Agama Dewasa Ini* (Several Questions of Religion at the Present Time). Jakarta: Rajawali, 1987.

Anshari, Endang Saifuddin. *Wawasan Islam* (The Credo of Islam). Jakarta: Rajawali, 1986.

Bahreisj, Hussein. *450 Masalah Agama Islam* (450 Questions of the Islamic Religion). Surabaya: Al-Ikhlas, 1980.

Bahreisj, Hussein. *Pedoman Fiqih Islam* (Handbook of Islamic Jurisprudence). Surabaya: Al-Ikhlas, 1981.

Bakry, Hasbullah. *Pedoman Islam di Indonesia* (Handbook of Indonesian Islam). Jakarta: Penerbit Universitas Indonesia, 1988.

Brockelmann, C. *Geschichte der Arabischen Litteratur* (History of Arabic Literature). 6 vols. Leiden: E.J. Brill, 1937-1942.

*Encyclopedia of Islam*. Leiden: E. J. Brill, 1913-1988.

*Encyclopedia of Islam*. Leiden: E. J. Brill, 1960-1992.

Glasse, Cyril. *The Concise Encyclopedia of Islam*. New York: Harper and Row, 1989.

Hamka. *Sejarah Umat Islam* (History of the Islamic Community). 4 vols. Jakarta: Bulan Bintang, 1981.

Hassan, Abdul Kadir. *Mushthalah Hadits* (Examination of Traditions). Bandung: Diponegoro, 1983.

Hughes, Thomas P. *A Dictionary of Islam*. Lahore: Premier Book House, 1964.

Indonesia. Departemen Agama. *Al Quraan dan Terjemahnya* (The Qur'an and Its Translation). Jakarta, 1974.

Indonesia. Departemen Agama. *Ensiklopedi Islam di Indonesia, 1987-1988* (Encyclopedia of Indonesian Islam for 1987-1988). Jakarta, 1987.

Indonesia. Departemen Pendidikan dan Kebudayaan. *Kamus Besar Bahasa Indonesia* (Great Dictionary of the Indonesian Language). Jakarta: Balai Pustaka, 1989.

Johns, Anthony H. "Quranic Exegesis in the Malay World," in A. Rippen (ed.), *Approaches to the History of the Interpretation of the Qur'an*. Oxford: Clarendon Press, 1988.

Juynboll, Th. W. *Handleiding tot de kennis van de mohammedaansche Wet volgens de leer der sjafi'itische school* (Handbook for the Understanding of Muslim Law according to the Shafi'i School). Leiden: E. J. Brill, 1930.

*Kiblat* (The Direction of Prayer). Jakarta, 1982-1987. Bimonthly magazine.

Koentjaraningrat. *Javanese Culture*. Kuala Lumpur: Oxford University Press, 1979.

*Leksikon Islam* (Islamic Lexicon). Jakarta: Penerbit Pustazet Perkasa, 1988.

Lubis, Arsyad Thalib. *Ilmu Fiqh* (The Science of Muslim Jurisprudence). Medan: Islamiyah, 1985.

Madjied, Nurcholis. *Islam Kemodernan dan Keindonesiaan* (Modernized and Indonesianized Islam). Bandung, 1987.

*Mizan* (The Scales of Righteousness). Jakarta, 1982 to 1990. Irregular magazine.

*Panji Masyarakat* (Banner of Society). Jakarta, 1981-1989. Bimonthly magazine.

Rais, M. Amien. *Islam di Indonesia* (Islam in Indonesia). Jakarta: Rajawali, 1986.

Rickelefs, M. C. *A History of Modern Indonesia*. Bloomington: University of Indiana Press, 1981.

Ash-Shieddieqy, M. Hasbi. *Sejarah dan Pengantar Ilmu Hadits* (The History and Handbook of the Science of Traditions). Jakarta: Bulan Bintang, 1980.

Sururi, I. A. *Kumpulan Istilah Agama* (A Collection of Religious Terms). Surabaya: Al-Ikhlas, 1984.

Syafi'i, Abd Karim. *Tanya Jawab Agama Islam* (Questions-Answers Concerning Islam). Surabaya: Al Ikhlas, 1981.

Wehr, Hans. *Arabisches Woerterbuch fuer die Schriftsprache der Gegenwart* (Arabic Dictionary for Contemporary Usage). Wiesbaden: Otto Harrossowitz, 1958.

Winstedt, Richard. *A History of Classical Malay Literature*. Kuala Lumpur: Oxford University Press, 1969.

Woodward, Mark R. *Islam in Java*. Tucson: University of Arizona Press, 1989.

Yunus, Mahmud. *Sejarah Pendidikan Islam di Indonesia* (History of Islamic Education in Indonesia). Jakarta: Mutiara, 1979.

Zainal Abidin, I. *Mushthalah Hadits* (Tradition Examination). Jakarta: Setia Karya, 1984.

Zaini, Syahminan. *Isi Pokok Ajaran Al-Qur'an* (The Essence of the Principal Teachings of the Qur'an). Jakarta: Kalam Mulia, 1986.

Zuhri, Saifuddin. *Sejarah Kebangkitan Islam dan Perkembangannya di Indonesia* (The History of the Rise of Islam and Its Development in Indonesia). Bandung: Al Maarif, 1981.

# A

**Abangan** (In.) Anthro. An Indonesian cultural group of Central Java that follows a lifestyle reflecting religious beliefs and practices popular during the Old Javanese, Hindu and Buddhist periods, albeit with some adaptation to Islamic and Western cultures that arrived later. Deeply pious Indonesian Muslims regard the abangan group as only superficially Muslim and in need of religious intensification to bring them into closer conformity with orthodox practices and beliefs.
*Usage*: *kaum* ___, *kelompok* ___, people in Indonesian society who relate to the abangan life style.

**'Abasa** (Ar:'abasa) Qur. "He Frowned," the eightieth chapter of the Qur'an. It is a lyrical chapter reproving Muhammad for not giving proper attention to an old man who visited him.

**Al 'Abbas bin Abdul Muththalib** (Ar: al-'abbas ibn 'abd al muṭṭalib) Biog. (d. 652). Uncle of the Prophet Muhammad and his protector while he lived in Makkah. A convert to Islam only near the end of the Prophet's life. Ancestor of the 'Abbasid dynasty.

**Abbasiyyah** (In.); Abbasiah (Ar: ad-dawlah al-'abbāsiyyah) Hist. Muslim Empire (750-1258) with its capital at Baghdad. Much of the development of Islamic theology, law, and philosophy occurred during its ascendancy. One of the two empires of classical Islam regarded as important in Sunni thought. *See* **Khalifah**.
*Usage*: ___ *kekhalifaan*, Abbasiyyah rulers; *bani* ___, the family from which the ruling family came; *dinasti* ___, the Abbasiyyah dynasty; *para raja* ___, the rulers of the Abbasiyyah dynasty.

**Abdhi Dhalem** (Jav.) Hist. Religious civil services in Java, headed by a kyai pengulu.

**Abdi** (In) (Ar: 'abd) Gen. vocab. Servant, slave. *Usage*: *meng___ kepada Tuhan*, to serve God; *peng___ kepada Tuhan*, submission to God.

**Abdillah**, Abdullah (Ar: 'abdullāh) Doct. "The Servant of God," a title ascribed to Muhammad.

**Abduh, Muhammad** (Ar: 'abduh, muḥammad) Biog. (d. 1905). Egyptian religious reformer; most noted spokesman of the Manar movement. Highly regarded among Indonesian Muslim Modernists. *See Tafsirul Manar.*

**Abdul Baqi, Muhammad Fuad** (Ar: muḥammad fu'ād 'abdul bāqī) Biog. (d. unk.). Egyptian scholar who prepared a synoptic version in Arabic of *Miftah Kunuzis Sunnah*, the monumental classification reference work on Traditions by A. J. Wensinck (d. 1939) in the 1940s.

**Abdul Fath Abdulfatah, Sultan**. *See* Tirtayasa, Abul Fath Abdul Fatah.

**Abdul Ghaffar, Haji** (Ar: 'abd al-ghaffār) Biog. The name taken by the Dutch scholar C. Snouck Hurgronje when he visited Makkah in the late nineteenth century. *See* **Hurgronje, C. Snouck.**

**Abdul Halim, K. H.** (In.) Biog (d. 1962). West Javanese scholar active politically in the nationalist period in several associations outlawed by the Dutch. Leader of the Persatuan Oemat Islam in the 1950s.

**Abdul Muththalib** (Ar: 'abd al-muṭṭalib ibn hāshim) Biog. (d. 578). Grandfather of Muhammad who raised him after he was orphaned until he was eight years old. Abdul was highly influential in Makkah for having rediscovered the Zamzam well and reincluding it in the pilgrimage procedures.

**Abdul Qadir Jailani** (Ar: 'abd al-qādir al jīlānī) Biog. (d. 1166). Persian mystic who founded the Qadiriyyah Order of Islamic mysticism, which had some followers in

Indonesia in the eighteenth and nineteenth centuries.

**Abdul Wahhab, Muhammad bin** (Ar: muḥammad ibn ‘abd al-wahhāb) Biog. (d. 1206H). Arab religious reformer whose followers were known as Wahhabis. He believed in return to the doctrines of the first four centuries of Islam as a means of purifying the religion. He made an alliance with the Saudi family, which has perpetuated his teachings until present-day Saudi Arabia.

**Abdul Wahab Hasbullah**. *See* **Hasbullah, Abdul Wahab**.

**Abdullah**. Spelling variant. *See* **Abdillah**.

**Abdullah, Abbas (Syekh H.)** (In.) Biog. (d. 1957). Minangkabau religious scholar educated in Egypt who introduced changes in Minangkabau schools to accord with the Egyptian model propounded at Al-Azhar university, notably the Ibtidaiyah and Tsanawiyah school years, each set at four years.

**Abdur Rauf Al Singkili** (In.) Biog. (d. 1693). The leading court scholar of Aceh in the last quarter of the seventeenth century. A member of the Syattariya Order, he is noted for providing the first Qur'anic commentary in Malay with his translation of the *Tafsirul Jalalayn*. Also known as Teungku Kuala. *See Tarjumanul Mustafid*.

**Abdurrahman Wahid**. *See* **Wahid, Abdurrahman**.

**Abdus Samad Al Palimbani** (In.) Biog. (d. 1244H/1828). Sumatran religious scholar who set a tone for Muslim intellectual activity in Indonesia with studies on theology (tauhid) and mysticism (tasawwuf). He introduced the Sammaniyyah mystical order to Sumatra from Makkah. *See Zuhratul Murid*.

**Abi Sa'ud** (Ar: abū su‘ūd ... al-‘imādī) Biog. (d. 1574). A Turkish scholar of jurisprudence and the Qur'an, who served as a judge and mufti of Istanbul. *See Irsyadul 'Aqlissalim* and *Tafsir Abi Sa'ud*.

**Abikusno Cokrosuyoso** (In.) Biog. (d. 1960). Muslim activist in the nationalist and early independence years of Indonesian history. With

Kartosuwirjo he advocated strong identification of Islam with a new Muslim state of Indonesia.

**Abu Bakar** (Ar: abū bakr) Biog. (d. 634). Close friend of Muhammad and the first Khalif of the Muslim Community following Muhammad's death. The collection of the Qur'an into a single document and the Arabic conquest of the Middle East both began during his leadership period. *Usage*: ___ *Ash Shiddiq*, Abu Bakar the veracious.

**Abu Bakar Aceh** (In.) Biog. (d. ca. 1980). Educator in higher education at Jakarta and Aceh. Writer of a series of books on Islam on the Qur'an and mysticism which were much used among the general Indonesian Muslim population in the second half of the twentieth century.

**Abu Darda** (Ar: abū ad-dardā') Biog. (d. 652). A companion of the Prophet Muhammad. Traced to him are 175 Traditions.

**Abu Dawud** (In.); Abu Daud (Ar: abū dāwūd) 1. Biog. (d. 875). One of six major collectors of Traditions (hadith), the sayings and actions of Muhammad. 2. Trad. Popular name among scholars for the collections of Traditions made by Abu Daud. *See* **As Sunan.**

**Abu Dzar Al-Giffari** (Ar: abū dhār al-ghifārī) Biog. (d. 652). A Companion of Muhammad. Traced to him are 281 Traditions.

**Abu Hanifah** (Ar: abū ḥanīfah) Biog. (d. 767). Classical Muslim scholar from Persia, who founded the Hanafi school of juris-prudence.

**Abu Hurairah** (Ar: abū hurayrah) Biog. (d. 678). A Companion of Muhammad. Over 5000 Traditions are traced to him.

**Abu Ishaq**. *See* **Asy Syirazi, Abu Ishaq.**

**Abu Musa Al Asy'ari** (Ar: abū mūsā al-ash'arī) Biog. (d. 664). A Companion of Muhammad. Traced to him are 260 Traditions.

**Abu Sa'id Al Khudri** (Ar: abū sa'īd al-khudrī) Biog. (d. 693). A companion of the Prophet Muhammad through whom 1170 different reports of Muhammad's words and behavior have been traced.

**Abu Shuja'**. *See* **Syarbini, Khatib.**

**Abu Sumah**. *See Hikayat Abu Sumah.*

**Abuhawat**. *See* **Cirebon.**

**Abul Fath, Sultan**. *See* **Bantam.**

**Abu Mufakir, Sultan**. *See* **Bantam.**

**Aceh** (In.) 1. Geog. Province of Indonesia on the northern tip of Sumatra, with special status to allow for the application of sacred law (syariat) to society. Popularly known as the "Verandah of Makkah" (Serambi Makkah) in part because of the close identification of the population with Islam. 2. Hist. Kingdom or sultanate controlling the Acehnese region, prominent during the sixteenth and seventeenth centuries and lasting until the twentieth century. The rulers, as sultans, during the zenith of its cultural and territorial expansion were: Ali Mogayat Syah 1507-22, Salahuddin 1522-37, Alauddin Riayat Syah 1537-68, Husein 1568-15, Alauddin Mansur Syah 1577-86, Ali Riayat Syah 1586-1604, Alauddin Riayat Syah 1588-1604, Iskandar Muda 1607-36 (separate entry), Iskandar Tsani 1636-41 (separate entry), (Sultana) Tajul Alam Safiatud Din Syah 1641-75 (separate entry).

**Aceh, Abu Bakar**. *See* **Abu Bakar Aceh.**

**Aceh, Perang**. *See* **Perang Aceh.**

**Achirat**. Spelling variation. *See* **Akhirat.**

**Achlak**; Achlaq. Spelling variations. *See* **Akhlak.**

**Ad**. Arabic prefix. *See* following word.

**Adab** (In.) (Ar: adab) 1. Hist. The concept of culture, refinement and civilization. In a religious sense, it connotes the standards and values of Islamic civilization. 2. Educ. The branch of knowledge in the National Islamic Studies Institutes (IAINs) and Indonesian universities that deals with literature, letters, and civilization. *See* **Institut Agama Islam Indonesia.**

**Adam** (Ar: ādam) Qur. The first man, created in God's image and original builder of the Kabah in Makkah. He is among the prophets sent to humankind, mentioned in the Qur'an.

**Adat** (In.) (Ar: 'ādah) Anthro. The mores and behavior of various cultural groups throughout the Indonesian islands. The term was given special meaning by Dutch ethnologists of the late nineteenth century, who held that each region had a customary law. They encouraged the Dutch administrators to codify and use adat as a means of regulating the groups themselves. There has been debate whether adat includes Islam or Islam includes adat.
*Usage*: *hukum* ___, the behavior incumbent on followers of adat law in the area of its use.

**Adat Bersendi Syara'** (Minang.) Anthro. Custom based on Islamic law as opposed to Islamic law based on custom.

**Adat Istiadat** (Fr. Ar: 'ādah) Anthro. The customs and practices of a specific cultural area. The term is often used in government office names in Indonesia and Malaysia.

**Adawiyah, Ibu Rabi'atul**. *See* **Rabi'atul Adawiyah.**

**Adh**. Arabic prefix. *See* following word.

**Adhan**. Spelling variant. *See* **Azan.**

**Adi Kesumo, Ahmad Najamuddin**. *See* **Palembang.**

**Adil** (In.) (Ar: 'adl) 1. Juris. The believer who is upstanding and characterized by good motives. 2. Trad. A characteristic assigned to certain transmitters whose character is considered upstanding and who have no motive for falsifying or altering information passed through them about the words and actions of the Prophet Muhammad.
*Usage*: *berlaku* ___, exhibit good conduct.

**Al Adil** (Ar: al-'adl) Theo. A name of God meaning "The Just."

**Adil, Yang Maha** (In.) Theo. A name of God meaning "The Most Upstanding."

**Adipati, Raden**. *See* **Pepatih Dalam**.

**Adiwidjaya, Sultan**. *See* **Cirebon**.

**Al 'Aadiyaat**, Al 'Adiyat (Ar:'ādiyāt) Qur. "Swift Horses," the 100th chapter of the Qur'an. It is a short lyrical chapter informing humans of God's knowledge concerning their unrighteousness.

**'Adn** (Ar: 'adn) Doct. Paradise, the Garden of Eden. Syn: Surga.

**Adz**. Arabic prefix. *See* following word.

**Adzab**. Spelling variant. *See* **Azab**.

**Adzan**. Spelling variant. *See* **Azan**.

*Al Adzhiem* (Ar: tafsīr al-qur'ān al-'aẓīm) Lit. title. A highly regarded commentary of the Qur'an by Ibnu Katsier (d. 1373) which has been translated into Indonesian on several occasions. It is prized for its succinctness in explaining the contents of the Qur'an. *See* **Tafsir**.

**Adzhim**. Spelling variant. *See* **Azhiem**.

**Afal** (In.); afdhal (Ar: afḍal) Gen. vocab. Better, the best, especially good, referring to behavior.

**Al Afghani, Seyid Jamaluddin** (Ar: jamāl ad-dīn al-afghānī) Biog. (d. 1897). A Persian/Afghani political activist who advocated Islamic unity under one caliph (Pan-Islamism) and the general modernization of the Muslim world.

**Al-'Afuw**; Al-'Afuw (Ar: al-'afū) Theo. A name of God meaning "The Pardoner." Syn: Yang Maha Pengampun.

**Agama** (In.) 1. Gen. vocab. Religion. 2. Doct. Religion, encompassing belief in some being greater than humans, ritual, and prescribed behavior for its followers. 3. Doct. The religion of Islam. Syn: din.
*Usage*: *ber___*, to practice a religion, often Islam; *ke___an*, matters of religion; ___ *Allah yang terachir*, God's final religion, i.e., Islam; ___ *celak*, ___ *kolot*, ___ *kuno*, ___ *sorban*, ___ *tasbis*, derogatory terms for Islam in the first part of the twentieth century

by Indonesian secular nationalists who regarded Islam a hindrance to national identity and development; ___ *Hadaramauti*, derogatory term depicting Islam as the religion of a backward people, excessively steeped in religion; ___ *Nasrani*, Christianity; ___ *Yahudi*, Judaism. *Amal-amal perjoangan* ___, actions undertaken for assisting the goals of religion; *cakrawala* ___, religious atmosphere; *dasar-dasar rituil ke___an*, basic religious rituals; *doktrin* ___, religious doctrine; *faham ke ___an*, religious thought or thinking; *Fakultas* ___, Faculty of Religion (in a university); *kuliah* ___, religion lesson; *lembaga ke___an*, religious institution; *masalah* ___, the question or matter of religion; *mempelajari* ___, to teach about religion; *memrevolusikan* ___, *mempermuda* ___, to renovate religion; *mendalam* ___ *Islam*, deepen oneself in Islam; *orang-orang* ___, orthodox Sunni Muslims (as opposed to the historical groups labeled as heretical); *penyiaran* ___, to spread a religion; *mempertahankan* ___, to defend religion; *pemeluk* ___, follower of a religion; *peradilan* ___, religious court; *perang* ___, a war in which religious values or practices are at stake, in some contexts, a "holy war"; *perkara* ___, religious matter; *pokok-pokok* ___, principles of religion; *rasa* ___, religious inclination or feeling; *soal* ___, the question or matter of religion; *tabligh* ___, lessons of the Islamic religion.

**Agama Jawa**. *See* **Kebatinan**.

**Agami Islam** (Jav.) Anthro. Followers of Islam that do not follow the principles of Islam seriously or follow dietary laws strictly while still taking the term "Muslim." Some do fast during Ramadan, however. This is in opposition to the Agami Islam Santri who are more devoted in their religious observances. *See* **Abangan**.

**Agami Islam Santri** (Jav.) Anthro. Followers of Islam who are devout in their observances of Islamic worship and ritual, as opposed to the Agami Islam, who are less observant of worship and ritual activities. *See* **Santri**.

**Agung, Cakrokusuma Ngabdurrahman** (Jav.) Biog.

(d. 1645). The third ruler of the Mataram dynasty of Central Java who expanded his control to most of Java. He used the title common to Javanese rulers of "Susuhunan." Late in his reign he adopted the title of Sultan confirmed by the Syarif of Makkah.

**Agung, Masjid**. *See* **Masjid Agung**.

**Agung, (Yang) Maha** (In.) Theo. An attribute of God meaning "the Most Exalted." Syn: Al Aziz.

**Ahad**. *See* **Yawmul Ahad**.

**Ahad, Ahaad**. *See* **Ilmu Mushthalah Hadis**.

**Al-Ahad** (Ar: al-aḥad) Theo. A name of Allah given in the Qur'an, meaning "The Only One." Same as Yang Maha Esa; Syn: Al Waahid.

**Ahkamul Khamsah** (Ar: al-ahkām al-khamsah) Juris. The five-fold division of human actions according to God's judgment: obligatory (fardu), recommended (sunnat), indifferent (mubah), reprehensible (makruh), and forbidden (haram).

**Ahli** (In.) (Ar: ahl) Gen. vocab. 1. People or group. 2. skilled, learned.
*Usage*: ___ *bidah*, groups in Muslim history advocating doctrine which was ultimately declared unacceptable and sinful, such as the Muktazilah and certain mystical orders; ___ *falak*, astronomers, especially those who calculate the arrival of the new moon at the beginning or end of the fasting month of Ramadan, rather than relying on actual sighting of the moon; ___ *fikih*, historical scholars learned in Muslim law; ___ *hadis*, historical scholars learned in the analysis of Traditions (hadis); ___ *ushuluddin*, historical scholars learned in Muslim law.

**Ahlul Bait Rasul** (Ar: ahl bayt rasūl) Expres. A symbolic phrase meaning "people of the house of the prophet [Muhammad]," i.e., Muslims.

**Ahlul Kitab** (In) (Ar: ahl al-kitāb) Doct. "People of the Book," monotheists other than Muslims, especially Jews and Christians. According to Qur'anic references, these people received messengers and books from God earlier

than Islam and, consequently, are to be respected by Muslims, even if the message given them has been distorted.
*Usage*: *kaum* ___, *para* ___, "the people of the book" collectively.

**Ahlus Sunnah Wal Jamaah** (In.) (Ar: ahl as-sunnah wa al-jamā'ah) Expres. A term used by Sunni Muslims to describe themselves, usually in distinction from the Syi'ah, as well as other sects regarded as heretics by the Sunni Muslims. Generally speaking the criteria for being able to use this epithet is to adhere to the religious teachings of Al Asyarie and/or Al Maturidi and the legal teachings of one of the recognized legal schools (mazhab).
*Usage*: *faham* ___, the principal points of doctrine and thinking acceptable to the group throughout Muslim history; *kalangan* ___, the Sunni scholars of history; *partai* ___, the group giving itself the title, i.e. traditionalist Muslims of Indonesia.

**Ahmad, Abdullah (Syekh H.)** (In.) Biog. (d. 1933). Leading educational reformer in Minangkabau in the early part of the twentieth century, noted for bringing secular subjects into Islamic schools. Educated in Egypt at Al Azhar University, he also edited the modernist Muslim magazine *Al-Munir* from 1911 to 1919.

**Ahmad Khatib Minangkabau** (In.) Biog. (d. 1916). Minangkabau scholar who became the leading Syafii shaykh at Makkah at the turn of the century. He exercised great influence on the Minangkabaui students at Makkah. He was the source of modernist Muslim thinking which they spread in Indonesia and Malaysia.

**Ahmad, Mirza Ghulam** (Urdu) Biog. (d. 1908). Indian Muslim who founded the Ahmadiyah movement, a modernist Muslim movement intended to modernize Muslims. He declared himself a prophet, a claim fervently denied by many Sunni Muslims since that time.

**Ahmadiyah** (Ar: Aḥmadiyyah) Relig. Contemporary sect asserting to be Islamic, whose followers and missionaries are found throughout the world,

including Indonesia. Many Sunni Muslims charge that the members of the Qadiyan group of this sect are not genuine Muslims, because of claims by some followers of the founder Mirza Ghulam Ahmad (d. 1908) that he was a prophet.
*Usage*: *aliran* ___, the followers of the Ahmadiyah in Indonesia; *golongan* ___ *Qadiyan*, the followers of the sect; *Jemaah* ___ *Qadiyan*, the association itself.

**Al Ahqaaf**; Al Ahqaf (Ar: al-aḥqāf) Qur. "The Dunes," the forty-sixth chapter of the Qur'an. It tells how God destroyed a wicked people with strong winds and storms.

**Al Ahzab**; Al Ahzaab (Ar: al-aḥzāb) Qur. "The Confederates," the thirty-third chapter of the Qur'an. It relates the attack of Islam's enemies on Madinah and the steadfast defense of that city anchored by the defenders' belief on Allah.

**Ainul Yakin, Maulana**. *See* **Giri (Raden Paku Sunan)**.

**'Aisyah binti Abu Bakar** (Ar: 'ā'ishah bint abī bakr) Biog. (d. 678). Favorite wife of Muhammad in his later years and political personality in the struggle for Muslim community leadership after his death. She was the source of 2210 different Traditions, the recorded words and behavior of Muhammad.
*Usage*: *Siti* ___, an Indonesian term of respect for 'Aisyah.

**Aisyiyah** (In) Assn. Women's unit of the Muhammadiyah Association in Indonesia, founded in 1917. It has been prominent in founding health care units and organizing women for social welfare purposes.

**Ajar** (In.) Educ. Learning, education.
*Usage*: ___*an Islam*, Islamic teachings; *mengamalkan* ___*an tasawuf*, performing mystical practices.

**Aji-Aji** (In.) Pop. Islam. Incantation and formulas intended to conjure magical powers or phenomena.
*Usage*: *meng*___, to recite formulas to invoke magical powers; *peng*___*an*, recitations used to incite magical powers.

**Ajimat**. *See* **Jimat**.

**Akad Nikah** (In.) Juris. Marriage contract.

**Akaid**; akidah (In.); aqa'id; aqidah; 'aqidah (Ar: 'aqīdah, 'aqā'id) Doct. Correct belief, in the sense of what is contained in the creed of Islam, which is intended to guide all Muslims. This includes the key doctrines regarding the nature of God and His creation and the necessity for worshiping and acting as God has commanded. Syn: Arkanul Iman.
*Usage*: ___ *Ahlus Sunnah wal Jama'ah*, the doctrines of the Sunni community; ___ *Hari Qiyamat*, standard beliefs regarding the Day of Judgment; ___ *Islamiah*, the standard beliefs among Sunni Muslims; ___ *tentang Allah Yang Maha Esa*, standard beliefs regarding God; ___ *tentang Nabi dan Rasul*, standard beliefs regarding Prophets; *pelajaran* ___, the teachings regarding the doctrines of Islam.

**Akekah** (In.); aqiqah (Ar: 'aqīqah) Pop. Islam. Ritual shaving of a baby's head for the first time, usually on the seventh day after birth.
*Usage*: *ber*___, to undertake ritual shaving of a new born baby's head.

**Akhir**. *See* **Yawmul Akhir**.

**Al Akhir** (Ar: al-ākhir) Theo. A name of God meaning "The Last." Syn: Yang Maha Akhir.

**Akhir, Yang Maha** (In.) Theo. A name of God meaning "God, the Very Last." Syn: Al Akhir.

**Akhir Sanad** (Ar: ākhir as-sanād) Trad. The last person on the line of transmission of a report preserving the Prophet Muhammad's words or behavior. The person is usually from among the Companions and is regarded as the real source of information from actual hearing or observation.

**Akhirat** (In.); achirat (Ar: ākhirah) Doct. The Hereafter, in distinction to the present condition of this world. Sunni Muslims believe Islam applies both in this world and in the Hereafter.
*Usage*: ___ *nanti, bahagia* ___, the happiness associated with the pious Muslim's life in the Hereafter; *dunia* ___, the continuing state of existence for Muslims in the Hereafter; *hari* ___, the Day of Judgment; *kelapangan di*__, the realm of the Hereafter;

*keselamatan dunia* ___, the joys and happiness associated with Muslim rewards in the Hereafter; *soal* ___, eschatology, matters of belief concerning just desserts in the Hereafter.

**Akhlak** (In.); achlak; achlaq (Ar: akhlāq) Doct. Behavior. The term connotes both individual behavior and the code of ideal behavior incumbent on all Muslims modeled on the commands and prohibitions laid down in the Qur'an and Traditions of the Prophet.
*Usage*: *ber___ tinggi*, to have behavior of a high quality; ___ *yang luhur*, ___ *mulia*, ___*ul karimah*, exemplary behavior; *memperbaiki* ___, to better or improve behavior.

**Akidah**. Spelling variant. *See* **Akaid**.

**Al**. Arabic prefix. *See* following word.

**Al Aksa**. *See* **Masjid Al Aksa**.

**Al A'laa**; Al A'la; Al A'la (Ar: al-'alā) Qur. "The Most High," the eighty-seventh chapter of the Qur'an. A short lyrical chapter asserting God's power over nature and His warning that a Day of Judgment will occur.

**'Ala Syar-thil Bukhari** (Ar: 'alā sharṭ al-bukhārī) Trad. An acknowledgement that a report preserving the words and behavior of the Prophet Muhammad was judged as in the "firm" category by Al Bukhari (d. 870). *See As Sahih*.

**'Ala Syar-thil Muslim** (Ar: 'alā sharṭ muslim) Trad. An acknowledgement that a report preserving the words and behavior of the Prophet Muhammad was judged as in the "firm" category by Muslim (d. 873). *See As Sahih*.

**'Ala Syar-thisy Syaikhain** (Ar: 'alā sharṭi al-shaykhain) Trad. An acknowledgement that a report preserving the words and behavior of the Prophet Muhammad was judged as in the "firm" category by both Al Bukhari (d. 870) and Muslim (d. 873). *See As Sahih*.

**Alaihissalam** (In.) (Ar: 'alayhi salām) Expres. "Upon him, peace," an expression said or written after mention of the name of a prophet other than Muhammad, an angel or some other revered figure mentioned in the Qur'an.

**Alam Nasyrah.** (Ar: alam nashraḥ) Qur. "Expanding World," the ninety-fourth chapter of the Qur'an. A medium-length lyrical chapter calling on Muslims to remember their obligations toward one another. It is also named Al Insyiraah and Asy-Syarh.

**Alamsyah, Ratu Perwiranegara.** *See* **Menteri Agama.**

**Al 'Alaq** (al-'alaq) Qur. "Congealed Blood," the ninety-sixth chapter of the Qur'an. A short lyrical chapter that contains the original revelation commanding Muhammad to receive the Word of God. It is also known as Iqra and Al Qalam.

**Alauddin.** *See* **Institut Agama Islam Negara.**

**Alauddin Mansur Syah, Sultan.** *See* **Aceh.**

**Alauddin Riayat Syah, Sultan.** *See* **Aceh.**

**Algemeene Middelbare School—AMS** (Dutch) Educ. Third form of Dutch education in twentieth century Colonial Indies, comprising grades 10 to 12. Open to pupils of European parentage and selected Indonesians.

**Alhamdulillah** (In.) (Ar: al-ḥamdu-lillāh) Expres. "Praise to God!" often used as "Thanks to God!," an utterance common among Muslims. It is known as tahmid.

**Al 'Ali** (Ar: al-'alī) Theo. Name of God meaning "The Most High."

**Ali, Abdul Mukti** (In.) Biog. (b. 1923). Educator and government administrator. Most noted for his term as Minister of Religion (Menteri Agama) (1971-78) when he reconciled Muslim religious and social goals with the government's policy of development.

**Ali, Maharaja.** *See Hikayat Maharaja Ali.*

**'Ali bin Abu Thalib** (Ar:'alī ibn abi ṭālib) Biog. (d. 661). A cousin of Muhammad, an important leader in the early

Muslim community and fourth caliph. The Syiah acknowledge him as their spiritual ancestor.

**Ali 'Imran**; Ali Imraan (Ar: āl 'imrān) Qur. "The Family of Imran," the third chapter of the Qur'an. It relates the story of Maryam, the mother of Isa (Jesus) and also outlines Islam's tolerance toward other monotheists.

**Ali Mogayat Syah, Sultan**. *See* **Aceh**.

**Ali Riayat Syah, Sultan**. *See* **Aceh**.

**'Alim**. *See* **Ulama**.

**Al Aliim**; Al 'Alim (Ar: al-'alīm) Theo. A name of God meaning "The All-Knowing."

**Aliran** (In.) 1. Anthro. Social-cultural division, used to differentiate major Indonesian groupings. Javanese society is often described as consisting of three broad groupings known as abangan, priayi and santri, a categorization accepted, with qualifications, by most observers of Indonesia society. 2. Doct. A group identified with an ideological or philosophical outlook.
*Usage*: ___ *Hamzah Fansuri*, the group associated with the viewpoint of Hamzah Fansuri; ___ *Kebatinan*, ___ *Kebatinan Jawa*, ___ *Kepercayaan*, nominally Muslim groups, primarily in Central and East Java who follow mystical practices from several religious traditions. Now protected by the national government, but considered "ignorant Muslims" by many pious Muslims, who want revivalist activities to inform the groups of proper Muslim beliefs; ___ *sufisme*, the grouping associated with Islamic mysticism, its outlook and practice.

**Alisjahbana, Takdir** (In.) Biog. (b. ca. 1908). Minangakabau-born scholar who set some of the standards for Indonesian language development and literary criticism.

**Allah** (In.) (Ar: Allāh) Doct. God in the Muslim religion. In the Qur'an He is described as the Creator of all things and as having command over all things. *See* **Tauhid, Takwa and Tuhan**.
*Usage*: ___ *hu Akbar*, "God is Great!"; ___ *umina Amin*,

"The Peace of God be Upon You"; ___ *berfirman*, the pronouncements of God (used when quoting from the Qur'an); ___ *haramkan*, God has forbidden; ___ *Maha Agung*, God the Supreme Being; ___ *Maha Esa*, God the Completely Unified; ___ *Maha Penerima*, God, the All-Receiving; ___ *Maha Penerima Taubat*, God the Great Receiver of requests for forgiveness; ___ *Maha Penyantun*, God, the Great Sympathizer and Sustainer; ___ *Maha Rahmat*, God, the All-Merciful; ___ *Pengetahui*, God, the All-Knowing; ___ *SWT*, "God the Most Holy;" ___ *Ta'ala*, "God exists above all!"
*Agama* ___, the religion of God, i.e., Islam; *ajaran* ___, the teachings of Islam; *bercaya kepada* ___ *dan rasulnya*, to believe in God and His Prophet Muhammad; *berdoa kepada* ___, praying to God; *berhamba(an) kepada* ___, to act as God's servant through obedience to his commandments; *berperang pada jalan* ___, to struggle or fight in the Way of God; bertawakkal ___, showing proper respect to God; *firman-firman* ___, the commands of God; *hadirat* ___, the presence of God; *hamba* ___, (Sufi) the servant of God; *hubullah*, love of God; *iman (ke)pada* ___ *dan rasulnya*, to believe in God and His messenger; *Insya* ___, "If God wills"; *La Ilaha illallah*, "There is no god but Allah"; *kadar* ___, the power of God to determine all things; *kekhalifan* ___, the stewardship of God [on earth], i.e. human role in tending the earth; *keridhaan* ___, the Grace of God; *kitab suci* ___, the holy book of God, i.e., the Qur'an; *memohon kepada* ___, to pray to God (for forgiveness); *mencintai* ___, (Sufi) to love God in mystical ecstasy; *mengabdi kepada* ___, to do God's will and act as His servant; *mentaati hukum* ___, obeying the laws of God; *perjuangan di jalan* ___, to struggle or fight in the way of God; *sifat Ilahi, sifat-sifat* ___, the attributes of God; *syukur* ___, Praise God!; *taat kepada* ___ *dan rasulnya*, obeying God and His Prophet [Muhammad]; *takdir* ___, God's predetermination of all things; *takwa kepada* ___, showing proper fear of God; *Tuhan* ___, God; *zat* ___, the nature of God.

**Allahu Akbar** (In.) (Ar: allāhu akbar) Expres. An

uttered expression used universally among Muslims, meaning "God is Great!" which occurs frequently in the Qur'an and in liturgies.

**Al Allamah** (In) (Ar: al-'allāmah) Title. "The Learned" (in religious knowledge).

**Al 'Aliyy**; 'Ali (Ar: al-'alī) Theo. A name of God meaning "The Most High." Same as Yang Maha Tinggi.

**Almarhum** (In.) (Ar: al-marḥūm) Title. "The late," "the deceased," indicated when speaking or writing about a person who is dead.

**Al Alusi** (Ar: abū ath-thanā' al-alūsī) Biog. (d. 1853). Hanafi scholar in Baghdad who attained high scholastic status as a young man for his commentary on the Qur'an. He was a member of the Naqsybandiyyah mystical order. *See Ruhul Ma'ani* and **Tafsir**.

**Aaly**. *See* **Ilmu Mushthalah Hadis**.

**Amal** (In.) (Ar: amal) Gen. vocab. Behavior that is exemplary and, often, pious. *Usage*: *meng__kan ajaran tasawuf*, undertake mystical practice; *__an bertawassul*, action undertaking to petition God for forgiveness or to help in a situation; ___ *bidah*, actions judged as innovative (and, usually, wrong) in religious performance; ___ *maulid*, observe the maulid recitations; ___ *mustahabah*, actions that are regarded in religious law as right and favorable; ___ *pahala*, undertake actions that gain merit; *memperbaiki* ___, to undertake good behavior; *menerjakan* ___ *kebaikan*, to perform exemplary behavior.

**Amangkubuwana**. Spelling variant. *See* **Hamengkubuwana**.

**Amangkurat**. *See* **Mangkurat**.

**Amar Ma'ruf Nahi Munkar** (In.) (Ar: amr ma'rūf nahi munkar) Juris. "promotion of good and banishment of evil." Islamic concept for community social action. *Usage*: *gerakan* ___, to belong to an effort which seeks to make Islamic values operative in society; *kegiatan* ___, activity involved in making Islamic values operative in society; ___ *melaksanakan*, to undertake efforts to make

Islamic values operative in society.

**Amarah** (In.) *See* **Nafsu.**

**Ameer Ali**, (Sayyid) (Urdu) Biog. (d. 1928). Syiah writer from India who inspired Modernist Muslims at the turn of the twentieth century. He accepted modern rationalism and saw much of the Qur'anic wording as symbolic. *See* also *Spirit of Islam*.

**Amil** (Ar: 'āmil) Hist. State administrators in early Islam and at other places in history charged with collecting and distributing funds connected with the poor tax (zakat). *Usage*: *orang* ___, officials in charge of poor tax collection and distribution.

**Al Amin**, Amiin (Ar: al-amīn) Doct. A name of Muhammad meaning "The Trusted."

**Amirul Mukminin** (In) (Ar: amir al-mu'minīn) 1. Hist. A title assumed by primary Muslim rulers throughout history, meaning "commander of the faithful." Claimed by the Mataram Sultan Agung in the seventeenth century. 2. Pol. In Indonesia used by Muslim intellectuals as a symbolic term for principal Muslim political authority, such as president, even though the president of Indonesia does not actually have access to the title either in law or by claim.

**'Amma, Juz** (Ar: juz 'amma) Qur. The last of the thirty reading sections of the Qur'an, consisting of surahs 78 to 114. Poetical in nature, this is often a favorite recitation section for Indonesian Muslims.

**Ampel, Sunan Raden Rahmat**; Ngampel ...; (Raden) Rachmat (In.) 1. Biog. (d. ca. 1470). One of nine Muslim sages who are popularly considered to have led the Islamization of Java through missionary activity. He opened a pesantren in Ampel, Surabaya, which allowed Islam to flow out to all of Java and to the Eastern islands of Indonesia. *See* **Wali Songo.** 2. Geog. Name of the National Islamic Studies Institute (IAIN) at Surabaya. *See* Institut Agama Islam Negara.

**Ampun** (In.) Doct. Forgiveness granted by God for transgressions against His law.

*Usage*: *minta* ___, to ask God for forgiveness.

**Amrullah, Abdul Karim** (In.) Biog. (d. 1945). Muslim reformer from western Sumatra who was the motivating force for educational change and modernist Muslim outlook, primarily on Sumatra in the early part of the twentieth century. Author of *Iqazhum Niyami fi Hukmil Qiyam*. Also known as Haji Rasul.

**Amrullah, Haji Adul Malik Karim**. *See* **Hamka.**

**AMS.** *See* **Algemeene Middelbare School.**

**An**. Arabic prefix. *See* following word.

**Al An'aam**; Al An'am (Ar: al-an'ām) Qur. "Cattle," the sixth chapter of the Qur'an. It tells about earlier prophets and the nature of God's revelation to those messengers of God.

**Anas bin Malik** (Ar: anas ibn mālik) Biog. (d. 710). A Companion of the Prophet Muhammad and a retainer in his household. There have been traced to him 2286 different reports regarding Muhammad's words and behavior.

**Al Anbiyaa'**; Al Anbiyaak; Al Anbia' (Ar: al-anbiyā') Qur. "The Prophets," the twenty-first chapter of the Qur'an. It explains the roles of prophets in God's scheme and relates information about many of them.

**Andalusia** (In.); Andalusiyyah (Ar: al-andalus) Hist. 1. A kingdom of the Umayyad dynasty in Spain from A.D. 661 to A.D. 750. It was free and separate from the Abbasids in the eastern Islamic world. 2. A general reference among Muslim intellectuals referring to the historical era of Andalusia, regarded as a major world civilization reflecting the success of Muslim culture.

**Al Anfaal**; Al Anfal (Ar: al-anfāl) Qur. "The Booty of War," the eighth chapter of the Qur'an. The chapter outlines the correct behavior for Muslims in warfare with others.

**Animisme** (In.) Relig. Belief that special powers exist in living things that can be drawn forth by adepts for supernatural purposes, such

as healing and casting spells. The concept has numerous believers in the Indonesian Archipelago.
*Usage*: *hidup* ___, the practice of animistic cults.

**Anis, Yunus**. *See* **Muhammadiyah**.

**An 'Ankabuut**; An Ankabut (Ar: 'ankabūt) Qur. "The Spider," the twenty-ninth chapter of the Qur'an. The parable is related about those taking other gods than Allah as building a flimsy house like that of a spider's web.

**Anshar**; Ansor (Ar: al-anṣār) Hist. "Helpers," a designator assigned to the people, mostly of Madinah, who became Muslims during the lifetime of the Prophet Muhammad in distinction to those people who accompanied Muhammad from Makkah.
*Usage*: *golongan* ___, *kelompok* ___, the collective group; *sahabat* ___, the group as distinguished from the Companions from Makkah.

**Al Anshari, Zakariah** (Ar: zakariyyā al-anṣārī) Biog. (d. 1520). Shafii legal scholar from Cairo whose works were used in Aceh in the seventeenth century. *See Fathur Rahman*.

**Ansor**. As a historical term, see **Anshar**. As a scriptural reference *see* **Anshar**. As an Indonesian association *see* **Gerakan Pemuda Ansor**.

**Antasari**. *See* **Institut Agama Islam Negara**.

**Anwaruddin, H**. *See* **Menteri Agama**.

*Anwarut Tanzil* (Ar: anwār at-tanzīl) Lit. title. "Light of the Revelation," a renowned commentary on the Qur'an by Al Baidhawi (d. 1291) long used in Indonesia. It is noted for its concise summary of earlier scholarship on Qur'anic interpretation.

**Appasunna** (Bugi) Pop. Islam. Circumcision ceremony marking the entry of both boys and girls to Islam in Sulawesi.

**Api Islam** (In.) Pol. A term in mid-twentieth century Indonesia referring to the essence of religion, used by President Sukarno (d. 1968) in the early 1960s as a challenge to Muslims to come to grips with modern technology and ways of doing things.

**Aqa'id**. Spelling variant. *See* **Akaid**.

**Aqidah**. Spelling variant. *See* **Akaid** and **Arkanul Iman**.

**Aqiqah**. Alternate spelling. *See* **Akekah**.

**Ar**. Arabic prefix. *See* following word.

**Arab** (Ar: 'arab) Lang. Name of a language, culture and people of the Middle East, that first received Islam. *Usage*: *Bahasa* ___, Arabic language; *berbahasa* ___, using the Arabic language; *huruf* ___, Arabic letters; *lisan* ___, in Arabic; *tulisan* ___, Arabic writing.

**Arabi**. *See* **Ibnu Arabi**.

**Al A'raaf**; Al A'raf; Al A'raf (Ar: al-a'rāf) Qur. "The High Place," the seventh chapter of the Qur'an. It tells about human relationship with God and the assignment of people to heaven and hell on the basis of belief toward God.

**Arbi'a'**. *See* **Yawmul Arbi'a'**.

**'Ardl** (Ar: 'arḍ) Trad. Transmission of a report preserving the words and behavior of the Prophet Muhammad by recitation and memorization.

**Arkanul Iman** (Ar: arkān al-īmān) Doct. The major beliefs of Islam, which recognize the existence of (a) Allah, (b) angels, (c) scriptures, (d) prophets, (e) the Day of Judgment, and (f) God's power to determine all things. Syn: Aqidah.

**Arkanul Islam** (Ar: arkān al-islām) Doct. The five pillars or actions incumbent on all Muslims: (a) confession that there is no God, but Allah and Muhammad is God's messenger, (b) undertaking prayer, (c) giving alms, (d) fasting during Ramadan, and (e) undertaking the pilgrimage to Makkah.

**Arrack** (Ar: 'araq) Juris. Alcohol or strong drink. Explicitly forbidden by scriptural injunction.

**'Arsy** (Ar: 'arsh) Gen. vocab. Chair or throne. *Usage*: ___ *Tuhan*, the throne of God.

**Arsylan, Amer Syakib** (Ar: shakib amir arslan) Biog. (d. 1946). Syrian writer of the Reformist Muslim school who wrote an important work titled *Lima dha ta'ahhara al muslimun* ... (Why the Muslims Slept), which modernist Muslims in Indonesia regarded as inspirational.

**Artinya** (In.) Gen vocab. A term used in making translations of Qur'an and Traditions to introduce the translation and indicate the meaning of the original Arab text.

**Arung Palakka**; Aru Palaka (In.) Biog. (d. 1696). Warrior commander from Sulawesi who led Bugi mercenaries for the Dutch East Indies Company in the middle third of the seventeenth century. He led forces against Gowa, elsewhere on Sulawesi, and on Java. As ruler at Bone (1677-96) he set aside customary councils and ruled as an arbitrary ruler. Also known as La Tenrittatia to Unru'.

**As**. Arabic prefix. *See* following word.

**Asbabul Wuruudil Hadits** (Ar: aṣbāb al wurūd al-ḥadīth) Trad. Consideration of conditions surrounding reports preserving the Prophet Muhammad's words and behavior, so that the report can be judged as valid or not.

**Asbabun-Nuzul**. *See* **Ilmu Tafsier**.

**Ash**. Arabic prefix. *See* following word.

**Ashabiyah** (In.); 'ashabiyah (Ar: 'aṣabiyyah) Hist. Earlier it meant political particularism, such as tribalism. In the twentieth century, it took the meaning of nationalism. Used by some Muslims as a pejorative term to indicate national allegiance detracting from Muslim solidarity. Syn: Ta'shub.
*Usage*: ___ *al Islamiyah*, Islamic spirit or identification; ___ *al jinsiyah*, ___ *al quamiyah*, identification with a people or ethnic group.

**Ashar** (In.) (Ar: 'aṣr) 1. Juris. The required daily prayer in the afternoon. 2. Al 'Ashr Qur. "Afternoon," the 103rd chapter of the Qur'an. A very short lyrical chapter urging people to do good out of love for God.

**Asmulhusna** (In.); asmaa-ul husna (Ar: al-asma' al-ḥusna) Doct. "The Most Beautiful Names," the characteristics of God and, hence, the various names assigned to Him as representing those attributes. Sometimes recited by individual Muslims as optional worship.

**Al-Asqalani.** *See* **Ibnu Hajar Al-Asqalani.**

**Asrama** (In.) Educ. A boarding house at a religious school, especially at rural areas on Java.

*Asrarul 'Arifin* (Ar: asrār al-'ārifīn) Lit. title. "Secrets of the Knowledgeable," a work on mysticism by Hamzah Fansuri (d. 1625) in which the mystic's journey to the discovery of God is given in allusions common to Persian mystics such as Al Hallaj (d. 922), Ar Rumi (d.1273) and Ibnu Arabi (d. 1240). The work came under attack by Ar Raniri (d. 1658) as pantheistic.

*Asrarul Insan* (Ar: asrār al-insān) Lit. title. "The Secrets of Perfect Man," a polemical work by Ar Raniri (d. 1658) denouncing mysticism of earlier Achenese mystics as pantheistic and unacceptable to Islam. Written at the behest of Sultan Iskandar Tsani of Aceh (d. 1641).

**Asura** (In) (Ar: 'āshūrā) Cal. The tenth day of the month of Muharram, celebrated with fasting as a special day of atonement. It has special meaning for the Syiites since it marked the date of the martyrdom of Husayn, the grandson of the Prophet Muhammad who was their pretender to the leadership of the Muslim community at the time.

**Asy.** Arabic prefix. *See* following word.

**Al Asy'ari, Abu Hasan Ali** (Ar: abū al-ḥasan ... al-ash'arī) Biog. (d. 935). Classical Islamic scholar who led the reaction to Free Thinkers with Al Maturidi (d. 944) and set the theological standards of Sunni Islam. *Usage*: *pembebasan ___isme*, the liberation of Asyarite theology; *teologi* ___, the theological principles set forth by Asy'ari in general use by Muslims.

**Al-Asy'ari, Abu Musa.** *See* **Abu Musa Al Asy'ari.**

**Asy'arie, K.H.M. Hasyim** (In.) Biog. (d. 1947). Noted Indonesian Muslim religious scholar, who undertook educational reforms at the Tebuireng Pesantren in East Java that allowed upgrading within the traditionalist standpoint. Also a founder and long-time leader (1926-53) of the Nahdlatul Ulama association. *See* **Shumubu.**

**Al Asy'ariyah** (In.); Asy'ariah (Ar: ash'ariyyah) Doct. The thinkers of the classical era favoring the philosophy and theology espoused by Al Asy'ari (d. 935).
*Usage*: *ajaran* ___, the teachings put forth by the Asy'ariyah; *golongan* ___, the orthodox believers of Sunni Islam; *skolastisisme* ___, the system of theological thinking followed by the intellectual successors of Al Asy'ari; *teologis* ___, the theology followed by the orthodox believers of Sunni Islam.

**Asyhadu an la ilaha illa'-Lah, wa asyhadu anna Muhammadan abdu-Hu wa rasulu-Hu** (Ar: ashhadu an lā ilāha illallāh wa ashadu anna muḥammadan rasūlu Llāh) Doct. The confession of faith meaning: "I confess that there is no god except Allah and Muhammad is His Messenger." The expression is referred to as tasyahud. Syn: kalimah kalih.

**Aszalamualaikum** (In.); as salam alaykum, as salamu 'alaikum (Ar: as-salāmu 'alaikum) Expres. Islamic greeting of one Muslim to another, meaning "peace be upon you," often with "wa Rahmatullahi wa barakatuh" (and the mercy of God and His blessings).

**At.** Arabic prefix. *See* following word.

**Ataturk, Mustafa Kamal** (Turk.) Biog. (d. 1938). Founder and first president of the modern state of Turkey. Known for his draconian reforms that made Islam subservient to nationalistic and state interests.

**Ateisme** (In.) Relig. The belief that there is no God.
*Usage*: *kaum* ___, indicating those who hold this philosophy or belief.

**Ath**. Arabic prefix. *See* following word.

**'Atid** (Ar: 'Atid) Doct. The name of a guardian angel.

**Atsar** (Ar: athar) Trad. Remnant or remainder, indicating the scattered reports concerning the words and behavior of the Prophet Muhammad, which form the raw material for Tradition analysis.
*Usage*: ___-___ *sahabat-sahabat nabi*, remnant reports of the Companions of the Prophet Muhammad concerning events during Muhammad's lifetime.

**Aulia** (In.); auliya (Ar: awlīyā', pl. of walī) Qur. Favorites of God, referring to those who are devoted to God's way.

**Aurat** (In.) Juris. Nakedness, actually the part of the human body that is to be covered when a person is outside the confines of the family. The aurat is different for males and females.
*Usage*: *menutupi* ___, to cover oneself properly in accord with Islamic requirements.

**Al-Awwal** (Ar: al-awwal) Theo. A name of God meaning "The Very First."

**Awwal Sanad** (Ar: awwal sanad) Trad. The first name on the line of transmission of a report preserving the Prophet Muhammad's words and behavior. The name is the last person to relate it orally; thereafter it is recorded by one of the great collectors.

**Awwamah**. *See* **Nafsu**.

**Ayah**, ayat [Ayah is usually singular and ayat plural] (In. fr. Ar: āyah) Qur. Verses of the Qur'an.
*Usage*: ___-___ *hukum*, ___ *ahkam*, verses dealing with legal injunctions; ___-___ *Madaniyyah*, verses of the Qur'an that were revealed at Madinah during the latter ministry of Muhammad; ___-___ *Makkiyah*, verses of the Qur'an that were revealed at Makkah during the early ministry of Muhammad; ___-___ *suci*, the holy verses; *menurunkan* ___, revelation of verses of the Qur'an.

**Ayah Kursi**; ayat kursi (In.); ayat kursi (Ar: āyat al-kursī) Pop. Islam. The common title given to Al Baqarah 255, a popular verse often recited by Muslims in times of danger and sorrow. The theme is that God never sleeps and is available to assist the reciter with his problems.

**Ayyub** (In.); Ayub (Ar: ayyub) Qur. Personal name of a prophet mentioned in the Qur'an. Equated with the Hebrew Job, he underwent severe trials by God and proved that he was a true believer.

**Az**. Arabic prefix. *See* following word.

**Azab** (In); adzab; azhab (Ar:'adhab) Doct. Punishment or torment, particularly that in the grave or the Hereafter for living a sinful life or failure to believe in Islam and follow its teachings.

**Azali** (Ar:azali) Doct. Punishment after death for having disbelief concerning Allah or for having badly transgressed His commands. Ant: kenikmatan.

**Azan**; adzan (Ar: adhān) Doct. The call to prayer given for the five prayers and for all community worship. *Usage*: ___ *kedua*, the second call to prayer; ___ *ketiga*, the third call to prayer; ___ *pertama*, the first call to prayer; *mendengar* ___, to hear the call to prayer.

**Azhab**. Spelling variant. *See* **Azab.**

**Al Azhar** (Ar: al-azhar) Educ. The name of a large mosque in Cairo, Egypt, and the center of Islamic learning located in the area of the mosque. For over two centuries it has been a favorite site for young Muslims from Southeast Asia to study Islamic sciences.

**Al Azhar, Masjid Agung**. *See* **Masjid Agung Al Azhar.**

**Al Azhiim**; Al 'Azhim; Al Azim (Ar: al-'aẓīm) Theo. A name of God meaning "The Greatest." Syn: Yang Maha Agung.

**Azimat**. Spelling variation. *See* **Ajimat**.

**Al Aziz**; Al Aziiz, Al 'Aziz (Ar: al-'azīz) Theo. A name of God meaning "The Just." Syn: Yang Maha Kuasa; Yang Maha Agung.

**Aziz.** *See* **Ilmu Mushthalah Hadis.**

**Azrail**. *See* **Izrail.**

# B

**Bab** (In.) Lang. A section of a book or compilation, usually dealing with similar material. The term is used in collections of Traditions and is often translated as "chapter."

**Babad** (In.) Hist. Chronicles, especially of Javanese, Hindu-Buddhist dynasties in early Indonesia, written to justify the ascension of particular rulers and glorify their regimes. The babads have limited direct historical information, but much indirect evidence of historical factors.

*Babad Tanah Jawa* (In.) Lit. title. "The Java Chronicles," a series of narratives and explanations about the dynasties of Java written in the Mataram period of the seventeenth century. It includes material about the Nine Saints (Wali Songo) who are reputed to have led the missionary activity that converted the Javanese population to Islam and about the Mataram dynasty.

**Babullah** (In.) Biog. (d. 1583) Sultan of Ternate (1570 to 1583) who destroyed the Portuguese political, economic and military power in the Moluccas and extended the empire of Ternate to its widest range. *See* **Ternate**.

**Baca**; membaca (In.) Qur. To read or recite. In Islam the meaning is generally to recite, a prayer or a selection from a scripture.
*Usage*: *mem___ ayat Qur'an*, to recite verses from the Qur'an in accordance with appropriate rules of recitation.

**Badal**. *See* **Ilmu Mushthalah Hadis**.

**Badan Amil Zakat dan Infaq/ Shadaqah—Bazis** (In.) Pol. "The Agency for Collecting the Poor Tax and Donations for the Needy," a quasi-government body in Jakarta District, founded in 1973, to act as an adviser to the district government on matters connected with collection and distribution of the poor tax (zakat).

**Badan Koordinasi Pemuda Masjid Indonesia** (In.) Assn. "The Indonesian Council for Coordinating Youth Mosque (Activity)," an association founded in the 1970s, with offices in Jakarta, to coordinate activities of youth, with its organizational focus on local mosques.

**Badan Persiapan Usaha Kemerdekaan Indonesia** (In.) Pol. "The Preparatory Council of the Indonesia Independence Effort" met in the Summer of 1945 under Japanese sponsorship to draft a constitution for declaring Indonesian independence. It was composed of 25 percent political Muslim delegates.

**Badar** (Ar: badr) Geog. A city ninety miles south of Madinah and the site of a major battle (17 March 623) between the early Muslim community of Madinah and its Makkan enemies. The Muslims won this battle. *Usage*: *peperangan* ___, the battle of Badar.

**Badaruddin, Sultan Mahmud**. *See* **Palembang**.

**Al Badawi**. Spelling variant. *See* **Al Baidhawi**.

**Badawi, Ahmad**. *See* **Muhammadiyah**.

**Al Badii'**; Al-Badii'un; Al-Badie' (Ar: al-badī') Theo. A name of God meaning "The Originator."

**Ba'diyah** (Ar: ba'ḍiyyah) Juris. To do in parts. *Usage*: *sembahyang sunnat* ___ *zuhur*, the permissibility of performing the midday prayer in parts at different times; *sunnat* ___, the permissibility of performing worship in parts.

**Badruddin, Sultan**. *See* **Demak**.

**Al Baedhowi**. Spelling variant. *See* **Al Baidhawi**.

**Al-Baghawi** (Ar: abū muḥammad ... al-baghawī) Biog. (d. 1117). A Khurasani scholar renowned for his knowledge of Traditions, who also wrote an important commentary of the Qur'an used in Southeast Asia during the twentieth century. *See Ma'alimul Tanzil* and **Tafsir**.

**Al-Baghdadi, Juneid** (Ar: junayd al-bagdādī) Biog. (d. 910). Noted mystic and writer of the classical Islamic period, whose views of the importance of legal obligation alongside mystical action was popular among traditional religious scholars in Southeast Asia for several centuries.

**Bagus Hadikusumo**. *See* **Muhammadiyah**.

**Bahagia** (In.) Doct. Happiness, welfare.
*Usage*: *ke__an manusia*, human prosperity or human welfare, usually used in the sense of benefits obtained from following God's commands.

**Bahauddin, Sultan Muhammad**. *See* **Palembang**.

**Bahimiah** (In.); bahimiyah (Ar: bahīmiyyah) Theo. Animal-like in being able to only perform basic functions of survival.
*Usage*: *sifat* ___, character of animalness found in humans according to mystics.

**Bahira; Buhaira** (Ar: Baḥirah) Biog. (d. unk.). A Christian teacher in Syria at the time of Muhammad. Historically accusations have been made by Muhammad's detractors that Bahira was Muhammad's source for the substance of the Qur'an. This charge has been vigorously denied by Muslims throughout Islamic history.

**Al Baidhawi**; Al Badawi; Al Baedhowi; Baydawi (Ar: 'abd allāh ... nāṣiruddīn al-bayḍawī) Biog. (d. 1291). An Arab scholar of the middle period renowned for the soundness of his commentary on the Qur'an and for its condensed views of earlier scholars on the subject. *See Anwarut Tanzil*.

**Al Ba'its** (Ar: al-bā'ith) Theo. Name of God, meaning "The Awakener."

**Baitullah** (In.) (Ar: baytullāh) Arch. Mosque in Makkah within the Holy Area (Masjidal-Haram). The term is also applied to several other places such as the Al Aksa Mosque in Jerusalem and the Mosque of the Prophet in Madinah.

**Baitulmukadas** (In.); Baitul Maqdis (Ar:al-bayt al-muqaddas) 1. Relig. Holy place; 2. Geog. Temple site in Jerusalem where Muhammad was taken during the Night Journey (mikraj) and ascended to heaven. After discussions there he descended and returned to Makkah with the flying horse Al Burak.

**Bakhtiar**. *See Hikayat Baktiar.*

**Al Balad** (Ar: al-balad) Qur. "The City," the ninetieth chapter of the Qur'an. It is a short lyrical chapter calling on the people of Makkah to change their moral indifference over to pious actions demanded by God.

**Balaghah** (Ar: balāghah) 1. Doct. Religious literature for intensifying the faith of believers. 2. Lang. Rhetoric. *See* **Ilmu Balaghah**.

**Baldatun Thayyibatun Warabbun Ghafur** (Ar: baldatun ṭayyibatun wa rabbun ghafūr) Pol. "A Fair Land Blessed by God," a motto by political Muslims in the liberal democratic era (1950-57) for their aspirations concerning the role of Islam and the Indonesian state.

**Bandungan**. *See* **Halaqah.**

**Bangsa** (In.) Pol. The concept of nation in Indonesian nationalism, indicating Indonesian identity. Earlier in the century the term indicated ethnic identity and was a symbol to Muslims of the divisiveness of nonreligious movements of the time.

**Bangweton** (In.) Hist. In the early Mataram Empire (sixteenth century), the march areas where imperial control was under dispute.

**Bani** (Ar: banī) Gen. vocab. Clan, tribe, descendents or house. *See* following word.

**Bani 'Abbas** (Ar: banī 'abbās) Hist. Descendents of Al 'Abbas bin Abdul Muththalib (d. 652) who formed an important elite in Islam and rose politically to form the second ruling dynasty, the Abbasids (749 to 1258)

**Bani Israel** (Ar: banū isrā'īl) Qur. The Children of Israel in the Qur'an, who are presented as troublesome people to whom the Prophet Musa (Moses) was sent.

**Banjar, Kerajaan** (In.) Geog. Sultanate located in Kalimantan with its capital at various sites including Banjarmasin. It opposed the Dutch trade expansion into its territory but ultimately signed a treaty. The Dutch abolished the sultanate in 1860. *See* **Kesultanan**. The rulers are as follows: Suriansyah 1595-1620, Rahmatullah 1620-42, Hidayatullah 1642-50, Musta'in Billah 1650-78, Inayatullah 1678-85, Sa'dillah 1685-1700, Tahlilillah 1700-45, Tamjidillah 1745-78, Tahmidillah 1778-1808, Sulaiman 1808-25, Adam Al Wasi' Billah 1825-57, Tamjidillah 1857-59.

**Al Banjari, Muhammad Arsyad** (In.) Biog. (d. 1812). Sufi Shaykh from Banjarmasin who introduced the Samaniyya Sufi Order to South Kalimantan. He wrote works in the vernacular for use by Indonesians. *See* *Sabilal Muhtadin*.

**Bank** (In.) Econ. Financial institution for currency transactions, saving and investing money.
*Usage*: ___ *haji*, a type of bank established to assist Muslims to save money for undertaking the pilgrimage but following investing procedures which do not involve the charging of interest; ___ *Al Islam lil Tananiyah*, ___ *Pembangunan Islam*, Islamic Development Bank.

**Bank Matahari** (In.) Econ. A bank founded by the Muhammadiyah at Jakarta which provides capital to Muslims consistent with historical Islamic concerns regarding interest and usury.

**Bank Muamalat Indonesia** (In.) Econ. A bank with government backing founded in 1991 to provide capital to Muslims consistent with historical Islamic concerns regarding interest and usury.

**Bank Summa**. *See* **Summa Bank**.

**Bantam**; Banten (In.) Geog. Port city on the Northwest coast of Java that was the site of a Muslim sultanate in the fifteenth and sixteenth centuries and which was active in East Asian trade. It was opposed to the monopolistic trade practices of the European traders and eventually lost it sovereignty to the Dutch as a result of

Dutch monopolistic practices. Rulers used the title "kunmat" and the Muslim titles of "maulana" and "sultan." *See* **Kesultanan** and **Kunmat**. The royal line of that sultanate was as follows: Hasanuddin 1552-70, Maulana Yusup 1570-80, Maulana Muhammad 1580-96, Abul Mufakir 1596-[ca 1625], Abul Fath [ca 1625]-51, (Sultan Agung) Abulfath Abulfatah Tirtayasa 1651-83, (separate entry), (Sultan) Haji 1682-87.

**Al Bantani**. *See* **Nawawi Banten, Muhammad**.

**Al Baqarah** (Ar: al-baqarah) Qur. "The Cow," the second chapter of the Qur'an. It contains the story of the Israelites and the golden calf and is the source of many verses in Muslim law regarding forbidden behavior.

**Al-Baqi** (Ar: al-bāqī) Theo. A name of God meaning, "The Eternal."

**Baqi, Muhammad Fuad Abdul**. *See* **Abdul Baqi, Muhammad Fuad**.

**Al Baqilani** (Ar: abu bakr muḥammad ibn aṭ-ṭayyib al-bāqillānī) Biog. (d. 1013). A Maliki jurist from Basra (Iraq) whose views of God included heavy emphasis on the creation, destruction and re-creation cycle. *See I'jaz Al Qur'an*.

**Al-Baar**; Al-Barr; Al-Barru (Ar: al-barr) Theo. A name of God meaning "the Beneficent." Syn: Yang Maha Dermawan.

**Barakah**. Spelling variant. *See* **Berkat**.

**Barat** (In.) 1. Gen. vocab. West, as a direction. 2. Anthro. West, as the name of the people and culture centering on Europe and North America. Used as a point of contrast with Islamic peoples and culture, often negatively.
*Usage*: *kebudayaan* ___, Western culture; *kepentingan penakluk* ___, the importance of dependency on the West; *kolonialisme-imperialisme* ___, the colonialism-imperialism of the West (toward Third World countries); *orang* ___, a Westerner, that is a European, American or Canadian; *proses pem___an*, the process of Westernization.

**Al Baari'**; Al-Bari; Al-Baar-un (Ar: al-bāri')

Theo. A name of God meaning "The Producer." Syn: Yang Mencipta Jiwa.

**Bari, Syekh**. *See Het Boek van Bonang.*

**Barisan Hizbullah**. *See* **Hizbullah, Barisan**.

**Barkat**, barakah, barakat. Spelling variants. *See* **Berkat**.

**Al Barru**. Spelling variant. *See* **Al Baar**.

**Al Barrun**. Spelling variant. *See* **Al Baari'**.

**Barzakh** (In. fr. Ar: barzakh) Doct. A state of being between death and the Day of Judgment when all dead souls remain in their graves. *Usage*: *alam* ___, the state after life, marked by the grave.

**Barzanji**; berzanji (In.) Pop. Islam. Special prayers given on the birthday of the Prophet Muhammad, named for the formulator of the genre, Ja'faar Al Barzanji (d. 1766). Long a popular action in Indonesia, modernist Muslims regard barzanji as unwarranted innovation in worship, while traditionalists support it as laudatory behavior. *Usage*: *membaca* ___, to recite the special prayers; *maulid* ___, the special prayers.

**Al Barzanji, Jaafar (Syekh)** (Ar: ja'far al-barzanjī) Biog. (d. 1766). Writer of the *Mawlid An-Nabi*, a collection of readings for the birthday of the Prophet Muhammad.

**Al Bashiirun; Al Bashir** (Ar: al-baṣīr) Theo. A name of God meaning "The Seeing." Syn: Yang Mempunyai Daya Lihat.

**Al Baasiqaat** (Ar: al-bāsiqāt) Qur. "The Palm Trees," an alternate title for the fiftieth chapter of the Qur'an. The chapter states that the Qur'an is a reminder for the people who correctly fear God. The usual title is "Qaf."

**Al Basith** (Ar: al-bāsiṭ) Theo. Name of God meaning "The Sustainer of Life."

**Basmalah**. Spelling variant. *See* **Bismillah**.

**Basri, Hasan** (Ar: ḥasan al-baṣrī) Biog. (d. 728). An early Arab mystic who formulated initial doctrines of

Islamic theology, law, philosophy and mysticism.

**Baswedan, A. R.** (In.) Biog. (b. 1908). Arab-Indonesian who founded the Arab Indonesian Union (Persatuan Arab Indonesia—PAI) early in the Independence era and was involved generally with modernist Muslim causes. He was minister of information in an early Republican cabinet.

**Batavia** (Dutch) Geog. Place name given by the Dutch to Jakarta or Jakatra (probably a corruption of the word Jayakarta) in 1619, a port on the north coast of Java also known as Suuda Kelapa. It became the headquarters of the Dutch East India Company and later capital of the Dutch East Indies administration. With the place name of Jakarta it became capital of the Republic of Indonesia in 1950.

**Al Baathin**; Al Baathinun (Ar: al-bāṭin) Theo. A name of God meaning "The Most Secret." Syn: Yang Gaib.

**Batin** (In. fr. Ar: bāṭin) 1. Pop. Islam. That which is not apparent in the Qur'an or in life in general, but hidden or secret. Ant: lahir. 2. Myst. The internal world of mystical experience where nonrational experience is sought and nonmaterial existence prevails.

**Al Battah** (Ar: al-battah) Juris. A type of permitted divorce where the wife initiates proceedings and a divorce is granted if the husband agrees to the conditions.

**Bayan**. *See* **Ilmu Bayan.**

**Al Baydawi**. Spelling variant. *See* **Al Baidhawi**.

**Al Bayyinnah**; Al Baiyinah (Ar: al-bayyinah) Qur. "Evidence," the ninety-eighth chapter of the Qur'an. A short lyrical chapter stating that prophets have been sent with clear proof of God's message for correct living.

**Bekel** (In.) Pol. The functionary in charge of a village (desa) on Java. Syn: lurah.

**Belanda** (In) Geog. The Netherlands, both in a contemporary and historical sense. Historically the term is closely tied to the colonial

system operated by the Dutch East India Company and the Dutch Government from the seventeenth to twentieth centuries.
*Usage*: *golongan* ___, the Dutch; *Hindia* ___, The Dutch Indies, the common name used by the Dutch to designate their colonial holdings in Southeast Asia; *kompeni* ___, Dutch East India company (VOC); *pemerintah kolonial* ___, the Dutch colonial government; *penjajahan* ___, Dutch colonialism.

**Belih** (In.) Juris. Sacrifice.
*Usage*: *pem___an hewan*, to sacrifice an animal as part of a religious festival, usually at Idul Adha.

**Benar** (In.) Gen. vocab. Term for "good" or "correct." Often used in a religious sense with "salah" to denote good and bad actions and thoughts.

**Benar, Yang Maha** (In.) Theo. Name of God meaning "The Most Fair."

*Bendera Islam* (In.) Lit. title. "The Banner of Islam," an Indonesian-language newspaper published from 1924 to 1927 under Sarekat Islam sponsorship. It changed its title to *Fajar Asia* in 1927.

**Berhala** (In.) Relig. Idolatry.
*Usage*: *menjembah* ___, worshipping idols.

**Berkat** (In.); barkat, barakat, barakah (Ar: barakah) Pop. Islam. Special blessing assigned by God to certain individuals, usually mystics, rural scholars, and other holy people.
*Usage*: *doa* ___, a prayer of blessing; *kelimpahan* ___, abundance of blessing; *membawa* ___, to carry a blessing; *meminta* ___, to ask for a blessing.

**Bersih** (In.) Juris. Purify, ritually cleanse.
*Usage*: *mem___kan ... ajaran bidah dalam Islam*, to delete and purge innovative doctrines and actions from Islamic practice; *me___kan budi pekerti*, character and behavior cleansed of evil or badness; *pem___*, the act of cleaning and purification for religious purposes.

**Besar, Yang Maha** (In.) Theo. A name of Allah meaning "The Greatest." Same as Al Kabir.

**Beureueh, Muhammad Dawud** (In.) Biog. (d. 1987). Acehnese political leader who favored the establishment of an Acehnese state based on Islamic principles with loose ties to the Republic of Indonesia. He waged guerrilla warfare against the central government during the 1950s to successfully achieve that goal.

**Bhiauddin, Sultan Husin**. *See* **Palembang.**

**Bhinneka Tunggul Ika** (In.) Pol. "Unity in Diversity," an Indonesian national motto.

**Bidah** (In.); bid'ah (Ar: bid'ah) Juris. A practice taken into religious activity that is not countenanced by religious sources but which has wide acceptance as being a legitimate activity. According to modernist Muslims nothing is allowed in matters of worship except that which is expressly commanded by God, while in other matters all actions are allowable except those which have been expressly forbidden by God. Traditionalists differentiate between different kinds of innovation, regarding some as beneficial even in matters of worship.
*Usage*: *mem___kan*, to undertake actions of worship involving new forms; *pem___*, the commission or act of bringing innovation into Islam.
___ *hasanah*, innovation regarded as beneficial; ___ *madzmumah*, innovation regarded as blameworthy; ___ *sesat*, innovation considered in error; ___ *tercela*, innovation regarded as blameworthy; ___ *yang boleh*, innovation regarded as permitted; ___ *yang haram*, innovation regarded as forbidden by God; ___ *yang makruh*, innovation regarded as neither harmful nor beneficial but neutral; ___ *yang sunnat*, innovation regarded as beneficial; ___ *yang wajib*, innovation regarded as essential.
*Ahli* ___, sects in Islamic history with doctrines unacceptable to mainstream Sunni Islam; *amal* ___, performance of innovation in devotional matters; *hal* ___ case of innovation; *mengerjakan* ___ *hasanah*, to perform a worthwhile innovative action in matters of worship; *menerangi* ___ *dan khurafat*, to strenuously oppose innovation and superstition;

*soal-soal* ___, matters of innovation under scrutiny.

*Bidayatul Mujtahid* (Ar: bidāyat al-mujtahid wa nihāyat al- muqtaṣid) Lit. title. An important book on Maliki jurisprudence by Ibnu Rusyd (d. 1126) cited mostly by postmodernist Indonesian writers in the late twentieth century.

**Bilal** (In.) (Ar: bilāl) 1. Biog. (d. ca. 639) An Ethiopian member of Muhammad's community who was assigned the task and honor of giving the call to prayer. 2. Juris. A symbolic allusion to a muezzin, the caller to prayer.

**Billah, Sultan Adam Al Wasi**. *See* **Banjar**.

**Billah, Sultan Musta'in**. *See* **Banjar**.

**Bima**. *See* **Kesultanan**.

**Bintoro, Raden**. *See* **Fattah, Raden**.

**Bismillah** (In.); basmalah (Ar: bismillāh) Pop. Islam. "In the name of God....," a phrase used by Muslims for various occasions and considered an act of piety. *Usage*: *membaca* ___, *mengbacakan* ___, *mengucapkan* ___, to recite the bismillah; *kalimat* ___, the *bismillah* as an Islamic creed; *masalah* ___ *dalam Al Fatihah*, the issue of including the *bismillah* in the recitation of Al Fatihah during normal prayer.

*Het Boek van Bonang* (Dutch) Lit. title. "The Book by Bonang," ascribed to Sunan Bonang (d. 1525) or Syeh Bari (d. unk) outlining the attributes of God and the behavior necessary to become a model human. Used as a religious primer for several centuries on Java.

**Boleh** (In.) Juris. The general word for permission to do something, indicating a classification of behavior. *Usage*: *mem___kan*, undertaking that category of behavior

**Bonang, Sunan** (In.) Biog. (d. 1525). One of nine legendary missionaries who are popularly believed instrumental in converting the population of Java to Islam. He worked primarily in East Java. Also known as Maulana Makdum Ibrahim. *See Het Boek van Bonang* and **Wali Songo**.

**Bonjol, Imam** (In.) Biog. (d. ca.1837) Leader of the Paderi Movement in West Sumatra in the early nineteenth century, a movement which attempted to alter local customs to conform with Islamic rules of jurisprudence. Because of his war against Dutch forces, he is considered by many modern Indonesian Muslim historians as a forerunner of the heroes who gained Indonesian Independence. *See* **Paderi** and **Institut Agama Islam Negara**.

**Al Boraq**. Spelling variant. *See* **Al Burak**.

**Bratakesawa** (Jav.) Assn. Javanese mystical sect basing its teaching on the Qur'an as explained through the book *Kunci Swarga*.

**Budaya** (In.) Anthro. Culture; civilization.
*Usage*: *ke___an Barat*, the civilization of the Western nations in the twentieth century, regarded by Muslims as technically and materially advanced, but as containing serious excesses and lapses of religious and moral values; *ke___an sekular*, secular culture, usually considered as "godless" and associated with the (decadent) West.

**Budi Utomo** (Jav.) Assn. "High Endeavor," a cultural association, founded on Java in 1908, which was seminal in providing intellectual direction for Indonesian nationalism. It was a forerunner of the Indonesian Nationalist Party (Partai Nasional Indonesia).

**Bugis** (In.) Anthro. The name of a ethnic Muslim group, originally located on Sulawesi, which migrated throughout the Southeast Asian region in the seventeenth century, serving as mercenaries, slave traders, and regular traders.
*Usage*: *raja-raja* ___, Buginese kings; *tanah* ___, South Sulawesi.

**Buhaira**. Alternate spelling. *See* **Bahira**.

**Al Bukhari**; Al Bukhary (Ar: al-bukhārī) 1. Biog. (d. 870). Central Asian scholar who was, with Muslim, one of the two foremost analysts of Traditions of the Prophet. His collections of "verified" or "firm" Traditions set the standard for other collectors. 2. Juris. A short title for the

collection of firm Traditions verified by Al Bukhari. The use of the short title indicates use of a collection whose veracity is not disputed among Sunni Muslims. *See* Ash Shahih and Ala Syar-thil Bukhari.
*Usage*: *Imam* ___, a frequently used reference to the scholar Al Bukhari.

*Bulughul Maram* (Ar: bulūgh al-marām) Lit. title. "Attainment of Desire," a well-known text on Tradition criticism and usage by Ibnu Hajarul Asqalani (d. 1448) which has had long usage in Indonesia.

**Bumi** (In.) Gen. vocab. Earth or world. Used by Muslims to indicate life on earth; usually used in distinction to heaven (langit) for life in the Hereafter.

**Bunga** (In.) Econ. Interest or increase in money from investment. This is a questionable practice according to Muslim jurisprudence.
*Usage*: ___ *uang*, interest or increase from investment.

**Bupati**. Spelling variant. *See* **Pepatih**.

**Al Burak**; Al Buraq (In.); Al Boraq (Ar: al-burāq) Qur. A winged, horse-like creature which carried Muhammad from Makkah to Jerusalem and return on the Night Flight when Muhammad ascended to heaven for consultations with God and other prophets. *See* **Baitulmakadas**.

*Burdah* (Ar: qaṣīdat al-burdah) Lang. Short title for *Kawaakibul Durriyya*. Poems in praise of the Prophet, often recited on the occasion of the Prophet Muhammad's birthday in many mosques in Indonesia and elsewhere. The most famous are by Ka'b bin Zuhayr (d. 10H) and Al Bushiri (d. 1294).

**Al Burhan** (Ar: al-burhān) Qur. A name of the Qur'an, indicating it contains the correct beliefs for humans to accept.

*Al Burhan fi 'Ulumil Qur'an* (Ar: al-burhān fī 'ulūm al-qur'ān) Lit. title. "The 'Guide' in the Sciences of the Qur'an", a commentary on the Qur'an by Zarkasyi (d. 1392).

**Burhanuddin, Syekh** (In.) Biog. (d. 1691) The carrier of

Islam to the Minangkabau area in the seventeenth century after study in Aceh. He established a school as the base of his conversion efforts.

**Al Buruuj** (Ar: al-burūj) Qur. "Celestial Signs," the eighty-fifth chapter of the Qur'an. A short, lyrical chapter emphasizing the greatness of God and the need for humans to recognize His existence.

**Buruk** (In.) Gen. vocab. Bad, evil.
*Usage*: *ke___an*, evilness, wickedness.

**Al Buruq**. Spelling variant. *See* **Al Burak**.

**Bushido** (Jap) Anthro. The code of conduct of the Japanese warrior class in medieval Japan. The code was one of the symbols used by the Japanese armed forces in World War II and was also used as an ideological component of Japanese governance in its occupation of Indonesia.

**Al Bushiri, Muhammad** (Ar: muḥammad sā'id ... al-buṣirī) Biog. (d. 1294). Arab writer of a famous poem called the *Kawaakibul Durriyya*, commonly referred to as the *Burdah*, which eulogized the Prophet Muhammad. It is recited in some mosques on the occasion of the Birthday of the Prophet Muhammad.

*Bustanul Salatin* (In. fr. Ar: bustān as-salāṭin) Lit. title. "Garden of Kings," by Ar Raniri (d. 1658) is intended as a history of Aceh, but it ranges far afield to give a complete system of religion, life, and political styles of past Muslim rulers.

# C

**Cakrokusuma Ngabdurrahman Agung.** *See* **Agung, Cakrokusuma Ngabdurrahman.**

**Cek Ko Po.** *See* **Demak.**

**Ceki** (In.) Juris. A card game, usually involving gambling. *Usage*: *main* ___, playing cards.

**Cela** (In.) Juris. Defect, flaw. *Usage*: *ter*___, culpable, blameworthy in character, a term applied to some transmitters of reports preserving the words and behavior of the Prophet Muhammad who were of questionable character and motivation, so that the reports transmitted through them cannot be relied on for accuracy or truth.

**Celak Mata** (In.) Pol. Cosmetically darkened eyes imputing sensuous qualities of the oriental harem. A derogatory term for Islam in the second part of the nationalist era (1920-38). *Usage*: *agama* ___, derogatory term for Islam.

**Cempe**; Campe (In.) Hist. Champa, a Hindu kingdom of Indochina important from the second century to the fourteenth century A.D. In the last century of its rule the court converted to Islam and furnished a consort to the Majapahit ruler who was allowed to practice her religion at the Majapahit court.

**Cendikiawan** (In.) Educ. Scholar, intellectual. Among Muslims the term means intellectual, often with modern philosophical, scientific, or humanistic specializations, in distinction to religious scholar (ulama) trained in standard religious sciences of Islam. *Usage*: ___ *Barat*, Western intellectuals; *kalangan* ___, the collective group of such scholars; ___ *Muslim*, Muslim intellectuals; ___ *Timur*, intellectuals from Asia.

**Centini**. *See* **Serat Centini**.

**Cerai** (In.) Juris. Separation in marriage. In Indonesia this is handled by an Islamic court when the marriage partners are Muslim.
*Usage*: *men___kan*, to undergo separation from one's spouse; *pen___an*, separation from one's spouse.

**Ceramah** (In.) Lang. A lecture. In Islamic practice in Indonesia the term designates a special lecture given on a holy occasion, such as given at many mosques by special speakers during the month of Ramadan.

**Chabar**. Spelling variant. *See* **Kabar**.

**Chalid, Idham**. *See* **Khalid, Idham**.

**Chalifah**. Spelling variant. *See* **Khalifah**.

**Chalil, Moenawar**. *See* **Munawar Khalil**.

**Al Chaaliq**. Spelling variant. *See* **Al Khaaliq**.

**Chatib**. *See* **Khutbah**.

**Cheng Ho** (Chin.) Biog. (d. unk). Chinese Muslim admiral dispatched with large fleets by the Ming Emperor in the early fifteenth century to Southeast Asia and the Indian Ocean to establish a Chinese presence and promote Chinese suzerainty. Responsible for conversion of local groups to Islam, particularly on the North Coast of Java.

**Cinta** (In.) Myst. The love of the mystic for God, often expressed in erotic verse, prose, or other expression.

**Cipayung** (In.) Geog. A resort area in West Java, the site of a series of conferences in the 1970s by Muslim student groups working as a think tank to provide inspiration for Muslim involvement in national improvement. Under the leadership of the Himpunan Mahasiswa Islam a series of recommendations were produced that had a profound and positive affect on the relations between Muslims and national government officials.

**Cirebon** (In.) Geog. City on the north central coast of Java and a site of a sultanate during the sixteenth century. *See* **Kesultanan**. The rulers during its prominence were: Mertawidjaya, unknown dates, Adiwidjaya, unknown dates, Abuhawat, unknown dates.

**Coen, Jan Pietersen** (Dutch) Biog. (d.1629). First Dutch governor general of the East India Company (VOC) in the Indies twice (1619-23 and 1627-29) and an architect of VOC power in the early years. He successfully defended the new factory at Batavia against British and local Indonesian opposition.

**Cokroaminoto, Haji Umar Said** (In.) Biog. (d. 1934). Javanese founder and long-time leader of the Sarekat Islam political movement from about 1908. Although leader of an umbrella nationalist party, he advocated close attention to Islamic principles, which led to a split with more militant members in the mid-1920s.

**Cokrosuyoso.** *See* **Abikusno Cokrosuyoso.**

**Cultuurstelsel** (Dutch) Hist. "Cultivation System," the major Dutch colonial policy applied to economic, political and social areas in nineteenth century Netherlands East Indies beginning in 1830. The Cultivation System was designed to make agricultural production of the Indies an important part of the international economic system and an important source of funds for the Netherlands. Indonesian and Dutch historians regard the system as exploitive of local labor.

# D

**Dachlan, (K.H.) Ahmad** (In.) Biog. (d. 1923). Javanese founder of the Muhammadiyah, a modernist Muslim association, in 1912. He was the foremost Muslim reformer on Java and his organization has remained one of several premier Muslim associations in Indonesia dedicated to education and social welfare. *See* **Muhammadiyah.**

**Dachlan, (K.H.) Muhammad.** *See* **Menteri Agama.**

**Dadu** (In.) Juris. Dice. *Usage*: *main* ___, playing dice, gambling.

**Daendels, Herman Willem** (Dutch) Biog. (d. 1818). French governor general of the Indies (1808-11), an appointee of Napoleon who laid the basis for a modern administration and infrastructure of the colonial administration in the Netherlands Indies.

**Dahar Klimah** (Jav.) Pop. Islam. Wedding meal on Java observed by pious Muslims (santris) at which goats are sacrificed. The ceremony is regarded as more Islamic than the slametan meal which is held at the weddings of the less devout (Agami Islam).

**Ad Dahr** (Ar: ad-dahr) Qur. An alternate title for the seventy-sixth chapter of the Qur'an, meaning "Time." A medium-length, lyric chapter describing the paradise that awaits those who believe in God and do the charitable works that He has commanded. Its usual title is Al Insaan.

**Dai** (In.) (Ar: dā'in) Educ. Missionary, revivalist, propagandist. A Muslim undertaking religious intensification activities. *See* **Dakwah.**

**Daif** (In.); dlaif; dha'if (Ar: ḍaīf) Trad. Weak; in examination of Traditions (hadis), it means that a story preserving the words and behavior of the Prophet Muhammad is unsupported by the usual methods of confirmation and cannot be regarded as true.

**Dakwah** (In.); da'wah (Ar: da'wah) 1. Educ. Efforts to improve thought and behavior to be in accord with ideal Islamic standards. 2. Educ. The public effort by Islamic groups to upgrade the general behavior of the Muslim community. The person who promotes such activities is known as a dai. 3. Educ. A program of study offered at the national Islamic Studies institutes (IAIN's) and other Indonesian institutions of higher education in which stress is placed on techniques for spreading and intensifying the teachings of Islam. *Usage*: *ber___*, *melakukan ___* to undertake faith and practice upgrading activities; *men___kan Islam di seluruh Sulawesi*, to spread Islam throughout Sulawesi; ___ *pembangunan*, improving faith and practice among believers; *ilmu* ___, the subject of study on how to perform effective efforts to renew religious faith and practice; *jiwa* ___, spirit of Islamic intensification; *metode* ___, techniques in upgrading faith and practice; *pergerakan* ___, the general movement toward intensifying renewed commitment to Islamic faith and practice; *pusat kegiatan* ___, center for Islamic upgrading activities; *rangka* ___, scheme or plan for Islamic intensification activities.

**Dalil** (In) (Ar: dalil) Doct. The basis of an argument that rests on a principle of the Qur'an.

**Damai**. *See* **Kedamaian, Yang Maha**.

**Dansa-Dansi** (In.) Pop. Islam. Dancing. Used among some Muslims in reference to Western style dancing where men and women embrace during social dating. Such behavior is viewed among some Muslims as violating religious tenets regarding the unauthorized touching between unrelated members of different sexes.

**Dar** (Ar: dār) Gen. vocab. House, place of residence; in writing on Islam often used in the figurative sense for identification with a religion or grouping. *See* entries on **Darulharab** and **Darul Islam**.

**Darajat, Sunan**; Drajat .... (In.) Biog. (d. unk.). One of nine leading missionaries popularly believed to have led the conversion of Java to Islam in the fifteenth century. He worked particularly with the orphans and the sick. Also known as Syarifuddin and Masih Munat.

**Ad Dari, Tamin**. *See Hikayat Tamin Ad Dari.*

*Darmogandul* (Jav.) Lit. title. Important book on Javanese mysticism appearing in Yogyakarta in the post-independence period (1950s). The confession of faith and other Islamic teachings are interpreted with sexual references common in some strains of Javanese mysticism.

**Darul Islam** (In.) (Ar: dār al-islām) Juris. "House of Islam," or home of believers in Islam, in distinction to "house of war" (dar al-harb), the area populated by nonbelievers.

**Darul Islam** (In.) Pol. The name of an Indonesian political movement which, in 1948, declared Indonesia a religious state subject to religious law. Known by the acronym DI/TII (Darul Islam/ Tentara Islam Indonesia), it was in rebellion against the Indonesian Republic until 1963 when the Indonesian military eradicated it.

**Darulharab** (In.); Darul Harb (Ar: dār al-ḥarb) Juris. "House of war" indicating the regions populated by non-Muslims, in distinction to "Darul Islam," which Muslims occupy.

**Darurat** (In.); darurah (Ar: ḍarūrah) Juris. Emergency, dire circumstances. A situation in which actions forbidden by God may be undertaken by Muslims because of emergency conditions. Usually involves eating forbidden food or cleansing with clean dirt rather than water for ablution.
*Usage*: *hukum* ___, the principle that emergency conditions negate normal patterns of religious life.

**Darussalam** (In.) (dār as-salām) Qur. "The Abode of Peace," a reference in the Qur'an to the dwelling place of believers in the Hereafter.

**Dato'ri** (Bug.) Title. Title of respect given a religious scholar on Sulawesi, especially in the early period of Islamization in the fifteenth and sixteenth centuries.

**Datu** (In.) 1. Title. In precolonial Southeast Asia a title common throughout Indonesia, Malaysia, Brunei, and the Philippines for a high ranking official attached to a ruler's court. The term survives as a historical concept and as a title of respect or heritage in Malaysia, Brunei, and the Philippines. 2. Pop. Islam. Title given a shaman in some areas of Southeast Asia.

**Daud**; Dawud (Ar: dāwūd) Qur. Personal name for a prophet mentioned in the Qur'an. He was one of six major prophets who brought a revelation to man, in this case the *Zabur*, equated with the Psalms of the Old Testament.

**Daulah**; daulat (Ar: dawlah) Pol. Political power, sovereignty, especially of the Southeast Asian Islamic states of the fifteenth to seventeenth centuries. *Usage*: ___ *Bani 'Abbas*, the Abbasiyyah Empire (eighth to thirteenth centuries); ___ *Fathimiyah Mesir*, the Fatimid Empire of Egypt (tenth to twelfth centuries).

**Daulah Islamiah** (Ar: dawlah al-islāmiyyah) Pol. Islamic state, in which sacred law (syariah) would be operative and the teachings of Islam apparent in public policy. This has been a primary point of discussion among Indonesian Muslims during most of the twentieth century.

**Da'wah**. Spelling variation. *See* **Dakwah**.

**Dayah** (Aceh.) Educ. In Aceh and north Sumatra the common term for an Islamic religious boarding school, similar to the pesantren of Java.

**Dayah Lihat, Yang Mempunyai**. (In.) Theo. Name of God meaning "The All Seeing." Syn: Al Bashiirun.

**Ad Dayyaan** (Ar: ad-dayyān) Theo. A name of God meaning "The Reciprocator."

**Demak** (Jav.); Cek Ko Po (Chin.) Geog. 1. A place

name for a city in central Java which was the center for the first Muslim state on Java in the fifteenth century. Site of an important mosque. *See* **Kesultanan** and **Masjid**. The rulers of Demak during its period of ascendancy were as follows: Al-Fattah 1478-1518 (separate entry), Badruddin 1504, Yunus of Jepara 1518-21, Trenggana 1505-18, 1521-46 (separate entry), Prawata 1546-61. 2. Pol. A term used symbolically for "national Islam" which looks within the Indonesian context rather than to the Middle East for inspiration.
*Usage*: *masjid* ___, a famous mosque established in 1428 which served as the seat of government for the first Islamic kingdom on Java.

**Demokrasi Liberal** (In.) Pol. "Liberal Democracy," a name given the period of political history from 1950 to 1957 when the governmental system was based on a multiparty parliament with cabinet coalitions. It is generally regarded by Indonesians as a period of political weakness and disarray.

**Demokrasi Terpimpin** (In.) Pol. "Guided Democracy," a name given the period of political history from 1958 to 1966 when President Sukarno ruled the country as chief arbiter of the political factions. It is generally regarded by Indonesians as a period of leftist domination of government and a low point in Muslim political fortunes. Also called Orde Lama.

**Departemen Agama R.I** (In.) Pol. "Department of Religious Affairs," the proper name of an Indonesian Government agency charged with the religious well being of various religious groups in Indonesia and with carrying out certain functions associated with the religious communities. It is headed by a minister of religious affairs. *See* **Menteri Agama**.

**Dermawan, Yang Maha** (In.) Theo. Name of God meaning "The Most Beneficent." Syn: Al Baar.

**Desa** (In.) 1. Anthro. Village, town. The basic village unit on Java. It has been the center of communal life since before recorded time. Land belonged to the desa, although it was worked in different arrangements by its inhabitants. It was headed by a lurah or bekel. 2. Pol. In the writing on development by recent Indonesian Muslim scholars desa refers to the historic rural lifestyle of the countryside, particularly on Java, where traditional Muslim values played an important part in the daily lives of the inhabitants.

**Dewan Masjid Indonesia** (In.) Pol. "The Council of Indonesian Mosques," a quasi-official agency, founded in 1972, to act as coordinator with national and international organizations concerning use of mosques as a center of revivalist activity (dakwah).

**Dewan Perwakilan Rakyat** (In.) Pol. "The Peoples' Consultative Assembly," the Indonesian parliament. Currently it is partly elected, partly appointed by presidential choice. Muslims of various political viewpoints have been members since it was formed in 1945.

**Dewantara, Ki Hadjar** (In.) Biog. (d. 1959). Javanese educator and nationalist figure during the nationalist era (1908-45). One of the four Indonesian government leaders during the Japanese Occupation Government (1942-45).

**Dha'if**. Spelling variant. *See* **Daif**.

**Dhalah** (Ar: ḍalālah) Juris. To be in error.

**Ad Dhar** (Ar: aḍ-ḍārr) Theo. Name of God meaning: "The Punisher."

**Dhudhur**. Spelling variant. *See* **Zuhur**.

**Adh Dhuhaa**; Adh Dhuha (Ar: aḍ-ḍuḥa) Qur. "The Morning Hours," the ninety-third chapter of the Qur'an. A short, lyrical chapter in which God assures the believer of His care and good will.

**Dhu'l Karnain**. *See* **Hikayat Iskandar Zu'l Karnain**.

*Di Bawah Bandera Revolusi* (In.) Lit. title. "Under the Banner of Revolution," a collection of speeches and writings of President Sukarno issued in the 1960s. It emphasized his nationalistic stance, his sympathy toward Islam, and the need for Islam to undergo a transformation to be applicable to contemporary conditions.

**DI/TII**. *See* **Darul Islam**.

**Din** (In.); dien (Ar: dīn) Relig. A term for the religion of Islam in general along with its beliefs, practices, and rituals. Syn: agama.

**Dinamisme** (In.) Relig. Attempts to explain the phenomena of some immanent force or energy that resides in all objects. Dynamists seek to control or propitiate that power. Control allows them magical energy to use in casting spells and foretelling events. Propitiation involves worship. *Usage*: *hidup* ___, to practice dynamism.

**Diponegoro, (Pangeran)**; Dipanegara (Jav.) Biog. (d. 1855). Javanese prince of the House of Mataram who led a war, known as the Java War (1825-30), against his brother, the ruler of Yogyakarta and the Dutch. He believed himself to be the Ratu Adil, a legendary Javanese savior, and also convinced the Muslim ulama to assist him.

**Dirayat**. *See* **Ilmu Dirayat Hadis**.

**Divide Et Empera** (Latin). Hist. "Divide and Rule," an expression used by Indonesian historians concerning European political actions in Southeast Asia, especially in the sixteenth and seventeenth centuries. Their historians held that Europeans fomented divisions so that they could intervene and control Southeast Asia.

**Djajadiningrat, Hoesin**. *See* **Jayadiningrat, Husein**.

*Djago! Djago!* (In.) Lit. title. "Up and At'em," a news-paper published at Pandang Panjang in the 1921-25 period aimed at a Muslim audience. It advocated militant action to gain nationalist goals and was considered by Dutch authorities to be communist controlled.

**Djarnawi Hadikusuma**. *See* **Partai Muslimin Indonesia**.

*Al Djihad* (In.) Lit. title. "Striving [in the Way of God]," a daily newspaper reflecting the views of the Masjumi political party, published in 1945 and 1946.

**Dlaif**. Spelling variant. *See* **Daif**.

**Doa** (In.) (Ar: du'ā') Juris. Prayer, usually in the sense of supplication to God, as opposed to liturgical prayer. *Usage*: *ber*___, to address God in private prayer; *ber*___ *kunut*, to undertake the standing prayer, as done in the night prayer; *men*___, to undertake prayer; *men*___ *bertawassul*, *men*___ *dengan tawassul, masalah tawassul dalam men*___, to undertake prayer petitioning God for His assistance in a matter. ___ *berkat*, a blessing given by an older person or a religious person; ___ *istighfar*, to pray for forgiveness; ___ *iftihah*, opening prayer; ___ *maulid*, to recite the Prophet's birthday prayer. *Kedudukan* ___ performance of prayer; *masalah* ___, the question or matter of prayer; *membaca* ___ *kunut*, to recite the standing prayer; *mengajarkan* ___ *tawassul*, to undertake prayer petitioning God concerning some personal matter; ___ *(di malam)*, to continuously pray (as during the night); *merendahkan* ___, to submit oneself (to God) in prayer.

**Dosa** (In.) Juris. Sin, that is, the product of failing to observe God's commands and prohibitions. This can be dissolved through God's pardon or through the application of merit earned at some other time. *Usage*: *ber*___, *ber*___ *melakukan*, to commit sin. ___ *(yang paling) besar*, a mortal sin; ___ *hati*, a sin of the heart; ___ *lidah*, a spoken sin; ___ *kemaluan*, a shameful sin; ___ *syirik*, the sin of disbelief; ___ *tubuh*, a sin of the body. *Hal* ___, a situation involving sin; *mengerjakan* ___ besar, to commit a major sin; *menampuni* ___, to pardon sin; *perbuatan* ___, the commission of sin.

**Drajat, Sunan**. Spelling variant. *See* **Darajat, Sunan**.

**Ad Dukhaan**; Ad Dukhan (Ar: dukhan) Qur. "Smoke," the forty-fourth chapter of the Qur'an. It refers to an incident when the Prophet Muhammad prayed for ending a famine.

**Dukun** (In.) Cult. On Java a practitioner of magic who claims to possess secret powers which he or she employs in a variety of functions. The dukun mostly treats illness with herbs and native medicines. Some dukuns foretell the future, other cast spells to create good or bad fortunes, and a few are practitioners in black magic.

**Dukunisme** (In.) Cult. The art of magic.

**Dunia** (In.) (Ar: dunya) Doct. Earth, world. In religious meaning the life of this world as opposed to the Hereafter.
*Usage*: *harta benda* ___, worldly possessions; *masalah ke___wan, soal ke___an, urusan ___wi*, matters concerned with earthly life, that is, non-religious matters; *meninggal* ___, to die; *urusan* ___, a temporal matter.

*Dunia Baru Islam* (In. Fr. Eng.) Lit. title. "The New World of Islam," a leading work on contemporary Muslim responses to political problems in the 1920s. *The New World of Islam* by L. Stoddard (d. 1950) is cited by postmodernist Muslims as an indication of patronizing Western scholarly attitudes toward Islam in the modern era.

*Dunia Islam* (In.) Lit. title. "The World of Islam," a newspaper of the 1920's that reflected the views of the Muslim leadership of the Sarekat Islam.

*Ad Durrul Mantser* (Ar: ad-durr al-manthūr) Lit. title. "Scattered Pearls," one of three major commentaries on the Qur'an written by As Sayuthi (d. 1505). Especially important among Indonesian religious scholars during the twentieth century. *See* **Tafsir**.

**Dusta** (In.) Juris. Lie, falsehood.
*Usage*: *ber___*, proving the falsehood of a report purporting to be a record of the prophet's words or behavior; *men___kan*, to defame someone.

**Dzahabi** (Ar. shams ad-dīn ... adh-dhahabī) Biog. (d. 1348) Arab historian and theologian from Syria. His major work, *Ta'rikh Al Islam*, is an extensive history compiled by decades. *See Mizanul Iktidal.*

**Adz Dzaariyaat**; Az Zaariyaat; Adz Dzariat; Adz Dzariyat (Ar: adh-dhariyāt) Qur. The sixty-first chapter of the Qur'an, titled "Scattering Winds." It tells how God manifests Himself and promotes prosperity and peace on earth.

**Dzaat**. Spelling variant. *See* **Zat**.

**Dzikir**. Spelling variant. *See* **Zikir**.

**Dzimmi**. Spelling variant. *See* **Zimmi**.

**Dzulhijjah**. Spelling variant. *See* **zulhijah**.

**Adz Dzuljalaali Wal Ikraam** (Ar: dhū-l jalāl ikrām) Theo. A name of God meaning "Full of Majesty and Generosity."

**Dzulqaidah**. *See* **zulkaidah**.

**Adz Dzuntiqaam** (Ar: dhuntiqām) Theo. A name of God meaning, "He Who Retaliates."

# E

**Ejaan** (In.) Lang. Spelling, orthography. An important consideration in the transliteration of Arabic terminology into Bahasa Indonesia.

**Endeh** (In.) Geog. An island in the Lesser Sundas, known historically for being the place of exile for Sukarno after his treason trial by the Dutch in the 1920s. He wrote a series of letters from here explaining his views on Islam. *See Surat-Surat Islam Dari Endeh.*

**Esa, Yang Maha** (In.) Theo. Unity or Oneness of God. Syn: Al Ahad.
*Usage*: *Tuhan Yang Maha* ___, God the Only One, the first principle of the national motto (Pancasila) of Indonesia.

**Ethical Policy** (Dutch) Hist. Dutch government policy at the turn of the nineteenth century aimed at correcting earlier exploitive policies followed by the Dutch government in regard to the East Indies. The Ethical Policy altered some practices, but changing economic conditions led to the institution of the Cultuur System, which extended economic exploitation rather than limiting it.

**Evolusi** (In.) Relig. The theory that complex life forms evolved from lower life forms and that man is a product of development from other creatures. Many Muslims hold the theory to be at odds with the version of creation presented in the Qur'an, which they claim indicates God made all creatures independent of one another.

# F

**Fadhal.** *See* **Riba.**

**Faedah** (In.) (Ar: fa'idah) Juris. The purpose of doing something. Used frequently in setting out religious exercises. Syn: tsamrah. *Usage*: *ber*___, usefulness, advantage.

*Faithul Mu'in. See Kitab Faithul Mu'in.*

**Al Fajr** (Ar: al-fajr) Qur. "Dawn," the eighty-ninth chapter of the Qur'an. A medium-length, lyric chapter in which humans are informed of God's earlier punishment of people who went astray and warned that if they do not do what is right, they too will be punished.

**Fakhruddin, Abdurrazak.** *See* **Muhammadiyah.**

**Fakhruddin Ar Razi.** *See* **Ar Razi, Fakhruddin.**

**Fakir** (In.); faqir (Ar: fākir) 1. Juris. Poor, destitute person, eligible for distribution from the poor tax. 2. Myst. A mendicant, living a life of poverty. Historically, some sufi practitioners turned their backs on all material things to devote their energies to the search for God. *Usage*: *menolong* ___ *miskin*, to give aid to the poor; ___ *miskin*, poor and miserable person and, hence, eligible for alms or receiving the proceeds of the poor tax.

**Al Falaq**; Al Falak (Ar: al-falaq) Qur. "Daybreak," the 113th chapter of the Qur'an. It urges humans to call on God in times of trouble and when confronted by evil. It is often cited as a guard against demons and the unknown in general.

**Falsafah**; filsafat (In.); falsafat (Ar: falsafah) Doct. Philosophy as it relates to the

logical deduction of concepts and ideas, particularly in regard to absolutes, such as God and eternity. In Islam it is the system built by one group of classical scholars who based their thought on Greek and Hellenistic models. It was made subservient to theology by Al Ghazali (d. 1111).
*Usage*: *ber*___, thinking within the structure of a set of rules and guidelines that consider the norms and ends of human existence.
___ *amalan*, situational ethics; ___ *Islam*, Muslim theology, especially of the classical period; ___ *modern Islam*, Muslim thinking of the twentieth century; ___ *Islam tradisional*, standard Sunni philosophical thinking.
*Ahli* ___, philosophers, usually referring to those of the classical period; *alam* ___, among philosophers; *buku-buku* ___, books on philosophy; *golongan* ___, *kalangan* ___-___ *Islam*, philosophers, especially those of the classical period.

**Falsafah** (In.) Pol. Ideology or perception, an expression used in popular Indonesian political parlance in the 1950s as the program or platform of a political group.

**Fana** (In.); fana' (Ar: fanā') Myst. Extinction of the "soul" of the mystic into God as the ultimate goal of mystical searching.

**Fansuri, Hamzah**; Fansyuri (In.) Biog. (d. 1625). Acehnese mystic of the Qadiriyyah order who introduced the ruba'i and sha'ir poetry forms to the Malay-Indonesian area. He also introduced philosophical and metaphysical language. His works were branded as heretical after his death by Al Raniri (d. 1658). Among his works were *Asrarul 'Arifin*.

**Faqih Usman**. *See* **Usman, Faqih**; **Menteri Agama**; and **Muhammadiyah**.

**Faqir**. Spelling variant. *See* **Fakir**.

**Al Farabi** (Al Farabius) (Ar: abu naṣr muḥammad ... al-farābī) Biog. (d. 950). Muslim philosopher of Turkic origin. He translated many works from Greek and wrote *Ihsan'l-'Ulum*.

**Faraid** (Ar: fara'iḍ) Juris. Compulsory matters in inheritance regulations.

**Fardu** (In.); fardlu (Ar: farḍ) Juris. That which is strictly prescribed and obligatory, the omission of which will be punished, while its execution will be rewarded.

**Fardu Ain** (In.); fardlu' ain (Ar: farḍ 'ayn) Juris. A matter to which all believers are obligated.

**Fardu Kifayah** (In.); fardlu kifayah, fardhu kifāyah (Ar: farḍ al-kifāyah) Juris. A matter in which it is demanded that a sufficient number of Muslims should fulfill the religious duties concerned, such as a holy war, and the performance of communal prayer. *Usage*: *pekerjaan-pekerjaan* ___, obligatory communal matters.

**Faruqi, Ismail** (Ar: fārūqī, ismā'il) Biog. (d. 1986). Palestinian-born intellectual who taught in North America and was a key organizer of the Muslim community there. He advocated the Islamization of knowledge as a Muslim means to tame Western influence on science and technology.

**Fasah** (Ar:faṣkh) Juris. Divorce by judicial decree when the husband has taken on abnormal physical or mental disorders, such as leprosy, venereal disease, madness, or impotence.

**Fasik** (In.); fasiq (Ar: fāsiq) Juris. A transgressor; a believer who behaves contrary to practice established by sacred law (syari'ah).

**Fata** (Ar: fata') Hist. A Muslim warrior of the middle period in certain sections of the Middle East who lived by a special code, much like the code of chivalry among European knights of the same era. *See* **Futuwuh**.

**Fatah Intan**. *See* **Institut Agama Islam Negara.**

**Fatahillah**. *See* **Gunung Jati, Sunan.**

**Fatayat Nadhlatul Ulama** (In.) Assn. "Young Women of the Orthodox Scholars Association," an organization, established in the 1950s. It is active in revivalist activities (dakwah), social welfare activities, sports, and Qur'an reading.

**Fatetehan**. *See* **Gunung Jati, Sunan.**

**Al Fat-h**; Al Fath; Al Fat-hu (Ar: al-fatḥ) Qur. "Victory," the forty-eighth chapter of the Qur'an. It predicted that Muhammad and his followers would be victorious in their wars against the Mekkans.

**Faathir**; Fathir (Ar: fāṭir) Qur. "Creation," the thirty-fifth chapter of the Qur'an. It affirms the role of God as perpetual creator and sustainer of the earth and all things in and on it.

*Fathul Bari* (Ar: fatḥ al-bārī fī sharḥ al-bukhārī) Lit. title. "Prologue of the Pure," a well known study on Tradition criticism and interpretation of the collection of Al Bukhari. The work is by Ibnu Hajarul Asqalani (d. 1448).

*Fathul Rahman* (Ar: fatḥ ar-raḥmān) Lit. title. "The Victory of God," a text on mysticism by Al Anshari (d. 1520), which is a commentary on the *Risalat fil Tauhid* by Al Dimashqi (d. 540H). It frequently has been translated into Malay-Indonesian.

**Fathur Rahman**. *See* **Menteri Agama**.

**Fatihah** (In.); Al Faatihah (Ar: fātiḥah) Qur. "The Opening," the first chapter of the Qur'an. It is considered to contain the essence of the Qur'anic message in its seven verses. It is revered by Muslims and included in its entirety in the standard prayer. It is also used to solemnize contracts.
*Usage*: *masalah bismillah dalam* ___, the matter of including the phrase "In the name of God the Merciful, the Compassionate" in the recitation of Al-Fatihah.

**Fatimid**. *See* **Khalifah**.

**Al-Fattaah**; Al-Fattah (Ar: al-fattāḥ) Theo. A name of God meaning "The All-Powerful."

**Al Fattah, Sultan**. *See* **Demak**.

*Fattah, Raden*, (Sunan Bintara) (In.) Biog. (d. ca. 1527). Javanese political activist of the early fifteenth century who became the first Muslim ruler of the kingdom of Demak and Bintoro. He took the title of Sultan ... Alamsyah Akbar. *See* **Demak** and **Wali Songo**.

*Fatuhatul Makiyah. See Jami'ut Tafshil.*

**Fatwa** (In.) (Ar: fatwā) Juris. A pronouncement by a qualified religious scholar on an issue of belief or practice. The decision is made in the context of past interpretations of other religious scholars of the same school of jurisprudence. The fatwa is not binding on any Muslim but is advisory of how the giver of the fatwa regards religious sources pertinent to the matter at hand.
*Usage*: *ber* ___, *memberi* ___ to undertake the process of formulating and issuing a fatwa; *mem*___*kan*, to be of the opinion that. ___ *mubaligh-mubaligh*, the opinion of popular preachers of Islam. *melontarkan* ___, to generate a legal formulation; *membaca* ___, to consider a legal opinion; *mendengar* ___, to receive a legal opinion.

**Feodalisme** (In.) Hist. A premodern system in which control of land is the key factor and social status is determined by the relationship of people to the land as land-holders or as workers bound to the land. The system was used with variations world-wide.

**Fi Ri'ayattilah** (In.) (Ar: fī ri'āyat illāh) Expres. "May you enjoy the protection of God," a popular expression given by one Muslim to another.

**Fi Sabillah**. *See* **Sabilillah.**

*Fi Zhilailul Qur'an* (Ar: fī ẓilāl al-qur'ān) Lit. title. "In the Shadow of the Qur'an," a neofundamentalist commentary on the Qur'an by Sayyid Qutub (d. 1966), stressing the values of the Qur'an as the absolute guide for the Muslim community and all humans. Translations in Indonesia have been popular during the 1980s. *See* **Tafsir.**

**Fidyah** (In.); fid-yah (Ar: fidyah) Juris. A fine for failure to perform required religious actions, such as prayer or fasting.
*Usage*: *cara* ___, a fine for failure to undertake religious actions; ___ *puasa*, a fine for failure to fast; ___ *sembahyang*, a fine for failure to worship.

**Fikih** (In.); fiqih, fiqh (Ar: fiqh) Juris. The codification of principles of conduct drawn by religious scholars from the Qur'an, Traditions, analogy of those two sources, and consensus of Legalists. In Indonesia fikih usually follows the dictates of the Syafi'i school which is common to Egypt and the coastal areas of India. Modernist Muslims downgrade fikih in their insistence on direct interpretation of the scriptures. *See* **Mazhab**. *Usage*: ___ *Islam*, Muslim jurisprudence; ___ *kuno*, jurisprudence labeled as "old fashioned" (by detractors). *Ahli-ahli* ___, Muslims historically believing in the importance of jurisprudence; *hukum* ___, the laws of Muslim jurisprudence; *ilmu ushul* ___, the science of assembling the jurisprudential codes; *istilah* ___, instrument of jurisprudence; *kaidah-kaidah* ___, the principles of jurisprudence; *kitab-kitab* ___, standard books of jurisprudence; *mazhab-mazhab* ___, the schools of jurisprudence; *para ahli* ___, *para ahli usul* ___, people of the Sunni sect who have historically believed that fikih properly regulates religious action; *qaw'idh* ___, the principles of jurisprudence; *ushul* ___, the basic principles of the science of codification.

**Fikih Mazhab Nasional** (In.) Juris. "National Indonesian School of Islamic Jurisprudence," an aspiration voiced by Hazairin (d. 1975), Ash-Shiddieqy (d. 1975) and other scholars in the 1960s and 1970s for formulation of a new code of jurisprudence built around Islamic principles reflecting the Indonesian environment.

**Fikih Muamalat** (Ar: fiqh mu'āmalāt) Juris. Principles of Muslim jurisprudence relating to matters of trade.

**Fikih Munakahat** (Ar: fiqh munākaḥāt) Juris. Principles of Muslim jurisprudence relating to matters of marriage.

**Al Fiil**; Al Fil (Ar: al-fīl) Qur. "The Elephant," the 105th chapter of the Qur'an. A very short, lyrical chapter recalling the invasion of Makkah by the Abyssinian ruler in the year of the Prophet's birth and how the invaders were driven away by flying creatures.

**Fi'liyyah**. *See* **Sunah Amaliyyah**.

**Filsafat**. Spelling variant. *See* **Falsafah**.

**Filsuf** (In.) Doct. Philosopher. *See* **Filsafah.**
*Usage*: ___-___ *Muslim*, the philosophers of Islam.

**Fiqh**, fiqih. Spelling variants. *See* **fikih**.

**Fir riqah** (Ar: fi raqīq) Juris. The emancipated or runaway slave, eligible for proceeds from the distribution of the poor tax (zakat).

**Fir'aun** (Ar: fir'awn) Qur. The ruler of Egypt at the time of the Israelites captivity there. The name is used symbolically for stubbornness and obduracy.

**Firdaus**. *See* **Surga**.

**Firman** (In.) Qur. Command or order. The term is used to announce a quote from the Qur'an, i.e. "Firman Allah" and equates to Christian expression "Word of God."

**Firqah** (Ar: firqah) Relig. Group or sect.
*Usage*: ___ *Syiah*, the Syiite faction of Islam; ___ *tasawwuf*, the mystics or Sufis.

**Fitrah**; pitrah (In.) (Ar: fiṭrah) Juris. The donation of a Muslim at the end of the fasting month, usually to a mosque, Muslim association, or particular religious scholar for distribution to the poor. According to jurisprudence the donation should be made as an assessment varying on different possessions and wealth.

**Fityah** (Ar: fatā) Juris. A slave, especially one who is emancipated and, accordingly, eligible for proceeds from distribution of the poor tax (zakat).

**Fulan** (Ar: fulan) Trad. A reference to an anonymous person, usually as an example to illustrate a specific case or situation. In Tradition analysis it is used to classify people in early Islam who relayed reports transmitting information about the words and behavior of the Prophet Muhammad from one generation to another. ___ **Dzabt** (Ar: ... thabt) A dependable relator of a report. ___ **Dhabitz** (Ar: ... ḍābiẓ) A person judged to have a strong memory in relaying a report. ___ **Dziqat** (Ar: ... thiqah) A person judged to be completely reliable in relaying a report. ___ **Hafidz** (Ar: ... ḥāfiz) A person judged to have memorized a large number of reports. *See*

**Hafidz.** ___ **Hujjah** (Ar: ... ḥujjah) A person judged to have memorized whole collections of reports. *See* **Hujjah.** ___ **Mutkin** (Ar: ... mutqin) A person judged to have been extremely careful in correctly transmitting reports.

**Fundamentalis** (In.) Relig. The principle of returning to the primary sources of a religion and making those principles the basis for contemporary life. In Islam this means emphasis on the Qur'an and the Way (sunnah) of the Prophet Muhammad.
*Usage*: *gerakan* ___, neo-orthodox movement in Islam.

**Fuqaha** (In.) (Ar: faqīh) Juris. Practitioner of Islamic jurisprudence. Fuqaha constituted a group of religious scholars in the classical and middle periods of Islamic history, who formulated the Muslim codes of behavior and expanded them through the centuries.
*Usage*: *para* ___, the practitioners of Islamic jurisprudence, often used in a historical sense.

**Furqan** (Ar: furqān) Qur. A name of the Qur'an meaning "The Criterion."

**Al Furqaan**, Al Furqan (Ar: furqān) Qur. 1. "The Distinction" or "The Scales," the twenty-fifth chapter of the Qur'an. It contains lessons about the nature of God and His relationship with His prophets. 2. A name given to the Qur'an, as the criterion for weighing right and wrong.

**Furu'**. *See* **Khilafiah.**

**Furuk**. *See* **Khilafiqah**.

**Fushshilat** (Ar: fuṣṣilat) Qur. "The Explanation," the forty-first chapter of the Qur'an. It states that God's power is the basis of faith and revelation. Also known as Haa Miim As Sajdah.

*Futuhatul Makiyah* (Ar: al-futūḥāt al-makkiyyah) Lit. title. "The Mekkan Opening," a major work on all phases of Islam by the Syiite mystic Ibnu 'Arabi (d. 1240), which has wide acceptance among Sunni Muslims, although his identifications of the mystic with the godhead during mystical exercises are regarded as overstated and even heretical by some groups.

**Futuwah**; futuah (Ar: futuwwah) Hist. Ethic of the middle period among certain warrior orders, such as the Ikwan Ash Shafa'. The ethic espoused piety, humility, generosity and hospitality, somewhat similar to the code of chivalry of medieval Europe of the same period.

# G

**Gabungan Sarikat Buruh Islam Indonesia—Gasbiindo** (In.) Assn. "The Indonesian Muslim Labor Alliance," a major labor organization founded in the late 1940s as a special member of Masjumi. Under the leadership of Yusuf Wibisono (b. 1908) in the 1950s it achieved considerable independence of action and won its own seat in parliament. It survived into the 1960s as an independent organization.

**Gabungan Usaha Pembinaan Pendidikan Islam—GUPPI** (In.) Assn. "The Working Group for Promoting Islamic Education," an organization founded in 1950. In the late 1960s it came under the umbrella of the Golkar political party and became an unofficial government instrument for promoting private Muslim (pesantren) education.

**Gadjah Mada** (Jav.) 1. Biog. (d. 1364). Javanese vizier of the Majapahit Empire at its greatest expansion, credited with policies leading to that period of greatness. In modern Indonesia he is recognized as a symbol of Indonesian nationalism. 2. Educ. A national university located at Yogyakarta.

**Al Gaffar** (In.); Al Ghaafir (Ar: al-ghāfir) Qur. "He Who Forgives," an alternative name for the fortieth chapter of the Qur'an. The usual name is Al Mu'min.

**Gaffar, Yang Maha** (In.) Theo. A name of God meaning "The Forgiver."

**Al Gafur** (In.); Al Ghafuur; Al Ghafur (Ar: al-ghafūr) Theo. A name of God meaning "The Forgiver."

**Gaib** (In.); Ghaib (Ar: ghayb) Myst. Secret matters known only to God. The power of amulets, spells, charms, and mysterious beings are

sometimes featured in this category.
*Usage*: *Maha* ___, A name of God meaning "The Most Secret."

**Gaib, Yang Maha**; Ghaib .... (In.) Theo. Name of God meaning "The Most Secret." Syn: Al Baathin.

**Garebek** (In.); Garebeg; Gerebeg (Jav.) Cult. Large public festivals held in Yogyakarta for the celebration of Idul Fitri (Gerebeg Poso) and the birthday of the Prophet (Garebeg Mulud). They began in the early seventeenth century on orders of Sultan Agung.

**Garuda** (In.) Pol. A mythical bird which carried the God Vishnu. The garuda as an eagle is the official seal of the Republic of Indonesia.

**Gasbiindo.** *See* **Gabungan Sarikat Buruh Islam Indonesia.**

*Gatoloco* (Jav.) Lit. title. Book on Javanese mysticism, written in the post-independence era (1950-65) in which the rites of Islam are viewed symbolically and placed within the anatomy of the worshiper. Hence religion is an internal matter, not an outward manifestation.

**Generasi Muda Islam—Gemuis** (In.) Assn. "The Young Islamic Generation," a front organization of all Muslim student groups formed in December 1964 to counter communist youth activities. In 1966 it surrendered its role to KAPPI and concentrated its attention on international Muslim events.

**Gerakan Mahasiswa Islam Indonesia—Germahi** (In.) Assn. "The Movement of Indonesian Muslim Students," a youth affiliate of the Muslim association Pergerakan Tarbiyah Islamijah (Perti), founded in 1962.

**Gerakan Pemuda Ansor—Ansor** (In.) Assn. "The Young 'Helper' Movement," the youth section of the Nahdlatul Ulama, founded in 1935. It works for the establishment of an Islamic society in Indonesia built on traditional Islamic jurisprudence (mazhab). It was a leader in countering Communist efforts to weaken Islamic public strength in the 1963-65 period and took part in student marches which brought the Sukarno regime to an end.

**Gerakan Pemuda Islam Indonesia—GPII** (In.) Assn. "The Indonesian Islamic Youth Movement," an Islamic youth movement founded in 1945, originally affiliated with Masjumi. After Masjumi's demise, it survived as an independent entity until 1963 when it was banned by presidential decree as an obstacle to the "Revolution," a reference to the anti-communist activities of the association.

**Gerhana Bulan**. *See* **Salat**.

**Gerhana Matahari**. *See* **Salat**.

**Germahi**. *See* **Gerakan Mahasiswa Islam Indonesia**.

**Al Ghaafir**. Spelling variant. *See* **Gaffar**.

**Al Ghafuur**; Al Ghafur. Spelling variants. *See* **Gafur**.

**Ghaib**. Spelling variant. *See* **Gaib**.

**Al Ghaniyy; Al-Ghaniy; Al Ghani** (Ar: al-ghanī) Theo. An attribute of God's essence, meaning "The Independent."

*Gharaibul Qur'an* (Ar: tafsir ghara'ib al-qur'ān) Lit. title. "Wonders of the Qur'an," a commentary on the Qur'an by An Nisaburi (d. 1328H) The work is one of a standard list in use in twentieth century Indonesia. *See* **Tafsir**.

**Al Gharib**. *See* **Ilmu Mushthalah Hadis**.

**Gharim** (Ar: ghārim) Juris. A debtor or creditor who is destitute due to a transaction and thereby eligible for funds from the poor tax distribution. The person is eligible only if the poverty was not due to a disreputable cause.

**Al Ghaasyiyah; Al Ghasyiah; Al Ghasiyyah** (Ar: al-ghāshiyah) Qur. "The Overwhelming," the eighty-eighth chapter of the Qur'an. A short, lyrical chapter contrasting the fate in the Hereafter of those who obey God's commands with those that do not.

**Al Ghazali, Syekh Abu Hamid** (Ar: abū ḥāmid muhammad al-ghazālī) Biog. (d. 1111) classical philosopher, theologian, and mystic from Tus, Persia. He reunited the various tendencies of religious thought at the close of the classical period and is accordingly known as a renovator of Islam. *See Ihya' Ulumuddin* and *Minhajul Arifin*.

**Gip, K. H.** *See* **Nahdlatul Ulama.**

**Giri, (Raden Paku Sunan)** (Jav.), Biog. (d. Unk.) One of nine prominent missionaries popularly believed to have been responsible for the conversion of Java to Islam. He established a mosque at Giri, which became the center of conversion in East Java, Sulawesi, and Nusa Tenggara. Also known as (Maulana) Ainul Yaqin and (Raden) Paku. *See* **Wali Songo.**

**Goens, Rycklof Van** (Dutch) Biog. (d. 1681). Ranking staff member of the East India Company in the mid-seventeenth century. He undertook numerous missions on behalf of the governor. His writings about the Mataram kingdom are an important scholarly contribution to the understanding of the kingdom. *See Vijf Gesandschaps Reizen.*

**Goldziher, Ignaacs** (Ger.) Biog. (d. 1936). An Austrian Jewish scholar noted for his study of the folk habits of the Arabs and for his analytical and skeptical studies of the Qur'an and Islamic subjects in general. He is cited currently both as an insightful observer of Islam and as a biased critic.

**Golkar.** *See* **Golongan Karya.**

**Golongan Karya—Golkar** (In.) Pol. Functional Groups, the political party associated with the Suharto government, gathering its primary strength from administrators and the military. Its strength has increased dramatically since the mid-1960s to the point where it dominates elections.

**Gontor.** *See* **Pondok Modern Gontor Ponorogo.**

**GPII.** *See* **Gerakan Pemuda Islam Indonesia.**

**Granada.** *See* **Khalifah.**

**Gresik** (In.) Geog. Name of a city on the north coast of Java. It was an entry point for Islam and the center of early Muslim political activity in the fifteenth century.

**Gujerat** (In.) Geog. A peninsula on the northeast coast of India that served as an important part of the Islamic lines of communication in the extension of Islam along the Indian Ocean-Southeast Asia trade routes. It was a stopover place for Arab scholars. Many other people originated there who came to Southeast Asia in the fifteenth and sixteenth centuries.

**Guna-guna** (Jav.) Pop. Islam. The practice of sorcery.

**Gunung Jati, Sunan** (Jav.) Biog. (d. ca. 1570). One of nine legendary figures popularly believed to have been responsible for the conversion of Java to Islam. He was from Aceh and worked at Jepara, Banten, and Cirebon converting the population of West Java. Also known as Fatatehan and Fatahillah. *See* **Institut Agama Islam Negara** and **Wali Songo**.

**GUPPI**. *See* **Gabungan Usaha Pembinaan Pendidikan Islam**.

**Guru** (In.) Educ. Teacher, in both a formal sense as a general description of a profession and in an informal sense as one who relays any kind of learning to another. *Usage*: *para* ___, teachers as a group.

**Gus** (Jav.) Educ. Title popularly given to the eldest son of a religious scholar (kiai) on Java, indicating a status as possible successor.

**Gusti** (In.) Title. 1. Title of respect assigned to Javanese rulers in the Sultanate period, often in combination with other titles. 2. Title of respect given a religious scholar on Kalimantan.

# H

**Haa Miim As Sajdah** (Ar: hā mīm as-sajdah) Qur. An alternate title of the forty-first chapter of the Qur'an, titled the Hā Mīm Prostration. The two Arabic letters are included to distinguish it from the thirty-second chapter, titled Al Sajdah. The forty-first chapter is generally known as Fushshilat.

**Hablullah** (Ar: ḥabullāh) Qur. A name of the Qur'an, indicating it has descended directly from God.

**Had** (In.); Hadd (Ar. ḥadd, ḥudūd) Juris. Stern punishments involving dismemberment, stoning and the death penalty for certain behavior condemned by Islam, such as adultery, strong drink, stealing, apostasy, and defamation of God.

**Hadaramaut** (Ar: ḥaḍramawt) Geog. Region in Southern Arabia. Large numbers of Arabs from the Hadramaut came to the Dutch East Indies in the nineteenth century, where they became independent merchants and religious teachers. Although highly revered as coming from the homeland of Islam, they were sometimes regarded as overbearing and exploitive of the local population.
*Usage*: *masyarakat* ___, reference to the Arab society from the Hadramaut; *agama* ___, religion of the Hadramaut, a pejorative reference by nationalists in the 1920s to Islam, associating it with backwardness and ultraconservative values.

**Hadaramautisme** (In.) Pol. A derogatory reference to the culture and religion practiced by the peoples from Southwest Asia who settled in Southeast Asia and followed a traditional lifestyle, eschewing modernism. In the 1920s and 1930s secular nationalists often applied this stereotype to political Muslims in general.

**Al Hadi** (Ar: al-hādi) Theo. Name of God meaning "The Guide."

**Hadiah**. *See* **Pahala**.

**Al Hadiid**; Al Hadid (Ar: al-ḥadīd) Qur. The fifty-seventh chapter of the Qur'an, titled "Iron." It tells about the nature of God.

**Hadikusuma, Djarnawi**. *See* **Partai Muslimin Indonesia**.

**Hadikusumo, Bagus**. *See* **Muhammadiyah**.

**Hadis** (In.); hadits; hadiets (Ar: ḥadīth) Trad. Traditions of the Prophet. Those reports from the first generations of Muslims regarding the words and actions of the Prophet Muhammad, judged as genuine, constitute a second scripture in Islam, ancillary to the Qur'an. The major classical collections are by Al Bukhari (d. 870), Muslim (d. 873), An Nasai'i (d. 915), Ibnu Majah (d. 886), Abu Dawud (d. 875) and At Turmudzi (d. 892). *See* especially **Ilmu Hadis Mustalah**. The major categories of Hadis are: ___ **Dhaif** (Ar: ḍa'īf) "Weak," a category of reports not able to be confirmed as authentic. ___ **Hasan** (Ar: ḥasan) "Good," a category of reports that do not fit absolutely the standards for regarding them as true, but still can be judged as probably true. ___ **Maudlu**; mau-dlu (Ar: mauḍū') "False," a category of reports known to have been fabricated. Such reports may not be used for any purpose in Islam. ___ **Qudsi**; Qudsy (Ar: qudsī) "Sacred," a category of reports in which the Prophet cites God as the source of his statements. These were not regarded by Muhammad or his Companions as belonging to the Qur'an, even though from the same source. They are classified as firm, good, weak, or rejected depending on the examination. ___ **Shahih**; shohih (Ar: ṣaḥīḥ) "Firm," a category of reports regarded as authentic. This is the highest category. ___ **Syarif** (Ar: sharīf) "Noble," a category of reports which directly relate the acts and utterances of the Prophet Muhammad himself.
*Usage*: ___-___ *palsu*, references to Muhammad's words and actions which are

considered not to be valid because of their failure to pass the textual examination of the scholars; ___ *nabi*, a reference to the firm and good Tradition collections which are considered accurate; ___ *talkin*, reports of the Prophet Muhammad's words and behavior that deal with the issue of sermonizing to the dead at graveside. *Ahlis* ___, the classical and medieval scholars who analyzed Traditions and compiled the collections; *berdasar* ___, based on Hadis; *dalah* ___ *nabi*, a report of Muhammad's words and actions found to be lacking in authenticity; *dalil-dalil* ___, on the basis of (Qur'an and) reports about the Prophet; *ilmu* ___, the field of knowledge in Islam which deals with the examination of the collected sayings and behavior of the Prophet Muhammad and applying textual examination to determine whether those sayings and behavior can be considered true; *istilah ahli* ___, the methodology of the scholars who analyzed reports about the Prophet's words and behavior; *kumpulan* ___, the extensive collections of reports of the Prophet Muhammad's words and behavior made by classical scholars; *memalsu* ___, to judge reports of Muhammad's words and actions as lacking in authenticity; *membaca* ___, to recite reports about the Prophet Muhammad's words and behavior; *meriwayatkan* ___, to cite a report about the Prophet Muhammad's words and behavior, usually as a source of support for a religious argument; *rowi-rowi* ___, the people in the first generations of Islam who preserved reports about the Prophet Muhammad's words and behavior and passed them on to the next generations.

**Hadis Arbain** (Ar: arba'ūn ḥadīth) 1. Trad. Name of a genre of reports transmitting information about the words and behavior of the Prophet Muhammad, in which forty reports on a subject are brought together for edification or inspiration of a believer. 2. Lit. title. A famous collection of forty-two Traditions by An Nawawi (d. 1278), which has enjoyed numerous translations into Indonesian in the last century after use in Arabic for several centuries.

**Hafiz** (In.); hafidz; hafid (Ar: ḥāfiẓ) 1. Qur. A person who has memorized the entire Qur'an and can recite any part of it at will. A hafiz memorizes the Qur'an through a methodology laid down in Muslim tradition; he must be certified in Indonesia by the Department of Religion. 2. Trad. Persons who memorized a collection of reports about the words and behavior of the Prophet Muhammad. Such people knew the subject matter, chain of transmission, biographical data, and other judgments for each of no less than 100,000 reports. Syn: al muhaddits. *See* **Fulan** and **Lafal**.

**Al Hafiz** (Ar: al-ḥāfiẓ) Theo. A name of God meaning "The Guardian."

**Al Hafizah**. Feminine form of Hafiz.

**Haid**; haidh (In.) (Ar: ḥayḍ) Juris. Menstruation, considered in Muslim jurisprudence to constitute uncleanness in certain ritual matters.
*Usage*: *masa* ___, period of menstruation.

**Hairun, Sultan**. *See* **Ternate**.

**Haiwa** (Ar: ḥawwā') Qur. The first woman, wife of Adam. She was tempted by Iblis and, with Adam, was driven out of paradise.

**Hajat** (Aceh) Pop. Islam. The Acehnese name for the ritual meal known throughout Southeast Asia to bring psychic forces in harmony with an individual's own destiny. *See* **Sedekah** and **Kenduri**.

**Haji** (In.) (Ar: ḥajj) 1. Doct. The pilgrimage, obligatory for all Muslims, to the shrines and sites of visitation in and near Makkah. There is a pilgrimage season and a prescribed ritual for participants. Participation is required once for each Muslim, subject to health and finances of the individual. In Indonesia most trips are arranged by Department of Religion personnel and a lottery is used to determine who will be allowed to participate. 2. Pop. Islam. (Ar: ḥājī) A title for a person who has undertaken the pilgrimage to Makkah and participated in the rites of pilgrimage prescribed for all Muslims. 3. Pol. A designator of such a person; sometimes used in a

derogatory sense by those who challenge whether such trips are worthwhile religiously. The term is sometimes used to indicate one who is naive, vain-glorious, or fanatic about his religion.
*Usage*: ___ *kecil*, to undertake the pilgrimage outside the pilgrimage season; ___ *nazar*, vow to undertake the Pilgrimage; ___ *orang lain*, to undertake the Pilgrimage on behalf of another because of old age or physical incapacity; ___ *Umrah*, to undertake the pilgrimage outside the pilgrimage season.
*Bank* ___, the Pilgrimage Bank (where funds are deposited in preparation of the Pilgrimage); *calon* ___, to be committed to go on the Pilgrimage and be in a state of preparation; *menerjakan* ___, *melaksanakan ibadah* ___, *menunaikan ibadah* ___, to undertake the religious rite of pilgrimage; *musim* ___, Pilgrimage season; *naik* ___, *pergi* ___, to go on the Pilgrimage; *urusan* ___, Pil-grimage arrangements.

**Haji, Sultan**. *See* **Bantam**.

**Haji Bawarkaroeng** (Bugi.) Pop. Islam. Prepilgrimage ritual in South Sulawesi in which prospective pilgrims visit local mountain shrines and make offerings on the basis that local legends states that Makkah was once located there.

**Haji Miskin**. *See* **Miskin, Haji**.

**Haji Rasul**. *See* **Amrullah, Abdul Karim**.

**Al Hajj**, Al Hajji (Ar: ḥajj) Qur. "The Pilgrimage," the twenty-second chapter of the Qur'an. It relates information about the Pilgrimage to Makkah and states that it constitutes a required action for all Muslims.

**Al Hakam** (Ar: al-ḥakam) Theo. Name of God meaning "The Arbitrator."

**Hakikat** (In.); hakekat; haqiqah (Ar: ḥaqīqah) Myst. Religious truth, usually relating to that discovered by mystics in the course of their reveries.
*Usage*: ___ *tasawuf*, mystical knowledge and truth; ___ *Tuhan*, truth as revealed by God in mystical experience.

**Hakim** (In.) 1. Pol. A judge, including those in charge of Muslim family matters. 2.

(Ar: ḥakīm) Trad. Title assigned to certain scholars who have memorized all literature pertinent to reports transmitting the words and behavior of the Prophet Muhammad.
*Usage*: ___ *agama*, a judge of religious matters.

**Al Hakim** (Ar: al-ḥakīm) Theo. A name of God meaning "The Wise."

**Halal** (In.) (Ar: ḥalāl) Juris. A category of behavior in Muslim jurisprudence indicating that an action is permitted. The term is frequently applied to foods that may be consumed by believers.
*Usage*: *meng___kan perbuatan*, an action or behavior permitted in jurisprudence.

**Halalbihalal** (fr. Ar: ḥalāl) Pop. Islam. Just after Ramadan the forgiveness of transgressions and general blessings by family members toward one another or by close associates in nonfamily situations. In Indonesia it is common to have food and drink and a general open house for such purpose.

**Halaqah** (In.) (Ar: ḥalqah) Educ. A system once used in Islamic schools where the teacher read a text and clarified what had been read. Students heard the lesson, but did not see the text. Many repetitions were necessary for students to master the material. Syn: bandungan; weton.

**Al Haliim**; Al Halim (Ar: al-ḥalīm) Theo. A name of God meaning "The Kindly." Syn: Yang Maha Penyantun.

**Halim, Abdul**. *See* **Abdul Halim**.

**Al Hallaj** (Ar: ḥusayn ibn manṣūr al-ḥallāj) Biog. (d. 922). A Persian mystic, put to death by Abbasid authorities for his statement relating his own mystical essence to that of God's. He is regarded among Muslim scholars in general as a deeply committed mystic representing the commitment of Islam to that form of worship, even if his description of his mystical experience was misunderstood by authorities.

**Hamba** (In.) Myst. Servant, that is, the mystic who serves God through his attention and search for what God truly desires.

**Hambali**; hambaliyyah. Spelling variants. *See* **Hanbali**.

**Hamdalah**; hamdalat (In) (Ar: ḥamdu lillāh) Pop. Islam. Acronym for the Arabic phrase "al-ḥamdu li-Llāh" meaning "Praise to Allah," used by Muslims to open prayer, a writing, a speech and in the death agony.

**Al Hamid**; Al Hamied (Ar: al-ḥamīd) Theo. A name of God meaning "The Praiseworthy." Syn: Yang Maha Terpuji.

**Hamengkubuwana**; Amangkubuwana (In.) Biog. Name of a series of Javanese rulers in the Yogyakarta dynasty, ruling with the title of sultan. The various rulers had the following reign dates: I: 1749-92, II: 1792-1810, III: 1810-14, IV: 1814-22, V: 1822-55, VI: 1855-77, VII: 1877-1921, VIII: 1921-39, IX: 1939-.

**Hamka, Dr.** (Acronym for Haji Abdul Malik Amrullah) (In.) Biog. (d. 1981). Son of Abdul Karim Amrullah (d. 1945) and leading Indonesian intellectual from Minangkabau in the first three decades of independent Indonesia. He wrote novels, essays, history, and works on Islamic subjects, including a Qur'anic commentary (tafsir).

**Hanafi**; Hanafiyah (Ar: ḥanafī) Juris. Founded about 150H/767. The name of one of the four schools of Muslim jurisprudence whose rulings dominated the thinking of religious scholars from classical times until the current century. It tends toward rationalism based closely on Qur'an and Sunnah. It is prominent in Turkey, Afghanistan, Central Asia, Pakistan, India, and Egypt. *Usage*: *golongan* ___, reference to the religious scholars and their followers who adhere to the legal codes and rulings of the Hanafi school of Muslim jurisprudence (fikih).

**Hanafiah, Muhammad**. *See Hikayat Muhammad Hanafiah.*

**Hanbali**; Hambali; Hambaliyah (Ar: ḥanbalī) Juris. Founded about 241H/855. The name of one of the four schools of Muslim jurisprudence whose rulings dominated the thinking of religious scholars from classical times until the current century. It is heavily oriented toward the Traditions of the Prophet and seeks to avoid using human reasons in its decisions. It is prominent in Central Arabia, Syria, and parts of Africa.

*Handleiding de Mohammedaansche Wet* (Dutch) Lit. title. "Handbook of Muslim Law," by Th. Juynboll (d. 1861) outlines the major writings of the Syafii School of Muslim law with major references to Indonesia. It remains an important resource for the study of traditionalist Islam in Indonesia.

**Hanifah**. *See* **Abu Hanifah**.

**Al Haq**; Al Haqq; Al Haqqu (Ar: ḥaqq) 1. Qur. A name of the Qur'an, indicating that it carries the truth for the benefit of humans. 2. Theo. Name of God meaning "The Truth". Syn: Yang Sejati.

**Haqiqah**; haqiqat. Spelling variants. *See* **Hakikat**.

**Al Haaqqah**; Al Haqqah (Ar: al-ḥāqqah) Qur. "Reality," the sixty-ninth chapter of the Qur'an. A medium-length, lyrical chapter describing the events of Judgment Day.

**Al Haqqu**. Spelling variant. *See* **Al Haq**.

**Haram** (Ar: ḥarām) Juris. A category of behavior which absolutely should not be undertaken by believers. Performing such action constitutes a sin.
*Usage*: *meng___kam*, judge as forbidden; *bidah yang ___*, innovation which is forbidden; *bukti pen___an*, the proof of what is prohibited.

**Haram, Masjidil**. *See* **Masjidil Haram**.

**Harfiyah** (Ar: ḥarf) Myst. Medium through which the Truth speaks to one.
*Usage*: *ilmu harf*, cabalistic exposition of letters in a magical square.

**Hari Akhirat** (In.) Pop. Islam. The Day of Judgment.

**Hari Kiamat** (In.) Pop. Islam. The Day of Judgment.

**Hari Raya** (In.) Cal. The name of the Indonesian holiday celebrating the Muslim celebration of Idul Fitri, the feast ending the fasting month of Ramadan. *See* **Idul Fitri**.

*Usage*: *ber* ___, to participate in the rites and celebration of Idul Fitri.

**Hari Raya Kurban.** *See* **Idul Adha.**

**Harimau Nan Selapan** (Minang.) Hist. "The eight tigers," a term for Haji Miskin (d. ca. 1850) and his associates during the Paderi Wars in Minanagkabau in the early nineteenth century because of their ferocity and brutality toward enemies. Their names were (Tuanku) Kubu Sanang, (Tuanku) Kota Ambalau, (Tuanku) Ledang Lawas, (Tuanku) Lubuk Aur, (Tuanku) Padang Luar, (Tuanku) Bang Sah (Nan Rinceh), (Tuanku) Galung, Hadji Miskin.

**Harta** (In.) Juris. Wealth; property. Consists of assets which are subject to the Muslim poor tax.
*Usage*: ___ *benda, dunia*, worldly goods; ___ *yang dizakatkan*, goods subject to the poor tax.

**Harun** (Ar: hārūn) Qur. Personal name of a prophet mentioned in the Qur'an. He was the brother of Musa (Moses) and is connected by scholars with the Biblical Aaron.

**Harunul Rasyid** (Ar: hārūn ar-rashīd) Biog. (809). The fifth ruler of the Abbasid Empire, a major Arab-Muslim state from the eighth to thirteenth centuries, whose rule is regarded as the cultural and political apex of the dynasty.

**Hasan.** *See* **Hadis.**

**Hasan, Teuku Mohammed.** *See* **Menteri Agama.**

**Hasanul Banna** (Ar: ḥasan al-bannā') Biog. (d. 1949). Egyptian Muslim activist who formed the Muslim Brotherhood (Ikhwan Al Muslimun) in the mid-twentieth century, which became an important political spokesman for Islamic values in many Middle Eastern countries, often as an underground movement.

**Hasanuddin** (In.) Biog. (d. 1669). Sultan of Gowa (1653-69) in Sulawesi whose trading alliances with the Portuguese brought him into conflict with the Dutch East India Company. The long Dutch campaigns necessary to subdue Hasanuddin made him a hero to Indonesian Muslim historians.

**Hasanuddin, Sultan**. *See* **Bantam**.

**Hasbullah, Abdul Wahab** (In.) Biog. (d. 1971). East Javanese religious scholar who was a delegate to the Makkah Conference in 1926 and was prominent for many years in leadership councils of the Nahdlatul Ulama including a long term as general chair (1947-71).

**Al Hasiib**; Al Haasib; Al Hasib (In. al-ḥasīb) Theo. A name of God meaning "The Great Accountant of All Things." Syn: Yang Maha Menghisab.

**Hassan, Ahmad** (In.) Biog. (d. 1958). Singapore-born Muslim scholar who gave the Persatuan Islam Association its modernist and fundamentalist tone. One of Indonesian Islam's most outspoken voices in the 1930s and 1950s. Authors of numerous tracts and books outlining basic Muslim beliefs.

**Hasyim, (Ki) Wahid** (In.) Biog. (d. 1953). Son of Hasyim Asy'ari; noted religious scholar from Java who was a leader of a national religious affairs office during the Japanese Administration (1942-45) and Minister of Religion (1950-53) in the first years of Indonesian independence. *See* **Menteri Agama.**

**Hasyim Asy'ari**. *See* **Asy'ari, K.H.M. Hasyim.**

**Al Hasyr** (Ar: al-ḥashr) Qur. "The Assembly", the fifty-ninth chapter of the Qur'an. It warns hypocrites and back-biters who assail Islam as doomed to failure and to eventual punishment.

**Hatta, Mohammad** (In.) Biog. (d. 1980) Minangkabau-born politician and secular nationalist leader of the 1920s and 1930s; one of the four government leaders during the Japanese occupation (1942-45) and first vice president of Indonesia. Devoted Muslim.

**Hawa Nafsu**. *See* **Nafsu.**

**Hawari** (In.); Hawariyyun (Ar: ḥawārī) Qur. The twelve disciples of Nabi Isa (Jesus) mentioned in the Qur'an. *Usage*: *orang-orang* ___, the apostles of Isa.

**Hawiah**. *See* **Neraka**.

**Hayam Wuruk** (Jav.) Biog. (d. 1389). Javanese ruler of the Majapahit Empire at the height of its power during its golden age in the fourteenth century. He is famous in Indonesian history as a symbol of a proto-Indonesian leader.

**Al Hayy**; Al Hayyu (Ar: al-ḥayy) Qur. A name of God mentioned in the Qur'an, meaning "The Living."

**Hayatan**. *See* **Hajat**.

**Hazairin** (In.) Biog. (d. 1975). Professor of law at the University of Indonesia and a specialist on the use of Islamic jurisprudence within Indonesia. Advocated the redefinition of jurisprudence to constitute a new school (mazhab) for the Indonesian environment. *See* **Fikih Mazhab Nasional.**

**Het**. Dutch article. *See* following word.

**Van Heutz, J. B.** (Dutch) Biog. (d. 1922). Dutch governor of Aceh from 1894 to 1904 who ended the Acehnese War through military and political action. He then served as governor general of the Netherlands Indies (1904-09).

**Hibbah** (Ar: hibah) Juris. A gift of property.

**Hidayah** (Ar: hidāyah) Qur. A title given the Qur'an, meaning "God's Guidance."

**Hidayatullah, Sultan**. *See* **Banjar** and **Institut Agama Islam Negara**.

**Al Hijr** (Ar: al-ḥijr) Qur. The fifteenth chapter of the Qur'an named for an area of land in the Middle East, now unknown, inhabited by a people known as the Tsamud, and where the prophet Syu'aib was active.

**Hijrah** (Ar: hijrah) Doct. "The Flight." Because of persecution, Muhammad moved his community from Makkah to Madinah in A.D. 622. This marks the base date of the Muslim calendar. *Usage*: *ber___ ke Madinah*, reference to the act of undertaking the flight from Mecca to Madinah with the Prophet Muhammad; *melakukan ___ ke...*, to flee to another place because of persecution.

**Hijriyah** (Ar: hijriyyah) Cal. After a date, the term indicates reference to the Muslim calendar, with a base date of A.D. 622.

**Hikayat** (In.) 1.Hist. Chronicle of kingdoms and princely houses in Southeast Asia. Like *babads* they glorify a ruler for whom they were written and deal symbolically with historical events. 2. Lang. A genre of popular literature consisting usually of cycles of stories or tales, generally popular in the recited version, but also written. Most are from Arabic, Persian, and Indian languages and many accompanied the arrival of Islam in Indonesia during the fourteenth and fifteenth centuries. 3. Lang. A genre of popular literature consisting of the miracles and sayings of holy persons in Islam.

*Hikayat Abu Samah* (In.) Lit. title. "The Tale of Abu Samah," the adventures of a son of Caliph Umar in early Islam, popular in Southeast Asia for the past several centuries.

*Hikayat Amir Hamza* (In.) Lit. title. "The Tale of Amir Hamza," the adventures of a Persian hero in a Persian court of early Islam. This rendition from Persian was used in the fifteenth and sixteenth centuries as a recruiting device for Islam in Southeast Asia and has remained popular.

*Hikayat Baktiar* (In.) Lit. title. "The Tale of Baktiar," one of several variations of the *Baktiar Nama* from Persian about a man facing execution, who tells stories to delay execution. Popular in Southeast Asia for the past several centuries. Similar to *Hikayat Maharaja 'Ali* and *Hikayat Ruspa Wiraja*.

*Hikayat Iskandar Zu'l Karnain* (In.) Lit. title. "The Tale of Iskandar the Horned," the adventures of Alexander the Great and how his descendants came to Southeast Asia as rulers of local kingdoms. Popular in Southeast Asia for the past several centuries.

*Hikayat Maharaja 'Ali. See Hikayat Baktiar.*

*Hikayat Muhammad Hanafiah* (In.) Lit. title. "The Tale of Muhammad Hanafiah," a popular story of the events surrounding the life of Muhammad and the succeeding era. It is a translation of a popular Persian cycle, which has been popular in Southeast Asia since the fifteenth century.

*Hikayat Puspa Wiraja. See Hikayat Baktiar.*

*Hikayat Raja-Raja Pasai* (In.) Lit. title. "Records of the Pasai Rulers," by an unknown court writer of the fourteenth century, describing the early Muslim kingdom and its eventual subjugation by the Javanese empire of Majapahit about 1350.

*Hikayat Sama'un* (In.) Lit. title. "The Tale of Sama'un," an original Malay adventure translated into various local languages of the Indonesian archipelago. It relates the adventures of a hero at the time of the Prophet Muhammad.

*Hikayat Shaikh Muhammad Samman* (In.) Lit. title. "The Narratives of Shaykh Muhammad Samman," an account of the miracles and deeds of an Arab mystic for pious readings, particularly in times of adversity.

*Hikayat Tamin Ad Dari* (In.) Lit. title. "The Tale of Tamin Ad Dari," a translation of an Arab romance (kissah) through an Indian language long popular in Southeast Asia. It outlines the adventures of a young man among spirits and prophets and has been translated into most local languages of the Indonesian archipelago.

**Hikmah** (In.); hikmat (Ar: ḥikmaḥ) Educ. A term, meaning "wisdom," used in reference to religious matters. Mystics maintain there are four varieties—that which is spoken, that which is intuitively known, that which God alone knows, and that which is collective concerning knowledge of the truth.

**Al Hikmah** (Ar: al-ḥikmah). Qur. A name of the Qur'an indicating the wisdom it contains as the Word of God.

**Himmah.** *See* **Himpunan Mahasiswa Al Jamiatul Washliyah.**

**Himpunan Mahasiswa Islam—HMI** (In.) Assn. "The Islamic Students' Association," founded in 1947. Title of the leading university Islamic students' movement, most noted for its activism during the 1960s and 1970s.

It was a supporter of the Suharto government in its crucial first years and rallied other Muslims to its support.

**Himpunan Mahasiswa Al Jamiatul Washliyah—Himmah** (In.) Assn. "The Student Association of the Washliyah Society," founded in May 1961 as part of the Muslim effort to mobilize politically in the guided democracy era.

**Himpunan Santri Pengusaha Indonesia—Hispi** (In.) Assn. "The Association of Indonesian Muslim Entrepreneurs," a group of small traders formed in 1990 in Magelang to promote small traders interests with larger enterprises and with the government.

**Himpunan Seniman Budayawan Islam—HSBI** (In.) Assn. "The Islamic Cultural Association," founded in the 1950s as a special member of the Masjumi political party to organize politically intellectuals, artists, and writers.

**Hindia Belanda** (Dutch) Geog. The Dutch East Indies, a name by which the Dutch referred to Indonesia during the colonial period when Indonesia slowly came under Dutch mercantile and political control beginning about 1619 and ending in 1949.

**Hindu-Bali** (In.) Pol. The people of Bali, who follow Hinduism as a religion and cultural system. The term, used solely by Muslims, indicates another community in Indonesia which must be recognized and accepted in national politics.

HIS. *See* **Hollandsche Inlandsche School.**

**Hisab (In.)** (Ar: ḥisāb) Juris. Calculation of the appearance of the moon to mark the beginning and end of fasting; as opposed to actual sighting (ruyah).
*Usage*: *meng___*, to calculate the arrival or end of fasting mathematically; *berdasarkan ___ (ahli falak)*, basing the arrival or end of fasting on calculations (of the mathematicians); *masalah ___ dan ru'yah*, the matter of determining the beginning and end of fasting with calculation or sighting.

HISPI. *See* **Himpunan Santri Pengusaha Indonesia.**

**Hissi.** *See* **Mukjizat.**

*History of Java* (Eng.) Lit. title. Important Western work on the Mataram Empire by Thomas Stamford Raffles (d. 1826), which includes material from law codes and other local historical sources.

**Hisyam, H.** *See* **Muhammadiyah.**

**Hitti, P. K.** (Eng.) Biog. (b. 1886). The American-Syrian author Philip K. Hitti noted for his works on the history of the Middle East, particularly the Syria-Lebanon area. Cited by postmodernist Indonesian Muslim writers.

**Hizb** (Ar: ḥizb) Pop. Islam. Repetition of God's name as a pious act. Syn: zikir, wirid. *Usage*: *membaca* ___, to recite God's name or names.

**Hizbullah, Barisan** (In.) Pol. "The Ranks of God," a home defense force composed of Muslim youth founded in December 1943 by Japanese authorities. It was associated with Masjumi during the Indonesian revolution and fought alongside units of the Indonesian army during that period. *Usage*: *anak-anak* ___, the young men of the Hizbullah.

**HMI.** *See* **Himpunan Mahasiswa Islam.**

**Hollandsche Inlandsche School—HIS** (Dutch) Educ. Lowest level of Dutch education in early twentieth century East Indies comprising grades 1 to 7. Open to pupils with European parentage and select Indonesians.

**HSBI.** *See* **Himpunan Seniman Budayawan Islam.**

**Hubb** (Ar: ḥubb) Myst. Love of the mystic for God, sometimes expressed in erotic visualizations.

**Huud**; Hud (Ar: hūd) 1. Qur. Personal name of a prophet mentioned in the Qur'an. He was a descendent of Nuh (Noah) and a prophet to the people of Ad. 2. Qur. The eleventh chapter of the Qur'an, named after the Prophet Hud. It deals with stories about various prophets in history.

**Al Huda** (Ar: hudā) Qur. "The Guide," a name of the Qur'an, indicating that it constitutes a plan for humans to follow.

**Al Hujjah** (Ar: hujjah) Trad. A title assigned to certain scholars in Tradition examination. The scholar had to memorize the subject matter, chains of transmission, and other important matters for each of about 300,000 reports. *See* **Fulan**.

**Hujjatul Islam** (Ar: ḥujjat al-islām) Title. Title for a renovator of the Islamic religion, applied to Al Ghazali and a number of other outstanding scholars in Muslim history who were regarded as providing insights on how to restore meaningfulness to the standard religious teachings and practices for that time.

**Al Hujuraat**; Al Hujurat (Ar: al-ḥujurāt) Qur. "The Chambers," the forty-ninth chapter of the Qur'an. It deals with the deportment of Muslims with one another in the early Muslim community.

**Hukum** (In.) 1. Pol. Law, legal precept. 2. (Ar: hukm) Juris. In Islamic law (*fiqh*) a decision or ruling by a judge on a question of religious import. *Usage*: *meng___ syirik*, to judge a matter as constituting disbelief.
___-___ *agama*, the general rules and regulations incumbent on Muslims as believers; ___ *darurat*, the law of emergency in which the Islamic rules of behavior do not necessarily apply; ___ *fikih*, Islamic jurisprudence; ___ *Islam*, the general rules and regulations incumbent on Muslims as believers; ___ *kias*, the rules on use of analogy in Islamic jurisprudence.
*Ahli-ahli* ___, reference to the historical scholars of Islam who have regarded the law of Islam as important and worked with its structure and implementation; *bergaulan* ___, societal law; *mengabdikan* ___ *Islam*, to submit oneself (humbly) to the laws of Islam; *menetapkan* ___-___ *Islam*, to apply the laws of Islam; *segi* ___ *Islam*, from the angle of Islamic law.

**Al Hukum** (Ar: al-hukm) Qur. A name of the Qur'an, referring to the regulations it contains for correct human behavior.

**Hukum Syarah** (Ar: ḥukm sharī'ah) Juris. Name of a law category among the

Minangkabau for matters dealing with Islam. This stands alongside customary law (*hukum adat*) as one of the two primary standards of Minangkabau society.

**Al Humazah** (Ar: al-humazah) Qur. "The Slanderer," the 104th chapter of the Qur'an. A very short, lyrical chapter in which the efforts of Muhammad's enemies to demean him is labelled as unrighteous.

**Hurairah**. *See* **Abu Hurairah**.

**Hurgronje, Christiaan Snouck** (Dutch) Biog. (d. 1936). Dutch scholar of Islam, known for his study at Makkah in the late nineteenth century and his subsequent role as internal affairs adviser to the Dutch East Indies administration. His studies on Acehnese society are frequently quoted by modern Indonesian scholars, but his views about the taming of political Islam are regarded as an unwarranted use of his knowledge of Islam. *See* **Abdul Ghaffar** and **Islam Policy**.

**Huruf** (In.) (Ar: ḥurūf) Lang. Letter of the alphabet. *Usage*: *menulis ___ Arab bahasa Melayu*, Malay written in Arabic script, known as Jawi script; *menulis Qur'an dengan ___ Latin*, writing the Qur'an in Arabic utilizing a Latin script.

**Huruf-Huruf Hijaaiyyah** (Ar: aḥruf hijāiyyah) Lang. The letters of the Qur'an and the Arab alphabet, including the numbers. Historically the letters have been the basic lessons of teaching at Islamic primary schools so that reading of the Qur'an can proceed from that knowledge.

**Hussein, Sultan**. *See* **Aceh**.

**Hutamah**. *See* **Neraka**.

# I

**IAIN**. *See* **Institut Agama Indonesia Negara.**

**Ibadah** (In.); Ibadat (Ar: 'ibādah) Doct. Worship, constituting a wide number of matters, especially prayer, pilgrimage, alms giving, and fasting. *See* **Kaidah.**
*Usage*: *ber___ (kepada Allah), meng___ti*, to perform worship.
___ *Batin*, secret prayer of the Syiahs; ___ *haji*, the pilgrimage; ___ *kaidah*, standards of worship; ___ *keramat*, mysticism; ___ *pribadi*, individual worship; ___ *muamalah*, matters of worship; ___ *puasa*, fasting during Ramadan; ___ *salat*, prayer; ___ *shiyam*, fasting during Ramadan; ___ *tawaf*, circumambulation of the Kabah the proper number of times, kissing the black stone and praying appropriately; ___ *wirid*, special worship during Ramadan.
*Amal* ___, act of worship; *aturan-aturan per___*, regulations regarding worship; *cara-cara ber___*, to perform worship; *masalah* ___, questions of worship; *mengerjakan (amal), menjalankan* ___, to perform worship; *soal* ___ *(salat)*, matters of worship.

**Iblis** (In.) (Ar: iblīs) Doct. The leader of the demons. He was created from fire and was the "father" of the jinn, another race created by Allah. His domain is hell (neraka).

**Ibnis Sabil** (In.) (Ar: ibn as-sabīl) Juris. The wayfarer; the person who is lost or destitute. This person may be a recipient of the distribution of the poor tax (zakat).

**Ibnu Abbas** (Ar: 'abdallāh ibn 'abbās) Biog. (d. 688). Uncle of the Prophet Muhammad. From his line came the Abbasid caliphate. Traced to him are 1660 stories about the words and behavior of Muhammad.

**Ibnu Arabi**; Ibnu Araby (Ar: abū bakr muḥ ... ibn 'arabī al-haytamī) Biog. (d. 1240) Shi'ite Arab from Muslim Spain, considered the preeminent proponent of metaphysical doctrine. He set forth the doctrine that all existence is an extension of God. *See Futuhatul Makiyah*; *Al Jam'iut Tafshil*; and **Tafsir**.

**Ibnu Battuthah** (Ar: abū 'abdullāh ibn bāṭūṭah) Biog. (d. 1368) North African Muslim traveler who visited much of the Muslim world, including Indonesia, and published his observations of Muslim life and society.

**Ibnu Hajarul 'Asqalani** (Ar. ibn ḥajar ... al-'asqalānī) Biog. (d. 1448). Arab legal scholar whose works have been extensively studied in Indonesian religious schools for over two hundred years. His study of the Traditions of the Prophet have been popular among modernist Muslim scholars. *See Bulugh Al Maram* and *Fathul Bari*.

**Ibnu Hajarul Haitami** (Ar: ibn ḥajar ... al-haitāmī) Biog. (d. 1567) A leading scholar of Syafii jurisprudence. His *Tuhfah* is a renowned text studied in religious schools in the nineteenth and twentieth centuries and consulted by present day scholars when dealing with questions of Islamic law. *See Tuhfah.*

**Ibnu Hanbal** (Ar: ibn ḥanbal) Biog. (d. 855). A leading Arab scholar of the classical period, who, inter alia, founded the Hanbali school of jurisprudence, and who was a compiler of a Tradition collection called the *Muwaththa*.

**Ibnu Hazm** (Ar: 'alī ibn Aḥmad ibn ḥazm) Biog. (d. 1064) Arab-Persian theologian from Muslim Spain. He was a Ẓāharī, holding that there are no hidden meanings in the text of the Qur'an.

**Ibnu Katsier** (Ar: abū fidā' ibn kathīr ad-dimashqī) Biog. (d. 1373). Arab writer on history, law, and the Qur'an whose works have been used extensively in Southeast Asian Islamic schools for over two hundred years. *See Al Adzhiem* and **Tafsir**.

**Ibnu Khaldun** (Ar: 'abd ar-raḥmān ibn muḥ ibn khaldūn) Biog. (d. 1406). Tunisian Arab who set forth protomodernist views of historiography and sociology. *See Muqaddimah.*

**Ibnu Majah** (Ar: abū 'abdullāh ... ibn mājah) 1. Biog. (d. 886). One of the six major compliers of Tradition collections, the sayings and actions of the Prophet Muhammad. 2. Trad. Title assigned by scholars to the collection of Traditions made by Ibn Maja. *See Sunan.*

**Ibnu Qayyimul Jauziyyah** (Ar: muḥammad ibn abī bakr ibn qayyim al-jawziyah) Biog. (d. 1350). Teacher of Ibn Taimiyah, imprisoned for a time for the unpopularity of his teaching. A scholar of Tradition literature. *See Zadul Ma'ad.*

**Ibnu Rusyd** (Ar: abū-l-walīd ...ibn rushd) Biog. (d. 1198). Arab philosopher from Muslim Spain known mostly for his translations of Aristotle. He also stated that two truths exist: one for philosophers and one for the masses known as religion. *See Bidayatul Mujtahid.*

**Ibnu Sina** (Ar: abū 'alī ḥusayn ... ibn sīnā) Biog. (d. 1037). Renowned Arab philosopher and physician from Central Asia. He based much of his philosophy on the writings of the ancient Greek physician Galen.

**Ibnu Taimiyah**; Ibnu Taymiyyah (Ar: taqī ad-dīn ... ibn taymiyyah al-ḥarrānī) Biog. (d. 1328). Hanbali legal scholar from Syria who wrote extensively about the use of innovation in religious matters. A forerunner of fundamentalism and frequently cited by modernist Muslim and postmodernist scholars.

**Ibnu Tufail** (Ar: abū bakr muḥammad ...ibn ṭufayl) Biog. (d. 1185). Muslim doctor and philosopher of Moroccan origin who lived in Granada. His book, *Hay bin Yaqzhan*, a philosophical novel, was influential in seventeenth century Europe.

**Ibnu Umar** (Ar: ibn 'umar ibn khaṭṭāb) Biog. (d. 73H). A Companion of the Prophet Muhammad who is reported to have freed over one thousand slaves as acts of piety. Traced to him are 2630 reports of the words and behavior of Muhammad.

**Ibrahim** (Ar: Ibrāhīm) 1. Qur. A prophet mentioned in

the Qur'an. Related by scholars to the Old Testament Abraham, he is one of six great prophets given special laws for humankind. 2. Qur. The fourteenth chapter of the Qur'an named for the Prophet Ibrahim (Abraham). It contains the prayer of Ibrahim at the time he established the shrine (Ka'bah) at Makkah as a site for worship.

**Ibrahim, H.** *See* **Muhammadiyah.**

**Ibrahim, Makhdum.** *See* **Bonang, Sunan.**

**Ibrahim, Maulana Malik.** *See* **Malik Ibrahim (Maulana).**

**Ibu** (In.) Title. Title of common respect given a woman in Indonesian society. By extension applied to certain Muslim women in Islamic history. *See* next word.

**ICMI.** *See* **Ikatan Cendekiawan Muslim Indonesia.**

**Idah** (In.); iddah (Ar: 'iddah) Juris. 1. A major section of Muslim jurisprudence dealing with the termination of a marriage. 2. The waiting period after a woman is divorced during which she must wait before being eligible for remarriage. It is normally fulfilled at the onset of the next menstruation, indicating that she is not pregnant from the dissolved marriage. If pregnancy occurs, it is a factor in the divorce settlement and the child belongs to the marriage.

**Ideologi** (In.) Pol. A political viewpoint with both a philosophical rationalization and a prescribed course of action for achieving certain goals in society. Nationalism, socialism, and communism are examples.
*Usage*: ___ *modernisasi*, the drive for modernization as a compelling political force.

**Idham Chalid**; Idham Khalid. *See* **Khalid, Idham.**

**Idris** (Ar: idris) Qur. Prophet mentioned in the Qur'an. Related by scholars to the Biblical Enoch, he is a forefather of the Prophet Nuh (Noah).

**Idul Adha** (In.); Iedil Adha (Ar: 'īd al-aḍḥā) Cal. A major feast day, held on the 10th day of the month of

Zulhijjah, celebrating the pilgrimage, when every family is expected to sacrifice an animal and share it with the poor. Also known as Idul Kurban.

**Idul Fitri** (In.); Iedil Fithri (Ar: 'īd al-fiṭr) Cal. The celebration marking the end of the fasting month of Ramadan on the first two days of the month of Syawal. In Indonesia it is a major national holiday known as Hari Raya. The two-day celebration is marked by public religious ceremonies on the first day and by social visits among homes on both days of the celebration. It is the popular high point of the Muslim year. Also known as Idus Sagir and Lebaran. *Usage*: *melakukan shalat* ___, *mengerjakan shalat* ___, to perform the communal prayer on Idul Fitri; *sembahyang* ___, *Idul Fitri* worship; *shalat* ___, the communal prayer held at mid-day on Idul Fitri; *shalat* ___ *dimesjid*, the communal prayer held in the mosque; *shalat* ___ *dilapangan*, the communal prayer held in the open.

**Idul Kurban**; Idul Qurban. *See* **Idul Adha**.

**Idus Sagir**. *See* **Idul Fitri**.

**Ifrit** (In.) (Ar: 'ifrīt) Pop. Islam. Demon. An ifrit is an evil jinn and is regarded as especially dangerous to humans. *See* **Setan**.

**Ihnayn**. *See* **Yawmul Ihnain**.

**Ihsan** (Ar: iḥsān) Juris. To perform an action in a perfect manner; sincere worship of God. Syn: akhlak. *Usage*: *ke___an*; good results; *arah* ___, for the purpose of achieving correct behavior.

*Ihsan'l 'Ulum*. *See* **Al Farabi**.

*Ihya Ulumuddin* (Ar: iḥyā 'ulūm ad-dīn) Lit. title. "Revival of the Religious Sciences," a leading work on theology by Al Ghazali (d. 1111), who attempted to reconcile mysticism with orthodox Sunni rationalism.

**Ijab** (In.) (ījāb) Juris. To celebrate or solemnize a contract or an arrangement. *Usage*: ___ *nikah*, to celebrate or solemnize a wedding; ___ *qabul*, in Syafii law, a transaction which must have met specific requirements to be valid.

*I'jaz fil Qur'an* (Ar: iʻjāz fī-l-qur'ān) Lit. title. "The Incomparability of the Qur'an," a commentary on the Qur'an by Al Baqilani (d. 1013) which reflects the orthodox (Ash'arite) position on theology and lays heavy stress on God's power over human endeavor.

**Ijazah** (Ar: al-ijāzah) Trad. Further use of a report transmitting information about the words and behavior of the Prophet Muhammad with the permission of a person serving as a transmitter of the report.

**Ijmak** (In.); ijma' (Ar: ijmā') Juris. One of the four sources from which Muslim law is derived. It frequently is defined as the agreement of the mujtahids of the people (i.e. those who have a right, by their knowledge, to form a judgment of their own), of any age, on any matter of faith. It is also defined by some as "agreement of the Muslim community."
*Usage*: *ber___*, to undertake the process of gathering a consensus on a matter of Islamic law; ___ *ulama*, the consensus of the early scholars of Islam; *berdasar* ___, to base a religious decision on analogy; *dalil-dalil* ___, analogy as the basis of a religious decision; *istilah* ___, the use of consensus as a tool in the development of Muslim jurisprudence.

**Ijtihad** (In.) (Ar: ijtihād) Juris. Intellectual striving. 1. Among legal scholars (fuqaha) in the middle period, it implied using reason to develop religious principle. 2. In the modern era it implies setting aside the interpretations of past scholars (ulama) for a fresh look at an issue in light of religious sources. Among modernists the term is contrasted to the practice of taklid, the doctrine of accepting an older jurist's thinking.
*Usage*: *ber___*, to undertake an examination using the principle of fresh interpretation of sources, usually the Qur'an and, sometimes, Traditions.

**Ikamah** (In.); iqamah (Ar: iqāmah) Juris. The second call to ritual prayer pronounced by the muazzin in the mosque before each of the five daily prayers.

**Ikatan Cendekiawan Muslim Indonesia—ICMI** (In.) Assn.

"The Association of Indonesian Muslim Intellectuals," founded 7 December 1990 at a meeting in Malang under the auspices of Minister Habibie with governmental support. It is an effort to harness Muslim intellectuals for the development drive of the nation.

**Ikatan Mahasiswa Muhammadiyah—IMM** (In.) Assn. "The Muhammadiyah Student Alliance," founded in April 1964 is a grouping of students in the high schools and higher-education institutions of the Muhammadiyah association. A strong participant in the anticommunist activities of the Guided Democracy period (1957-66).

**Ikatan Masjid Mushalla Indonesia Muttahidah—IMMIM** (In.) Assn. "The Rightly Guided Association for Mosques and Prayer Houses," founded in 1964 in Ujung Pandang to encourage the use of mosques for a wide range of religious activities, especially education and other learning activities.

**Ikatan Pelajar Muhammadiyah—IPM** (In.) Assn. "The Muhammadiyah Pupils' Association," a grouping of pupils in the lower level schools of the Muhammadiyah.

**Ikatan Pelajar Nahdlatul Ulama—IPPNU** (In.) Assn. "The Student Alliance of the Nahdlatul Ulama," a student front started in the 1950s.

**Ikatan Sarjana Islam Indonesia—ISII** (In.) Assn. "The Indonesian Muslim Teachers' Alliance," an affiliation of the Nahdlatul Ulama active in the 1960s.

**Ikhlas** (In.); Al Ikhlash, Al Ikhlaash (Ar: ikhlāṣ) Doct. Absolute devotion to God in religious faith, practice and action. Ikhlas is often used as a contrast to disbelief (shirk).

**Ikhwanul Muslimun** (Ar: al-ikhwān al-muslimūn) Pol. "Brotherhood of Believers," an association in Egypt beginning in the 1950s, first legal and then outlawed for its militant espousal of neofundamentalist principles.

**Ikhwanush Shafa** (In.); Ikwan Ash Shafa'; Ikwanus Safa (Ar: ikhwān aṣ-ṣafā') Hist.

"The Brothers of Purity," a part mystical, part philosophical group of the eleventh century A.D. that adapted certain neoplatonic doctrines, particularly the return of the soul to the ultimate being.

**Ikmal** (Ar: ikmāl) Juris. Sighting the moon so that the fasting month can begin or end; as opposed to mathematical reckoning (hisab) as a method of determination.

**Iktiqad** (In.); i'tikad; i'tiqad (Ar: i'tiqād) Doct. Belief in Islam.
*Usage*: *ber*___ to be pious and faithful to the teachings of Islam; *meng*___*kan*, to act in accordance with correct beliefs; *meluruskan* ___, to act in accordance with correct beliefs; *menganut* ___, to be a convinced believer of Islam; *soal* ___, the question of (correct) belief.

**Ilahi** (In.) (Ar: ilāhī) Theo. God.
*Usage*: *takdir* ___, the will or determination of God in human affairs; *wahyu* ___, the revelation of God.

**Ilham** (In.) (Ar: ilhām) Doct. Inspiration of God to humans, particularly to his emissaries and prophets, although others are not excluded. The term is different than revelation (*see* **wahyu**) which is reserved for the passage of scripture to prophets.

**I'lam** (Ar: al-a'lām) Trad. A term indicating that a report relaying the words and behavior of the Prophet Muhammad was transmitted from one transmitter to the next by direct reporting.

**Ilmu** (In. fr. Ar: 'ilm) Educ. Science; knowledge. The term is generic and can infer modern science or, more often in a religious context, traditional Islamic knowledge. In the religious context the term is assigned to a whole series of historical religious sciences in Islam.

**Ilmu Akhlak,** Ilmu Achlak (Ar: 'ilm al-akhlāq) Educ. Ethics and morals; the approach to good character and morality.
*Usage*: ___ *laduni*, knowledge of morality coming directly from God (through revelation).

**Ilmu Aqoid**; Ilmu Aqaid. *See* **Ilmu Tauhid**.

**Ilmu Badi** (Ar: 'ilm badī') Educ. The science of metaphors in the study of the Arabic language.

**Ilmu Bahasa** (In.) Educ. The study of language, usually Bahasa Indonesia. In Islam, this means the study of the structure of Arabic, regarded as the key for undertaking the proper studies of the scripture and explanations of religion.

**Ilmu Balaghah** (Ar:'ilm al-balāghah) Educ. The science of rhetoric in the study of the Arab language. It is divided into **Ilmu Badi** and **Ilmu Bayan.**

**Ilmu Bayan** (Ar: 'ilm bayān) Educ. The science of word meaning in the study of the Arabic language.

**Ilmu Dirayat Hadis** (Ar: al-ḥadīth dirāyatān) Educ. One of the two major subgroups of Ilmu Mushthalah Hadis. It deals with the transmissions of the reports about Muhammad's words and behavior and judges the accuracy of the information based on the probabilities of accurate transmission.

**Ilmu Fikih** (In.); ilmu fiqh; ilmu fiqhi. *See* **Ilmu Ushul Fikih.**

**Ilmu Hadis.** *See* **Ilmu Mushthalah Hadis.**

**Ilmu Haqiqah.** *See* **Ilmu Mukasyafah.**

**Ilmu Huruf** (Ar: 'ilm al-ḥurūf) Myst. The mystical practice of assigning important and holy phrases with numerical values for interpretation of personal and communal affairs.

**Ilmu Isnad.** *See* **Ilmu Mushthalah Hadis.**

**Ilmu Isytiqaq** (Ar: 'ilm al-ishtiqāq) Educ. Etymology in the study of the Arabic language.

**Ilmu Kalam.** *See* **Ilmu Tauhid.**

**Ilmu Keakhiratan** (In.) Educ. The science of eschatology; the study of the things of the Hereafter.

**Ilmu Keislaman** (In.) Educ. The collective sciences of Islam, dealing primarily with belief, ritual, practice, jurisprudence and Arabic language study.

**Ilmu Kerokhanian** (In.) Educ. The study of the angels of God.

**Ilmu Ketuhanan** (In.) Educ. The science of metaphysics or the study of the nature of God.

**Ilmu Lughat** (Ar: 'ilm al-lughah) Educ. Philology in the study of the Arabic language.

**Ilmu Ma'ani** (Ar: 'ilm al-ma'ānī) Educ. A section of the study of the Arabic language which deals with the use of appropriate vocabulary. It is divided into **Ilmu Isytiqaq** and **Ilmu Lughat**.

**Ilmu Mantiq** (Ar: 'ilm al-manṭiq) Educ. The science of logic, an important subject in the traditional Islamic education pattern.

**Ilmu Mukasyafah** (Ar: 'ilm al-mukashāfah) Educ. In mysticism, the knowledge of finding the absolute truth that transcends human and theological limitations. Syn: Ilmu Haqiqah.

**Ilmu Mushthalah Hadis** (Ar: 'ilm muṣṭalah al-ḥadīth) Educ. The master science of examining the collected reports about the life of the Prophet Muhammad to determine the probable accuracy and acceptability, for use in doctrine, jurisprudence, and general guidance of Muslims, of reports circulating among the early generations of Muslims concerning the words and behavior of the Prophet Muhammad. Syn: Ilmu Atsar, Ilmu Hadis, Ilmu Isnad. It is divided into two major subgroups: **Ilmu Dirayat Hadis** and **Ilmu Riwayat Hadis**.

In the actual examination of reports the following classifications, inter alia, were made to indicate the type of report and its degree of authenticity. ___ **Aahaad** (Ar: al-āḥād) A report which is related through no more than four lines of transmission. ___ **Aaly** (Ar: al-'ālī) A report judged accurate because of the lessons found in it or the sureness of the lines of transmission. ___ **Aziz** (Ar: al-'azīz) A report coming through two distinct lines of transmission. ___ **Badal** (Ar: al-badal) A report recorded in a very early collection with a flawed line of transmission. It may be firm, good, or weak. ___ **Gharib** (Ar:

al-gharīb) A report communicated through a single line of transmission. It may be firm, good, or weak. ___ **Jayyid** (Ar: al-jayyid) A report judged as having good characteristics in all phases of investigation. It may be firm or good. ___ **Mahfudz** (Ar: al-maḥfūẓ) A report having a flaw in its line of transmission concerning one transmitter. It may be firm or good. ___ **Majhul** (Ar: al-majhūl) A report in which complete information about the transmitters is not known. It is weak. ___ **Ma'lul** (Ar: al-ma'lūl) A report that appears authentic on the surface but has flaws detected only by thorough examination. It is weak. ___ **Mansukh** (Ar: al-mansūkh) A report which has been superseded by later actions or words of the Prophet. It is not included in collections. ___ **Maqlub** (Ar: al-maqlūb) A report with subject matter that is directly contradicted by another report with a valid line of transmission. It is weak. ___ **Maqthuu'** (Ar: al-maqṭu') A report whose first transmitter is from the second generation of Muslims without any confirming report coming through the first generation. It cannot be the basis of any jurisprudential formulations. ___ **Marfu** (Ar: al-marfū') Any report whether the chain of transmission is complete or not. ___ **Masruq** (Ar: al-masrūq) A report in which the line of transmission has clearly been altered. It is weak. ___ **Matruk** (Ar: al-matrūk) A report which begins with a person of questionable reputation. It is weak. ___ **Mauquf** (Ar: al-mawqūf) A report regarding the Qur'an that says something beyond the opinion of the reciter. ___ **Maushul** (Ar: al-mawṣul wa muttaṣil) A report with a continuous line of transmission and clear verification at all points of the transmission. ___ **Mu'allaq** (Ar: al-mu'allaq) A report in which the initial person in the line of transmission is missing. It may be firm, good, or weak. ___ **Mu'an'an** (Ar: al-mu'an'an) A report which has two transmitters from the same generation. It is weak. ___ **Mubham** (Ar: al-mubham) A report which contains an unknown name among the transmitters, but a later transmitter asserts the veracity of the unknown person. It is firm. ___ **Mudabbaj** (Ar: al-mudabbaj)

A report which has two transmitters reversed in two different versions of the report. It may be firm, good, or weak. ___ **Mudallas** (Ar: al-mudallas) A report in which an unknown name appears among the transmitters. It is weak.___ **Mu'dlal** (Ar: al-mu'aḍal) A report in which two or more points in the chain of transmission are missing. It is not included in collections and has no authority. ___ **Mudltharib** (Ar: al-muḍṭarib) A report in which lines of transmission or information cannot be reconciled. It is weak. ___ **Mudraj** (Ar: al-mudraj) A report in which there is an unusual name among the transmitters or the information relates to events that did not happen. It is weak. ___ **Muhkam** (Ar: al-muḥkam) A report which is very clear and is not contradicted by another report. It may be firm, good, or weak. ___ **Muhmal** (Ar: al-muhmal) A report in which a transmitter cannot be distinguished from another person of the same name. It is weak. ___ **Mukhtalaf** (Ar: al-mukhtalaf) A report in which two lines of transmission yield different information. The one with the stronger line of transmission prevails. If equal in authority, they both stand. ___ **Mu'lal** (Ar: al-mu'ḍal) A report in which there are weak points in the lines of transmission. It is weak. ___ **Munkaar dan Ma'ruf** (Ar: al-munkar wa ma'rūf) In reports judgment is based on the character of the transmitters. Reports with good transmitters are rated as good and those with bad transmitters are rated as bad. ___ **Munqathi** (Ar: al-munqaṭi') A report which has gaps in the line of transmission after the first generation. It has no validity in Islamic jurisprudence. ___ **Mursal** (Ar: al-mursal) A report begun by the second generation after Muhammad. The legalists use selected reports from this group with great caution. ___ **Musalsal** (Ar: al-musalsal) A report in which the proper transmission has been fully authenticated. It is firm. ___ **Mushafahah** (Ar: al-muṣāfaḥah) A report found in an early book of collection with a transmission from a student of the author. It may be firm, good, or weak. ___ **Mushahhaf dan Muharraf** (Ar: al-muṣaḥḥaf wa al-muḥarraf) A report in which examination shows the information to have been garbled and/or the line of transmission to have been altered. It is weak. ___ **Musnad** (Ar: al-musnad) A report which has a continuous line of transmission. It may be firm, good, or weak. ___ **Mustafiidl** (Ar: al-mustafīḍ) A report which is known to have three lines of transmission from the time of the first generation. It is firm. ___ **Mutabi'** (Ar: al-mutabi') A report which has two lines of transmission. It may be firm, good, or weak. ___ **Mutasyaabih; Al Mutasyabih** (Ar: al-mutashābih) A report which has unidentifiable names among the transmitters. It is weak. ___ **Mutawaatir** (Ar: al-mutawātir) A report from so many sources and through so many people that is almost impossible for the report to be inaccurate. ___ **Muttashil** (Ar: al-muttaṣil) A report relayed through two lines of transmission that split from the same single source. It may be firm, good, or weak. ___ **Muwafaqah** (Ar: al-muwāfaqah) A report found in a book of collections with a line of transmission only to that point. It may be firm, good, or weak. ___ **Naasikh dan Mansukh** (Ar: an-nāsikh wa al-mansūkh) A report which was negated by later words or behavior of the Prophet or by God's commands in the Qur'an. Such reports have no standing. ___ **Nazil** (Ar: an-nāzil) A report regarded as probably inaccurate because of excessive names in the line of tradition. Such reports have no standing. ___ **Saqim** (Ar: as-saqīm) A report which is opposed by a verse of the Qur'an. Such reports are rejected. ___ **Syahid** (Ar: ash-shāhid) A report which has two varieties of information contained in it. It may be firm, good, or weak. ___ **Szadz dan Mahfudz** (Ar: ash-shādh wa maḥfūẓ) A report which is in conflict with information given in another report with a better line of transmission. It is weak.

**Ilmu Nahwu** (Ar: 'ilm al-naḥw) Educ. The science of grammar, a branch of the study of Arabic.

**Ilmu Pengetahuan Modern** (In.) Anthro. Contemporary sciences, primarily from the West, dealing with science and technology. Term in modern Indonesian expression.

**Ilmu Qira-ah** (Ar: 'ilm al-qirā'ah) Educ. The science of the recitation of the Qur'an according to the seven accepted traditional styles. Syn: Ilmu Tajwid

**Ilmu Qur'an**. *See* **Ilmu Tafsier.**

**Ilmu Riwayat Hadis** (Ar: 'ilm al-ḥadīth ar-riwayat) Educ. One of the two subsciences of Ilmu Mushthalah Hadis. It examines the biographies of the early Muslims who transmitted reports about the words and behavior of the Prophet Muhammad. The sciences uses the assessments about the character of personalities as a tool in evaluating the reliability of the reports.

**Ilmu Sharaf**; Ilmu Saraf (Ar: 'ilm aṣ-ṣaraf) Educ. Morphology; a branch of the study of Arabic, an important subject in the traditional education pattern.

**Ilmu Syariat**. *See* **Ilmu Ushul Fikih.**

**Ilmu Tafsier** (Ar: 'ilm at-tafsīr) Educ. Studies of the Qur'an's assembly and major features. Stress is on commentary, which usually employs material from Traditions (hadis) that speak to interpretations of the Qur'an. Syn: Ilmu Qur'an. Its major subsciences are: ___ **Asbabun Nuzul** (Ar: asbāb an-nuzūl) Explaining verses of the Qur'an according to the conditions existing at the time of their revelation. ___ **Nasikh Mansukh** (Ar: an-nāsikh wa al-mansūkh) The knowledge of which verses take precedent over others in the Qur'an to avoid conflicts among God's commands. ___ **Qishah-Qishah** (Ar: al-qiṣṣah) The circumstances surrounding revelation.

**Ilmu Tajwid**. *See* **Ilmu Qira-ah.**

**Ilmu Tasawwuf** (In.) (Ar: 'ilm at-taṣawwūf) Educ. The principles of Islamic mysticism, dating from Al Ghazali (d. 1111) in the eleventh and twelfth centuries.

**Ilmu Tashrif** (Ar: 'ilm at-taṣrīf) Educ. Conjugation and morphology.

**Ilmu Taufiq** (Ar: ‘ilm at-tawfīq) Educ. The study of God’s attribute of forgiveness and the requirements for procuring His help and guidance.

**Ilmu Tauhid** (In.) (Ar: ‘ilm at-tawḥīd) Educ. The study of the attributes of God and their interrelationship as laid out in the standard creeds of Islam (akidah). To Sunni Muslims this connotes the works of Al Ash’ari and Al Maturidi, who set the theory, and others who commented on those basic doctrines. Syn: **Ilmu Aqoid** and **Ilmu Kalam**.

**Ilmu Teknologi** (In.) Anthro. The application of science to technical problems of civilization, primarily in production of goods and services.

**Ilmu Ushul Fikih**; Ilmu Ushul Fiqhi (Ar: ‘ilm uṣūl al-fiqh) Educ. The study of the principal sources of Muslim jurisprudence. Syn: Ilmu Fikih; Ilmu Syariat.

**Ilmu Usuludin** (In.); Ilmu Ushuluddin (Ar: ‘ilm uṣūl ad-dīn) Educ. The study of the principal doctrines of Islam. *See* **Arkanul Islam**.

**Ilmu-Ilmu Kealaman** (In.) Educ. In modern Indonesia the natural sciences, consisting of chemistry, physics, mathematics, biology, physical anthropology, geology, medicine, and astronomy.

**Ilmu-Ilmu Kemanusiaan** (In.) Educ. In modern Indonesia the humanities, consisting of psychology, philosophy, religion, language, and theatre.

**Ilmu-Ilmu Kemasyarakatan** (In.) Educ. In modern Indonesia the social sciences, consisting of anthropology, political science, geography, law, history, economics, and communication.

**Ilyas** (Ar: ilyās) Qur. A prophet mentioned in the Qur’an. Scholars relate him to the Biblical Elijah.

**Ilyas, K. H. Mohammad.** *See* **Menteri Agama**.

**Ilyasa’** (Ar: alyasa‘) Qur. A prophet mentioned in the Qur’an. Scholars relate him to the Biblical Elisha.

**Al Imadi**. *See* **Abi Sa’ud**.

**Imam** (In.) (Ar: imām) 1. Juris. The leader of Muslim ritual prayer, usually the senior or most respected person present. 2. Pol. The title assumed by the spiritual and secular head of a Muslim political unit, also called khalifah. 3. Pop. Islam. A title of respect given to a highly venerated religious figure, such as a mystic saint, a very learned scholar, or a person of great piety.
*Usage*: *ke__an*, leadership of Islam; ___ *mujtahid*, the religious leader who breaks new ground in religious law, usually applied to the great classical scholars.

**Imam Militer** (In.) Pol. A chaplain in the Indonesian armed forces.

**Imamah** (In.) Pol. "The Imamate," the leadership of a group, such as the Syiah, dedicated to continuing the principles of Islam.

**Imamul Khairi** (Ar: imām al-khayr) Theo. Title applied to Muhammad meaning the leader of all good things.

**Imamul Muttaqin** (Ar imām al-muttaqīn) Theo. Title applied to Muhammad meaning "Leader of All Righteous Believers."

**Iman** (In. and Ar: īmān) Doct. Proper belief or faith, implying the essence of the "true believer" among Muslims. The term often is used to distinguish those in the religion who take its dictates seriously and believe sincerely. Syn: keimanan.
*Usage*: *ber__*, to be a true believer of Islam; *ke__an*, Islamic faith and belief. ___ *Islam*, proper belief of Islam; ___ *kepada Allah Subhanahu wa Ta'ala*, belief in God, Praise Him Who is Most Exalted!; ___ *kepada Hari Qiamat*, belief in the Day of Judgment; ___ *kepada hukum takdir*, belief in the power of God over all things; ___ *kepada kitab suci*, belief in holy books; ___ *kepada rasul dan nabi*, belief in messengers and prophets; ___ *yang gelisah*, faith which is not firmly set.
*Arkanul* ___, the pillars of belief, i.e., God, angels, prophets, scriptures, Day of Judgment, and God's unlimited power; aspek *ke__an*, an aspect of Islamic faith and belief; *ber___ kepada Allah dan RasulNya*, to truly believe in Allah and His prophet (Muhammad); *orang-*

*orang Islam yang ber___*, Muslims who truly believe; *rasa ___*, a feeling of faith; *soal ke___an*, matters dealing with Islamic belief; *tujuh ___*, the seven basic beliefs of Islam.

**IMM.** *See* **Ikatan Mahasiswa Muhammadiyah.**

**IMMIM.** *See* **Ikatan Mesjid Mushalla Indonesia Muttahidah.**

**Imperialisme** (In.) Pol. The concept that Western countries, by the force of their economic and military strength, dominate the world and determine the most important political and economic matters. Third World nations struggle to compete but are usually victims of Western manipulation.

**Imraan**; Imran (Ar: 'imrān) Qur. 1. The father of the prophets Musa (Moses) and Harun (Aaron). 2. The father of Maryam (Mary), the mother of the prophet 'Isa (Jesus).

**Inayatullah, Sultan.** *See* **Banjar.**

*Indonesia Merdeka* (In.) Lit. title. "Free Indonesia" was a magazine of the 1920s which served as a voice of the politically important Indonesia Union (PI).

**Industrialisasi** (In.) Soc. Industrialization, a primary goal of most national economic plans followed by the colonial government and Indonesia since the 1920s.

**Al Infithaar**; Al Infithar (Ar: al-infiṭār) Qur. "Cleaving Asunder," the eighty-second chapter of the Qur'an. A short, lyrical chapter warning that a Day of Judgment will occur when all humans will be judged by God.

*Injil* (In.) (Ar: injīl) Qur. Title, meaning "gospel" or "message" referring to the New Testament of the Christians. Islam holds that the *Injil* was, like the Qur'an, originally a holy book containing divine law, revealed to the Prophet Isa (Jesus), but later corrupted by his followers. Also known as *Kitab Injil.*

**Insan** (In.); Al Insaan, Al Insan (Ar: insān) Myst. Humans, usually connected with being Muslim.

*Usage*: *kamil* ___, the perfect human, that is, the righteous Muslim, usually in the context of mystical practice; *watak* ___ *Muslim*, innate goodness of the Muslim believer.

**Al Insaan** (Ar: al-insān) Qur. "Humankind," the seventy-sixth chapter of the Qur'an. A medium-length, lyrical chapter which declares that God is All-knowing. He rewards and punishes according to human acceptance or rejection of His message. The chapter is also known as Ad Dahr.

**Inshafuddin** (In.) Assn. An Acehnese umbrella association of religious scholars, meaning "In the Name of The Religion." It seeks to coordinate the activities and provide standards of action for its members.

**Institut Agama Islam Negara—IAIN** (In.) Pol. "The National Institutes of Islamic Studies," the component institutes of the system of higher educational institutions for Islamic studies operated by the Indonesian Department of Religion. There are fourteen at various sites throughout Indonesia, with faculties of culture (adab), law (syari'ah), education (tarbiyah), principles of religion (ushuluddin) and revivalism (dakwah). Their locations are as follows: Aceh (IAIN Ar-Raniri), Medan (IAIN Sumatra Utara), Pedang (IAIN Imam Bonjol), Riau (IAIN Sultan Syarif Qasim), Jambi (IAIN Sultan Thaha Saifuddin), Lampung (IAIN Fatah Intan), Jakarta (IAIN Hidayatullah), Yogyakarta (IAIN Kalijaga), Semarang (IAIN Sanga), Bandung (IAIN Sunan Gunung Jati), Surabaya (IAIN Sunan Ampel), South Kalimantan (IAIN Antasari), and South Sulawesi (IAIN Alauddin).

**Institut Ilmu Qur'an** (In.) Educ. The Institute of Qur'anic Science, a private school operating at the higher education level. It was founded in 1977 to train professionals, especially women, in the recitation, singing, and expostulation of the Qur'an.

**Insya Allah** (In.); insya'allah (Ar: inshā' allāh) Pop. Islam. "If God Wills," an exclamation made while voicing an intention to do something in the future or speaking of a desired upcoming event. The phrase recognizes His control over all things.

**Al Insyiqaaq**; Al Insyiqaq (Ar: al-inshiqāq) Qur. "Rending Asunder," the eighty-fourth chapter of the Qur'an. It is a medium-length, lyrical chapter describing the Day of Judgment and the terror of the disbelievers on that day.

**Al Insyiraah**; Asy Syarh (Ar: al-inshirāh) Qur. "The Field," an alternate name for the ninty-fourth chapter of the Qur'an. The usual name is Alam Nasyrah.

**IPM**. *See* **Ibatan Pelajar Muhammadiyah**.

**IPPNU**. *See* **Ikatan Pelajar Nahdlatul Ulama**.

**Iqamah**. Spelling variant. *See* **Ikamah**.

**Iqbal, (Sir) Muhammad** (Urdu) Biog. (d. 1938) South Asian Muslim scholar influenced by Nietzche, Western orientalists and Muslim modernism. He regarded Islam as the highest state of human development. He is much cited by Indonesian Muslim scholars today.

*Iqazhun Niyami Fi Hukmil Qiyam* (Ar:iqāẓ an-niyām fī ḥukm al-qiyām) Lit. title. "Waking the People Who are Sleeping Concerning the Law Establishing a Time for Reciting Maubud," a modernist Muslim tract, written by H.A.K. Amrullah (Hadji Rasoel) (d. 1945). This had a great influence on modernist Muslim attention to practices in worship which had been added after Muhammad's time.

*Iqna'* (Ar: iqnā') Lit. title. "The Satisfactory Clarification," a Syafii book on jurisprudence by Al Syarbini (d. 1570) emphasizing basic legalist principles. It has had wide use by the Traditionalist religious scholars in Indonesia.

**Iqra** (Ar: iqra') Qur. "Read!" an alternate name for the ninety-sixth chapter of the Qur'an. The usual name is Al 'Alaq and another alternate name is Al Qalam.

**Al Irsyad**; Al Irshad. *See* **Jamai'yyatul Islam wal Irsjad**.

*Irsyadul 'Aqlissalim* (Ar: irshād 'aql as-salīm) Lit. title. "The Intellectually Correct Understanding," a Qur'anic commentary by Abi Sa'ud (d. 1574) which draws heavily on Al Baidhawi's (d. 1291) *Anwarul Tanzil* and restates it in the context of the other scholarship of the day. *See* **Tafsir.**

**'Isa**, Isa al Masih (Ar: 'īsā al-masīḥ or 'īsā ibn maryām) Qur. A prophet mentioned in the Qur'an. Associated with the New Testament Jesus, he is one of the six major prophets bringing special laws to humankind.
*Usage*: *masalah wafatnya nabi ___ alaihissalam*, the question of the Prophet Isa's death.

**Isa Anshary, Muhammad** (In.) Biog. (d. 1969). Religious scholar from West Sumatra active in the Persatuan Islam and leader of a fundamentalist faction in Masjumi during the 1950s.

**Ishaq** (Ar: isḥāq) Qur. A prophet mentioned in the Qur'an. Related by scholars to the Biblical Isaac.

**ISII.** *See* **Ikatan Sarjana Islam Indonesia.**

**Iskandar Muda** (In.) Biog. (d. 1636). Acehnese ruler (1609-36) at the height of Acehnese political power in the Malacca Straits and patron of religious learning and the arts. Highly regarded among modern Indonesian Muslim historians as the consummate Indonesian Muslim ruler, despite his sponsorship of pantheistic mysticism. *See* **Aceh.**

**Iskandar Tsani** (In.) Biog. (d. 1641). Acehnese ruler (1636-41, noted for his support of religious scholar and activist Ar Raniri (d. 1658) in his religious reforms. His reign marks the end of the Acehnese Golden Age. *See* **Aceh.**

**Iskandar Zulkarnain.** *See* *Hikajat Iskandar Zu'l Karnain.*

**Islam** (In.); (Ar: islām) 1. Relig. "The Surrendering," the general name for the religion instituted by Muhammad on instructions from God. It consists of two major orthodox divisions-Sunni and Syiah. 2. Doct. The collection of practices that mark the religion of Islam, particular the five pillars of Islam. *See* also **Arkanul Islam.**

*Usage*: ___*isasi*, Islamization; *ke*___*an*, Islamicness. ___ *murni*, pure Islam (i.e., Islam in a pure state).

*Agama* ___, the religion of Islam; *ajaran* ___, the basic teachings of Islam; *arkanul* ___, the pillars of Islam (i.e,. confession of God and His prophet, prayer, alms, fasting and the pilgrimage); *beragama* ___, to be an active believer of Islam; *berkembang* ___, to undertake a development or the restructuring of perceptions of Islam's applicability; *budayaan* ___, Islamic culture; *dakwah* ___, spreading or intensifying the Islamic message; *kedatang* ___, arrival of Islam to an area, such as Southeast Asia; *dinul* ___ the religion of Islam; *dunia* ___, the area of the world in which Muslims reside; *identitas ke*___*an*, identification with Islam; *izzul* ___ *wal Muslimin*, respect for Islam and Muslims; *kalangan masyarakat* ___, the area of the world in which the Muslims exist; *kebangkitan* ___, development or restructuring of perceptions of Islam's applicability; *kebudayaan* ___, Islamic culture; *masa keruntuhan kerajaan* ___, the period of the decline of Islamic kingdoms in Indonesia, (i.e., the sixteenth to eighteenth centuries); *masalah* ___, questions or matters of Islam; *masyarakat* ___ , Islamic society or the community of believers throughout the world to which all Muslims belong; *masyarakat* ___ *di Indonesia*, the community of believers living in Indonesia; *masuk* ___, to enter Islam as a convert; *menjalankan* ___, follow the dictates of Islam; *moralitas* ___, Islamic morality; *negara-negara* ___, the nations which are controlled by Muslim peoples; *nilai-nilai* ___, the fundamental values of Islam; *pejuang-pejuang* ___, campaigners for Islam; *pemahaman* ___, thinking about Islam; *pemikir* ___, Islamic thinker; *pempinan* ___, a leader of the Muslims; *penyiaran* ___, converting (an area) to Islam; *peradaban* ___, Islamic culture; *perjuangan* ___, the struggle of Islam for survival and progress in its mission; *pikiran* ___, Islamic thinking; *proses* ___*isasi*, the process of Islamization; *pusat penyebaran* ___, center for the spread of Islam; *reformasi* ___, the rethinking of Islam in a particular era to adapt the message to conditions existing then; *soal-soal* ___, matters concerning the Islamic religion; *umat* ___, the Muslim community of believers.

*Islam Bergerak* (In.) Lit. title. "Islam on the Move" was a newspaper between 1921 and 1925 in Surakarta. Edited by Haji Misbach (d. ca. 1940), it reflected the views of the faction that advocated the use of militant action to gain nationalist goals of the era.

**Islam Policy** (Eng.) Pol. The policy of the Netherlands Indies beginning in the late 1890s when its Office of Internal Affairs set forth a strategy of encouraging Muslim ritual and practice while hindering the spread of "politicized" doctrines, such as Pan Islamism. *See* **Hurgronje, Christiaan Snouck**.

**Ismail** (Ar: ismā'īl) Qur. A prophet mentioned in the Qur'an. Related by scholars with the Old Testament Ishmael, he was the son of Ibrahim (Abraham) and was one of six major prophets bringing special laws to humankind.

**Ismailiyah** (Ar: ismā'īliyah) Doct. An important grouping in Syiah Islam, who believe that there were seven imams before the Imamate became hidden. Syn: Sab'iyah.

**Isnad** (Ar: isnād) Trad. Reports transmitting the words and behavior of the Prophet Muhammad are examined for authenticity, in part, through the "chain" of transmitters that passed the report on from generation to generation in early Islam.

**Al Israa**; Al Israak; Al Isra' (Ar: al-isrā') Qur. "The Night Journey of the Prophet," the seventeenth chapter of the Qur'an. It describes an event in Muhammad's life when he was transported to Heaven to meet God.

**Isra** (In.); Isra'; Isra (Ar: isrā') 1. Doct. "The Night Journey," the miracle in which Muhammad was taken in a night's time by a winged steed to Jerusalem where he ascended to heaven (mikraj), spoke with God and earlier prophets, and then returned to Makkah. *See* **Mikraj** 2. Cal. The twenty-seventh day of the month of Rajab, which is a special day commemorating the anniversary of the Night Journey.

*Usage*: ___ *lakukan dengan mimpi*, (the contention that) the Night Journey was performed through dreaming. *kissah* ___, the story of the Night Journey; *merayakan* ___, to show respect and honor for the anniversary of the Night Journey; *masalah* ___, the question concerning (the correct interpretation) of the Night Journey.

**Israfil** (Ar: isrāfīl) Doct. In the Islamic pantheon, an archangel. On Judgment Day he will give a blast on his trumpet to destroy all mortal creation.
*Usage*: *malaikat* ___, the angel Israfil.

**Israil** (Ar: isrā'īl) Qur. The Jewish people, especially the Children of Israel in their exodus from Egypt.
*Usage*: *bani* ___, the Children of Israel.

**Istiadat**. *See* **Adat Istiadat**.

**Isti'azh**. *See* **Ta'awwudz**.

**Istighfar** (In.); (Ar: istighfār) Pop. Islam. Begging for divine pardon with the phrase "astagfirullāhal 'azhiim" meaning "grant forgiveness O Great God."

**Istikharah** (In.) (Ar: istikhārah) Juris. A prayer for special favors and blessings, especially in times of trial or when faced with difficult choices.
*Usage*: *ber*___, to ask for help from God.

**Istinja'** (Ar: istinjā') Juris. Purification, ritual washing.
*Usage*: *ber*___, to wash one's behind and private parts before undertaking regular preprayer washing.

**Istiqlal**. *See* **Masjid Istiqlal**.

**Istislah** (Ar: istiṣlāḥ) Juris. The principle of a good outcome. If no prohibitions or admonitions of God are transgressed and an action results in general good for an individual or the public, it is permissible.

**Istisqa** (Ar: istisqā') Juris. Prayer for rain.
*Usage*: *sembahyang sunat* ___, the prescribed prayer for rain.

**Istitsna'** (Ar: istithnā') Pop. Islam. Acronym for the phrase "insya Allah," "if God wills."

**Isya** (In.); (Ar: 'ishā') Juris. The night prayer recited after sundown and before morning, often undertaken as a community prayer in the mosque about an hour and a half after sundown.

**Isytiqaq**. *See* **Ilmu Isytiqaq**.

**I'tikad**; i'tiqad. Spelling variants. *See* **Iktiqad**.

**I'tikaf** (Ar: iʿtikāf) Juris. Spiritual retreat, especially during the last ten days of Ramadan when Muslim men often seclude themselves in mosques for prayer.

*Al I'tishan* (Ar: al-iʿtiṣām) Lit. title. A text by Asy Syathibi (d. 1388) concerning Muslim jurisprudence from the Maliki perspective. A work sometimes cited by twentieth-century Indonesian Muslim writers.

**Itsna Asyariyah** (Ar: ithnā ʿasyriyyah) Sect. "The Twelvers," constituting the majority group in Syiah Islam who believe that there were twelve imams before the Imamate became hidden.

**Ittiba'** (Ar: ittibāʿ) Juris. Literally "following"; some modernist Muslim groups maintained that those Muslims not trained to undertake original research and analysis (ijtihad) concerning matters of religious behavior might make a decision between the opinions of several legal schools.

*Al Ittifaqul Iftiraq* (In.) Lit. title. "Joining and Splitting," a magazine published in Padang in the early part of the twentieth century reflecting a modernist Muslim outlook.

**Ittihad** (Ar: ittiḥād) Myst. 1. Unity of creation with God; seeing all things visible as only existing in God. 2. Mystical union of the worshiper with God. The soul of the worshiper is consumed by God and reacts positively to the union.

**Al Ittihadiah**; Al Ittihadiyah (In.) Assn. "Unification," an organization founded in 1935 in Medan espousing modern Islamic principles and active in education, social welfare, and revivalist (dakwah) activities. A special member of the Masjumi party at its founding in 1945. It was still active in the 1980s.

**Ittisal** (In.) Myst. Opening the heart for reception of

knowledge which is secret between God and the receiver.

**Izrail**; Azrail (Ar: ʻizrāʻīl) Doct. In the Islamic pantheon, one of four archangels. He is known as the angel of death.

**Izzuddin** (Ar: ʻizz ad-dīn) Title. Honorific for princes and prestigious scholars of Islam. *See* following word.

# J

**Al Jabariyah** (Ar: jabriyyah) Doct. A historical group in Islam which held that humans had no power over their own destinies, but that God's power preempted any such control on humans' part. This was in contrast to the Qadariyyah, who believed humans had total control over their own actions.

**Al Jabbaar**; Jabbar (Ar: al-jabbar) Theo. Name of God meaning "The Irresistible."

**Jabir Bin 'Abdillah** (Ar: jābir ibn 'abdillāh) Biog. (d. 73H) A Companion of the Prophet. Traced to him are 1540 reports of the words and behavior of Muhammad.

**Jahanam**; Jahannam. *See* **Neraka**.

**Jahar** (In.) (Ar: jahr) 1. Myst. Use of the voice to pronounce the name or names of God, as contrasted to saying them silently (zikir khafi). 2. Qur. In recitation of the Qur'an, pronouncing with a strong voice.
*Usage*: *istilah* ___, repeating the names of God aloud.

**Jahat** (In.) Juris. Bad, evil, wicked, malicious.
*Usage*: *ke___an*, evilness, wickedness; *ke___an terhebat*, wickedness of a serious nature.

**Jahiliah** (Ar: jāhiliyya) 1. Doct. "Age of Ignorance," the historical age preceding the arrival of Islam. In general Muslims believe that age was marked by immorality and lack of religious responsibility. Conditions only changed when the teachings of Islam arrived. 2. Lang. Pejorative references, usually by neofundamentalists, to modern technological cultures that have some basis other than Islamic values and standards. The West is often portrayed as a Jahiliah culture.

*Usage*: *kaum* ___, the idolatrous people living in the time of the age of ignorance; *kebudayaan* ___, the way of life and cultural outlook dominant in the age of ignorance; *masa* ___, the time period of the age of ignorance.

**Jahim**. *See* **Neraka.**

**Al Jailani**. *See* **Abdul Qadir Jailani**.

**Jaiz** (In.) (Ar: jā'iz) Juris. An action considered to be neutral in regard to God's commands, which may or may not be performed with no harm or merit occurring either way. Syn: mubah.

**Jakarta** (In.) Geog. Capital of Indonesia and site of major nationalist buildings and monuments. A center of Islamic religious effort centering on the Department of Religion (Departemen Agama), the Independence Mosque (Masjid Istiqlal), the Masjid Agung Al-Azhar and many foundations supporting Islamic activity of various kinds. Earlier known as Jayakarta and Batavia.

**Jakfar Sadiq, Syekh**. *See* **Kudus, Sunan**.

**Al Jalal**; Al Jalil (Ar: al-jalāl) Theo. Name of God meaning "Characterized by Greatness." This is understood to mean that God is beyond the understanding of His creatures.

**Al Jalalain**. *See Tafsirul Jalalain*.

**Jalan Yang Lurus** (In.) Expres. "The straight path," a popular expression among Muslims for Islam.

**Al Jalil**. Spelling variant. *See* **Al Jalal**.

**Jama'ah**; Jemaah (In.); Jamaah (Ar: jamā'ah) 1. Assn. Group or association, used frequently by Muslim organizations. 2. Juris. The free association of Muslims in formal worship, usually associated with a mosque. *Usage*: ___ *Jum'at*, Friday communal prayer; *mengumpulkan* ___, gathering for public prayer.

**Jambek, Syekh M. Jamal** (In.) Biog. (d. 1947). A Minangkabau-born mathematician who taught mathematics to Minang students in Makkah and later in Minangkabau. He published almanacs (for prayers and

Ramadan) and undertook extensive efforts to propagate Islam in urban areas of west Sumatra.

**Al-Jami'** (Ar: jāmī') Theo. Name of God, meaning "The Collector of all creatures on the Day of Judgment."

**Jamiat Islam Wal Irsyad Al Arabia**; Jamiiyatul Irsyaddan (In. fr. Ar: jāmi'at wal irsyād al-'arabiyyah) Assn. "The Union for Reformation and Guidance," known generally as Al-Irsyad. An association of Arab Muslims in Indonesia, founded in the 1920s to further the reformist principles of Islam promoted by Muhammad Abduh (d. 1905). While not a leading movement in size of membership, it had significant intellectual influence on the development of modernist Islam in Indonesia.

**Jami'at Khair** (In. fr. Ar: al-jāmi'h al-khairiyyah) Assn. "The Benevolent Association," the first non-Dutch organization in the Netherlands Indies, dedicated to Arab education, started in 1895. It went out of existence in 1910 with the founding of Al Irsyad.

*Jami'ul Ahkam* (Ar: al-jāmi'h liaḥkām al-qur'ān) Lit. title. "The Qur'anic Legal Collection," a commentary on the Qur'an written by Al Qurthubi (d. 1273) which emphasizes the legal obligations on believers. Also known as the *Tafsir Qurthubi.*

*Jami'ul Bayan* (Ar: jāmi' al-bayān) Lit. title. "The Clarifying Collection," a commentary of the Qur'an by Ath Thabari (d. 932) noted for its broad approach and analysis. Especially well liked by later scholars and frequently imitated.

*Jam'iush Shaghir* (Ar: jāmi' aṣ-ṣaghīr) Lit. title. "The Modest Collection," an important compilation of Traditions assembled by As Sayuthi (d. 1505), long important as a text in Southeast Asia.

*Jami'ut Tafshil* (Ar: jāmi' at-tafṣīl) Lit. title. "The Representative Collection," a commentary of the Qur'an by Ibnu Arabi (d. 638H) which stresses the hidden meanings of the text as well as the obvious surface message. Part of a larger work called *Fatuhatul Makiyah.*

**Jamiyah Amaliah** (fr. Ar: jam'iyyah and 'amal) Doct. An association which seeks to promote good behavior of its members, a concept popular in Indonesian Muslim writings of the 1980s.

**Jamiiyatul Irsyaddan**. *See* **Jamiat Islam Wal Irsyad Al Arabia**.

**Jamiyatul Khairiyah** (Ar: jam'iyyah khairiyyah) Assn. "The Benevolent Association," an association of Indonesian and Malaysian students in 1923 in Cairo. It was one of several formed in the Middle East at the time, devoted to promoting religious ideals among its members to serve as a guide for the home countries. It changed its name to Persatuan Pemuda Indonesia-Malaya in 1924.

**Jam'iyatul Washliyah** (In.) Assn. "The Unshakeable Association," an organization in north Sumatra founded in 1930 dedicated to Islamic principles based on the Syafii interpretation. It is strong among the Karo Batak people.

**Janazah**. *See* **Jinazah**.

**Jannah**. *See* **Surga**.

**Jariah**. *See* **Sedekah**.

**Jasmani** (In.) (Ar: jismanī). Doct. Physical or human, especially in regard to emotions, life and being. *Usage*: *kebangkitan* ___, human development; *kesehatan* ___ *dan rohani*, physical and spiritual well-being.

**Jati, Sunan Gunung**. *See* **Gunung Jati, Sunan**.

*Jati, Wirid Hidayat. See Sirat Wirid Hidayat Jati.*

**Al Jaatsiyah**; Al Jatsiah; Al Jatsiyah (Ar: al-jāthiyah) Qur. "Kneeling," the forty-fifth chapter of the Qur'an. It relates how God will reward or punish in the Hereafter on the basis of behavior on earth. Also known as Asy Syari'ah.

**Al Jauziyyah, Ibnu Qayim**. *See* **Ibnu Qayyimul Jauziyyah**.

**Jawa** (In.) Geog. A major island of Indonesia with several different cultural regions. Central and East Java were the locations of several historically important kingdoms including Majapahit (1294-1527) which is the nationalist historians proto-Indonesian state. The Islamic kingdoms of Demak (1478-1561) and Mataram (1575-1755) have strong identification for Indonesian Muslim historians. The phenomenon of a dichotomous culture of close association with Islam by some (santri) and loose association by others (abangan) is a highly emphasized anthropological characteristic of the central portion of the island.

**Jawi** (In.) Lang. A script in which Arabic letters are used to write Malay, which was popular for several centuries throughout the Indonesian-Malay areas. It has been retained as one script in current-day Malaysia, Southern Thailand, and Brunei. Currently of importance for historical works in Indonesia.

**Jayadiningrat, Husein;** Djadjadingrat, Hoesin (In.) Biog. (d. 1960) Javanese scholar educated in the Netherlands noted for his studies on linguistics and Islamic law.

**Jayakarta**. *See* **Jakarta** and **Batavia.**

**Jayo, Sultan Kramo**. *See* **Palembang.**

**Jayo Wikramo, Mahmud Badaruddin**. *See* **Palembang.**

**Al Jayyid**. *See* **Ilmu Mushthalah Hadis.**

**Jaza'** (Ar: jazā') Pop. Islam. Merit for undertaking laudatory actions. Syn: pahala. *See* **Yawmul Jaza.**

**Jemaah**. Spelling variant. *See* **Jama'ah.**

**Jenar**. *See* **Siti Jenar, Syekh.**

**Jenayah**. Spelling variant. *See* **Jinayah.**

**Jenazah**. Spelling variant. *See* **Jinazah.**

**Jepara** (In.) Geog. City on the north central coast of Java and site of an Islamic kingdom in the sixteenth century that sought on three occasions to drive the Portuguese from Malacca (1513, 1551, 1574). All the attacks were unsuccessful.

**JIB**. *See* **Jong Islamieten Bond.**

**JIBDA.** *See* **Jong Islamieten Bond Dames Afdeling.**

**Jibrail** (In.); Jibril (Ar: jibrā'īl, jibril) Doct. The name of one of the four archangels. *See* **Malaikat.**
*Usage*: *malaikat* ___, the angel Jibrail.

**Jihad** (In.) (Ar: jihād) Doct. "The Way of God," the concept of striving to accomplish some religious end. It is often translated as "holy war," since it includes protection of the Islamic community, but sometimes transcends physical effort for more sophisticated means of further Islamic interests.
*Usage*: ___ *fi sabillah*, undertaking action to further the conditions or aims of Muslim society, nation or religious principles; *gerakan* ___, a cause undertaken for the sake of religion (Islam); *al kanunul* ___, the law of war and peace; *komando* ___, name of a number of breakaway groups in the Republic of Indonesia that espouse militant Islam.

**Jihad, Resolusi.** *See* **Resolusi Jihad.**

**Jilbab** (In.) (Ar: jilbab) Juris. Head covering worn by some Muslim women to cover all the head except the oval of the face. It has become popular in Indonesia over the past twenty years, especially among purist groups, who regard it as a sign of piety.

**Al Jili, Abdul Karim** (Ar: 'abd al-karīm al-jīlī) Biog. (d. 1428). Well known Persian mystic following the viewpoint of Ibnu Al Arabi (d. 1240) and author of *Al Insaanul Kamil* (The Perfect Human). His viewpoints and writings have had some use in Southeast Asia especially prior to 1900. *See* **Tajali.**

**Jimat**; ajimat; azimat (In) (Ar. 'azīmah) Pop. Islam. Talisman, amulet, written formula considered to have special blessing or magical properties.
*Usage*: *banyu* ___, water with magical powers.

**Jin** (In.); Jinn (Ar: jinn) 1. Qur. A race of creatures that inhabit the world in another dimension. Some are Muslims; others are ifrits, demonlike creatures who cause humans much suffering and grief. 2. Qur. The seventy-second chapter of the Qur'an, named after a type of being on a plane of existence

other than human. A lyrical chapter of the Makkan period.
*Usage*: ___ *kafir*, a Jinn remaining outside of Islam; ___*mukmin*, a Jinn converted to Islam as a result of Muhammad's preaching.

**Jinayah**; jenayah (In.); jinayat; jinajat (Ar: jināyah) Juris. The branch of jurisprudence dealing with criminal action, judgment, and punishment.

**Jinazah** (In.); jenazah; janazah (Ar: jināzah) Juris. Funeral rites which include detailed prescription for the preparation of the body and prayers for the deceased.
*Usage*: ___ *disembahkan*, to undertake the funeral rites, especially the prayer for the dead.

**Jiwa** (In.) Doct. Spirit or essence; soul.
*Usage*: ___*nya dibersihkan oleh Tuhan*, cleansing the soul by God. ___ *Indonesia*, the spirit of Indonesia; ___ *keabadian*, the eternalness of the spirit; *merusakkan* ___, to destroy the spirit (of someone or a cause); ___*ummat Islam*, the spirit of the Muslim community.

**Jiwa, Yang Mencipta** (In.) Theo. A name of God meaning "The Spirit which is the Great Creator." Syn: Al Baari.

**Jizyah** (Ar: jizyah) Juris. A tax placed on non-Muslims in early Islam.

**Joko Said**. *See* **Kalijaga, Sunan.**

**Jong Islamieten Bond—JIB** (In.) Pol. "The Young Muslims Union," a Muslim youth group started in 1924 as an offshoot of the Jong Jawa association. It served as an intellectual think-tank during the nationalist era and was absorbed into the general Islamic movement in the 1940s.

**Jong Islamieten Bond Dames Afdeling—JIBDA** (Dutch) Assn. "The Young Muslims Union, Women's Auxiliary," Women's section of the JIB, active from 1924 to 1942.

**Jubah** (In.); jubbah (Ar: jubbah) Pol. A cassock, often worn by saintly individuals among Muslims. A pejorative reference to Islam and Muslims as old-fashioned and espousing outmoded values in general. A term applied by the secular nationalists during the preindependence period.

**Judi** (In.) Juris. Playing with dice; usually used meaning gambling in general. Gambling is almost universally believed among Muslims to transgress God's law.
*Usage*: *ber___*, to gamble.

**Jumadil Kubra**. *See* **Malik Ibrahim (Maulana)**.

**Jumadilakhir** (In.); Jumadil Akhir (Ar: jumādā aththāniyah) Cal. Name of the sixth month of the Islamic calendar, meaning "the second month of dryness."

**Jumadilawal** (In.); Jumadil Awwal (Ar: jumādā al-ūlā) Cal. Name of the fifth month of the Islamic calendar, meaning "the first month of dryness."

**Jum'ah**. *See* **Yawmul Jum'ah**.

**Jum'at** (In.); jum'ah; jum'at (Ar: jumu'ah) Cal. Friday, the day of the communal prayer.
*Usage*: *khutbah* ___, the Friday sermon.

**Al Jumu'ah**; Al Jum'ah (Ar: al-jumu'ah) Qur. "Day of Prayer," the sixty-second chapter of the Qur'an. It clarifies the behavior of the ungodly.

**Jumud** (In.) Anthro. Static, non-progressive.
*Usage*: *ke___-kekunoan kiai-kiai*, old-fashioned religious teachers (an expression used by secular nationalists in the 1920s against Islam)

**Juynboll, Th. W.** (Dutch) Biog. (d. 1861). Dutch scholar of Islam who worked on Traditions and jurisprudence. *See Handleiding de Mohammedaansche Wet*.

**Juz** (In.) (Ar: juz') Qur. A section of the Qur'an, which crosses chapters (surah) intended to facilitate reading and recitation. There are thirty juz of equal length, each with its own number.

**Juz Amma** (Ar: juz' 'amma) Qur. The popular name for the last reading section of the Qur'an (number thirty), generally known for its short, poetical selections, often learned and read by children.

# K

**Ka'b bin Zubayr.** *See* **Burdah.**

**Kabah**; kabbah (In.); ka'bah; kaabah (Ar: ka'bah) 1. Doct. The shrine of Islam at Makkah, erected, according to the Qur'an, by the Prophet Ibrahim (Abraham). The Kabah is the center of religious activities in the pilgrimage held each year as part of the Muslim calendar. 2. Pol. The symbol of the Kabah was used by the National Development Party (PPP) in two Indonesian election campaigns as symbolic of its role as political spokesman for Muslim interests. Its use was denied in the third campaign by law, which saw the use of religious symbols as inflammatory and divisive of national unity.
*Usage*: ___ *Al Musyarrafah*, Kabah, the Honored.

**Kabar** (In.); khabar; chabar (Ar: khabar) Trad. The report transmitting the words and behavior of the Prophet Muhammad. Syn: matan.

**Al Kabiir**; Al Khabir (Ar: al-khabīr) Theo. A name of God meaning the "The Well Informed." Same as Yang Maha Agung.

**Kada**; kadha (In.); qada'; qadha; qadla (Ar: qaḍā') Juris. Performing a religious obligation outside of the normal place or time because it was not able to be performed normally.
*Usage*: *mengqada*, to perform a religious obligation out of place; *meng___ puasa*, fasting undertaken after Ramadan as a make-up for fasting missed; *meng___ salat*, *meng___ sembahyang*, ritual prayer held at a make-up time. ___ *sunnat subuh*, to make up the morning prayer.

**Kadar** (In.); qadar (Ar: qadar) Doct. The power of God to determine all events. It is an explicit point in the

Muslim creed that God has such power. As recognition of that power, many Muslims utter the term "insha Allah," i.e., "if God wills," when using the future tense. *See* **Takdir**.

**Kadha**. Spelling variant. *See* **Kada**.

**Kadi**; qadi, qadhi, qathi (In.); kadhi (Ar: qāḍī) Juris. A judge of a religious court.

**Kadim** (In.) Pop. Islam. The future.
*Usage*: *mengadimkan*, to predict, to prophesy.

**Kadiriah** (In.); Qadiriyah; Qodiriyah (Ar: qādiriyyah) Myst. Name of a Sufi order founded by 'Abdul Qadirul Jilani (d. 1166). The order has experienced a heavy influx of folk Sufism accounting for much of its wide popularity. It is influential in North Africa, Turkey, South Asia, and Indonesia.

**Kafan** (Ar: kafan) Juris. A wrapping for the corpse in use among Muslims.
*Usage*: *di__kan*, to undertake the wrapping after ritual washing of the corpse is completed.

**Al Kafi** (Ar: al-kāfī) Theo. A name of God meaning "The Sufficient One."

**Kafir** (In.) (Ar: kāfir) Juris. "Rejector;" a person who does not believe in Islam.
*Usage*: *ke__an*, disbelief; *meng__kan*, to pronounce judgment on someone as being a disbeliever (usually as a matter of faith or law). *Golongan ___ Kuraisy*, the people of Makkah at the time of the Prophet Muhammad who opposed him; *kaum ___*, people who do not believe in Islam; *mati ___*, disbeliever's death (i.e. condemned to hell); *orang ___*, unbelievers of Islam; ___ *zimmi*, Christians and Jews who reject Islam, usually in the context of early Islam.

**Al Kaafiruun**; Al Kafirun (Ar: al-kāfirūn) Qur. "The Infidels," the 109th chapter of the Qur'an. A very short, lyrical chapter dissociating the believer from the disbeliever.

**Al Kahfi**; Al-Kahf (Ar: al-kahf) Qur. "The Cave," the eighteenth chapter of the Qur'an. The chapter contains lessons about the "Unity of God" and the concept of His justice.

**Kaidah** (In.); qa'idah (Ar: qāwā'id) 1. Gen. vocab. Rule, guideline, regulation, standard. 2. Juris. The standards of worship, encompassing purification, prayer, almsgiving, and the pilgrimage.

**Kaidah 'Ibadah** (Ar: qawā'id 'ibādah) Juris. The standards of worship, encompassing purification, prayer, almsgiving, and the pilgrimage. *See* **Ibadah.**

**Kaidah Mu'amalah** (Ar: qawā'id mu'āmalah) juris. The standards of behavior regulating believers in relationship with other humans and with the physical world.

**Kaidah Tajwid** (Ar: qawā'id tajwīd) Qur. The appropriate method of reciting the Qur'an.

**Kalam** (Ar: kalām) Doct. Theology and theological thinking. *See* **Ilmu Tauhid.** *Usage*: *ahli* ___, theologians, particularly those of the classical period; ___ *Ilahi*, ___*ullah*, the theology of God.

**Kalijaga, Sunan**; Kalijago (In.) 1. Biog. One of nine leading missionaries of early Indonesian Islam, popularly believed to have led the conversion of Java to Islam. He is credited with using the shadow puppet (wayang) theatre as a means of spreading stories about Islam. He is often called the central figure of the nine walis. Also known as Orang Muda Muhammad Said and Joko Said. *See* **Wali Songo.** 2. Educ. Name of a national Islamic Studies institute (IAIN) at Yogyakarta. *See* **Institut Agama Islam Negara.**

*Kalilah Wa Dimnah* (Sanskrit) Lit. title. "The Two Jackels," a collection of animal fables which was famous throughout the Islamic world during the middle period. The collection was popular in Southeast Asia during the eighteenth and nineteenth centuries.

**Kalimah** (In) (Ar: kalimah) Doct. Creed, especially the Confession of Faith. *Usage*: *membaca* ___ *tauhid*, confessing the belief of the Unity of God.

**Kalimah Kalih** (Fr. Ar: kalimat) Pop. Islam. A term meaning the two confessions, i.e,. "asyhadu an la Ilaha illa 'Lah, wa asyhadu anna

Muhammadan Abdu-Hu wa Rasulu-Hu," meaning "I confess that there is no god except Allah and that Muhammad is His Prophet."

**Kalimah Syahadat** (Ar: kalimat ash-shahādah) Doct. The expression "asyhadu an la ilaha illa 'Lah wa anna Muhammadan rasūlu Lah;" "There is no God but Allah and Muhammad is the apostle of God." This is the first tenet of practical religious practice and is generally recognized by Muslim theologians and jurists as separating believers from unbelievers.

**Kalimah Zikir** (Ar: kalimat adh-dhikr) Pop. Islam. The expression "la ilaaha illal Lah," meaning "There is no god, but God."

**Kalipatullah** (Jav.) Title. Royal title of Javanese kings indicating their role as representatives of God on earth. *See* following word.

**Kamil Insan** (In.) (Ar: insān al-kāmil) Myst. Conceptualization of the perfect human. Among mystics the term denotes one who uses intuitive knowledge (ma'rifat) gained through mystical practice to lead a godly life. Muhammad is featured as a perfect person, as were several leading sufi shaykhs. In contemporary Islam the term has come to mean "the ideal or model Muslim."

**Kangjang** (Jav). Title. 1. Royal title often used with "gusti" at major Javanese courts during the sultanate and colonial periods. When used with office names it indicated the major government officials. 2. Title of religious scholars on Kalimantan. Syn: kiai, raden.

**Het Kantoor voor Inlandsche Zaken** (Dutch) Pol. "The Office of Internal Affairs," an administrative unit in the Dutch colonial administration of the Netherlands Indies. In the late nineteenth and early twentieth centuries it functioned as a security unit dealing with threats to the existing political order, which included concerns about the motives of Muslims on several occasions. Modern Indonesian Muslim historians regard its work as an unjust interference in the religious life of Muslims.

**Kanun** (In.); qanun (Ar: qānūn) Pol. Law, law code. Syn: hukum.
*Usage*: *al ___ul am*, public law; *___ul jihad*, the law of war and peace; *al ___ul khas*, civil law.

**Kapitalisme-Liberalisme** (In.) Pol. A philosophical or ideological underpinning of several Western nations, such as the United States. While recognizing the prosperity of such states, Muslim thinkers view such societies as suspect, because of their failure to clearly base their principles on eternal values which Muslim thinkers maintain Islam represents.

**Karamah**. Spelling variant. *See* **Keramat**.

**Karbela** (Ar: karbala) 1. Geog. Place name of a city in Iraq and site of a major Syi'ite shrine. 2. Hist. Site of the massacre in 61H/680 of Husayn, grandson of the Prophet Muhammad, and his retinue by Umayyad authorities. This established a matyrdom for Syiah Islam.

**Kari** (In.); qari' (Ar: qāri') Qur. A male reciter of the Qur'an. The professional reciter has memorized the Qur'an which he recites in a wide variety of contexts.

**Kariah** (In.); qariah (Ar: qari'ah). Qur. Female Qur'an reciter.

**Al Kariim**, Al Karim, Al Kariem (Ar: al-karīm) Theo. A name of God meaning "The Magnanimous." Same as Yang Maha Mulia.

**Kartosuwiryo, Sekarmaji Maryan** (In.) Biog. (d. 1962). Leader of the Darul Islam, a Muslim group in West Java that declared itself the government of an Islamic State of Indonesia in 1948. It fought against Republican forces until pacified in the early 1960s.

**Karya-Karya Rohani** (In.) Doct. Spiritual works.

**Kasidah** (In.); qasidah (Ar: qasidah) Qur. Songs in praise of religion sung usually by women. They accompany themselves with various musical instruments. In the 1980s this emerged as a popular form of religious expression in Indonesia.
*Usage*: *ber___*, to sing in kasidah style.

**Kasih Maha Yang** (In.) Theo. A name of God meaning "The All Loving."

**Kasman Singodimedjo** (In.) Biog. (d. 1982). A Masjumi leader from Central Java, educated in Dutch-language schools as an economist. Once member of the government's Central Economic Board in the 1950s.

*Al Kas-syaf* (Ar: al-kashshāf) Lit. title. "The Guide," a commentary of the Qur'an by Al Zamakhsyary (d. 1143), noted for its discussion of the language of the Qur'an and confirming its claim to be a miracle. *See* **Tafsir**.

**Katib**. Spelling variant. *See* **Khatib**.

**Kaum Muda** (In.) Pol. The modernist Muslim movement of the twentieth century which emphasized revitalization of Islamic thinking, particularly toward scientific and sociological modernization of Muslim societies, but based on a modern interpretation of the Qur'an and the Traditions of the Prophet.

**Kaum Tua** (In.) Pol. The traditionalist Muslim group of the twentieth century that insists on application of the teachings of the great religious teachers of the Islamic past. While not denying the need for modernization in general, members of the group deny that religious principles need review; those principles simply need to be applied.

**Al Kautsar** (Ar: al-kawthar) Qur. "Great Comfort,", the 108th chapter of the Qur'an. A very short, lyrical chapter acknowledging God's goodness to believers.

*Kawaakibul Durriyya. See Burdah.*

**Kawin** (In.) Juris. Marriage.

**KBIM**. *See* **Kesatuan Buruh Islam Merdeka**.

**Keakhiratan**. *See* **Ilmu Keakhiratan**.

**Kebatinan** (In.) Pol. Title given to a group of people, mostly in Central Java, who practice mystical rights based on a mixture of religions: Hinduism, Buddhism, Islam, Christianity, and animism. The term is sometimes confused with abangan, which is a more general cultural term. Also known as Kepercayaan.

**Kebudayaan.** *See* **Budaya.**

**Kedamaian, Yang Maha** (In.) Theo. Name of God meaning "The Most Peaceful."

**Kedaulatan.** *See* **Daulah.**

**Kehadirat Tuhan** (In.) Doct. To die; to stand in the presence of God for judgment.

**Keirei** (Japanese) Pol. Slight bowing in use among the Japanese in the form of greeting. During the Japanese occupation of Indonesia the keirei was required of all inhabitants, free or jailed, vís-a-vís any Japanese. Not to be confused with the sai keirei, which had ceremonial aspects.

**Kekal, Yang Maha** (In.) Theo. A name of God meaning "The Eternal."

**Keluarga** (In.) Juris. Family. In some Muslim writing the term is used in the sense of generational descent. *Usage*: *telah ber___*, to be already married.

**Kemal Ataturk, Mustafa** (Turkic) Biog. (d.1935). First president of modern Turkey, who undertook an intense modernization of the country, accompanied by secularization. His reforms limited the exercise and influence of Islam and, accordingly, had considerable appeal among the secular nationalists of Indonesia during the 1920s and 1930s.

**Kemas, Muhammad bin Ahmad** (In.) Biog. (d. 1763). Sumatran scholar from Palembang who wrote books on popular Islam, including the deeds of a mystic saint and one on future events. *See Hikayat Shaikh Muhammad Samman.*

**Kenduri** (In.); khanduri (Aceh) (Pers) Pop. Islam. Popular Islamic term of South and Southeast Asia, indicating a ritual meal given for any number of occasions. Islamic prayers and blessings often are part of the kenduri. Syn: garebek, sedekah. *Usage*: *ibadah* ___, inclusion of Islamic elements to the ritual meal to make it essentially an Islamic festivity.

**Kepenguluan.** *See* **Penghulu.**

**Kepercayaan**. *See* **Kebatinan.**

**Kerajaan** (In.). Hist. Kingdom, especially the political entities of the Indian period of Southeast Asian history predating the arrival of the Europeans, including many of the Muslim states. *See* **Raja** and **Kesultanan.**
*Usage*: *istana* ___, the ruler's palace; ___ *maritim*, maritime trading states.

**Keramat** (In.) Karamah (Ar: kāramāt) Pop. Islam. The term for magic, in the sense that a person or thing possesses special mystical powers. Keramat in Indonesian folk belief can be mastered by certain individuals for good fortune, protection, or foretelling the future.
*Usage*: *di__kan*, to regard something as having supernatural qualities; *orang* ___, blessed or honored person; *kuburan ulama yang* ___, the tomb of a famous saint regarded as a site of visitation for asking assistance with particular problems of life.

**Kerokhanian**. *See* **Ilmu Kerokhanian.**

**Kesatrian** (In.) Anthro. Noble, knightly.
*Usage*: *ke__an*, nobility, courtliness, an important consideration of courtier behavior at Javanese Muslim courts in the sultanate and colonial periods.

**Kesatuan Buruh Islam Merdeka—KBIM** (In.) Assn. "The Free Islamic Labor Union," a special member of the Masjumi political party in the 1950s.

**Keselamatan, Yang Maha** (In.) Theo. Name of God meaning "The Most Gracious."

**Kesultanan** (In.)(Ar: sulṭān) Hist. A form of government during the middle period and popular in Southeast Asia until the twentieth century. The primary form of Islamic government immediately prior to the arrival of the Europeans. In Indonesia they were located at the following places and times: Aceh 1520-1907 (separate entry), Banjar 1526-1852 (separate entry), Bantan 1526-1683 (separate entry), Bima 1640-1951, Cirebon 1302-1700 (separate entry), Demak 1478-1561 (separate entry), Kutai 1300-1960, Makasar

1603-66, Palembang 1659-1825 (separate entry), Siak 1723-1946, Ternate 1350-1585 (separate entry), Tidore 1495-1905 (separate entry).

**Ketuhanan**. *See* **Ilmu Ketuhanan**.

**Ketuhanan Yang Maha Esa;** Ketahunan YME (In.) Pol. "Belief in God the Only One," the first of five principles of Pancasila, the Indonesian national philosophy. This principle is taken by many Muslims to indicate that Islamic ideals are operative in Indonesian political life.

**Khabar**. Spelling variant. *See* **Kabar**.

**Al Khabir**. Spelling variant. *See* **Al Kabiir**.

**Khadijah** (Ar: khadījah) Biog. First wife of the Prophet Muhammad and mother of five children by him, including Fatimah. Khadijah is often idealized among Muslims as the model wife because of the support she gave her husband during his early ministry.

**Khafi** (In.); khafiy (Ar: khafī) 1. Myst. Silent in recitation, rather than aloud. 2. Doct. Hidden in meaning, especially in understanding the Qur'an, as opposed to meanings that are obvious.
*Usage*: *istilah* ___, devices for extracting hidden meanings of religious texts.

**Al Khafidh** (Ar: khāfid.) Theo. Name of God meaning "The Debaser."

**Khair** (In.) (Ar: khayr) Gen. vocab. Charity, a good work.
*Usage*: *Imamul* ___*i*, Title of Muhammad meaning "The leader of all good actions."

**Khairun, Sultan**. *See* **Ternate**.

**Khalaf** (Ar: khalaf) Hist. Referring to the scholars of the middle classical period, about 300H.
*Usage*: *aliran* ___, *gerakan* ___, the scholars of the middle classical period.

**Khalid, Idham; Chalid ...** (In.) Biog. (b. 1921). Managing chair (ketua) of the Nahdlatul Ulama and minister in the Guided Democracy cabinets of President Sukarno (d. 1968) between 1958 and 1965.

**Khalifah** (In.); chalifah; khalif (Ar: khalīfah) 1. Doct.

The term for "steward" or "regent of God" assigned to humans to designate their control over all things on earth. 2. Pol. The title of a series of rulers in Islam from just after the death of Muhammad until the early twentieth century. It meant the person who acted on behalf of the Prophet. The caliphates were in Iraq and Spain and their dates are as follows: Abbasid 750-1258 (separate entry), Fatimid 910-1160, Granada 1238-1492, Kordoba 755-1236, Umayyad 661-750, Usmaniyah 1299-1924.
*Usage*: *ke___an Turki*, the Turkish caliphs, of the Ottoman dynasty; ___ *Tuhan di bumi*, humans, as God's stewards on earth.

**Khalifah-Khalifah Rasyidin** (In.); khalifatur rasijjidun; khalifat rashidun (Ar: khulafā' ar-rāshidūn) Hist. The first four rulers of the Islamic peoples after the death of Muhammad, usually rendered as the "righteous caliphs." The historical epoch encompassing their combined rule, about forty years, is regarded by Muslims as a time when the "true" teachings of Islam were practiced.
*Usage*: *masa* ____, the period of the rule of the first four rulers of the Islamic community following the death of Muhammad.

**Khalifatullah** (In.) (Ar: khalīfat al-allāh) Pol. A title of the early sultans of Indonesia, recognizing the holder as "the shadow of God on earth."

**Khalil, Munawar**. *See* **Khalil Munawar**.

**Al Khaaliq**; Al Chaaliq (Ar: al-khāliq) Theo. A name of God meaning "The Creator." Syn: Yang Mencipta.

**Khalwat** (In.) (Ar: khalwah) 1. Myst. Removing oneself from external distractions to center on worship of God and thereby draw near to Him. 2. Juris. For people to go into private; usually used in a negative sense for nonmarried males and females to undertake sexual activity with one another.
*Usage*: *ber___, ber___ dua-duan*, to engage in unauthorized contact with the opposite sex; larangan *ber___*, the prohibition against unauthorized male-female contact.

**Khams**. *See* **Yawmul Khams**.

**Khan, (Sir Sayyid) Ahmad** (Urdu: shafā'at aḥmad khān) Biog. (d. 1898). Modernist Muslim of South Asia who founded the Aligarh School to train the Muslim elite in Western studies.

**Khanaqah**. *See* **Zawiyah**.

**Khanduri**. Spelling variant. *See* **Kenduri**.

**Khariji**. *See* **Khawarij**.

**Khatam** (In.); Khataman (Ar: khatmah) Qur. Reading the Qur'an from beginning to end at one session, often undertaken as a ritual by members of a mystical order (tarekat), or by worshipers at a mosque during Ramadan.

**Khatib**; katib (In.); chatib (Ar: khāṭib) 1. Doct. The term for the person giving the sermon at the Friday communal worship. While not licensed officially, usually a set group of people deliver the sermons; frequently they are religious scholars. 2. Title. Title of respect for a religious scholar.

**Khatib Minangkabau, Ahmad** (In.) Biog. (d. 1916) Minangkabau-born scholar of the Shafii order who became mufti of that order in Makkah. His writings and his personal teaching of Malay and Minangkabau students in Makkah was a key factor in the rise of the modernist Muslim movement in Southeast Asia.

**Khatimun Nabiyiin** (Ar: khātim an-nubūwah) Doct. "Seal of the Prophets," an accolade given Muhammad as the final prophet to humans. It is a point of belief among Sunni Muslims and leads to challenges of the Ahmadiyah Qadiyan's contentions that its founder is a prophet.

**Khauf** (In.) (Ar: khauf) Doct. Fear of God.

**Khawarij** (Ar: khawārij) Hist. A group in early Islam which opposed both the emerging Sunni and Syiah groups. In effect, a third group which elevated proper belief (iman) to the highest ideal and rejected all compromises with other values, standards, and customs.

**Al Khazin** ('alā' ad-dīn al-khāzin al-baghdādī) Biog. (d. 1340). Arab author of a well known commentary on the Qur'an, which is often cited by twentieth-century religious scholars of Indonesia. *See Lubabut Takwil* and **Tafsir**.

**Khidmat** (In.) (Ar: khidmah) Gen. vocab. Honor and respect.

**Khilafah** (Ar: khilāfāt) Juris. 1. Matters for decision in a particular community or group. Muslim political commentators regard the concept as the basis for Muslim political action. 2. Law dealing with state and governmental matters. Syn: hukum kenegaraan.

**Khilafiah** (In.); khilafiyah (Ar: khilāfiyyah) Juris. Matters of difference among persons and groups in Islam that do not affect basic belief and doctrine. In Indonesia the dispute concerning the correct use of taqlid and ijtihad was considered to be a khilafiyah dispute, while other differences such as pronouncing the Friday sermon (khutbah) in the vernacular or in Arabic, which was dependent on the taqlid-ijtihad debate, was considered an associated dispute (furu).

*Usage*: *meng___kan*, to experience differences in matters of interpretation; *masalah-masalah furu'* ___, matters of different interpretation.

**Khitahi** (In.); khittah (Ar: khiṭṭah) Pol. Basic goals and directions of effort. Sometimes used as a title of the program or aims of particular organizations.

**Khiyar** (In.) (Ar: khīyār) Juris. A period of grace in a transaction when revocation is possible according to the conditions of the original arrangement.

**Khotbah**. *See* **khutbah**.

**Khula**; khulu; khol (khul') Juris. Purchased divorce by a woman wishing to leave a marriage. Such purchase leaves the dower with the husband and the wife usually waves future support.

**Khulud**. *See* **Surga**.

**Khurafat** (In.) (Ar: khurāfāṭ) Doct. Superstition, often applied by purist Muslims to many aspects of popular Islam, particularly the use of amulets, consultation with

soothsayers, and saint worship.
*Usage*: *memerangi bidah dan* ___, to undertake efforts against innovation and superstition.

**Khusuf**. *See* **Salat**.

**Khusyuk** (In.); khusia; khusyu (Ar: khushū‘) Juris. Strict piety, attitude of humility.
*Usage*: *ke___an*, piety, humility; ___ *dan tawadu kepada Tuhan*, correct attitude of humility and piety toward God; *mendoa dengan* ___, praying with humility.

**Khutbah**; khotbah (In.) (Ar: khuṭbah) Doct. The sermon given at the Friday communal prayer. In Indonesia these are subject to official scrutiny and there are some limitations on political and social issues that may be discussed in them.
*Usage*: *ber___*, to deliver the Friday sermon; ___*Id*, the sermon given at the festival of Idul Fitri or Idul Adha; ___ *Jum'at*, the sermon given at the Friday prayer; *membaca* ___ *Jum'at*, to deliver the Friday sermon; *mengdengarkan* ___, to listen to the Friday sermon; *rukun* ___, the institution of the Friday sermon.

**KIAA**. *See* **Konperensi Islam Asia Afrika**.

**Kiai**; ki; kijai (In.); kyai; kijahi; kiyahi (Jav.) Title. A title given to religious scholars (ulama) of pesantren on Java. They are highly regarded by local people and sought out for their advice on all sorts of matters. In some cases they are believed to have special knowledge and powers that draw those wishing to receive blessings or supernatural assistance.
*Usage*: *kekunoan* ___-___, pejorative term used by secular nationalists in the 1920s meaning "old-fashioned teachers of religion"; *para* ___, the group of kiais as a generality; *sang* ___, reference to a single kiai.

**Kias** (In.); qias; qiyas (Ar: qiyās) Juris. Analogy; one of the four sources of Sunni Muslim jurisprudence. The analogy is to cases existing in the Muslim scriptures of the Qur'an and Traditions. *See* **Ushul Fikih**.
*Usage*: *meng___kan*, to base a decision on the principle of analogy; *peng___an*, drawing

forth an analogy for jurisprudential reasons. *Berdasar* ___, to base a decision on the principle of analogy; *dalil-dalil* ___, *hukum* ___, the principle of analogy.

**Kiblat**; qiblat (In.) (Ar: qiblah) Juris. The direction of prayer, i.e., the direction toward Makkah. In mosques it is marked by a niche in the wall, called a mihrab. In hotel rooms it is signified with a marker on furniture or on the ceiling.

*Kiblat* (In.) Lit. title. A popular Muslim magazine, issued monthly, starting in 1953 which issues articles concerning developments within the Indonesian Muslim community. Associated with the Yayasan Perjalanan Haji Islam.

**Kifayah**. *See* **Fardu Kifayah** and **Sunah**.

**Kijai**, Kijahi. Spelling variant. *See* **Kiai**.

**Al Kindi** (Ar: abū yūsuf ... al-kindī) Biog. (252H/870). A renowned Arab philosopher of the classical period, who wrote extensively. Included in his writings is a dictionary of philosophic terms.

**Kiraat**; kiraah; qiraat (In.); qiraah; qir'at, qira'ah (Ar: qirā'ah). Qur. Recitation of the Qur'an according to one of the established methods of doing so. The technique is learned from a certified teacher of the art.
*Usage*: ___-___ *nabi*, the forms sanctioned by the Prophet Muhammad; ___ *masyhur*, accurate recitation techniques transmitted by authoritative sources; ___ *maudlu*, recitation techniques transmitted by confused sources; ___ *mutawatir*, accurate recitation techniques transmitted by repetition of reliable sources; ___ *syadz*, recitation techniques of disputed authority; ___ *takhlif*, recitation techniques transmitted by different lines of authority.
*Ahli-ahli* ___, *imam-imam* ___, people who set the terms for recitation of the Qur'an in early Muslim history.

**Kitab** (In.) (Ar: kitāb) 1. Lang. "Book," used in titles of certain genre of religious literature outlining the principles of religion. 2. Juris. "Book," used in collections of Traditions and jurisprudence to note the first division of a study, that is, chapters. Kitabs are broken

further into sections, known as bab. 3. Doct. "Scripture," such as the Torah of the Jews and the Evangel of the Christians.
*Usage*: ___-___ *samawi*, ___-___ *suci*, holy books (revealed by God); ___-___ *tafsir*, commentaries of the Qur'an; ___ *Perjanjian Muda*, The New Testament; ___ *Perjanjian Lama*, the Old Testament.

*Kitab Dhammun* (Ar: kitāb ḍammūn) Lit. title. "The Collection," the name of a book by an anonymous author used in early Islamic education in Southeast Asia for teaching the elements of Arabic grammar.

*Kitab Fathul Mu'in* (Ar: fatḥ al-mu'īn) Lit. title. "Help of the Helper," a book on jurisprudence by Zainuddin Al Malibari (d. 1574) used by Southeast Asian scholars for over two centuries.

*Kitab Injil. See Injil.*

**Kitab Kuning** (In.) Educ. "The Yellow Books." Arab language works from Muslim writers of the middle period, which are studied in the pesantren and together set the standards and paradigms for the graduates of those schools. The works cover the subject of jurisprudence (fikih), nature of God (tauhid), Traditions of the Prophet (hadis), mystical practice (tasawuf), and the Arab language.

*Kitab Saribu Mas'alah* (In.) Lit. title. "Book of the Thousand Questions," a compilation on popular mysticism translated from Arabic into Indonesian by an anonymous scholar of the sixteenth century. It was popular throughout Southeast Asia during the following two centuries.

**Kitabi** (Ar: kitābī) Juris. Matters pertaining to "Peoples of the Book," that is, Christians, Jews and other peoples Muslims regard as having received revealed books of God.

*Kitabul Muhadzab* (Ar: al-majmū' sharḥ al muhadhdhab) Lit. title. "The Teacher," a text on Tradition selection and analysis by Asy Syirazi (d. 1083).

*Kitabul Umm* (Ar: kitāb al-umm) Lit. title. "The Source," a major legal compendium of Traditions assembled by Asy Syafii (d. 820) and one of the original texts of the Syafii school of jurisprudence. It is cited by contemporary Indonesian Muslims and copies are extant in Arabic and in Indonesian translation.

*Kitabun Nihayah* (Ar: nihāyat al-muḥtāj) Lit. title. "The End of Neediness," a leading jurisprudential text of the Syafii school, written by Ar Ramli (d. 1596), popular in Indonesia in the nineteenth and twentieth centuries.

**Kitabullah**; kitaabullah (Ar: kitābullāh) Doct. The message of God, revealed to humans, through a prophet. The Qur'an is the ultimate message, intended for all people at all times and places. The Torah, Zabur, and Injil are mentioned in the Qur'an as examples.

**Kiyahi**. Spelling variant. *See* **Kiai**.

**Kodrat** (In.); qudrat (Ar: qudrah) Doct. The power of God sufficient to form all of creation.
*Usage*: ___ *Tuhan*, God's omnipotence.

**Kolot** (In.) Pol. Ignorance, old-fashioned.
*Usage*: *kaum* ___, people of ignorance, a label given Muslims by secular nationalists in the 1920s.

**Komando Jihad** (In.) Pol. The generic name given by the Suharto government to radical, underground Muslim groups seeking to establish Islamic rule in Indonesia. They are discovered in small numbers from time to time. The government publicizes them as the "threat from the right."

**Komaruddin, Sultan Sri Teruno**. *See* **Palembang**.

**Kompeni Belanda**. *See* **Vereenigde Oostindische Compagnie (VOC)**.

**Komunisme** (In.) Pol. An ideology and movement calling for common, usually public, ownership of all means of production and a socialistic sharing of the proceeds of labor. Opponents, including most Indonesian Muslims, picture them as radical, destructive of society, and antireligious. One important theme in Indonesia's history in the twentieth century has dealt with the struggles between communist and non-communist groups.

**Kongres Al Islam.** *See* **Muktamar Alam Hindia As Syariyah.**

**Kongres Muslimin Indonesia** (In.) Pol. "The Indonesian Muslim Congress," a gathering of prominent Muslims in December 1949 on the eve of the passing of sovereignty to the Indonesian state to discuss common Muslim attitudes about the politics, economics, and social-cultural issues of the times.

**Kongres Ummat Islam Indonesia** (In.) Pol. "The Congress of the Indonesian Community of Believers," a gathering of prominent Muslims in November 1945 which converted the Masjoemi organization from the Japanese period into Masjumi as a united political party of Muslims for the period of independence which was then just beginning.

**Konperensi Islam Asia Afrika—KIAA** (In.) Pol. "The Asian-African Islamic Conference," held in March 1965 at Bandung as a means of eliciting Islamic support for President Sukarno's foreign policy goals calling for creation of a Third World force.

**Konperensi Pendidikan Agama** (In.) Educ. "The Religious Education Conference," held at Yogyakarta in April 1963, dealt with the direction that Islamic schools in Indonesia should take. It centered on evaluation techniques and renewal of curricula.

**Konstituante** (In.) Pol. The Constituent Assembly held from 1956 to 1959 at which all political elements of Indonesia were present to determine the major questions of state and to supply a permanent constitution. The body became deadlocked on several issues, including the role of Islam in the Indonesian state.

**Konstitusi Madinah** (In.) Pol. A contract made between Muhammad and all the tribes in Madinah when he became guardian and administrator of the city. It guaranteed autonomy in large areas of life, including religion. The contract has been promoted by Indonesian postmodernists as prototype legislation for the modern Muslim state. Also known as Perjanjian Madinah.

**Kor'an**. Spelling variant. *See* **Qur'an**.

**Korban**; kurban (In.); qurban (Ar: qurbān) Juris. Sacrifice of an animal as part of worship on Idul Adha, the 10th day of the month of Zulhijah.
*Usage*: *memberikan* ___, giving a sacrifice on Idul Adha.

**Korban Nazar**; Kurban Nazar (Ar: qurbān nazr) Juris. A sacrifice of an animal on Idul Adha in which the person making the sacrifice promises to give the meat as alms to the poor.

**Kordoba**. *See* **Khalifah**.

**Korps Pegawai Republic Indonesia—KORPRI** (In.) Pol. Civil service corps of the Republic of Indonesia, a quasi-official agency that looks after the career interests of its members, organizes them politically, and administers many free time activities, particularly sports and entertainment.

**Kotor** (In.) Juris. Ritual impurity.
*Usage*: *waktu* ___, menstruation.

**Kramo Jayo, Sultan**. *See* **Palembang**.

**Kraton** (Jav) Hist. The court of a ruler, particularly on Java, which owes its existence to the Hindu-Javanese era where it was the cosmological center of the realm, vested with symbolic significance that carried over into the Muslim and colonial eras.

**Kromo** (In.); krama (Jav.) Lang. A style of Javanese language in which the inferior addresses the superior with polite and obsequious phrases and terms.
*Usage*: *Tata* ___, high-Javanese, in which the inferior refers to the superior in indirect, superlative references.

**Kuasa** (In.) Theo. The concept of power, referring, for example, to God's power over all things.
*Usage*: *ke___an*, power.

**Kuasa, Yang Maha** (In.) Theo. A name of God meaning "The All Powerful." Syn: Al Aziz.

**Kuat, Yang Maha** (In.) Theo. Name of God meaning "The Most Powerful." Syn: Al Matiin; Al Qawiyy.

**Kubur** (In.) (Ar: qubūr) Juris. Grave.
*Usage*: *di__kan*, to undertake burying of a corpse; *ke__an*, burial. *__an ulama yang keramat*, the tomb of a Muslim saint believed to be empowered with magic; *berziarah ke* ___, visit a tomb, usually for the purpose of gaining supernatural powers; *menqizinkan menjembah* ___, to permit the burial worship ceremony to take place; *penziarahkan* ___, the act of visiting a tomb to gain supernatural powers.

**Kudus.** *See* **Masjid Menara Kudus.**

**Kudus, Sunan** (Jav.) Biog. (d. unk). One of nine noted missionaries popularly held to be responsible for converting Java to Islam in the sixteenth century. He worked in central Java and along the northern coast. Also known as (Syekh) Jakfar Sadiq. *See* **Wali Songo**.

**Kufur** (Ar: kufr) Juris. Disbelief, that is, rejection of any of the tenets of Islam and connoting disbelief in Islam itself as the religion of God.

**Kuliah** (In.) Educ. Talk, sermon, lesson. Often a special religious talk given in the evening after the required prayer or after optional night prayers.
*Usage*: *___-___ subuh*, a religious talk given after the morning prayer.

*Kunci Swarga*. *See* **Bratakesawa.**

**Kunmat** (Sunda.) Title. Title of Bantamese rulers of the fifteenth and sixteenth centuries indicating imperial authority.

**Kuno** (In.) Pol. Old, old-fashioned, outmoded.
*Usage*: *ke__an (Islam)*, term used by the secular nationalists of the 1930s declaring Islam to be out of date and incapable of responding to contemporary political conditions; *orang-orang* ___, people with old-fashioned notions, especially Muslims adhering to ideas no longer popular.

**Kunut**; qunut (In.) (Ar: qunūt) Juris. A special recitation made at the second part (rak'a) of the morning prayer. The modernist Muslims of the early twentieth century saw this recitation as unauthorized innovation in worship, but traditionalists saw the practice as meritorious. *Usage*: ___ *nazilah*, to give the special prayer when one has feelings of hatred toward someone else; ___ *subuh*, the special recitation during the morning prayer; ___ *witir*, calls for special action to prayer to overcome some obstacle to Muslims. *Masalah* ___ *sembahyang subuh*, the question about giving the recitation during the morning prayer; *membaca doa* ___, to give the special recitation.

**Kunut Nazilah** (Ar: qunūt nazilah) Pol. A form of exertion (jihad) undertaken against a foe threatening Islam through spiritual power, usually generated through prayer, often spontaneous. Indonesian organizations asked Indonesian Muslims to do this on behalf of the Palestinian cause in the last part of the twentieth century.

**Kuraisy** (In.); kureisy, quraisy, quraisj (Ar: quraysh) Hist. 1. The name of an Arab tribe that controlled Makkah and to which Muhammad belonged. 2. The enemies of the early Muslim community during Muhammad's prophethood, who resisted Islam and worked against it. 3. After the conversion of the tribe to Islam and the death of Muhammad, the elite of Islam and a term of respect. *Usage*: *bangsa* ___, *kaum* ___, the Kuraisy people; *keturun bangsa* ___ Kuraisy descent; *kafir* ___, the Kuraisy unbelievers, referring to those who opposed Muhammad during his ministry; *suku* ___, the Kuraisy people; *turunan* ___, Kuraisy descent.

**Kurban**. Spelling variant. *See* **Korban**.

**Kurban Nazar**. *See* **Korban Nazar**.

**Kuria** (Batak) Title. Title of an Islamic scholar, used in the Batak area of Sumatra.

**KurniaNya** (In.) Doct. God's mercy or blessing.

**Kusuf**. *See* **Salat**.

**Kutai**. *See* **Kesultanan**.

**Kyai**. Spelling variant. *See* **Kiai**.

**Kyai Pengulu** (Jav.) Title. Religious functionary. Leader of the religious civil service (abdhi dhalem), particularly in the late colonial period (eighteenth and nineteenth centuries) on Java.

# L

**La Beaume, Jules** (French) Biog. (d. 1878). French Arabist and Islamicist of the mid-nineteenth century who wrote works on the Qur'an in Arabic. *See Tafshil Ayatil Quranul Hakim.*

**La Hukma Illah Lillah** (Ar: lā ḥukma illā lillāh) Doct. "There is no law except God's," the motto of the Khawarij, a sect in early Islam laying stress on properly following God's commands.

**Lafal** (In.); lafadz; lafadh (Ar: lafẓ) 1. Gen. vocab. To speak, articulate, recite. 2. Qur. To recite the Qur'an from memory. 3. Trad. To recite from memory the important materials surrounding the collection of a particular Tradition. *See* **Hafiz.**
*Usage*: *me___kan*, to recite (often from memory); *me___kan niat sembahyang*, to recite the "intention" at the beginning of worship.

**Al Lahab** (Ar: al-lahab) Qur. The 111th chapter of the Qur'an, named after a person who opposed the Prophet Muhammad at Makkah. The chapter is also known as Al Masad.

**Lahir** (In.) 1. Doct. That which is apparent, as in the Qur'an or in life in general, in contrast to that which is not apparent or even secret. 2. Myst. The external world, the world of material forms where rationality prevails, as opposed to the mystical experience which is internal, secret, and not capable of perception or rational thought. Ant: batin.

**Al Lail** (Ar: al-layl) Qur. The ninety-second chapter of the Qur'an, titled "Night." A short, lyrical chapter in which God tells believers that He guides them.

**Lailatul Bara'ah** (Ar: layl al-barā'ah) Pop. Islam. The 15th night of the month of Syakban, when it is believed that the destinies of humans are set. It is observed by many Indonesians with intense prayer. *See* **Lailatul Qadar**.

**Lailatul Mikraj** (Ar: layl al-mi'rāj) Doct. The 27th of the month of Rajab when the Night Journey of Muhammad took place.

**Lailatul Qadar** (Ar: layl al-qadr) 1. Cal. The night of power, concealed in the last ten nights of the month of Ramadan. The 27th is celebrated as the descent of the Qur'an. 2. Pop. Islam. During lailatul qadar there is some confusion with lailatul bara'ah (15th of the month of Syakban) when destines are set, so the period of time is often accompanied by free prayer to ward off bad results.

**Langgar** (In.) Arch. Prayer house. Syn: mushalla.
*Usage*: *membangun* ___, establish prayer houses (as a pious act).

**Langit** (In.) Doct. Sky, firmament, heavens. Used by Muslims for the paradise of heaven in the Hereafter. *See* **Surga**.

**Lajnah Pentashih Al-Qur'an** (In.) Pol. "Office for Qur'an Standardization," a unit in the Department of Religion charged with producing a standard version of the Qur'an for Indonesia.

**Laqob** (Ar: al-laqab) Trad. The term for title or appelation, meaning that a person is usually known by another name.

**Al Lathif** (Ar: al-laṭīf) Theo. A name of God meaning "The Mysterious or Subtle One."

**Latin** (In.) Lang. Name of an ancient language of the Western world. The word is used as a descriptor for alphabet and writing for most Western languages.
*Usage*: *huruf* ___, Latin letters; *menulis Qur'an dengan huruf* ___, writing the Qur'an using Latin letters (instead of Arabic script).

**Laza**. *See* **Neraka**.

**Lebai** (In.) Pol. A functionary, usually outside of Java, who acts as a local prayer leader and analyzes religious questions that arise in the society. Syn: modin.

**Lebaran.** *See* **Idul Fithri.**

**Leknas.** *See* **Lembaga Ekonomi dan Sosial Nasional.**

**Lemah** (In.) Trad. Term used to characterize a report transmitting the words and behavior of the Prophet Muhammad as probably not accurate; weak. Syn: daif. *Usage*: *mem___kan*, to be categorized as weak; *sebab ke___annya*, points of weakness in analysis.

**Lemah Abang, Syekh.** *See* **Siti Jenar, Syekh.**

**Lembaga Ekonomi dan Sosial Nasional—Leknas** (In.) Pol. "The National Institute of Economic and Social Science." Leknas is a research unit established in the Indonesian Academy of Sciences (LIPI). Among other projects it does research on Islam in the contemporary era and publishes a variety of works on Islamic subjects.

**Lembaga Ilmu Pengetahuan Indonesia—LIPI** (In.) Pol. "The Indonesian Academy of Science." Among other topics, Muslim activity in the political, social and economic fields is a topic of research. *See* **Lembaga Ekonomi dan Sosial Nasional—Leknas.**

**Lembaga Seni Budaya Muslim Indonesia—Lesbumi** (In.) Assn. "The Indonesian Muslim Academy of Arts," an organization associated with the Nahdlatul Ulama, dealing with setting Muslim standards for theatre, literature, and manifestations of culture. Founded in the 1950s, but particularly active in the 1960s in countering communist attacks on religion.

**Lembaga Studi Agama dan Filsafat** (In.) Assn. "The Institute for the Study of Religion and Philosophy," a discussion group begun by Dawam Rahardjo (b. 1942) in 1983.

**Lembaga Swadaya Masyarakat—LSM** (In.) Assn. "The Institute for Society's Self Motivation," a non-government organization (NGO) of the 1980s with units active in health, home industries, birth control, and environment operating under an Islamic rubric.

**Lembut, Yang Maha** (In.) Theo. A name of God meaning "The Most Gentle."

**Lesbumi.** *See* **Lembaga Seni Budaya Muslim Indonesia.**

*Het Licht* (Dutch) Lit. title. "The Light," the name of a magazine, issued irregularly from 1925 to 1941 by the Jong Islamieten Bond, giving its intellectual views on Islam, and reflecting its members' Western educations. Also known as *An-Nur.*

**Liga Muslimin Indonesia** (In.) Assn. "The Indonesian Muslim League," a federation of the Nahdlatul Ulama, Perti, and the Partai Sarekat Islam Indonesia, formed in April 1952 for cooperation in political affairs. It lasted until the 1970s when the parties were absorbed into consolidating alliances of the New Order period.

*Lima dha ta'ahhara al-muslimun.* *See* **Arsylan, Amer Syakib.**

**LIPI.** *See* **Lembaga Ilmu Pengetahuan Indonesia.**

*Al Lisan* (Ar: al-lisān) Lit. title. "The Tongue," the name of a magazine, published by the Persatoean Islam in the 1920s in Bandung, offering interpretations of Islamic teachings from a fundamentalist and modernist Muslim perspective.

**Lohor** (In.) (Ar: ẓuhr) Juris. The obligatory prayer at mid-day. *See* **Zuhur.**

**LSM.** *See* **Lembaga Swadaya Masyarakat.**

*Lubabut Takwil* (Ar: lubāb at-ta'wīl fī ma'ānī at-tanzīl) Lit. title. "Quintessence of the Interpretation," a commentary on the Qur'an by Al Khazin (d. 1373), which is in use by Indonesian Muslim scholars in the twentieth century. *See* **Tafsir.**

**Lubang Buaya** (In.) Geog. The "Crocodile Hole," a site near Jakarta at Halim Air Base. In 1966 communist youth groups kidnaped six army generals and massacred them at Lubang Buaya. The term is used symbolically by Muslim writers to indicate the gross misconduct conducted in the political system of that time.

**Lughat.** *See* **Ilmu Lughat.**

*Al Lulu' Wal Marjan. See Miftah Kunuzis Sunnah.*

**Luqman** (Ar: luqmān) Qur. The thirty-first chapter of the Qur'an, named for the sage named Luqman. The chapter relates the advice of Luqman to his son about worship, good thinking and proper comportment.

**Lurah** (In.) Pol. 1. Historically, the functionary in charge of a village (desa) on Java. Syn: bekal. 2. Official in contemporary Indonesia in charge of a district equivalent to that of an American township.

**Luth** (Ar: lūṭ) Qur. A prophet mentioned in the Qur'an, related by scholars to the Old Testament Lot. He is known as the prophet to the "overwhelmed cities," a probable reference to Sodom and Gomorrah.

# M

**Ma'af** (In.) Gen. vocab. Excuse, pardon.
*Usage*: *di__kan*, to be forgiven.

*Ma'alimul Tanzil* (Ar: ma'ālim at-tanzil) Lit. title. "The Master Interpretation," a commentary on the Qur'an by Al-Baghawi (d. 1117), which draws heavily on the traditions of the Prophet Muhammad for its explanations. It has been widely used in Southeast Asia during the twentieth century. *See* **Tafsir.**

**Ma'ani.** *See* **Ilmu Ma'ani.**

**Al Ma'aarij**; Al Ma'arij; Al Ma'arij (Ar: al-ma'ārij) Qur. "The Steps," the seventieth chapter of the Qur'an. A medium-length, lyrical chapter contrasting the fate in the Hereafter of the righteous and the damned.

**Mabadi Khairi Ummah** (Ar: mabādi' khayr ummah) Juris. The welfare of the Muslim community of believers.

**Mabuk** (In.) Juris. Action regarded as neutral in behavior which is neither good nor bad, with neither reward nor punishment attached to it.
*Usage*: *me__kan*, to perform a neutral action.

**Machluk.** *See* **Makhluk.**

*Madarikut Tanzil* (Ar: madārik at-tanzīl) Lit. title. "The True Explanation," a commentary on the Qur'an by Abu Abdallah An Nasafi (d. 1245). Also known as *Tafsir Nasafi*. It has enjoyed wide usage in Southeast Asia for several centuries. *See* **Tafsir.**

**Madilog** (In.) Pol. Social and Islamic programs of Tan Malaka, a leftist of the nationalist and revolutionary periods.

**Madinah** (In.); Medinah (Ar: madīnah) Geog. Formerly Yasrib; the second city of Islam and the site where Muhammad developed the original Islamic community after his flight from Makkah. Muhammad's tomb is located there. In Islamic history it has been important as an intellectual center for Islamic sciences.
*Usage*: *masa* ___, the period of history in which Muhammad lived there; ___ *Al Munawwarah*, Madinah the Radiant.

**Madjelis**. Old spelling of Majelis. In addition to entries below, *See* under **Majelis**.

**Madjelis Islam A'la Indonesia—MIAI** (In.) Assn. "The Indonesian High Islamic Council," a federation of Islamic groups brought together in 1937 to unite political efforts of Indonesian Muslims. Headed by K. Mas Mansur and K. H. Dachlan. It lasted until 1943 when Japanese authorities converted it into Masjoemi.

**Madjelis Sjuro Muslimin Indonesia—Masjoemi** (In.) Assn. "The Consultative Congress of Indonesian Muslims," a union of Indonesian associations formed in 1943 by Japanese authorities in order to coordinate Muslim efforts in supporting the Japanese war effort. Transformed into Masjumi after the declaration of Indonesian independence in 1945.

**Madjelis Sjuro Muslimin Indonesia—Masjumi** (In.) Pol. "The Consultative Council of Indonesian Muslims," a major political party of an Indonesian Muslim group in the 1940s and 1950s. At first an umbrella organization of Muslim organizations, many of its leaders became spokesmen of Outer Island interests. It was disbanded by President Sukarno (d. 1968) in 1961. Its leaders were Sukiman Wirjosandjojo 1945-52 (separate entry), Muhammad Natsir 1952-59 (separate entry), Prawoto Mangkusasmito 1959-60.

**Madjied, Nurcholis** (In.) Biog. (b. 1939). Muslim writer who led the Himpunan Mahariswa Islam (1966-71) and made it a "think-tank" for Muslim reconciliation with the government's policy of development. His ideas on Islamic modernization remain controversial in some quarters.

**Madrasah** (In.) (Ar: madrasah) Educ. Schools for general Muslim education. At the present time in Indonesia these schools, operated by private organizations and foundations, receive government subsidies and constitute an alternate national education system for those students seeking an Islamic-based education. *Usage*: *lulusan* ___, madrasah graduate; *membuat* ___, to establish a school (as a pious act); *mewakafkan* ___, to donate land or funds for a school; *pelajar* ___, madrasah student.

**Madrasah Aliyah Negeri—MAN** (In.) (Ar: madrasah 'aliyyah) Educ. "The National Senior-level Islamic Academy," the official name given the third level of the madrasah system operated by the Department of Religion, consisting of grades ten through twelve.

**Madrasah Ibtidaiyah Negeri—MIN** (In.) (Ar: madrasah ibtidā'iyyah) Educ. "The National Beginners-level Islamic Academy," the official name given the first level of the madrasah system operated by the Department of Religion, consisting of grades one through six.

**Madrasah Thawalib** (In.) (fr. Ar: madrasah and ṭālib) Educ. The modernized Islamic school system established by the modernists (kaum muda), primarily the Muhammadiyah, in West Sumatra in the early part of the twentieth century.

**Madrasah Tsanawiyah Negeri—MTsN** (In.) (madrasah thānawiyyah) Educ. "The National Intermediate-level Islamic Academy," the official name of the second level of the madrasah system operated by the Department of Religion, consisting of grades seven through nine.

**Madzhab**. Spelling variant. *See* **Mazhab**.

**Mafakir, Abul**. *See* **Bantam**.

*Mafatihul Ghaibi* (Ar: mafātīḥ al-ghayb) Lit. title. "Revelation of the Secret," a commentary on the Qur'an by Ar Razi (d. 1209). Also known as *Tafsirul Kabir* (The Great Commentary). Highly respected commentary on the

Qur'an in general use among Southeast Asian Muslims. *See* **Tafsir**.

**Magrib** (In.); maghreb (Ar: maghrib) Juris. The daily required prayer performed in the early evening, near sunset.
*Usage*: *salat* ___, the early evening prayer.

**Magribi, Maulana**. *See* **Malik Ibrahim, (Maulana)**.

**Maha** (In. fr. Kawi) Indonesian prefix, meaning "greatest." *See* following word.

**Mahabbah** (In.) (Ar: maḥabbah) Myst. Devotee's love toward God and feeling of closeness to God. A feature of later mysticism replacing fear of God put forward by early Muslim ascetics.

**Al Mahalli, Jalaluddin** (Ar: jalāl ad-dīn muḥammad ... al-maḥallī) Biog. (d. 1389). An important Syafii legal scholar of the Middle East whose works were finished or incorporated by later scholars. His commentary on the Qur'an, finished by As Suyuthi (d. 1505), remains very popular after several centuries of use in Southeast Asia. *See Tafsirul Jalalain* and **Tafsir**.

**Maharaja** (In.) Title. Title for ruler, originating in India, used by some rulers in Southeast Asia, including those who were Muslim. *See* following name.

*Mahasinut Takwil* (Ar: maḥāsin at-ta'wīl) Lit. title. "Explanation of the Most Elegent," a commentary on the Qur'an by Al Qasimi (d. 1914). This work is part of the current bibliography of Arabic writings cited by contemporary Indonesian Muslim intellectuals. Also known as *Tafsirul Qasimi*. *See* **Tafsir**.

**Mahdi** (In.) (Ar: mahdī) Doct. In eschatology, a guide or leader. A messianic figure who will appear at the end of the world and usher in a new order.

**Mahfudz**. *See* **Ilmu Mushthalah Hadis**.

**Mahkum Alain** (Ar: maḥkūm 'alayna) Trad. A term used by authors presenting Traditions to indicate that a particular Tradition has been given a "firm" rating by the two great scholars of the field, Muslim and Bukhari and, hence, can be accepted without dispute as genuine.

**Mahmuz** (Ar: maḥmud) Gen. vocab. To be praised.

**Al Maa-idah**; Al Ma'idah; Al Maidah (Ar: mā'idah) Qur. "The Banquet," the fifth chapter of the Qur'an, which tells the story of the followers of Isa (Jesus) asking for a banquet of food to be sent to them from heaven. The chapter deals with Muslim relations with monotheists.

**Al Maisir** (Ar: maysir) Juris. A game of chance played with arrows specifically forbidden by the Qur'an.

**Maja Kjahi** (Jav.) Biog. Javanese Muslim teacher who was a close associate and confederate of Prince Diponegoro (d. 1855) in the Java War (1825 to 1830). Ultimately he broke ranks with Diponegoro and tried to arrange a peace with the Dutch.

**Majapahit** (In.) 1. Hist. A major kingdom of Java with influence on neighboring islands (1294 to 1527), and a major political entity of the classical Hindu-Buddhist era. It disintegrated when raiders from the Muslim ports captured its capital in 1527, ushering in a period of Islamic political control. It is seen as a predecesser state to the Indonesian Republic by Indonesian nationalist historians. 2. Pol. Modern Indonesian intellectuals regard Majapahit as a model for a highly centralized, self-sufficient agriculturally based state, in contrast to the Srivijaya model which is based on state trade with foreign nations.
*Usage*: *zaman* ___, the period of Majapahit rule.

**Majelis Dakwah Islamiyah—MDI** (In.) Assn. "The Islamic Propagation Council," a youth organization affiliated with the Golkar political organization, founded in 1978 to "defend Pancasila, promote the concept of God the Only one and promote social justice" through both physical and mental effort.

**Majelis Syuriyah** (In.) Assn. "The Consultative Council," a unit of the Nahdlatul Ulama, which deals with issues brought before the body concerning the application of Muslim law to current moral, ethical and religious concern. It issues decisions (fatwas) consistent with Syafii interpretation on those matters.

**Majelis Tarjih** (In.) Assn. "Council of Consideration," a unit of the Muhammadiyah composed of religious scholars that issues decisions (fatwas) on matters referred to it by the association and its members, usually dealing with moral, ethical and religious concerns. The council bases decisions on Qur'an and Traditions, with the insight of the important scholars of Islam.

**Majelis Ulama** (In.) Pol. "Religious Scholars' Council," a general name given to assemblies of religious specialists who meet to discuss matters of religious importance. The state sponsored *Majelis Ulama Indonesia* is one example. Most Muslim organizations also have such groups.

**Majelis Ulama Indonesia—MUI** (In.) Pol. "The Religious Scholars Council of Indonesia," a quasi-official body of religious scholars appointed by the national government to review issues of moral, ethical, and religious concern affecting the nation. The council issues decisions as general recommendation to the government and as guidance to believers. There are similar organizations in each province called Majelis Ulama Propinsi.

**Majelis Ulama Propinsi**. *See* **Majelis Ulama Indonesia.**

**Al Majhul**. *See* **Ilmu Mushthalah Hadis**.

**Al Majiid**; Al Majied; Al Majid (Ar: al-majīd) Theo. A name of God meaning "The Glorious." Syn: Yang Maha Megah.

**Majidal Haram**. *See* **Baitullah.**

**Makam** (In.); maqam; maqaam (In. from Ar: maqām) Pop. Islam. Grave, especially the holy grave of a person regarded as a saint. *Usage*: *di__kan*, to bury; ___ *Rasulullah*, the grave of the Prophet Muhammad; *ziarah ke ___ nabi*, visit the grave of the Prophet Muhammad.

**Makam Puteri Cempa** (In.) Hist. Gravestone of the Champa princess married to the Majapahit king in the late fourteenth century who practiced Islam at court prior to Java's conversion to Islam.

**Makasar**. *See* **Kesultanan**.

**Makdum** (In.); makhdum (Ar: makhdūm) Title. "The late, revered," a title assigned a pious Muslim who has already passed away. *See* following word.

**Makhluk** (In.); makhluq; Machluk (Ar: makhlūq) Doct. Creature, a term used in the Qur'an for angels, humans, animals, plants, jinn, and demons.
*Usage*: ___ *hidup*, living creatures; ___ *rohani*, angels.

**Makkah**; Mekkah (Ar: makkah) Geog. The first city of Islam, in Saudi Arabia, where Muhammad was born and began his ministry. It is the site of the Kabah, the shrine where the rites of pilgrimage are held each year.
*Usage*: ___ *Al Mukarramah*, Makkah the Blessed; *masa* ___, the period in history when Muhammad lived there; *serambi* ___, a popular appellation applied to Aceh, as the traditional Southeast Asian staging area for travel to Makkah, meaning "the veranda of Makkah"; *syarif* ___, ruler of Makkah, several of which issued investiture documents for Southeast Asian rulers assuming the title of sultan in the fifteenth century.

**Makmum** (In.) (Ar: ma'mūm) Juris. A follower, one who is led, as in prayer.

**Al Makmun** (Ar: abū al-abbās 'abdullāh al-ma'mūn). Biog. (d. 833). Arab ruler of the Abbasid dynasty (813-33) when the theological views of the Free Thinkers (Muktazalite) became the court-sanctioned version of Islam and leaders from other schools of thought were brought before an inquisition and punished for deviating beliefs. The trend was reversed under a later ruler.

**Makrifat** (In.); marifat, ma'rifat (Ar: ma'rifah) Myst. Intuitive knowledge, a level of understanding considered by mystics to be superior to that of acquired knowledge. Intuitive knowledge is concerned about the relationship of the worshiper to God.

*Usage*: *ber___*, to undertake mystical exercises that lead to intuitive knowledge.

**Makruh** (In.) (Ar: makrūh) Juris. Abhorrent. An action or behavior which should not be undertaken, but for which there is no sin if performed.
*Usage*: *bidah yang* ___, innovation which is undesirable, but not necessarily prohibited.

**Maksiat** (In.) (Ar: ma'ṣiyah) Doct. Badness and rebelliousness toward God.
*Usage*: *ahli* ___, people who break God's commands and undertake actions considered sinful.

**Malaikat** (In.) (Ar: malā'ikah) Doct. A special creature of God for carrying out His commands and praising Him; an angel.
*Usage*: ___ *Israfil*, ___ *Izrail*, ___ *Jibrail*, ___ *Mikhail*, the four archangels; ___ *Munkar [dan] Nakir*, the angels of punishment in the grave; *para* ___, angels.

**Malek**; Maalik; Malik (Ar: mālik) 1. Doct. The angel who is the guard of hell. 2. Title. A royal title from the Middle East, equivalent to king, taken by some early Southeast Asian Muslim rulers, such as those at Pasai.
*Usage*: *malaikat* ___, the angel Malek.

**Al Malibari, Zainuddin** (Ar: zayn ad-dīn al-malībarī) Biog. (d. ca. 1522). Indian scholar of jurisprudence associated with the Shafii school. *See* **Kitab Fathul Mu'in**.

**Al Maalik** (Ar: al-mālik) Theo. A name of God meaning "The King."

**Malik Ibn Anas** (Ar: mālik ibn anas) Biog. (d. 795). Personal name of an early Arab compiler of Traditions (hadis) collection, the *Muwaththa*, the sayings and actions of the Prophet Muhammad. He was also the founder of the Maliki school of Muslim jurisprudence.

**Malik Ibrahim, (Maulana)** (In.) Biog. (d. 1419). One of nine missionaries popularly believed to have led the conversion of Java to Islam in the fifteenth century. He is known to have lived in the Gresik area of Java. Also known as (Maulana) Magribi and Jumadil Kubra. *See* **Wali Songo**.

**Maliki** (Ar: mālikiyyah) Juris. A school of jurisprudence founded by Malik bin Anas (d. 795), which is based heavily on the words and behavior of the Prophet Muhammad. Its influence is most pronounced in North Africa, Egypt, and the Sudan.

**Al Malikil Mulki** (Ar: mālik al-mulk) Theo. A name of God meaning "Possessor of the Kingdom."

**Malim**. Minangkabau variant. *See* **Ulama**.

**Maluku** (In.) Geog. Place name for an island group in eastern Indonesia. During the fifteenth and sixteenth century, Muslim principalities there were confronted by Portuguese, Spanish, and Dutch traders seeking monopoly control over the clove, nutmeg, and mace spices and other goods from the area. A rich interaction occurred, especially at Ternate and Tidore, with the Dutch the ultimate victors.

**Ma'lul**. *See* **Ilmu Mushthalah Hadis**.

**MAN**. *See* **Madrasah Aliyah Negeri**.

**Manakib** (In.); manaqib (Ar: manāqib) Pop. Islam. Literature of the saints, their lives, records and stories about them.
*Usage*: *pembacaan* ___, literature of the saints.

*Al-Manar* (Ar: al-manār) Lit. title. "The Light," the name of a journal published from 1897 to 1935 in the Middle East, issued by Muhammad Abduh (d. 1905) and Rashid Rida (d. 1935). It espoused a reformist view of Islam, calling for the development of Islamic doctrines suitable to modern science and technology. *See Tafsir Al Manar* and **Tafsir**.

**Manawi**. *See* **Mukjizat**.

**Mandarsyah**. *See* **Ternate**.

**Mandi** (In.) Juris. to bathe, to wash.
*Usage*: ___ *janabat*, to ritually bathe the corpse.

**Mangkurat**; Amangkurat (Jav.) Biog. The name of a series of Javanese rulers with the title susuhanan of the Mataram kingdom and its successor, the Kartasura sultanate. The periods of the reigns were I: 1646-77, II:

1677-1703, III: 1703-08, and IV: 1719-23.

**Mangkusasmito.** *See* **Prawoto Mangkusasmito.**

**Al Mani'i** (Ar: al-māni') Theo. Name of God meaning "The Withholder."

**Mansukh.** *See* **Ilmu Mushthalah Hadis.**

**Mansur, A. R. Sutan.** *See* **Muhammadiyah.**

**Mansur, Mas** (In.) Biog. (b. 1896). Muhammadiyah leader from East Java active during preindependence and the Japanese period in promoting Indonesian Muslim unity. *See* **Muhammadiyah.**

**Mansyur, Sultan Muhammad.** *See* **Palembang.**

**Mansyur Syah, Sultan Alauddin.** *See* **Aceh.**

**Mantiq.** *See* **Ilmu Mantiq.**

**Mantja Negara** (Jav.) Geog. In the early years of the sixteenth century, the name for the Moslem Mataram empire and conquered territories outside the central lands of the kingdom.

**Manusia** (In.) Doct. Humans as a collective.
*Usage*: *ruh* ___, human spirit or the essence of human life in the moral and spiritual sense.

**Maqam**; maqaam. Spelling variant. *See* **Makam.**

**Maqamin Amin** (Ar: maqāmin amīn) Doct. Paradise. Syn: Surga.

**Maqbil** (Ar: maqbūl) Trad. Accurate and reliable; a term used in assessment of transmitters of reports concerning the words and behavior of the Prophet Muhammad.

**Maqlub.** *See* **Ilmu Mushthalah Hadis.**

**Maqthuu'.** *See* **Ilmu Mushthalah Hadis.**

**Al Maraghi** (Ar: aḥmad muṣṭafā al-marāghī) Biog. (d. 1945) Egyptian religious scholar and activist who was chief kadi of the Sudan and Rector of Al-Azhar University. Noted for his *Tafsir Al Maraghi*, which has been popular among some Indonesian intellectuals in the third quarter of the twentieth century.

*Marah Labid* (Ar: marāḥ labid) Lit. title. "Compact Bliss," a compilation of jurisprudential writings in Arabic about the Qur'an and its interpetation by Al Nawawi Al Bantami (d. 1888) drawing on Arabic and Turkish scholars of the late middle period.

**Marco Polo** (Italian) Biog. (d. 1324). Italian traveler who visited Perlak in North Sumatra in 1292 and provided a written sketch of a Muslim maritime kingdom headed by Sultan Abdul Jahl (d. 1300).

**Marfu.** *See* **Ilmu Mushthalah Hadis.**

**Marhaban** (In.) Pop. Islam. A poem in praise of the Prophet Muhammad usually sung or chanted at the celebration of the birthday of the Prophet.

**Marifat**; ma'rifat. Spelling variants. *See* **Makrifat.**

**Martabat** (In.) (Ar: martabah) Myst. Grade or level of human development. In most mystical systems in Southeast Asia seven distinct levels are featured.

**Ma'ruf.** *See* **Ilmu Mushthalah Hadis.**

**Maryam** (Ar: maryam) Qur. "Mary," the nineteenth chapter of the Qur'an named for the mother of the Prophet Isa (Jesus). It tells the story of the virgin birth of Isa. *Usage*: *Sitti* ___, The honored Maryam.

**Mas Mansur.** *See* **Mansur, Mas.**

**Al Masad** (Ar: al-masad) Qur. "Palm Fiber," an alternate title for the 111th chapter of the Qur'an. It is usually titled Al Lahab.

**Al Masehi** (In.); Al-Masih (Ar: al-masīh) 1. Qur. The messiah, identified with 'Isa b. Maryam' (Jesus). 2. Cal. After a date the term indicates the Christian calendar.

**Mashaf Utsman** (In.); mash-haf ...; mushhaf ...; mushaf ... (Ar: maṣḥaf al-'uthmān) Qur. The assemblage of the Qur'an into a single written document, completed at the time Utsman (644-656) was caliph. That version is regarded as the only authoritative version by Sunni Muslims. *Qur'an Al Karim*, a copy certified by the Egyptian government a half century ago, is the version of the mashaf utsman ordinarily used by Indonesian Muslims.

**Al Masih**. *See* **'Isa.**

**Masih Munat**. *See* **Darajat, Sunan**.

**Masjid**. Preferred spelling. In addition to entries immediately below, see also **Mesjid**.

**Masjid**; mesjid (In.) (Ar: masjid) Arch. The Islamic house of worship and local center of religious activity. Formally, it is the site of the communal prayer each Friday at mid-day, but it is used for prayer throughout the day on all days of the week. This contrasts with a prayer house (mushalla) which is intended for prayer by individuals and small groups with little formality. ___ **Agung Al Azhar**, a major mosque in Kebayoran, a prosperous suburb of Jakarta, founded by Dr. Hamka (d. 1981). Now known for its educational emphasis and its promotion of Muslim middle class views of Islam. ___ **Al Aksa**; Al Aqsha, a famous mosque in Jerusalem marking the spot where Muhammad ascended to heaven during the Night Journey. ___ **Agung**, an eighteenth century mosque at Yogyakarta which is still the center of religious celebrations in the region. ___ **Demak**, the mosque in Demak dating to the thirteenth century, used by the rulers of the first Islamic state in Java as the site of their government. ___ **Haram**, the Great Mosque in Makkah which contains the Kabah. ___ **Istiqlal**, a major mosque in Jakarta, often used for Indonesian national celebrations of Islamic holy days; ___ **Menara Kudus**, the founding mosque by Sunan Kudus for the movement that led to Islamic political control of Java. It has the doors from the palace of the defeated Majapahit ruler. ___ **Nabawi**, the mosque at Madinah originally built by the Prophet Muhammad and the early community of Islam. ___ **Salman**, a mosque on the campus of the Bandung Institute of Technology noted for its activities with students in promoting religious revival in the second half of the twentieth century. It is the site of frequent addresses by speakers using religious

themes and it has also a publishing outlet.
*Usage*: *fondasi* ___, mosque endowment foundation; *membangun* ___, *membuat* ___, *mendirikan* ___-___, to establish places of worship as evidence of Islamic identification; *mewakafkan* ___, to give money or land for the establishment and operation of a mosque.

**Masjkur, K. H.** *See* **Nahdlatul Ulama.**

**Masjoemi.** *See* **Madjelis Sjuro Muslimin Indonesia.**

**Masjumi.** *See* **Madjelis Sjuro Muslimin Indonesia.**

**Al Maslahatul Mursalat** (Ar: maṣlaḥat al-mursālat) Juris. A principle that examines positive and negative aspects of a matter at issue to determine its inclusion as a basis of law.

*Masnawi. See.* **Al Rumi, Muhammad Jalaluddin.**

**Masruq.** *See* **Ilmu Mushthalah Hadis.**

**Al Masudi** (Ar: abū al-ḥasan ʿalī al-maʿsūdī) Biog. (d. 956). Arab historian, ethnologist and encyclopedist, often cited by Indonesian Muslim writers of the late twentieth century.

**Ma'sum, K. H. Ali.** *See* **Nahdlatul Ulama.**

**Masyarakat** (In.) Anthro. Society.
*Usage*: ___ *Muslim*, Islamic society, meaning that the people in society undertake worship and live by the standards of Islam.

**Masyhur.** *See* **Kiraat.**

**Masykur, K. H.** *See* **Menteri Agama.**

**Matan Hadis** (Ar: matan hadīth) Trad. The substance of the report transmitting the words and behavior of the Prophet Muhammad, in differentiation to the chain of transmitters that precedes the report itself.

**Mataram** (In.) Hist. An important Indonesian Muslim kingdom on Java (ca. 1575 to 1755) which controlled much of the island at the time of the arrival of the Europeans and ultimately found itself forced to give political and economic concessions to the Dutch East India Company. Not to be confused with the

Buddhist kingdom of Mataram. *See* **Agung, Mangkurat, Pakubuwono,** and **Senopati.**

**Materialisme** (In.) Anthro. An outlook or approach to life that advocates acquisition of material goods and a high use of services as a means to promote common prosperity. Materialisme is a fundamental tenet of most modern approaches to economic and social life.
*Usage*: *orang materialis*, a person justifying the concept of materialisme in modern society.

**Al Matiin**; Al Matien (Ar: al-matīn) Theo. A name of God meaning "The Firm." Syn: Yang Maha Kuat.

**Matlaul Anwar** (In.) Assn. A modernist Muslim association of West Java founded in 1916 by Mohammad Yasin (d. unk.). Associated with Masjumi at its establishment in 1945 as a special member. By the 1980s it had established chapters nation-wide.

**Matruk**. *See* **Ilmu Mushthalah Hadis**.

**Maturidi, Abu Mansyur** (Ar: abū manṣūr al-māturīdī) Biog. (d. 944). Major Sunni Muslim theologian, who, with Al Asy'ari (d. 935), determined Sunni standards following the Free Thinker (Muktazalite) dispute in the tenth century.

**Maturidiyah** (Ar: māturīdiyyah) Doct. The philosophical followers of Maturidi (d. 944) who further developed his viewpoint and popularized his teachings.
*Usage*: *ajaran* ___, the teachings of the sect.

**Maudlu**. *See* **Hadis**.

**Maududi, Abul A'la** (Urdu) Biog. (d. 1974). South Asian scholar who developed many of the tenets of the neofundamentalist Islam, which have been so prominent in the second half of the twentieth century. He emphasized the importance of the Islamic state and sacred law. His books were popular reading among Indonesian Muslims in the late twentieth century.

**Al Maula** (Ar: al-mawlā) Theo. A name of God meaning "The Protection."

**Maulana**; mawlana. Title. A title for a Muslim religious scholar or for a Muslim ruler. *See* following name.

**Maulid** (In.); maulud (Ar: mawlid) Cal. The birthday commemoration of the Prophet Muhammad on the 12th day of the month of Rabiulawwal.
*Usage*: *amal* ___, activities marking the celebration; *doa* ___, ___ *barzanji*, the prayers marking the celebration of the birthday of the Prophet; *membaca* ___, to recite the prayers marking the celebration of the birthday of the Prophet; *merayakan* ___, to celebrate the birthday of the Prophet.

**Mauquf**. *See* **Ilmu Mushthalah Hadis.**

**Maushuul**. *See* **Ilmu Mushthalah Hadis.**

**Al Maa'uun** (Ar: al-mā'ūn) Qur. "Small Kindnesses," the 107th chapter of the Qur'an. A very short, lyrical chapter admonishing Muslims to be kind to the less fortunate.

**Ma'wa**. *See* **Surga.**

*Mawahibul Laduniyah* (Ar: al-mawāhib al-ladunniyyah) Lit. title. "The Sublime Gift (of God)," by Al Qasthallani (d. 1517). A famous biography of the Prophet Muhammad, much quoted by other scholars.

*Mawlid An Nabi. See* **Al Barzanji (Syeleh) Jaafar.**

**Mawlana.** Spelling variant. *See* **Maulana.**

**Mayat** (In.) Juris. Corpse, deceased.
*Usage*: *menjembahyangkan seorang* ___, perform the funeral worship for the deceased; *menyatakan talkin* ___, recite the "prompting" (of Islamic teachings) to prepare the deceased for the visits of the angels Nakir and Munkar.

**Mazhab** (In.); madzhab (Ar: madhhab) Juris. One of four major schools of jurisprudence prominent in Islam, which lay out proper action for religious ritual and other matters considered important by Muslims. Six prominent schools were founded about the tenth century and four remain important today—Syafii, Maliki, Hanafi, and Hanbali. The schools have been dominant in the following areas: Turkey, the

Balkans, the Eastern Mediterranean lands, India, Central Asia, and China (Hanafi); Arabia and Qatar (Hanbali); the Arab West and West Africa (Maliki); Egypt, the Indian Ocean area, and Southeast Asia (Syafii).
*Usage*: *anti-*___, to be an opponent of Muslim jurisprudence schools (i.e., to reject the schools for modernist Islam); *ber*___ *Hanafi*, to use the principles of the Hanafi school of jurisprudence as a guide for personal action.
___ *Empat*, the four standard schools of Muslim jurisprudence; *kitab-kitab fikih* ___, the well-known writings of the scholars of the four standard schools of Muslim jurisprudence; lingkungan ___ *Syafii*, the circle of influence of the Syafii school; *menganut* ___ *Syafii*, to be a follower of the Syafii school; ___ *Syiah*, the Syiah sect of Islam; *para imam* ___, the scholars of the various schools of Muslim jurisprudence; *pengikut* ___, an adherent of a Muslim jurisprudence school.

**MDI.** *See* **Majelis Dakwah Islamiyah.**

*Medan Moeslimin* (In.) Lit. title. "Among the Muslims," the name of a newspaper in the years 1921-25, published by Haji Misbach of Surakarta, which favored the left-wing of the Muslim movement and its communist allies.

**Medinah.** Spelling variant. *See* **Madinah.**

**Meer Uitgebreid Lager Onderwijs—MULO** (Dutch) Educ. "Expanded System of Lower Instruction," the name of a school system established by the Dutch in 1903. It consisted of grades seven through nine. MULO schools gave instruction in Dutch, English, German, history, science, mathematics, and drawing. Graduates were eligible to attend a higher course in mathematics or literature. Private groups could found MULO schools and were eligible for subsidy from the colonial administration so long as they maintained minimum standards.

**Megah, Yang Maha** (In.) Name of God meaning "The Most Glorious." Syn: Al Majiid.

**Mekkah**. Spelling variant. *See* **Makkah**.

**Melayu** (In.) Lang. A major language of Southeast Asia, which originated as a trade language in the coastal and riverine areas of Indonesia and in Malaysia. It became the basis of modern Malay, used in Malaysia, Singapore, Southern Thailand, and Brunei. It also is the basis of Bahasa Indonesia used throughout the archipelago. Earlier Melayu was written in Arab script (jawi), but now it is almost entirely used in modified Latin characters.
*Usage*: *ditulis huruf Arab Bahasa* ___, Malay written in Arabic script.

**Mencipta, Yang** (In.) Theo. A name of God meaning "The Creator." Syn: Al Khaaliq; Al Baari'.

**Mendengar, Yang Maha** (In.) Theo. A name of God meaning "The Great hearer." Syn: As Samii.

**Mengetahui, Yang Maha** (In.) Theo. A name of God meaning "All-Knowing."

**Menghisab, Yang Maha** (In.) Theo. A name of God meaning "The Great Reckoner." Syn: Al Hasiib.

**Menstruasi** (In.) Juris. Menstruation; considered to be a ritually impure period for women.
*Usage*: *saat* ___, the period of menstruation.

**Menteri Agama** (In.) Pol. The minister of religion in Indonesia who heads the Department of Religion (Departemen Agama). The appointment is political and reflects the position of the national government leadership which makes the appointment. The ministers of the Department were H. M. Rasyidi (1946), Fathur Rahman (1946-47), H. Anwaruddin (1947), K. H. Masykur (1947-48), Teuku Mohammed Hasan (1948-49), K. H. A. Wahid Hasyim (1949-52) (separate entry), K. H. Faqih Usman (1952-53) (separate entry), K. H. Mohammad Ilyas (1955-56, 1957-59), K. H. Wahid Wahab (1959-62), K. H. Saifuddin Zuhri (1962-67) (separate entry), K. H. Mohammad Dachlan (1967-71), H. A. Mukti Ali (1971-78) (separate entry), H. Alamsyah Ratu Perwiranegara (1978-82), and

H. Munawir Sjadzali (1982-92).

**Menyayangi, Yang** (In.) Theo. A name of God meaning "The Most Gentle." Syn: Al Rauuf.

**Merauke** (In.) *See* **Sabang ke Merauke**.

**Mertawidjaya, Sultan**. *See* **Cirebon**.

**Mesir** (In. from Ar: misr) Geog. Egypt.

**Mesjid**. Alternate spelling. In addition to entries below, *see* **Masjid**.

**Mesjid Desa** (Jav.) Hist. A decree of Sultan Agung in the early seventeenth century established a central mosque in every village of the Mataram kingdom. It was headed by a modim with four assistants.

**Mesjid Gede** (Jav.) Hist. A decree of Sultan Agung in the early seventeenth century established a major mosque in every province in the Mataram kingdom on Java, headed by a pengulu with forty assistants.

**Mesjid Kawedaan** (Jav.) Hist. A decree of Sultan Agung in the early seventeenth century established a central mosque in every district of the Mataram kingdom on Java. It was headed by a naib with eleven assistants.

**Messianisme** (In.) Anthro. Belief of people in the arrival of a noted person who will usher in a period of justice and prosperity. In Islam this is associated with the Imam Mahdi and in Indonesian folklore it is the Ratu Adil. Syn: millenarisme.

**Meujalaee** (Aceh.) Qur. The act of reading the Qur'an from beginning to end, often with a group of people taking turns. Performed often in the mosque during Ramadan as a act of piety.

**MIAI**. *See* **Madjelis Islam A'la Indonesia**.

*Miftah Kunuzis Sunnah* (Ar: muftāh kunūz as-sunnah) Lit. title. "The Key for Opening the Treasure of Traditions," a major reference work on Traditions of the Prophet by A. W. Winsinck (d. 1939), published Paris, 1934 in Arabic. A later abbreviated rendition, also in Arabic, was undertaken by M.F. Abdul Baqi (d. unk) with the title *Lu'lu' wal Marjaan*, which has been translated into Indonesian by several publishers.

**Mihrab** (In.) (Ar: mihrāb) Juris. A small recess in the front of a mosque, indicating the direction that worshipers face in performing prayer.

**Mikhail** (Ar: mikā'īl) Qur. In the Islamic pantheon, one of four archangels.

**Mikraj** (In.); mi'raj (Ar: mir'āj) Doct. The ascent of Muhammad to heaven during the Night Journey to meet the other prophets and approach God. A historical debate continues on whether the ascent was physical, psychological, or spiritual, with the physical ascent being the doctrinal position in Sunni Islam. *See* **Isra**. *Usage*: ___ *dengan ruh dan tubuh*, ascent with both body and spirit; *merayakan* ___ *Nabi*, to celebrate the occasion of the Ascent.

**Millenarisme** (In.) Anthro. Belief in the establishment of a just and prosperous society through divine will, usually connected with the arrival of a noted personage. Syn: messianisme.

**Mimbar** (In.) (Ar: minbar) Juris. The pulpit in the mosque from which the Friday sermon (khutbah) is given. The term is used symbolically, similar to the word "pulpit" in English.

**MIN**. *See* **Madrasah Ibtidaiyah Negeri**.

**Minangkabau** (In.) Geog. People of Western Sumatra around the city of Padang. Society is based on matrilineal inheritance patterns, some degree of matriarchy and a rich tradition of local custom. It has been a major site for the entry of Islamic trends from the Middle East to Southeast Asia. It has also provided a number of national leaders and intellectuals of the Islamic and nationalist movements.

**Minangkabau, Ahmad Khatib**. *See* **Khatib Minangkabau, Ahmad**.

*Minhajul Abidin* (Ar: minhāj al-'ābidīn) Lit. title. "Instructions for the Servant [of God]," by Al Ghazali (d. 1111). A defense of classical

Islamic values written late in the life of an important renovator of Islam.

*Minhajut Thalibin* (Ar: minhāj aṭ-ṭālibīn) Lit. title. "Instructions for the Seeker," a major Syafii legal text, written by Al Nawawi (d. 1277), used in Indonesian Islamic schools prior to 1900 to teach students the elements of Muslim jurisprudence.

**Mintaredja, M. S.** (In.) Biog. (b. 1921) Muhammadiyah activist and leader of the Parmusi organization from 1970 to 1973. *See* **Partai Muslimin Indonesia** and **Partai Persatuan Pembangunan**.

**Minum** (In.) Juris. Drink, Beverage.
*Usage*: ___ *khamar*, ___ *minum keras*, alcoholic beverages generally forbidden by Muslim jurisprudence.

**Mi'raj**. Spelling variant. *See* **Mikraj**.

*Mir'at Al Mu'min* (Ar: mir'āt al-mu'min) Lit. title. "Mirror of the Believer," a study outlining the commonly held doctrines of Islam regarding God, prophets, holy books, and the Hereafter by Shams Al Din Pasai (d. 1630).

**Mirza** (Urdu: mīrzā) Title. In South Asia a title given to persons of highly respected families.

**Mirza, Ghulam Ahmad**. *See* **Ahmad, Mirza Ghulam**.

**Misbach, Haji** (In.) Biog. (d. ca 1940). Political leader at Surakarta during the early twentieth century, associated with the communist movement. He controlled two leftist Muslims newspapers—The *Medan Moeslimin* and *Islam Bergerak*—which often interpreted the Qur'an through communist dogma. He was sent into internal exile in 1924 by Dutch colonial authorities.

**Miskin** (In.) (Ar: miskīn) Juris. Poor. In Islam special consideration is to be shown toward the poor, primarily by extending alms to them.
*Usage*: *fakir* ___, person eligible for alms because of his very poor economic state.

**Miskin, Haji** (In.) Biog. (d. ca 1850). A Minangkabau religious scholar and an important person on the Paderi side in the Paderi War against established Minangkabau society and their Dutch allies in the early nineteenth century.

**Missi.** *See* **Zending.**

**Mistik** (In.); mystiek (Eur.) Relig. Worshipers who undertake exercises designed to examine their own inner souls as a means of coming into contact with God.
*Usage*: *ber*___, to engage in mysticism; ___ *Islam*, Muslim mystic. *aliran* ___, that sector of society that engages in regular mystic practice; *benih-benih* ___, mystical tendencies; *orang* ___, Muslim mystic; *soal-soal* ___, mystical matters.

**Mistisisme** (In.) Relig. Religious belief and activity which stresses trances as a means of gaining insight about the inner being and its relationship with God or nature.
*Usage*: ___ *Jawi*, Javanese mysticism.

**Mizan.** *See* **Yawmul Mizan.**

*Mizan* (Ar: mīzān) Lit. title. 1. "The Scales," a Muslim magazine in Bukittinggi in 1939 employing Indonesian written in Jawi (Arabic) script. 2. "The Scales," a Muslim magazine published in English by the Library of the Istiqlal Mosque, Jakarta, in the late 1980s and early 1990s outlining the state of contemporary Islam in Indonesia.

*Mizanul Iktidal* (Ar: mīzān al-i'tidāl) Lit. title. "The Scales of Righteousness," a text on Traditions written by the Arab scholar Abu Abdallah Dzahabi (d. 1348). The work deals with Islamic genealogy as a key to the preservation of early Tradition literature in Islam.

**Modernisasi** (In.) Anthro. The process of adapting life styles and economic outlooks that stress materialism and technology. The entire Muslim world is in the midst of such emphasis. In Indonesia most Muslims agree with the theme of modernization, but want limits on the degree of materialism that accompanies it.
*Usage*: *proses* ___, the modernization process.

**Modin** (In.) (Ar: mu'adhdhīn) Pol. A religious figure in many Javanese villages who analyzes religious questions and undertakes prayers at funerals and ritual feasts. Syn: lebai. *See* also **Muazin.**

**Mogayat Syah, Sultan Ali**. *See* **Aceh.**

**Mohammed, Maulana**. *See* **Bantam.**

**Monotheisme** (In.) Relig. Belief in one, sole God.

**M.T.Q.** *See* **Musabaqah Tilawatil Qur'an.**

**MTsN.** *See* **Madrasah Tsanawiyah Negeri.**

**Al Muakhiru** (Ar: almu'akkhir) Theo. Name of God meaning "The Deferrer."

**Muakhodah**. *See* **Sunah.**

**Mualaf** (In.); muallaf (Ar: mu'allaf) Juris. A person who has newly entered Islam. Such a person is eligible for poor tax assistance if needy. *Usage*: *orang* ___, a convert to Islam.

*Mu'alimul Tanzil. See Ma'alimul Tanzil.*

**Mu'allaq**. *See* **Ilmu Mushthalah Hadis.**

**Muamalah** (In.); muamalat (Ar: mu'āmalah) Juris. 1. Those actions and matters dealing with human relationship with other humans and the physical world. 2. Those actions and matters dealing with trade and business. *Usage*: *kaidah* ___, *soal-soal* ___, matters concerning human relationships.

**Mu'an'an**. *See* **Ilmu Mushthalah Hadis.**

**Mu'awiyah bin Abi Sufyan** (Ar: mu'āwiyah ibn abū sufyān) Biog. (d. 680). Sixth caliph and founder of the Umayyah dynasty. He took the office from Ali, the son-in-law of the Prophet and Ali's son.

**Muazin** (In.); mu'adzin; muadzin; mu'azin (Ar: mu'adhdhīn) Juris. The person who gives the call to prayer that is recited or broadcast from the minaret of a mosque. In current Indonesia the task is sometimes shared among good Arabic reciters and includes young men learning Arabic.

**Mubah** (In.) (Ar: mubāḥ) Juris. A category of behavior in Muslim jurisprudence, indicating an action that is regarded as neutral, neither liked nor disliked by God. Syn: jaiz.

**Mubalig** (In.); muballigh; mubaligh (Ar: muballigh) Doct. The name for a speaker at a religious exercise, such as a gathering in the mosque during the fasting month of Ramadhan. The term can also be applied to a person involved in missionary or revival activity (dakwah).
*Usage*: ___ *Islam*, a Muslim revivalist speaker; ___-___ *Islam*, the Muslim missionaries in early Southeast Asia; *orang* ___, a Muslim revivalist speaker; *para* ___, *gabungan* ___, Muslim revivalists as a group.

**Al Mubdi** (Ar: al-mubdi') Theo. Name of God meaning "The Beginner and the Restorer."

**Mubham**. *See* **Ilmu Mushthalah Hadis.**

**Mudabbaj**. *See* **Ilmu Mushthalah Hadis.**

**Mudallas**. *See* **Ilmu Mushthalah Hadis.**

**Al Mudaqqiq** (Ar: al-mudaqqiq) Theo. A name of God meaning "The Exact."

**Al Muddatstsir** (Ar: al-muddaththir) Qur. "The Cloaked Ones," the seventy-fourth chapter of the Qur'an. A medium-length, lyrical chapter in which God charges Muhammad to publicly proclaim the lessons of Islam.

**Mu'dlal**. *See* **Ilmu Mushthalah Hadis.**

**Mudltharib**. *See* **Ilmu Mushthalah Hadis.**

**Mudraj**. *See* **Ilmu Mushthalah Hadis.**

**Al Mudzil** (Ar: al-mudhil) Theo. Name of God meaning "The Debaser."

**Mufakir, Sultan Abul**. *See* **Bantam.**

**Mufti** (Ar: muftī) Juris. A Muslim, learned in science and methodology of Muslim jurisprudence, who issues advisory opinions (fatwas) on matter of Muslim law.

*Al Mughni Muhtaj* (Ar: al-mughnī muḥtāj) Lit. title. "The Helper of the Seeker," by Asy-Syarbini (d. 1570). An important legalist work by a Shafii scholar, which has been important in Indonesia for over a century.

**Al-Mughniyu** (Ar: al-mughnu) Theo. A name of God meaning "The Enricher."

**Al Muhaddits.** *See* **Hafiz.**

*Al Muhadzab. See Kitab Al Muhadzab.*

**Al Muhaimin** (Ar: al-muhaymin) Theo. A name of God meaning "The Vigilant."

**Muhajirin** (Ar: muhājirūn) Doct. Name of a group of early Muslims, meaning "migrants," who accompanied Muhammad from Makkah to Madinah. They constituted the backbone of his support in the building of the community of believers. *Usage*: ___ *al uwwal, golongan* ___*, kelompak* ___, the "migrants" (muhajirun) as a collective group.

**Muhammad** (Ar: muḥammad) 1. Biog. (d. 632). The chief figure in the religion of Islam, who is recognized as the last of a long line of prophets. The Qur'an, as the word of God, was revealed to him. He formed a community of believers at Makkah and then at Madinah. The words and behavior of Muhammad have come to be regarded as a second scripture supporting the Qur'an. His life itself is regarded as exemplary and as a model of emulation by Muslims. 2. Qur. The forty-seventh chapter of the Qur'an, named for the Prophet Muhammad. It states that the martyred Muslim will enter Paradise.

**Muhammad, Maulana.** *See* **Bantam.**

**Muhammadiyah** (In.) Assn. The name of the premier Muslim movement of the modernist Muslim (kaum muda) outlook. In existence since 1912, it has been involved in religious, educational, and social welfare activities. It probably is the most respected Islamic association in Indonesia and is also well known abroad. It issues *Suara Muhammadiya* as a regular publication. The Chairmen of the Muhammadiyah were K. H. A. Dachlan 1912-23 (separate entry), H. Ibrahim 1923-33,

H. Hisyam 1932-37, Mas Mansur 1936-44 (separate entry), Bagus Hadikusumo 1944-53, A. R. Sutan Mansur 1953-59, Yunus Anis 1959-62, Ahmad Badawi 1962-68, Faqih Usman 1968-71 (separate entry), and Abdurrazak Fakhruddin 1971-90.
*Usage*: *golongan kaum* ___, the membership of the Muhammadiyah; *pengikut golongan* ___, members of the Muhammadiyah; *organisasi* ___, the Muhammadiyah as an association; *persyarikatan* ___, the Muhammadiyah as an association; *perguruan* ___, Muhammadiyah schools.

**Muhaqqiq** (Ar: al-muḥaqqiq) Theo. A name of God meaning "The Final Examiner."

**Muharraf**. *See* **Ilmu Mushthalah Hadis.**

**Muharram** (In.) (Ar: muḥarram) Cal. Name of the first month of the Islamic calendar, meaning the "sacred month." The first of Muharram is the Muslim New Year. The tenth is the celebration of Ashura, a special fasting day and a day of atonement.

*Al Muharrar* (Ar: al-muḥarrar) Lit. title. "The Blessed," a major Syafii work on jurisprudence by Ar Rafie (d. 1226) with a long record of use in Southeast Asia. It is a summation of several books by Al Ghazali (d. 1111) on legal matters, along with the decisions of several older Syafii scholars.

*Muhibah. See* **Termas Mahfuz.**

**Al Muhith** (Ar: al-muhiṭ) Theo. A name of God meaning "The Omnipotent."

**Muhkam**. *See* **Ilmu Mushthalah Hadis.**

**Muhmal**. *See* **Ilmu Mushthalah Hadis.**

**Muhrim** (In.) Juris. 1. (Ar: maḥram) People whom it is forbidden to marry because of family relationship. 2. (Ar: muḥrim) The pilgrim after assuming the dress of a pilgrim.

**Al Muhsi** (Ar: al-muḥṣī) Theo. A name of God, meaning "The Reckoner."

**Muhsin**; muhsinun (Ar: muḥsin) Doct. A believer who carries out behavior with sincere desire to please God in its performance.

**Al Muhyi** (Ar: al-muḥyī) Theo. A name of God meaning "The Giver of Life."

**MUI.** *See* **Majelis Ulama Indonesia.**

**Al Mu'iz** (Ar: al-mu'izz) Theo. A name of God meaning "The Restorer."

**Al Mujaadilah**; Al Mujaadalah; Al Mujadilah (Ar: al-mujādilah) Qur. "Women Who Plead," the fifty-eighth chapter of the Qur'an. It deals with the reconciliation of a husband and wife who have separated.

**Mujahadah,** Mujahadat (Ar: mujāhadah) Juris. Undertaking an important effort on behalf of Islam. Syn: Jihad.

**Al Mujib** (Ar: al-mujīb) Theo. Name of God meaning "The Answerer of Supplications."

**Mu'jizat.** Spelling variant. *See* **Mukjizat.**

**Mujtahid** (In.) (Ar: mujtahid) Juris. A thinker, writer, and scholar of Islamic jurisprudence who undertook expansion of the law based on religious sources. The term is used historically for the early jurists and also for more recent scholars who attempt to define law for new situations.
*Usage*: *imam* ___, an early Muslim jurist; *para* ___, the early Muslim jurists as a collective entity.

**Mukalaf** (In.); mukallaf (Ar: mukallaf) Juris. A person making a formal opinion about Islam who scrupulously observes decisions made by previous writers of his own school of jurisprudence.

**Mukasyafah.** *See* **Ilmu Mukasyafah.**

**Al Mukhadlaramun** (Ar: al-mukhḍarmūn) Trad. People who lived as non-Muslims in the time of Muhammad and then converted to Islam, but did not see Muhammad after their conversion. For purposes of their recollections of Muhammad, they are placed among the second generation of Muslims and their reports are not given high credence.

**Al Mukharrij** (Ar: al-mukharrij) Trad. The

person who published reports of the Prophet Muhammad's words and behavior in formal collections, such as Muslim and Bukhari.

**Mukjizat** (In.); mu'jizat; mu'jizat (Ar: mu'jizah) Doct. A miracle, that is, a happening prompted by God, which is a deliberate variation from usual occurrence, in order to indicate to humans that a particular person is a prophet. Miracles are of two varieties. Hissi are those dealing with matters of the five senses. Manawi are those in which thought and reasoning are necessary to perceive the miracle.
*Usage*: *ke___an Al Qur'any*, the revelation of the Qur'an as a miracle; ___-___ *rasul rasul*, the miracles of the prophets; *sifat* ___, characteristic of a miracle.

**Mukmin** (In.); mu'min; mumin (Ar: mu'min) 1. Doct. A true believer, in contrast to a Muslim, who is a pro forma member of the religion. 2. Qur. "The Believer," the fortieth chapter of the Qur'an. It relates the story of a member of Pharaoh's court who was a believer of the Prophet Musa, when Pharaoh was not. The chapter is also known as Ghafir and Ath Thaul. 3. Theo (In: Yang Memberi Keamanan). A name of God meaning "The Believer."
*Usage*: ___ *yang mutlak*, absolute belief; *amirul* ___*in*, a title of the chief Muslim political authority in Islamic history; *seorang* ___, a believer; *umat* ___*in*, the community of believers.

**Al Mukminun**; Al Mu'minun (Ar: al-mu'minūn) Qur. "The Believers," the twenty-third chapter of the Qur'an. The chapter asserts that believing is an important part of Islam in this world and in the Hereafter.

**Al Muktabah** (Ar: al-mukātabah) Trad. An official letter of authorization given by a transmitter of a report about the words and behavior of the Prophet Muhammad to the next person in the line of transmission, indicating it is an authentic report.

**Mukhtalaf**. *See* **Ilmu Mushthalah Hadis**.

**Muktamar** (In.) (fr. Ar: mu'tamar). Assn. Congress, a term used for major meetings of general membership by many Indonesian Muslim organizations.

**Muktamar Alam Islam Hindia As Syariqiyah** (In.) Hist. A series of conferences sponsored by the Sarekat Islam in 1922 at Cirebon, 1924 in Garut, 1924 in Surabaya and 1925 in Yogyakarta to deal with common activities of Indonesian Muslims. The meetings ended with internal problems put aside for preoccupation with the caliphate question in Middle Eastern affairs. Syn: Kongres Al Islam.

**Muktazilah** (In.); Mu'tazilah (Ar: mu'tazilah) Hist. "Free Thinkers," the term for a group of Muslim writers and thinkers of the tenth century who believed reason to be the supreme value of Islam. In their thinking, reason could be used to interpret the Qur'an and was superior to it. The group's view was rejected by other scholars who established the "orthodox" Sunni interpretation that the Qur'an, as God's word, was superior to human reason.
*Usage*: *aliran* ___, the Muktazilah group; *faham* ___, thinking of the Muktazilah; *golongan* ___, *kaum* ___, *orang-orang* ___, *partai* ___, the Muktazilah group.

**Mukti Ali, H. A.** *See* **Ali, Abdul Mukti** and **Menteri Agama.**

**Mu'lal.** *See* **Ilmu Mushthalah Hadis.**

**Mulia, Yang Maha** (In.) Theo. A name of God meaning "The Most Magnanimous." Syn: Al Kariem.

**Al Mulk** (Ar: al-mulk) Qur. "The Sovereign," the sixty-seventh chapter of the Qur'an. A medium-length, lyrical chapter proclaiming the greatness of God and His ability to know and do all things. It is also known as Tabaarah.

**MULO.** *See* **Meer Uitgebreid Lager Onderwijs.**

**Mumin**; Mu'min. Spelling variant. *See* **Mukmin.**

**Al Mumit** (Ar: mumit) Theo. A name of God meaning "The Extinguisher of Life."

**Al Mumtahanah**; Al Mumtahinah (Ar: al-mumtaḥinah) Qur. "She

Who is to be Examined," the sixtieth chapter of the Qur'an. It puts forth the principle that good relations with those who attack Islam is not possible.

**Munafik** (In.) (Ar: munāfiq) Juris. Hypocrite; the term has been used in Islam, especially during the time of the Prophet Muhammad, to designate those persons who, while outwardly professing to accept Islam, have secretly denied the faith.
*Usage*: *ke___an*, hypocrisy; *kaum ___in*, hyprocrites as a general group; *orang-orang* ___, hypocrites.

**Munakahat** (Ar: munākaḥāt) Juris. Law of marriage and family matters.

**Munasabah** (Ar: munāsabah) Qur. The technique of Qur'anic commentary in which a verse is seen in relationship with the verses which precede it.

**Munat, Masih**. *See* **Darajat, Sunan**.

**Munawalah** (Ar: al-munāwalah) Trad. Transmission of a report containing information concerning the words and behavior of the Prophet Muhammad by a formal transfer.

**Munawar Khalil, Muhammad**; Moenawar Chalil,... (In.) Biog. (d. 1961). A leading Indonesian modernist Muslim scholar of the 1950s whose works were quoted extensively from that time until the present. Wrote, inter alia, *Al Qur'an dari Masa ke Masa* (The Qur'an from Age to Age) and *Peristiwa Isra' dan Mi'raj* (The Incident of the Night Journey and the Ascension).

**Munawir Sjadzali**. *See* **Menteri Agama**.

**Mundur** (In.) Hist. Decline, stagnation.
*Usage*: *ke___an Islam*, the decline of Islam (i.e., a charge made by modernist Muslims in the first part of the twentieth century that Islam had fallen behind the West and needed renovation)

*Al Munir El Manar* (In.) Lit. title. "Light of the Victors," an Islamic magazine published in Padang, between 1911 and 1916, edited by H. Abdullah Ahmad (d. 1933). It reflected the values of Modernist Islam put forth by

Al Afghani (d. 1897) and M. Abduh (d. 1905) in *Al- Manar* published in Egypt. It used Indonesian in Arabo-Melayu (Jawi) script.

**Munkar** (In.) (Ar: munkar) Doct. In eschatology one of two angels who asks pertinent questions of the recently deceased to determine whether the person is truly a Muslim. If the deceased fails to answer the questions satisfactorily, Munkar and his associate, Nakir, inflict painful punishment. *Usage*: *malaikat* ___, the angel Munkar.

**Munkar**. *See* **Ilmu Mushthalah Hadis**.

**Al-Muntaqim**, Al Muntaqin (Ar: al-muntaqim) Theo. A name of God meaning "The Avenger."

**Munqathi**. *See* **Ilmu Mushthalah Hadis**.

*Muqaddimah* (Ar: kitāb al-'ibar muqaddimah) Lit. title. "Introduction (to the Book of Examples)" a historical study using a proto-sociological methodology by Ibn Khaldun (d. 1406). Internationally famous work which is considered a forerunner of modern sociology.

**Al Muqaddimu** (Ar: al-muqaddim) Theo. A name of God meaning "The Preceder of All Things."

**Al Muqallid** (Ar: al-muqallid) Juris. A legal scholar who applies jurisprudence to a new problem by interpolating from decisions of previous jurists, without any reference to primary religious sources. *See* **Taklid**.
*Usage*: *para* ___, the jurists of this type as a collective whole.

**Al Muqiit** (Ar: al-muqīt) Theo. Name of God meaning "The Giver of Sustenance."

**Al Muqsith** (Ar: al-muqsīṭ) Theo. Name of God meaning "The Equitable."

**Muqtadir**. *See* **Al Qaadir**.

**Muraqabah** (Ar: murāqabah) Myst. Devotion undertaken as part of mystic ritual.

**Murdud** (Ar: murdūd) Trad. Inaccurate and unreliable; a category of reports transmitting information concerning the words and behavior of the Prophet Muhammad.

**Muria, Sunan** (In.) Biog. (d. unk). One of nine legendary personages popularly believed to have led the conversion of Java to Islam in the sixteenth century. He is reputed to have used the Javanese orchestra (gamelan) and the popular theatre as instruments of propagation. Also known as (Raden) Prawoto. *See* **Wali Songo.**

**Murjiah** (In.) (Ar: al-murji'ah) Doct. An early Islamic sect which believed that once association with Islam was made, no further act of searching for truth was necessary. This contrasted with the Khawarij, who believed that special efforts were necessary to place God's commands into practice in human life.

**Mursal.** *See* **Ilmu Mushthalah Hadis.**

**Al Mursalaat**; Al Mursalat (Ar: al-mursalāt) Qur. "The (Angel) Messengers," the seventy-seventh chapter of the Qur'an. A medium-length, lyrical chapter proclaiming that the message brought by angels to humans is correct and that the rewards and punishments proclaimed will really happen.

**Murtad** (In.) (Ar: murtadd) Juris. An apostate to Islam. Apostasy may either be verbal by denying a principle of belief or by action in treating things religious with disrespect.
*Usage*: *ke___an*, apostasy; *orang* ___, an apostate.

**Musa** (Ar: musa) Qur. A prophet mentioned in the Qur'an, equated by scholars with the Old Testament Moses. He was one of six major prophets bringing special laws to humankind.

**Musa, Ibrahim** (In.) Biog. (d. ca. 1945) Religious scholar in Minangkabau who took a leading role in changing teaching techniques and introducing new subject matter to Islamic schools. Active from the turn of the twentieth century through the Japanese occupation.

**Musabaqah Tilawatil Qur'an—MTQ** (In.) (Ar: musābaqah tilawat al-qur'an) Qur. "Qur'an Reading Competition," the official name of the Qur'an

Recitation Competition conducted annually in Indonesia. Founded in 1962 with the first national competition in 1967, it now sponsors several categories of competition at area, city, provincal and national levels.

**Musafir** (In.) (Ar: al-musāfir) Juris. Traveler; certain ritual matters are changed for the Muslim traveler, such as prayer and fasting.

**Musalsal.** *See* **Ilmu Mushthalah Hadis.**

**Mushaf.** *See* **Mashhaf Utsman.**

**Mushafahah.** *See* **Ilmu Mushthalah Hadis.**

**Mushahhaf.** *See* **Ilmu Mushthalah Hadis.**

**Mushalla**; mushollah (Ar: muṣallā) Arch. Prayer house. *See* **Masjid.**
*Usage*: *mebuat* ___, to establish or build a prayer house, usually as a pious act.

**Al Mushawwir** (al-mus.awwir) Theo. A name of God meaning "The Shaper."

**Muslim** (In.) (Ar: muslim) Doct. The name assigned to followers of Islam; literally one who has surrendered to God. *See* **Mukmin.**
*Usage*: *kaum cendekiawan* ___, Muslim intellectuals as a group; *kaum* ___ *dan Muslimat, kaum* ___*in*, Muslims (male and female) as a collective group; *keluarga* ___, the Muslim family; *masyarakat* ___*in*, Muslim society; *para pemimpin* ___, Muslim leadership groups; *pribadi* ___, a person who has genuinely accepted Islam as a guide in life; *sarjana-sarjana* ___, Muslim scholars.

**Muslim** (Ar: abū al-ḥusayn muslim ibn al-ḥajjāj) 1. Biog. (d. 873) Arab compiler of a major collection of Traditions (hadis), the sayings and actions of the Prophet Muhammad. 2. Trad. A major collection of Muslim (d. 870), known as the *Sahih*, which, with the collection by Bukhari, is regarded as one of the two authoritative collections of Traditions. *See* **Sahih** and **'Ala Syar-thil Muslim.**
*Usage*: *Imam* ___, a title for the scholar Abu ... Muslim.

**Muslimat** (In.) Assn. "Muslim Women," a woman's organization affiliated with the Masjumi political party, founded at Masjumi's inception in 1945.

**Muslimat Nahdlatul Ulama** (In.) Assn. "The Muslim Women of the Nahdlatul Ulama," a women's association affiliated with the Nahdlatul Ulama, founded in 1938. It has been concerned with education, family matters, and indoctrination of Islamic teachings.

**Musnad** (Ar: al-musnad) Trad. Books of reports containing information about the words and behavior of the Prophet Muhammad collected by the first generation of Muslims.
*Usage*: *hadis* ___, early collections of Traditions; *kadang-kadang* ___, conscientious collections of Traditions of the period.

**Musnad.** *See* **Ilmu Mushthalah Hadis.**

*Al-Musnad* (Ar: al-musnad) Lit. title. "The Transmission," a short title of a collection of Traditions made by Ibnu Hanbal (d. 855). The collection is noted among Muslims as a primary book of jurisprudence because it was collected earlier than most other Tradition collections.

**Al Musnid** (Ar: al-musnid) 1. Trad. Any person in the chain of transmission of a report concerning the words and actions of the Prophet Muhammad. 2. Trad. A title assigned to certain scholars who examined collections of reports transmitting the words and behavior of the Prophet Muhammad. The scholar had extensive knowledge of a collection but had not completely memorized its material.

**Mustafa, Kemal Ataturk.** *See* **Kemal Ataturk, Mustafa.**

**Mustafidl.** *See* **Ilmu Mushthalah Hadis.**

**Mustahabah** (Ar: mustaḥabb) Juris. An action or behavior which is preferred. There is no sin attached if it is not done, but merit gained if it is done.
*Usage*: *amal* ___, a good action.

**Musthalah.** *See* **Ilmu Mushthalah Hadis.**

**Mustahil** (In.) (Ar: mustahil). Theo. What is not possible, such as certain attributes which cannot be assigned to God.

**Musta'in Billah, Sultan.** *See* **Banjar.**

**Mustawa** (Ar: mustawa) Doct. Place in the top level of heaven visited by Muhammad during the Night Journey.

**Musyabbihah** (Ar: mushabbihah) Doct. "The Assimilators." A group in early Islam who believed that God had body parts like humans and was capable of local motion.
*Usage*: *golongan* ___, the Assimilators.

**Musyawarah Nasional Islam** (In.) Hist. "The National Assembly of Islam," a meeting of leading religious figures in Indonesia in July 1975. It called for the establishment of the Council of Indonesian Ulama (Majelis Ulama Indonesia—MUI).

**Musyawarah Nasional Santri** (In.) Hist. "The National Gathering of Conscientious Believers," a meeting of prominent private religious educators and officials of the Department of Religious Affairs as a follow-up to the All-Indonesia Seminar on Private Religious Education (Seminar Pondok Pesantren) in 1965. It noted shortages of adequately trained personnel in teaching and administration in traditional Muslim schools and called for methodological renewal of curriculum.

**Musyrik** (In.) (Ar: mushrik) Juris. A person following a religion wherein idols are worshiped, more than one God exists or God is seen in ways that divide his personality and attributes.
*Usage*: *golongan* ___, *orang-orang* ___, polytheists; *sikap* ___, polytheistic belief or inclination.

**Al Muta'aal**; Al Muta'al (Ar: al-muta'ālī) Theo. A name of God meaning "The Self Exalted." Same as Yang Maha Tinggi.

**Mutabi.** *See* **Ilmu Mushthalah Hadis.**

**Al Mutakabbir** (Ar: al-mutakkabir) Theo. A name of God meaning "The Superb."

**Mutakallimin** (Ar: al-mutakallimun) Theo. The theologians of Sunni Islam in the classical period, who wrote in defense of Sunni principles against a variety of views, most of which were later classified as heresies. *Usage*: *kaum* ___, theologians as a collective group.

**Mu'talif dan Mukhtalif** (Ar: al-mu'talif wa-l-mukhtalif) Trad. A technical phrase used in the examination of reports about the Prophet Muhammad's words and behavior. It refers to Arabic words where the vowels have not been included and words could have different meanings depending on which vowels are to be used.

**Mutasyaabih**; mutasyabih. *See* **Ilmu Mushthalah Hadis.**

**Mutawaatir**. *See* **Ilmu Mushthalah Hadis.**

**Mu'tazilah**. Spelling variant. *See* **Muktazilah.**

**Al Muthaffifiin**; Al Muthaffifin (Ar: al-muṭaffifūn) Qur. "Those Giving Short Measure," the eighty-third chapter of the Qur'an. A short, lyrical chapter stating that those who give short measure and otherwise transgress God's law will be punished in the Hereafter.

**Mutmainah**. *See* **Nafsu.**

**Mutraf** (Ar: mutraf) Doct. A person not sincere in devotion to the principles of religion, but seduced by such worldly considerations as wealth or power.

**Muttafiq dan Muftariq** (Ar: al-muttafiq w-l-muftariq) Trad. "Examination and Judgment," a technical phrase used in the examination of reports about Muhammad's words and behavior. It refers to common names and the need to differentiate among people with family descent when they appear as transmitters of such relatings.

**Muttaqi** (Ar: muttaqin) Doct. A person who fears God and honors Him in all belief and behavior.

**Muttaqin, E. Z.** (In.) Biog. (d. 1985). Muslim intellectual and activist leader from Java and leading member of the Majelis Ulama Indonesia during the early 1980s.

**Muttashil**. *See* **Ilmu Mushthalah Hadis.**

**Al Mu'ti** (Ar: al-mu't.ī) Theo. A name of God meaning "The Giver."

**Muwafaqah**. *See* **Ilmu Mushthalah Hadis.**

*Al Muwaththa* (al-muwaṭṭa') Lit. title. The short title of an early Tradition collection by Malik Ibn Anas (d. 795), that has been given high respect among Sunni Muslims as a book of jurisprudence.

**Muzakkar, Kahar** (Ind.) Biog. (b. 1921) A Muslim leader in Sulawesi who led a revolt against the central Indonesian government in the 1950s concerning regional economic rights and the non-Islamic basis of the Indonesian state.

**Al Muzzammil** (Ar: al-muzzammil) Qur. "The Enshrouded One," the seventy-third chapter of the Qur'an. A short, lyrical chapter in which Muslims are instructed to voluntarily exert themselves to worship God in special night vigils to show the seriousness of their commitment.

**Mystiek**. Spelling variant. *See* **Mistik**.

# N

**An Naba'**; An Nabaa'; An Nabaak; An Nabaa (Ar: an-naba') Qur. "News," the seventy-eighth chapter of the Qur'an. A short, lyrical chapter outlining the role of God as creator and asserting human duty to obey His injunctions.

**Nabawi**. *See* **Masjid Nabawi**.

**Nabi** (In.) (Ar: nabī) Doct. Prophet; a messenger from God sent to a particular people—or in Muhammad's case to all humankind—with a revealed message to indicate what is right and wrong, and to serve as a guide for human behavior. Sunni Muslims hold that Muhammad was the final or seal (khatam) of the prophets.
*Usage*: *ke*___*an*, prophethood. ___ *Besar Muhammad*, the great Prophet Muhammad; ___ *Muhammad*, the Prophet Muhammad. *kisah para* ___, the stories of the prophets; *masa* ___, the era of the Prophet Muhammad; *para* ___, the collective term for all prophets; *qaul* ___, prophets saying; *shahabat* ___, the Companions of the Prophet Muhammad; *sifat* ___, prophetic characteristic; *taqrir* ___ prophetic confirmation; *tawassul dengan* ___, ask for intercession of the Prophet; *zaman* ___, the era of the Prophet Muhammad.

**Nadir** (Ar: an-nadīr) Hist. A Jewish tribe residing in Madinah, which Muhammad expelled as constituting a security threat.

**Nadzar**. Spelling variant. *See* **Nazar**.

**An Nafi** (Ar: an-nāfi') Theo. A name of God meaning "The Giver of the Advantage."

**Nafsi** (In.); Nafsiyah (Ar: nafsiyyah) Theo. Matters concerning the human soul in relationship to God.

**Nafsu** (In.) (Ar: nafs) Juris. Desire, lust, passion; sinful action relating to human passion.
*Usage*: ___ *amarah*, anger and an inner impulse to vent rage through bad action; ___ *awwamah*, an inner impulse for undertaking good action; *hawa* ___, passions; ___ *mutmainah*, an inner impulse to protect oneself from all evil by bringing God into the mind's eye.

**Nagara Islam**. Spelling variant. *See* **Negara Islam**.

**Nahdlatul Ulama** (In.) Assn. "Renaissance of the Religious Scholars," a name of an Islamic association, founded in 1926. It is the premier advocate of the traditionalist (kaum tua) viewpoint. It is closely tied to the religious scholars who operate private Islamic schools (pondok/pesantren) especially in Java and in Southern Kalimantan. It has a double leadership: a general chair (rais am), who is a religious scholar and spokesman and a chair (ketua), who is the association's administrator. Historically those offices have been held by the following people: *Rais Am*, K. H. Hasyim Asy'ari 1926-53 (separate entry), K. H. Wahab Hasbullah 1947-71 (separate entry), K. H. Bishri Syamsuri 1972-80, K. H. Ali Ma'sum 1981-83, K. H. Achmad Siddiq 1983- (separate entry); *Ketua*, K. H. Gip 1926-34, K. H. Nur 1934-(42), K. H. Masjkur 1947-56, K. H. Idham Khalid 1956-83 (separate entry), Abdurrahman Wahid 1983- (separate entry).

**Nahdlatul Wathan** (In.) Assn. "Renaissance of the Nation," an organization founded in 1935. It is dedicated to the promotion of private religious training, particularly in establishing and operating pondoks, pesantren, and madrasah. Active initially on Lombok, it has expanded to the entire East Java and Nusa Tenggara regions.

**Nahdliyin**, Nahdliyyin (In.) Assn. The general membership of the Nahdlatul Ulama association.

**Nahi Munkar**. *See* **Amar Ma'ruf Nahi Munkar**.

**An Nahl** (Ar: naḥl) Qur. "The Bee," the sixteenth chapter of the Qur'an. The characteristics of the bee, such as its industriousness, are put forward as an exemplar for human behavior.

**Nahwu.** *See* **Ilmu Nahwu.**

**Naib** (In.) Pol. On Java the official in charge of a central mosque at the district level (kewedanaan) during the Islamic periods and Dutch colonial era. He was to have eleven assistants, according to orders issued in the seventeenth century.

*Nailul Authar* (Ar: nayl al-awṭār) Lit. title. "Satisfaction of the Hopeful," a widely used collection of Traditions focusing on Muslim obligations by Asy Syaukani (d. 1832), a Middle Eastern Islamic scholar, frequently used and cited by Indonesian Muslim legalists.

**Na'im.** *See* **Surga.**

**Najamuddin, Sultan.** *See* **Palembang.**

**Najis** (In.) Juris. Feces, excrement; ritually unclean.

**An Najm** (Ar: an-najm) Qur. "The Star," the fifty-third chapter of the Qur'an. It stresses the principle that a person is alone responsible for his or her own sins.

**Nakir** (In.) (Ar: nakīr) Pop. Islam. The name of an angel who visits the deceased upon internment in the ground and asks questions to ascertain the piousness of the deceased during life. For those who have sinned greatly Nakir and his fellow angel Munkar exact painful retribution.
*Usage*: *malaikat* ___, the angel Nakir.

**An Naml** (Ar: an-naml) Qur. "The Ant," the twenty-seventh chapter of the Qur'an. It relates information about the Prophet Sulaiman (Solomon) and his census of the animals.

**Naqshabandiyyah** (Ar: naqshbandiyyah) Myst. Name of a sufi order founded by Muhammad ... Bahaud Din Naqshband (d. 1389). The order uses silence, special prayers, and silent recitation of God's name (zikir) as its means of gaining spiritual awareness. The order is especially influential in Central Asia and Indonesia.

**Naro, J.** *See* **Partai Persatuan Pembangunan.**

**Nas** (In.); Nash (Ar: naskh) Qur. Verses of the Qur'an which require careful interpretation because they appear to be in conflict with other verses. Earlier Western Orientalists referred to this phenomenon as "abrogation," asserting that one set of verses was replaced by a later revelation. Contemporary Muslim scholars deny this interpretation noting that in any system some points take precedence over other, lesser points.
*Usage*: ___-___ *yang suci*, Qur'anic verses requiring knowledgeable interpretation.

**An Naas;** An Nas (Ar: an-nāss) Qur. "Humans," the 114th and last chapter of the Qur'an. A very short, lyrical chapter telling humans to seek their refuge in God.

**An Nasafi** (Ar: abū 'abdullāh ... an-nasafī) Biog. (d. 1310). Hanafi legalist and theologian who taught at Kirman and Baghdad. Famous for a Muslim creed, a Qur'anic commentary and many works on jurisprudence. *See Madarikut Tanzil* and **Tafsir**.

**An Nasa'i** (Ar: aḥmad ibn 'alī an-nasā'ī) 1. Biog. (d. 915). A major Arab compiler of Tradition (hadis) collections, the sayings and actions of the Prophet Muhammad. 2. Lit. title. The common reference to the collection of Traditions assembled by the scholar An Nisa'i. *See As Sunan*.

**Nasakom**. *See* **Nasionalisme-Agama-Komunisme**.

**Nasehat** (In.) Doct. Lessons, advice or other worthy information for living a pious life in accordance with the teachings of Islam.

**Nash**. Spelling variant. *See* Nas.

**An Nashiir** (Ar: an-nāṣir) Theo. A name of God meaning "The Helper."

**An Nashr** (Ar: an-naṣr) Qur. "Assistance," the 110th chapter of the Qur'an. A very short, lyrical chapter proclaiming that God is the Lord to be acknowledged.

**Nashrani**. *See* **Nasrani**.

**Nasiah** (Ar: nasīah) Juris. Credit in financial transactions. Generally regarded as permissible, but, if carrying-charges are added, it is considered as usury (riba) by some Muslim jurists. *Usage*: *riba* ___, credit considered as usury.

**Naasikh.** *See* **Ilmu Mushthalah Hadis** and **Ilmu Tafsier.**

**Nasionalisme** (In.) Pol. Identification with a nation-state and its symbols (i.e. flag) so that all other ideologies and values are regarded as subservient to that identification. Indonesian nationalism has been a powerful force in claiming independence and building an Indonesian nation. *Usage*: ___ *Islam*, Islamic nationalism.

**Nasionalisme-Agama-Komunisme—Nasakom** (In.) Pol. "(Unity of the Political Philosophies of) Nationalism, Religion and Socialism," an ideological slogan and aspiration put forward by President Sukarno in the period from 1955 to 1965 in which political segments of Indonesia would cooperate and fuse their efforts and outlooks for the national good. In the later years of Guided Democracy it became a litmus test for continued participation in the Sukarnoist political system.

**Nasrani** (In.); nashrani (Ar: naṣrānī) Relig. A name for Christians, referring to the birthplace of Isa (Jesus). *Usage*: *agama* ___, Christianity.

**Nasution, Abdul Haris** (In.) Biog. (b. 1918). Indonesian general and minister of defense (1959-66) in the time of Guided Democracy. Privately a devout Muslim, but as a career army leader an advocate of Indonesian nationalism and army professionalism. He was responsible for attempts to build Muslim political activism as part of a counterbalance to communists during the Guided Democracy period.

**Nationaal Indonesisch Panvinderij—NATIPJ** (Dutch) Assn. "National Indonesian Guides," a scouting organization for boys founded by the Jong Islamieten Bond in the 1920s.

**Natsir, Mohammad** (In.) Biog. (b. 1908) Indonesian intellectual and politician from Sumatra. In particular, leader of a modernizing wing of the Masjumi political party in the 1940s and 1950s. Prime minister of Indonesia, 1950-51. *See* **Madjelis Sjuro Muslimin Indonesia** and *Panji Islam.*

**Al Nawawi**; Al Nawawij (Ar: abū zakariyyā' muhyi ad-dīn an-nawawī) Biog. (d. 1278). Shafii legal scholar in the Middle East whose works have been extensively used in Indonesian religious schools for the past two hundred years. *See Minhajut Thalibin, Riyadhush Shalihin*, and *Hadis Arba'in.*

**Nawawi Banten, Muhammad** (Ar: muḥammad ibn 'uthmān an-nawawī al-jāwī al-bantānī) Biog. (1315H/ 1888). An Indonesian-born scholar who lived and taught in Makkah in the late nineteenth century. He wrote extensively, including a Qur'anic commentary, with many of his books being used in Indonesian Islamic schools. *See Marah Labid.*

**Nazar** (In.); nadzar (Ar: nadhr) Pop. Islam. A vow to undertake a religious action, often as the return for God's favorable intervention in a particular problem confronting the worshiper making the vow.
*Usage*: *haji* ___, vow to undertake the pilgrimage.

**An Naazi'aat**; An Nazai'at, An Nazi'at (Ar: an-nāzi'āt) Qur. "(Angels) Who Drag Forth," the seventy-ninth chapter of the Qur'an. A medium-length, lyrical chapter emphasizing the vengeance of God on those who spurn His guidelines for proper belief and behavior. Also known as Ath Thaamah.

**Nazil.** *See* **Ilmu Mushthalah Hadis.**

**Negara** (In.) 1. Pol. a nation, a nation-state. 2. Geog. In the sixteenth century Mataram empire the area located in the capital district, directly under control of the court.
*Usage*: ___ *kaum Muslimin*, a Muslim nation.

**Negara Agung** (Jav.) Geog. In the sixteenth century Mataram empire the area located in the hinterland of the capital, but still firmly under the empire's control.

**Negara Islam** (In.) Nagara Islam. Pol. "Islamic state," a twentieth century term indicating a nation-state deliberately operated on the principles of Islam. Indonesian Muslims have come to no consensus on just what principles and structure a Islamic state should take despite considerable discussion and several national experiments elsewhere over three-quarters of a century.

**Negeri** (Min.) Anthro. In Minangkabau history a unit of several villages forming a basic political and social unit.

**Neofundamentalisme** (In.) Relig. A term applied to several Islamic movements of the 1970s and 1980s which emphasize the early teachings of the religion and application of those principles to current conditions. Neofundamentalists are viewed by many outsiders as militant and intolerant of nonreligious considerations of society and nation.

**Neokolonialisme** (In.) Pol. The concept that Western nations assert economic and cultural domination over most of the world including the Muslim world and Indonesia. The term was consistently used as a point of ideology during the Guided Democracy era (1957 to 1966) and less used as a point of reference under the New Order era (1966 to the present).

**Neomodernisme** (In.) Anthro. A movement of Muslim intellectuals in the latter quarter of the twentieth century which rests on modernist calls for return to basic scripture, but regards historical efforts of Muslim intellectuals as having relevance to interpretations of Islamic principles to contemporary conditions.

**Neraka** (In.) Doct. The name of the place for eternal punishment for those who disbelieve and those who rebelled against God during their lifetimes. Syn: jahannam, jahim, hawiah, wail, sa'ir, sagar, hutamah, laza.
*Usage*: *masuk* ___, enter hell (as punishment).

*Neratja* (In.) Lit. title. "The Scales," a newspaper of the 1920s reflecting views of the Islamic leadership of the Sarekat Islam nationalist movement.

**Ngampel, Sunan**. Spelling variant. *See* **Ampel, Sunan**.

**Ngelmu** (Jav.) Pop. Islam. Magical practice. *See* **Dukunisme**.

**Niat** (In.) niyah (Ar: niyyah) Juris. Purpose; intention. A short declaration of intention pronounced audibly or mentally, immediately prior to prescribed religious ritual in which the performer states his intent to perform the act with piety and religious purpose. Syn: usali.
*Usage*: *melafalkan* ___ *sembahyang*, pronouncing the "intention" prior to the beginning of required prayer.

*Nihayah. See Kitab Nihayah.*

**Nikah** (In.) (Ar: nikāh) Juris. Marriage and the legal issues pertaining thereto. In Indonesia legal questions regarding marriage matters are under the jurisdiction of an Islamic court system.
*Usage*: *me___kan*, to marry.

**Nikmat** (In.) Doct. Comfort, luxury.
*Usage*: *ke___an*, eternal reward in the Hereafter for being a Muslim and living a pious life. Ant: azali.

**Nilai** (In.) Doct. Standard or value.
*Usage*: ___-___ *kemanusiaan*, human standards, as opposed to those of God.

**An Nisaa'**; An Nisaak, An Nisa' (Ar: an-nisā) Qur. "The Women," the fourth chapter of the Qur'an. It is one of several chapters centering on the role, responsibilities and expected behavior of women in Muslim society.

**An Nisaburi** (Ar: niẓām ad-dīn ... al-qummī an-nisabūrī) Biog. (d. 1328H) Middle Eastern author of a prominent commentary of the Qur'an which is modeled after that of Ibn Jarir Ath Thabari (d. 923). *See Gharaibul Qur'an* and **Tafsir**.

**Niyah**. Spelling variant. *See* **Niat**.

**Nuh** (Ar: nūḥ) 1. Qur. Personal name of a prophet mentioned in the Qur'an, who is associated by scholars with the Old Testament Noah. He was prophet when God visited the earth with a great flood to purge it of sinners. 2. Qur. "The (Prophet) Noah," the seventy-first chapter of the Qur'an. A short, lyrical chapter telling of God's distress and punishment with sinners before the Great Flood.

**Nun** (Ar: Nun) Qur. The Arabic alphabetical letter "Nun," an alternative title for the sixty-eighth chapter of the Qur'an. The usual name for the chapter is Al-Qalam.

**An Nuur**; An Nur (Ar: an-nūr) Qur. 1. "The Brilliance (of God)," the twenty-fourth chapter of the Qur'an. The chapter deals with societal and family matters. 2. A name of the Qur'an, indicating that it is like a "ray" of light from God. 3. Jounal of the Jong Islamieten Bond. *See Het Licht*.

**Nur, K. H.** *See* **Nahdlatul Ulama**.

**Nur Muhammad** (Ar: nūr muḥammad). Doct. A primordial light created by God that existed prior to all other creation to shape all things and provide their essence. A key concept of mysticism in much of the Islamic world, including Indonesia.

**Nusantara** (In.) Geog. The geographical area of the Indonesian archipelago and alternate name for Indonesia used in literary allusions. *Usage*: *bumi* ___, the Indonesian Archipelago; ___ *Indonesia*, the Indonesian homeland.

**Nuzulul Qur'an** (Ar: nuzūl al-qur'ān) Doct. The descent or revelation of the Qur'an to Muhammad, in parts, over a lengthy period of time. This is an important part of Islamic doctrine.

**Nyawa** (In.) Relig. Spirit, soul.

# O

*Oetoesan Hindia* (In.) Lit. title. "Messenger of the Indies," a newspaper of the 1920s reflecting the views of Islamic leadership of the Sarekat Islam nationalist organization.

**OKI**. *See* **Organisasi Konperensi Islam**.

**Orang Muda Muhammad Said**. *See* **Kalijaga, Sunan**.

**Orde Baru** (In.) Pol. "New Order," a term assigned by the Suharto government to the era of its own rule (1966-). The era is featured as a time of attainment, of national unity, and of economic and political development. Orde Baru is used in contradistinction to Orde Lama (Old Order) indicating the preceding era of President Sukarno. *Usage*: *masa* ___, the time period of the New Order.

**Orde Lama** (In.) Pol. "Old Order," a term given by the Suharto government to the regime of President Sukarno, which preceded the Suharto government. That earlier period is featured as leftist, corrupt, and marked by national disunity. The period extends either from 1958 to 1965 or 1945 to 1965. *See* **Demokrasi Terpimpin**. *Usage*: *masa* ___, the time period of the Old Order.

**Organisasi Kemasyarakat—Ormas** (In.) Pol. General term in Indonesian national life indicating associations with a public mission and identity. Muslim associations are included in this category and are subject to the political rules established by the government for their operation.

**Organisasi Konperensi Islam—OKI** (In.) Pol. "Organization of the Islamic Conference," an international grouping of forty-five nations where Muslims constitute a majority of the population, founded in 1969. It has dealt with political, social and economic issues facing Muslim nations. Indonesia is a member.

**Orientalis** (In.) Relig. Western scholars interested in Asian religious traditions, who studied and wrote about them in the nineteenth and twentieth centuries. A number were missionaries and colonial officials whose findings sometimes reflected their official positions and judged the Asian religions as inferior or flawed. The term "Orientalist" is currently a term of approbation among Muslims of Asia. However, Orientalists, in general, have written works of great interest to Muslims and they have also trained many Muslim scholars.
*Usage*: ___ *Barat*, Western Orientalists; *kaum* ___, *para* ___, the group of Orientalists as a whole.

**Ormas.** *See* **Organisasi Kemasyarakat.**

# P

**Paderi** (In.) Hist. "White," a name assigned to a group of Islamic activists in the early 1800s in the Minangkabau area of Sumatra, who modeled themselves on the Wahhabi Movement of Arabia, and who wished to purify the society there of non-Islamic practices and strengthen Islam. *See* **Bonjol, Imam.**
*Usage*: *perang* ___, the war between the Dutch and the Paderi forces lasting from 1821 to 1830.

**Paguyuban Ngestu Tunggal—Pangestu** (Jav.) Relig. Javanese mystical sect under Christian influence.

**Paguyuban Sumarah** (Jav.) Relig. Javanese mystical sect.

**Pahala** (In.) Juris. Merit for certain pious actions, usually seen in religious terms. Nonobligatory prayer and participation in Ramadan services are two popular actions undertaken to gain merit. Modernists believe pahala is earned by an individual for self alone, while some traditionalists believe merit may be transferred to a loved one. Syn: jaza'.
*Usage*: *ber*___, to be involved with activities that gain religious merit.
___ *amal kebaikan*, good actions that earn merit; ___ *bacaan ayat suci*, gaining merit through recitation of Qur'anic verses; ___ *sedekah*, merit through giving alms; ___ *tahlil*, merit in reading the last prompting to the dead; ___ *wakaf*, merit through giving a pious endowment to the support of a religious purpose.
*Diberi* ___, to be given merit; *hadiah* ___, the gift of merit (granted by God); *masalah hadiah* ___, the question of (God's) granting merit for pious actions of believers; *mendapatkan* ___, to be involved with activities that

gain religious merit; *menerima ___ dari amalan orang lain*, receive merit from the pious action of another person.

**Pajajaran** (Sunda.) Hist. A Hindu kingdom of West Java founded in 1333, which was tributary to Majapahit empire initially, but converted to Islam about 1550. It was then usually tributary to one of the north coast Muslim kingdoms. *Usage*: *kerajaan* ___, the Kingdom of Pajajaran.

**Paku** (Jav.) Prefix or suffix to other titles. *See* following noun.

**Paku, Raden**. *See* **Giri, Sunan.**

**Pakubuwono**; Pakubuwana (Jav.) Biog. In the Mataram dynasty the name of several rulers with the Javanese title of susuhunan, who ruled at Surakarta in the eighteenth, nineteenth, and twentieth centuries. The dates of reigns are as follows: I: 1705-19, II: 1725-49, III: 1749-88, IV: 1788-1820, V: 1820-23, VI: 1823-30, VII: 1830-58, VIII: 1858-61, IX: 1861-93, X: 1893-xxxx, XI: xxxx-1944, XII: 1944-44.

**Palaka, Aru; Palakka, Arung**. *See* **Arung Palakka.**

**Palembang** (In.) Geog. City in south Sumatra and site of a state which began before the arrival of Islam (ca. 1455) and ended in 1825. Its Muslim rulers, using the title of sultan, were as follows: Muhammad Mansyur Jayo Ing Lago 1706-14, Agung Komaruddin Sri Teruno 1714-17, Mahmud Badaruddin Jayo Wikramo 1724-58, Ahmad Najamuddin Adi Kesumo 1758-76, Muhammad Bahauddin 1776-1803, Mahmud Badaruddin 1803-21, Husin Bhiauddin 1813-17, Ahmad Najamuddin Pangeran Ratu 1819-21, Ahmad Najamuddin Prabu Anom 1821-23, Kramo Jayo 1823-25.

**Al Palimbani, Abdus Samad**. *See* **Abdus Samad Al Palimbani.**

**Pan Islamisme** (In.) Hist. The philosophy of certain Muslim activists, such as Al Afghani (d. 1897) and Al Kawakibi (d. 1903), in the late nineteenth century calling for unity across the Muslim world in reasserting Islam religiously and politically. It was regarded as a nascent threat by colonial governments of the period and security steps were taken against its adherents by many governments, including the Dutch East Indies administration.

**Panatagama**. Spelling variant. *See* **Panotogama**.

**Pancasila** (In.) Pol. "Five Principles," a term assigned for the state motto of Indonesia. National law calls for it to be the single basis for all political and social organizations in Indonesian national life. The principles are "Belief in God the Only One, Humanitarianism, National Unity, Democracy as expressed through Representatives of the People and Social Justice." *Usage*: *soal* ___, matters concerning the state motto.

**Pandu Ansor** (In.) Assn. "Scout Movement of the Helpers' Association," a scouting organization operated by the Nahdlatul Ulama.

**Panembahan** (Jav.) Title. A title of Javanese rulers of the Majapahit and Mataram periods in the twelfth to seventeenth centuries, meaning "Object of Respectful Veneration."

**Pangeran** (Jav.) Title. 1. "Prince," or "Exalted" a title of the Muslim kingdoms and in the colonial era, often used in combination with other titles to indicate "regent," "governor" and other functions. 2. Title for ruler on Kalimantan in the precolonial era.

**Pangeran Mangkubumi** (Jav.) Title. "Prime Minister," a title used historically on Java by Muslim and non-Muslim kingdoms and principalities.

**Pangestu**. *See* **Paguyuban Ngestu Tunggal**.

**Panitia Persiapan Kemerdekaan Indonesia** (In.) Hist. "Committee for Preparing Indonesian Independence," a body meeting in 1945 on behalf of a larger congress with the task of preparing a draft constitution. Of the ten members two were from political Muslim organizations.

*Panji Islam* (In.) Lit. title. "The Islamic Banner," a Muslim magazine of the late 1930s, edited by Mohammad

Natsir (b. 1908) and others, reflecting a Westernized approach to the study of Islam.

*Panji Masyarakat*—Panjimas (In.) Lit. title. "The Banner of Society," a contemporary Muslim magazine beginning publication about 1970, edited by Rusjdi Hamka (b. 1935), presenting views primarily reflecting modernist and postmodernist Muslim thinking.

**Panotogomo**; pantagama; panatagama (Jav.) Title. Title assumed by the sultans of Yogyakarta and Surakarta meaning "regulator of religion."
*Usage*: ___ *Agama Islam*, regulator of the Islamic religion.

**Panotogomo Kalipatullah.** *See* **Saidina Panotogomo Kalipatullah.**

**Panteisme** (In.) Relig. To associate God's creation with God. It marked a stage in the development of Islamic mysticism, particularly under Ibnu Arabi (d. 1240), and was labeled as heretical (syirik) by later theologians and mystics.
*Usage*: *faham-faham* ___, pantheistic thinking.

**Parmusi.** *See* **Partai Muslimin Indonesia.**

**Partai Demokrasi Indonesia—PDI** (In.) Pol. "Indonesian Democratic Party," a name taken by a union of several parties in the political party simplification of 1973. It consists of old-line nationalists, Sukarnoists, Christians and many university students.

**Partai Demokrasi Islam Indonesia—PDII** (In.) Pol. "Indonesian Muslim Democratic Party," a proposed party put forward by former Vice President Hatta (d. 1980) in the late 1960s, which was turned aside by the authorities on the grounds that party simplification was about to occur and new parties at that time would not be appropriate.

**Partai Komunis Indonesia—PKI** (In.) Pol. "Indonesian Communist Party," a name taken by an association of leftists in Indonesia at several times during the twentieth century. It was first prominent in the 1920s and outlawed for militant activity by the Dutch authorities. Again important during the 1960s as a principal political force in the Sukarno era, it became involved in a power move against the military, after which it was outlawed. The acronym is used by contemporary Muslim writers as a symbol of perfidy and illegal clandestine activity by the left against the nation and against Muslim interests.

**Partai Muslimin Indonesia—Parmusi** (In.) Pol. "Indonesia Muslim Party," a title of a Muslim political party in the late 1960s that was formed by former members of Masjumi, which had been banned a few years earlier. It entered the Partai Persatuan Pembangunan in a simplification of political parties in 1973. Its chairs (ketua) were Djarnawi Hadikusuma 1968-70 and H. M. Mintaredja 1971-73 (separate entry).

**Partai Persatuan Pembangunan—PPP** (In.) Pol. "National Development Party," a name taken by a union of Muslim political associations which became one of the three legal political parties in contemporary Indonesia. Over the past fifteen years its share of seats in parliament has declined to about 20 percent of the total. Its general chairs (ketua) were H. M. Mintaredja 1973-79 (separate entry) and H. J. Naro 1981--.

**Partai Sarekat Islam Indonesia—PSII** (In.) Pol. A continuation of the Sarekat Islam in the Liberal Democracy period of the 1950s when it had been a minor party, generally in alliance with the Nahdlatul Ulama Association.

**Paryana Suryadipura** (Jav.) Relig. Javanese mystical sect based on anthropological-biological teachings.

**Pasai.** *See* **Samudera-Pasai** and *Hikayat Raja-Raja Pasai.*

**Pasallang** (Bugi) Pop. Islam. The initiation of boys and girls to Islam in Sulawesi through circumcision.

**Pasisiran** (Jav.) Geog. In the Mataram empire (sixteenth century) the region of the north coast where independent, trade-based cities had considerable autonomy.

**Patih** (In.) Hist. In the early Mataram period (sixteenth century) the title of the chief government official in the provinces, who administered for the petty prince (pepatih).

**Patuntung** (Bugi) Doct. In Sulawesi, investigation of the Islamic religion in an attempt to reconcile local values with those of Islam.

**PDI.** *See* **Partai Demokrasi Indonesia.**

**PDII.** *See* **Partai Demokrasi Islam Indonesia.**

**Pecah** (In.) Trad. Broken, ruptured.
*Usage*: ___-___*kan*, the broken line of transmission in the preservation of reports about the Prophet's words and behavior.

**Pelajar Islam Indonesia—PII** (In.) Assn. "Indonesian Muslim Students" a name taken by a student organization founded in 1947, affiliated with the Masjumi political party. It was active as an ally of the army leadership during the Guided Democracy period, but retreated from political activism in the 1970s for attention to education and revivalism.

*Pemandangan* (In.) Lit. title. "Islamic Outlook," a newspaper published at Padang Panjang from 1921 to 1925 aimed at expressing a radical and generally procommunist outlook regarding Indonesian politics of the time.

**Pembaharuan** (In.) Relig. Renewal, renovation.
*Usage*: *proses* ___, the renewal process in religion or national development.

**Pembangunan** (In.) Econ. Development of economic, political, and social institutions fitting with twentieth century models of modernism, resting on materialistic and technological themes. Syn: perkembangan.
*Usage*: ___ *mental/spiritual*, development that encompasses moral and spiritual values.

*Pembela Islam* (In.) Lit. title. "Defense of Islam," a magazine published by the Persatoean Islam, Bandung from 1929 to 1935 reflecting a modernist, fundamentalist view of Islam which took issue with groups it considered unsympathetic to its views of proper belief and behavior.

**Pembela Tanah Air** (In.) Assn. "Defense of the Homeland," an association of leading Muslims founded October 1943 to present Muslim aspirations to the Japanese authorities concerning Indonesian independence.

**Pembentuk, Yang Maha** (In.) Theo. A name of God meaning "The Most Described."

**Pemberi, Yang Maha** (In.) Theo. A name of God meaning "The Most Generous." Syn: Al Wahhaab.

**Pembina Iman Tauhid Islam.** *See* **Persatuan Islam Tionghoa Indonesia.**

**Pemerintah Revolusioner Republik Indonesia/Piagam Perjuangan Semesta Alam—PRRI/Permesta** (In.) Pol. "Revolutionary Government of the Republic of Indonesia/ Charter of Inclusive Struggle," a name adopted by a political group which represented an Outer Island rebellion against the central government from 1957 to 1962. The term is often used symbolically by contemporary Indonesian writers to indicate ethnic and regional diversity of the country and the fragile nature of political relationships.

**Pemikiran Baru** (In.) Hist. "New Thinking," a title often assigned to a group of Islamic thinkers, active in the 1970s, characterized by their attention to political and economic development of the nation.

**Pemilihan Umum—Pemilu** (In.) Pol. General elections in the Indonesian Republic, since 1972 held regularly every five years for seats in parliament. Muslims have been successful candidates and Muslim parties have participated regularly.

**Pemuda Mahasiswa Pelajar Islam—PMPI** (In.) Assn. "The Islamic Students (Association)," a youth movement formed in 1967 as a unity organization for Muslim youth. It conducted demonstrations concerning international Muslim issues and local cases involved with what members considered slander of Islam.

**Pemuda Persatuan Islam** (In.) Assn. "Youth of the Persatuan Islam," the youth wing of the Persatuan Islam.

**Pencipta, Yang Maha** (In.) Theo. A name of God meaning "The Greatest Creator."

**Pendidikan** (In.) Educ. Education.
*Usage*: *lembaga-lembaga* ___ *agama*, religious educational institutions.

**Pendidikan Guru Agama Negara—PGAN** (In.) Assn. "National Religious Teachers' Institute," a type of general Muslim education founded in 1951 by the Department of Religion to combine Islam and secular subjects in secondary education.

**Penerima, Yang Maha** (In.) Theo. A name of God meaning "The All Receiving."

**Pengadilan Agama** (In.) Pol. Islamic courts in Indonesia which handle cases of family law.

**Pengadilan Tinggi Agama** (In.) Pol. The Islamic appeals court in Indonesia which deals with cases of family law.

**Pengajian** (In.) Pop. Islam. Private or semiprivate religious services, as in a government office, which workers perform during work hours.

**Pengampun, Yang Maha** (In.) Theo. A name of God meaning "The All-Forgiving."

**Pengantur Agama Islam**. *See* **Panotoagama.**

**Pengasih, Yang Maha** (In.) Theo. A name of God meaning "The All Merciful."

**Pengetahui, Yang Maha** (In.) Theo. A name of God meaning, "The All Knowing."

**Penghabisan, Yang Maha** (In.) Theo. A name of God meaning "Last beyond Everything Else."

**Penghulu**; pengulu (Malay) 1. Anthro. In Minangkabau the head of a family who arranges all internal matters, with due consideration of the customs that govern family behavior. 2. Hist. In Mataram a person in charge of a major mosque at the provincial level on Java. As established by royal orders in the seventeenth century, he was to be assigned forty assistants. He was in charge of all religious matters in the province and was also known as religious affairs judge (Pengulu Hakim). 3. Kepenguluan. Pol. On Java the division of civil service for officials dealing with Islamic affairs.

**Pengingat** (In.) Geog. A town on the island of Riau which was the site of a center for the study of mysticism in the early nineteenth century. A number of translations of Arabic titles were made for distribution in the Southeast Asian region.

**Penyantun, Yang Maha** (In.) Theo. A name of God meaning "The Most Kindly." Syn: Al Haliim.

**Penyayang, Yang Maha** (In.) Theo. A name of God meaning "The All Compassionate."

**Pepatih** (Jav.) Pol. Petty prince of the Mataram empire who had control over a region where villages paid taxes to him. They were called regenten by the Dutch and later integrated into the Indonesian republic with the title of bupati.

**Pepatih Dalam** (Jav.) Pol. In the early Mataram empire (early sixteenth century) the chief political official equivalent to vizier or chief councillor, called rijksbestierder by the Dutch. Syn: raden adipati; rijksbestierder.

**Peradilan** (In.) Pol. Court. *Usage*: ___-___ *agama*, religious courts (dealing with inheritance and family matters); *ketua-ketua* ___ *agama*, judges of the religious courts.

**Perang Aceh** (In.) Hist. (1873-1904) A series of hostilities (known as the Aceh War) between Dutch and Acehnese guerrilla forces. The immediate cause was Dutch occupation of the territory after two centuries of exercising indirect, protectorate control. The Aceh king called for a holy war and the religious scholars (ulama), believing the Islamic way of life in danger, led the population in armed opposition to the Dutch occupation. *See* **Van Heutz** and **Tiro, Cik de.**

**Perang Badar** (In.) Hist. A battle in the year 2H on the Western side of the city of Madinah undertaken by the Muslims under Muhammad against the Makkans.

**Perang Jawa** (In.) Hist. (1825-30) A war of succession in which Prince Diponegoro (d. 1855) united court dissidents and rural Muslims against his brother who was supported by Dutch forces. The brother and the Dutch were victorious. The war is pictured by nationalist historians as an early patriotic effort against Dutch colonialism.

**Perang Kejil** (In.) Hist. Limited tactical encounters, or guerrilla warfare. Used primarily in historical descriptions of the Aceh War at the beginning of the twentieth century.

**Perang Paderi**. *See* **Paderi**.

**Perang Sabil** (In.) Doct. Warfare between believers and non-believers, in which the faith of Islam or the welfare of Muslims as believers is at issue. A believer falling in such a war is believed to be awarded paradise regardless of other factors. Perang Sabil was used by Indonesians against the Portuguese in the sixteenth century and later several times against the Dutch.
*Usage*: *orang* ___, a person undertaking a cause considered to be holy in nature.

**Perang Salib** (In.) Hist. The Crusades of the European Christians against the Saracens to control the Holy Land of Christianity (1097 to 1291).

**Percaya** (In.) Doct. Faith, belief in God.
*Usage*: *ke___an*, in Tradition (hadith) analysis the accurate passage of a report on the Prophet Muhammad's words and behavior from one generation to another; *ke___an-ke___an*, beliefs. *Aliran-aliran ke___an*, the religious sects of Java which constitute a special category of treatment in Indonesian political life; *memperbaiki ke___an*, improving or deepening belief in God; *mempertahankan ke___an*, defending the faith of Islam; *menyiarkan ke___an*, spreading the faith of Islam.

**Perdata** (In.) Juris. Matters of civil law in the Republic of Indonesia.
*Usage*: *hukum* ___, civil law.

**Pergerakan Mahasiswa Islam Indonesia—PMII** (In.) Assn. "Indonesian Muslims Student Association," a prominent Muslim student association founded in 1956, affiliated with the Nahdlatul Ulama.

**Pergerakan Sarjana Muslimin Indonesia—Persami** (In.) Assn. Independent student group, active in the 1960s as a mass organization for political Islam.

**Pergerakan Wanita Islam Indonesia** (In.) Assn. "The Indonesian Islamic Women's Movement," founded in the early 1950s and affiliated with the Partai Sarekat Islam Indonesia (PSII).

**Perguruan** (In.) Educ. An educational institution emphasizing educational sciences; a teachers' institute.
*Usage*: ___ *Tinggi Islam Swasta*, private Islam teachers training university.

**Perguruan Tinggi Agama Islam Negeri—PTAIN** (In.) Educ. "National Islamic Teaching Institute," founded at Yogyakarta in September 1951 to provide postsecondary training in Islamic subjects. It was the predecessor to the Institute Agama Indonesia Nasional (IAIN) system.

**Perguruan Tinggi Ilmu Al-Quran** (In.) Educ. "Qur'anic Science Teaching Institute," founded in Jakarta in 1971, for the study of the Qur'an, especially recitation, singing, and memorization.

*Peristiwa Isra' den Mi'raj. See* **Munawar Khalil, Muhamma.**

**Perjalanan Haji Islam—PHI** (In.) Pol. "The Pilgrims' Transportation Service," an agency in the Indonesian Department of Religion, begun in 1825, which arranges transportation and associated services for the annual pilgrimage to the Islamic Holy Land for Indonesians undertaking the pilgrimage.

*Perjanjian Baru* (In.) Lit. title. "The New Testament" of the Christians.

*Perjanjian Lama* (In.) Lit. title. "The Old Testament" of the Christians.

**Perjanjian Madinah.** *See* **Konstitusi Madinah.**

**Perjuangan** (In.) Pol. 1. Struggle, effort, direction, aim. 2. Used during the Indonesian revolution for the national effort of Indonesians to achieve independence. 3. Used in the 1950s by politically active groups for indicating their aims. *Usage*: *amal-amal ___ agama*, actions taken for the sake of an Islamic purpose.

**Perkembangan** (In.) Pol. Development, often used in the economic, political and social sense for creation of modern institutions based on Western models. Syn: pembangunan.

**Permi.** *See* **Persatuan Muslimin Indonesia.**

**Persami.** *See* **Pergerakan Sarjana Muslimin Indonesia.**

**Persatuan Guru Agama Islam Republik Indonesia—PGAIRI** (In.) Assn. "The Union of the Islamic Teachers of the Republic of Indonesia," a special member of the Masjumi political party in the 1940s.

**Persatuan Guru Islam Indonesia—PGII** (In.) Assn. "The Indonesian Islamic Teachers' Union," formed in 1949 at the Kongres Muslim Indonesia as a unity organization of teachers' associations.

**Persatuan Islam—Persis;** Persatoean Islam (In.) Assn. "Islamic Union," the name of an Islamic association founded in 1926, belonging to the modernist Muslim (kaum muda) faction. It followed the view of Muslim "radicalism," an early expression of Islamic neofundamentalism. *See Al Lisan* and *Pembela Islam*.

**Persatuan Islam Tionghoa Indonesia—PITI** (In.) Assn. "The Indonesian Chinese Muslim Association," an organization founded in 1961 in Jakarta as a social and educational association. In 1972 it changed its name to Pembina Iman Tauhid Islam—PITI.

**Persatuan Mahasiswa Islam Indonesia—PMII** (In.) Assn. "The Indonesian Islamic Student Association," founded in 1956 was affiliated with the Nahdlatul Ulama. It was active in the Guided Democracy period in the interest of Muslims and took part in the Cipayung forums for promoting a role for Islam in national development in the 1970s.

**Persatuan Muslimin Indonesia—Permi** (In.) Assn. "The Indonesian Muslims Association," a West Sumatran political movement founded in 1932 and broken up by the Dutch in 1937 as a threat to internal order.

**Persatuan Organisasi Buruh Islam Seluruh Indonesia—PORBISI** (In.) Assn. "The All-Indonesia Islamic Workers Association," was a special member of the Masjumi political party in the 1950s.

**Persatuan Sarjana Muslim Indonesia** (In.) Assn. "The Indonesian Muslim Intellectual's Association," formed in 1964 as a means of politically organizing Muslims for the Guided Democracy period.

**Persatuan Tarbiyah Islamiyah—Perti** (In.) Assn. "Islamic Education Union," an association, founded in 1928 at Bukittingi, representing the interests of traditionalist Muslims of Minangkabau, organized in reaction to modernist Muslim calls for change in matters regarding worship. An independent political party in the 1950s, in the 1990s it was associated with Golkar.

**Persatuan Ulama Seluruh Aceh—PUSA** (In.) Assn. "The All Aceh Union of Religious Scholars," the name of a noted organization that coordinated anti-Dutch activity in the Acehnese area beginning in 1939.

**Persatuan Ummat Islam—PUI** (In.) Assn. "The Islamic Believers' Union," a West Javanese Muslim movement centering on education, economics, and social welfare activities founded in 1952.

**Persis.** *See* **Persatuan Islam.**

**Pertama, Yang Maha** (In.) Theo. A name of God indicating He precedes all other things in time and status.

**Pertanian Nadhlatul Ulama** (In.) Assn. "Farmers of the Nahdlatul Ulama," an association of agriculture freeholders founded in the 1950s, which represents small farmers' interests and promotes traditionalist religious activities.

**Perti**. *See* **Persatuan Tarbiyah Islamiyah.**

**Perubahan** (In.) Anthro. Change, usually in the sense of modernization. *Usage*: ___ *sosial*, social change.

**Perwiranegara, H. Alamsyah Ratu**. *See* **Menteri Agama.**

**Pesantren** (In.) Educ. Boarding schools for the study of Islamic sciences with a long history dating back to the Buddhist period. Stress is placed on traditional techniques of learning—repetition and memorization—in mastering standard religious sources. Pesantren have a high reputation in the Indonesian Muslim community for producing able graduates with a good grounding in moral values. *Usage*: *anti-*___, expressions of dislike of pesantrens and the religious system they represent, made from various quarters over time. *Dunia* ___, the world of the pesantren; *kehidupan* ___, life in the pesantren; *kurikulum* ___, curriculum of the pesantren; *lingkungan* ___, the environment and living in a pesantren; *lurusan* ___, the morality of the pesantren; *masalah ke*___*an*, the subject of pesantren education and its value; *pendidikan* ___, pesantren education.

**Pesantren Tebuireng**. *See* **Pondok Pesantren Tebuireng**.

**Pesta** (Jav.) Pop Islam. Formerly a ritual meal in which spiritual powers were at issue. Islamic prayers and the concept of alms were incorporated so that the feasts could be regarded as "Islamic." Syn: selamatan, kenduri.

**Petangan** (Jav.) Pop. Islam. In Javanese religious practice, the use of numbers for forecasting auspicious and inauspicious occasions.

**PGAIRI**. *See* **Persatuan Guru Agama Islam Republik Indonesia.**

**PGAN**. *See* **Pendidikan Guru Agama Negara.**

**PGII**. *See* **Persatuan Guru Islam Indonesia**.

**PHI**. *See* **Perjalanan Hadji Islam.**

**Piagam Jakarta** (In.) Pol. "Jakarta Charter," a name used by Muslim political activists to refer to a document produced in 1945 by a council of Muslim political leaders. It called for Muslims to be governed by Islamic law in the new state of Indonesia. Although leaders of the assembly preparing independence documents agreed to its inclusion in the new constitution, the assembly at large was unwilling to accept it.

**Pidana** (In.) Pol. Criminal matters.
*Usage*: *kitab undang-undang* ___, criminal code; *perkara* ___, criminal matters.

**PII**. *See* **Pelajar Islam Indonesia**.

*Pilihan Timoer* (In./Mal.) Lit. title. "Choice of the East," a periodical of Malayan and Indonesian students studying at Al Azhar University in Cairo, 1927-1928.

**Pitrah**. Spelling variant. *See* **Fitrah**.

**PITI**. *See* **Persatuan Islam Tionghoa Indonesia**.

**PKI**. *See* **Partai Komunis Indonesia**.

**PMII**. *See* **Pergerakan Mahasiswa Islam Indonesia**.

**PMPI**. *See* **Pemuda Mahasiswa Pelajar Islam**.

**Poligami** (In.); Polygamy (Eur.) 1. Juris. The social concept, practiced historically by Muslims and justified by Islamic scriptures, for marriage by men to more than one woman at a time. 2. Pol. The practice of multiple marriages by men and the discussion and debate surrounding the issue in the press and in policy bodies during most of the twentieth century.

**Pondok** (In.) (Ar: funduq) Educ. The name given religious boarding schools in some parts of Southeast Asia, usually outside of Java. Syn: pesantren.

**Pondok Modern Gontor Ponorogo** (In.) Educ. A madrasah founded in 1926 in East Java which stressed a melding of religious subjects, Arabic language, and general subjects.

**Pondok Pesantren Tebuireng** (In.) Educ. A pesantren school located in Jombang, East Java. Founded 1899 it came under the influence of K.H. Hasyim Asy'arie (d.1947), who reformed the teaching of Arabic and made other changes in teaching to provide better understanding of subject matter. The Pesantren Tebuireng has maintained a reputation of progressivism while remaining traditionalist in doctrine.

**PORBISI**. *See* **Persatuan Organisasi Buruh Islam Seluruh Indonesia**.

**Portugis** (In.) Hist. The seafarers from Portugal who explored and established trading activities in South and Southeast Asia in the sixteenth century. Using Malacca as their strong point and commercial center they established an active presence in the affairs of Indonesian kingdoms for about 100 years. Ultimately they were expelled from Malacca by the Dutch in 1641 and the Portuguese influence waned after that time. *Usage*: ___ *bangsa*, the Portuguese; *armada* ___, Portuguese fleet; *imperialisme* ___, Portuguese imperialism; *kekuatan militer* ___, Portuguese military power; *orang-orang* ___, the Portuguese; *serdadu* ___, Portuguese soldiers.

**PPP**. *See* **Partai Persatuan Pembangunan**.

**Prawata, Sultan**. *See* **Demak**.

**Prawirodirjo, Sentot**. *See* **Sentot Prawirodirjo**.

**Prawoto, Raden**. *See* **Muria, Sunan**.

**Prawoto Mangkusasmito** (In.) Biog. (d. 1970). Last leader of the Masjumi political organization in 1945 and a leading economist associated with the Muhammadiyah movement. *See* **Madjelis Sjuro Muslimin Indonesia**.

**Priayi** (In.); priyayi (Jav.) Anthro. A sociological group found primarily in the areas dominated by Javanese. The term identifies a group of people characterized by status in the traditional Javanese civil service. *Usage*: *golongan* ___, priayi grouping of society.

**Primbon** (In.) Lit. title. Books published by early religious scholars on Java for teaching Islamic matters. They contained various Islamic quotations, various prayers and dealt with medicine, secret matters and mystical themes. Syn: suluk.

**Priyayi**. Spelling variant. *See* **Priayi**.

**PRRI/Permesta**. *See* **Pemerintah Revolusioner Republik Indonesia**.

**PSII**. *See* **Partai Sarekat Islam Indonesia**.

**PTAIN**. *See* **Perguruan Tinggi Agama Islam Negeri**.

**Puasa** (In.) Juris. Fasting, indicating the ritual fast undertaken during the month of Ramadan. Syn: saum, shiyam.
*Usage*: *ber*___, to undertake the fast; *buka* ___, to end or break the fast; *bulan* ___, *Ramadan*, the month of fasting; *masuk dan keluar* ___, to begin and end fasting; *melakukan ibadah* ___, to undertake the fast; *permulaan ibadah* ___, the beginning of the rite of fasting; *terus ber*___, to continue fasting.

**Puasa Sunnah**; puasa sunnat (In.) Doct. "Meritorious Fasting," undertaken outside of the obligatory period of Ramadan. This is usually done on the 10th day of the month of Muharram, on the 9th of Zulhijah in connection with the pilgrimage, the first four days of Syawal, or other times, such as two days a week, for piety.

**PUI**. *See* **Persatuan Ummat Islam**.

**Puji** (In.) Trad. Praiseworthy. *Usage*: *ter*___, praiseworthy in character, a term applied to some transmitters of Traditions (hadis), who are unlikely to have modified or fabricated reports of the Prophet Muhammad's words and behavior.

**Purdah** (Urdu) Juris. Wearing clothing that covers the body and hair, done by Muslim women out of piety. Syn: jilbab.

**PUSA**. *See* **Persatuan Ulama Seluruh Aceh**.

**Pusaka** (In.) Hist. 1. Royal regalia of the Islamic kingdoms of Southeast Asia. The term included weapons, emblems of office, betel-use instruments, and books, all regarded as blessed and containing power (keramat) for the support of the ruler and his court.

*Puspa Wiraja. See Hikayat Baktiar.*

**Putihan** (Jav.) Anthro. The Muslim who seriously observes Islamic worship and behavior. Syn: santri.

# Q

**Al Qabidh** (Ar: al-qābiḍ) Theo. A name of God meaning "The Restrainer."

**Qabliyah** (Ar: qābiliyyah) Juris. Preparation. *Usage*: *sembahyang sunnat* ___, the allowable voluntary prayer prior to required worship; *sunnat* ___ *juma'at*, the allowable preparatory phrases addressed to God prior to the Friday prayer.

**Qada'**; qadha; qadla. Spelling variants. *See* **Kada**.

**Qadar**. Spelling variant. *See* **Kadar**.

**Al Qadar** (Ar: al-qadar) Qur. "(Night of) Power," the ninety-seventh chapter of the Qur'an. A very short, lyrical chapter telling how God sets the fate of all humans.

**Qadariyah**; Qodariyah (Ar: qadariyyah) Doct. A group in early Islam which believed that humans had complete control over their own actions, in contrast to the Jabbariyah, who believed God determined all actions.

**Qadha**. Spelling variant. *See* **Kada**.

**Qadhi**; Qadi. Spelling variants. *See* **Kadi**.

**Al Qadim** (Ar: al-qadīm) Theo. A name of God meaning "The Eternal."

**Al Qaadir**; Al Qadiir (Ar: al-qādir) Theo. A name of God meaning "The All Powerful." Syn: Yang Maha Berkuasa; Muqtadir.

**Qadiriyah**. Spelling variant. *See* **Kadiriah**.

**Qadiyan**; qadian (Urdu) Doct. The branch of the Ahmadiyah sect which maintains its founder, Mirza Ghulam Ahmad (d. 1908), was a prophet. This claim and the missionary activities of

the Ahmadiyah Qadiyan have consistently alarmed Indonesian Muslims and each generation has spoken out against its presence in the region.
*Usage*: *faham* ___, the thinking of the Qadiyan Sect.

**Qadla**. *See* **Kada**.

**Qaaf**; qaf (Ar: qāf) Qur. The fiftieth chapter of the Qur'an, named for the Arabic letter Qaf. The chapter states that the Qur'an is a reminder for the people who correctly fear God. It is also known as Al Baasiqaat.

**Al Qahhaar**; Al Qahhar (Ar: al-qahhār) Theo. A name of God meaning "The Victorious." Syn: Yang Maha Tinggi.

**Qa'idah**. Spelling variant. *See* **Kaidah**.

**Al Qalam** (Ar: al-qalam) Qur. 1. "The Pen," the sixty-eighth chapter of the Qur'an. A medium-length, lyrical chapter in which God affirms that Muhammad is indeed His Messenger and that his detractors will ultimately suffer for their ridicule of his mission. It is also known as Nun, after the Arabic letter.
2. An alternate title for Surah Al 'Alaq, the ninety-sixth chapter of the Qur'an.

**Al Qamah** (Ar: al-qāmah) Trad. A title assigned to a person from the second generation of Muslims. Syn: Tabi'in.

**Al Qamar** (Ar: al-qamar) Qur. "The Moon," the fifty-fourth chapter of the Qur'an. It tells of the Day of Judgment and God's punishment of those who have gone astray.

**Qanun**. Spelling variant. *See* **Kanun**.

**Qari'**. Spelling variant. *See* **Kari**.

**Qariah**. Spelling variant. *See* **Kariah**.

**Al Qaari'ah**; Al Qari'ah; Al Qari'ah (Ar: al-qāri'ah) Qur. "The Calamity," the 101st chapter of the Qur'an. A short, lyrical chapter describing the terror of humans on the Day of Judgment.

**Qarun** (Ar: qārūn) Qur. The leader of a rebellion against the Prophet Musa and a general detractor of Musa as a prophet.

**Al Qashash** (Ar: al-qaṣaṣ) Qur. "Stories," the twenty-eighth chapter of the Qur'an. The chapter tells those who fled from Makkah to Madinah to save the religion that their effort would be rewarded.

**Al Qashthalani** (Ar: abū al-'abbās al-qasṭalānī) Biog. (d. 1517). Arab scholar of the middle period who wrote on Tradition analysis, theology, and the life of the Prophet Muhammad. *See Mawahibul Laduniyah.*

**Qasidah**. Spelling variant. *See* **Kasidah**.

**Al Qasimi** (Ar: muḥammad jamāl ... ad-dīn al-qāsimī) Biog. (d. 1914). Egyptian writer and scholar on history and the Qur'an. *See Mahasinut Takwil* and **Tafsir**.

**Qathi**. Spelling variant. *See* **Kadi**.

**Qauliyyah**. *See* **Sunan**.

**Al Qawiyy**; Al Qawy (Ar: al-qawī) Theo. Name of God meaning "The Strong." Syn: Yang Maha Kuat.

**Qaynuqa'** (Ar: qaynuqā') Hist. A Jewish tribe residing in Madinah, that Muhammad expelled as constituting a security threat.

**Al Qayyum**; Al Qayyuum (Ar: al-qayyūm) Theo. A name of God meaning "The Self-Subsistent."

**Qias**, Qiyas. Spelling variant. *See* **Kias**.

**Qiblat**. Spelling variant. *See* **Kiblat**.

**Qimar** (Ar: qimār) Juris. Dice or any game of chance. Muslim jurisprudence holds such games to be an infraction of correct conduct.

**Qira'at; qir'at; qiraat**; qira'ah. Spelling variants. *See* **Kiraat**.

**Qiradh** (fr. Ar: qirḍ) Juris. Borrowing or lending money, which could involve the person in unauthorized financial practices known as riba.

**Qishah-qishah**. *See* **Ilmu Tafsier**.

**Al Qiyaamah**; Al-Qiamah; Al-Qiyamah (Ar: al-qiyāmah) Qur. "Resurrection," the seventy-fifth chapter of the

Qur'an. A short, lyrical chapter asserting God's power to create and ultimately to bring all creatures to judgment.

**Qiyas**. Spelling variant. *See* **Kias**.

**Qodariyah**. Spelling variant. *See* **Qadariyah**.

**Qodiriyah**. Spelling variant. *See* **Kadiriah**.

**Al Qudduus**; Al Qudus (Ar: al-quddūs) Theo. A name of God meaning "The Holiest." Yang Maha Suci.

**Qudrat**. Spelling variant. *See* **Kodrat**.

**Qudsi**; qudsy. *See* **Hadits**.

**Qunut**. Spelling variant. *See* **Kunut**.

**Quraisy**, Quraisj. Spelling variants. *See* **Kuraisy**.

*Al Qur'an; Al-Quran* (In.); *Al Kor'an* (Ar: Qur'ān) Doct. The primary scripture of Islam which Muslims believe was revealed by Allah to Muhammad through the medium of the angel Jibrail. Muslims believe the Qur'an was a miracle and that it serves as a guide for human conduct.

*Usage*: *ayat hukum* ___, the verses of the Qur'an dealing with injunctions incumbent on believers; *berdasar* ___, to base a decision on the Qur'an; *dalil-dalil* ___, the Qur'an as basis of a decision; *digariskan oleh* ___ *dan hadis*, as outlined by Qur'an and Traditions; *hafal* ___, to memorize the Qur'an; *kitab suci* ___, the Qur'an as a holy book; *membacakan* ___, to recite the Qur'an; *penjelasan* ___, *pentafsiran* ___, commentary provided on the contents of the Qur'an; *tafsir* ___, commentary on the Qur'an.

**Qur'an Bahriyah** (fr. Ar: qur'ān and al-baḥriyyah) Qur. A Qur'an with a format especially intended for memorization.

*Al Qur'an dari Masa ke Masa*. *See* **Munawar Khalil, Muhammad**.

*Al Qur'an Kariem; Al Quraanul Karim* (Ar: al-qur'ān al-karīm) Qur. The name given to the contemporary versions of the Qur'an that are considered descendants of the Utsman standard version. Indonesia adopted its version in 1980.

**Qur'an Stambul** (In.) Pop. Islam. A miniature Qur'an often given blessing by a soothsayer and worn as an amulet against danger or against supernatural interference with the wearer.

**Qurayza** (Ar: al-qurayẓah) Hist. A Jewish tribe residing in Madinah whose members Muhammad had massacred or sold into slavery as punishment for siding with external enemies.

**Qurban** (In.); kurban; korban (Ar: qurbān) Juris. Sacrifice of an animal as part of worship on the festival of Idul Adha.

**Al Qurthubi** (Ar: shams ad-dīn muḥammad ... al-qurṭubī) Biog. (d. 1273). A Syafii legalist in the Middle East who wrote important works on eschatology, Tradition analysis, and the Qur'an. *See Jami' Akham* and **Tafsir**.

**Qutub, Sayyid** (Ar: sayyid quṭb) Biog. (d. 1966) A martyred Egyptian journalist known for his writings which gave ideological direction to neofundamentalist thinking. In particular he wrote about the West as the modern "Age of Ignorance" (jahiliah). *See Fi Zhilailul Qur'an* and **Tafsir**.

# R

**Rabb** (Ar: rabb) Theo. "Lord," often used in the sense of divine being or God. *Usage*: ___*ul 'alamin*, Lord of the Worlds; ___*ul 'Izzah*, Lord of Might.

**Ar Rabbun** (Ar: ar-rabb) Theo. A name of God meaning "The Possessor."

**Rabi'atul Adawiyah** (Ar: rābi'ah al-'adawiyyah) Biog. (d. 801). An early saint of Islam who lived an ascetic life and explored a mystical relationship which extolled love and intimacy with God. She is also famous for her short and pithy poetry and proverbs.

**Rabithah Alam Islamy Kerohanian** (Ar: ar-rābiṭah al-islāmiyyah) Assn. "The World Muslim League," an association of Muslims, based in Makkah, with chapters in various regions of the world, to promote cooperation among Muslims. It is nongovernmental.

**Ar Rabithah Al Alawiyah** (Ar: ar-rābiṭah al-'alawiyyah) Assn. "The Alawite League," an association of Arabs primarily from Southern Arabia with a traditionalist Muslim viewpoint who, in 1938, joined with the more modernist Al Irsyad to form the Persatuan Arab Indonesia.

**Rabiulakhir** (In.) (Ar: rabī' al-ākhir, rabī' ath-thānī) Cal. The fourth month of the Islamic calendar, with the meaning "the second spring."

**Rabiulawwal** (In.) (Ar: rabī' al-awwal) Cal. The third month of the Islamic calendar, with the meaning of "the first spring." On the 12th is Maulid, the birthday of the Prophet Muhammad.

**Rachmat, Raden**. *See* **Ampel, Sunan Raden Rahmat**.

**Ar Ra'd**; Ar Ra'ad (Ar: ar-ra'd) Qur. "Thunder," the thirteenth chapter of the Qur'an. This chapter deals with God's relationship with humans, who are pictured as His chief creation.

**Raden** (In.) Title. 1. Title of respect, indicating descent from royalty. *See* following word. 2. Title of religious scholars on Kalimantan. Syn: kiai, kangjang.

**Raden Adipati**. *See* **Pepatih Dalam**.

**Raffles, Sir Stamford** (English) Biog. (d. 1826) Lieutenant governor of Java under the English inter-regnum in the Indies 1811-16. He reformed the administration and took a deep interest in Javanese history and folkways. Later, he founded modern Singapore. *See History of Java.*

**Al Rafi'i** (Ar: ar-rāfi') Theo. Name of God meaning "The Exalter."

**Rafi'i, Muhammad** (Ar: 'abdulkarim muḥammad rāfi'ī) Biog. (d. 1226). Arab scholar of the late middle period known for his writings on Syafii jurisprudence. *See Thabaqaatusy Syafiiyah* and *Al Muharrar.*

**Raafi'ud Darajaat**; Rafi'l Darajat (Ar: ar-rāfi' ad-darajāt) Theo. Name of God meaning "The Giver."

**Al Rahim** (Ar: ar-raḥīm) Theo. Name of God meaning "The Compassionate."

**Rahimullah** (In.); Rahimullah (Ar: raḥīmullāh) Expres. "The Compassion of God," said or written after the mention of the name of an important personage of early Islam.
*Usage*: *Imam Syafii* ___, Imam Syafii, the Mercy of God [on him].

**Ar Rahmaan** (Ar: ar-raḥmān) Qur. "The Merciful," the fifty-fifth chapter of the Qur'an. It tells of God's mercy to humankind and His blessings to them on earth and in the Hereafter.

**Ar Rahman** (In.) Theo. A name of God meaning "The Merciful."

**Rahman, Fathur**. *See* **Menteri Agama**.

**Rahmat** (In.) (Ar: ar-raḥmah) Gen. vocab. Mercy and compassion.
*Usage*: *pulang ke* ___*ullah*, to die; *rasufir* ___, a title of Muhammad, meaning "The Carrier of Mercy."

**Rahmat, Yang Maha** (In.) Theo. A name of God meaning "The Most Merciful."

**Rahmatullah, Sultan**. *See* **Banjar**.

**Rais Am** (Ar: ra'īs 'āmm) Title. "General Chair (of the Consultative Council of the Nahdlatul Ulama)," the highest position among religious scholars in the organization. For a roster of holders of that office, see Nadhlatul Ulama.

**Raja** (In.) Hist. 1. "Ruler," of a petty kingdom of the Malay-Indonesian world in the precolonial era. The term was somewhat confused with and supplanted by "sultan" with the arrival of Islam. It remains a title of royalty throughout Muslim Southeast Asia. 2. Historical reference by twentieth-century Indonesian writers referring to the rulers of the Islamic states period of history, i.e., the fifteenth to seventeenth centuries, regardless of the actual titles in use by individual rulers at the time.
*Usage*: *ke*___*an*, royalty, royalness; ___-___ *anak negeri*, local rulers.

**Rajab** (In.) (Ar: rajab) Cal. The seventh month of the Islamic calendar, with the meaning "the revered month." The 27th is Lailatul Mikraj, the celebration of the Night Journey of Muhammad.

**Rakaat** (In.) (Ar: rak'ah) Juris. The cycle of postures in the ritual prayer, consisting of standing, bowing, prostrating, and sitting.

**Ramadan**; Ramadhan (In.); Ramadlan; Romadhan (Ar: ramaḍān) Cal. The ninth month of the Islamic calendar, meaning "the month of great heat." It is also the fasting month for Muslims in which all healthy adult Muslims abstain from food, water, and sexual activity from sunrise to sunset. The month is considered holy because the first section of the Qur'an was revealed in it. The 27th is widely believed to be Lailatul Qadar, the night of power, when the Qur'an was

originally revealed to Muhammad.
*Usage*: *bulan* ___, the month of Ramadan.

*Ramayana* (In.) Lit. title. The great cycle of stories from Hinduism popular in Central Java and adapted to the various theatre productions there. Sunan Kalijaga used variations of the story along with shadow puppets (wayang kulit) to spread lessons of Islam. He used the following figures as examples of various doctrines: Puntadewa and Samiaji (Confession of faith), Bima and Werkudara (Five daily prayers), Arjuna (Poor tax), Nakula and Sahadenja (Fasting and Pilgrimage).

**Ar Ramli, Syamsuddin** (Ar: shams ad-dīn muḥammad ar-ramlī) Biog. (d. 1596). Arab scholar of the middle period whose works on Syafii jurisprudence have been popular among religious scholars in Indonesia. *See Kitabun Nihayah*.

**Ar Raniri, Nuruddin** (Ar: nūr ad-dīn ar-ranīrī) 1. Biog. (d. 1658). Arab missionary-scholar who stressed orthodox mysticism in the Indonesian-Malay world in the seventeenth century. Prolific writer of standard Islamic books in Malay. *See Bustanul Salatin*. 2. Educ. Name of a national Islamic studies institute (IAIN) at Banda Aceh. *See* **Institut Agama Islam Negara**.

**Raqib** (Ar: raqīb) Doct. The name of an angel who records all the good actions of humans.

**Al Raqib** (Ar: ar-raqīb) Theo. A name of God meaning "The Vigilant."

**Rasufir Rahmah** (Ar: rasul ar-raḥmah) Doct. Title of Muhammad meaning, "The Carrier of Mercy."

**Rasul** (In.) (Ar: rasūl) Doct. The messenger of God, indicating one sent by Allah with a message for humans. Muhammad is considered to be the last messenger.
*Usage*: *masa* ___*ullah*, the era of Muhammad, the Prophet of God; *sunnah* ___, *sunnat* ___, the manner in which the Prophet Muhammad lived as an example to other Muslims.

**Rasul, Haji**. *See* **Amrullah, Abdul Karim**.

**Rasulilahu** (In.); Rasulullah (Ar: rasūlullāh) Doct.

Muhammad, the Messenger of God.
*Usage*: *keturunan* ___, descent of the Prophet Muhammad's descendants; *makam* ___, the tomb of the Prophet Muhammad; *mentaati* ___, follow the injunctions of Islam derived from the words and behavior of the Prophet Muhammad preserved in Traditions (hadis).

**Rasyid.** *See* **Khalifah-Khalifah Rasyidin.**

**Al Rasyid** (Ar: ar-reshid) Theo. A name of God meaning "The Just."

**Rasyid Ridha**; Rasyid Redha (Ar: muḥammad rashīd riḍā') Biog. (d. 1935). Syrian Arab who taught in Egypt and founded a modernist Muslim school of thought that emphasized modernization in accord with the teachings of Muhammad's Companions. *See Tafsirul Manar* and **Tafsir**.

**Rasyidi, H. M.** *See* **Menteri Agama.**

**Ratib Saman** (fr. Ar: rātib) Myst. A Sufi recitation session, often held on Monday night, in which the recitations of the religious formulas (zikir) are chanted in a loud and noisy manner so as to induce excitement and euphoria.

**Ratib Zikir** (Ar: dhikr rātib) Myst. Special recitations of various phrases undertaken by mystics as part of their religious exercises. *See* **Zikir**.

**Ratu Adil** (Jav: ratu adil) Pop. Islam. In Javanese folklore the future savior who will arrive to usher in an age of peace and prosperity. He is sometimes related to the popular Muslim concept of the Imam Mahdi. *See* **Mahdi** and **Diponegoro.**

**Ar Rauuf**; Ar Ra-uuf; Ra'uf (Ar: ar-ra'ūf) Theo. A name of God meaning "The Gentle." Same as Yang Menyayangi.

**Rawatib** (In.) Juris. Optional prayer undertaken before or after required prayer.
*Usage*: *sembahyang sunnat* ___, permissible optional prayer.

**Raya** (In.) Anthro. To celebrate, to observe.
*Usage*: *me___an*, to celebrate the birthday of the Prophet Muhammad; *me___an mikraj nabi*, to observe the ascension of the Prophet Muhammad.

**Ar Razi, Fakruddin** (Ar: fakr ad-dīn ar-rāzī) Biog. (d. 1209). A Syafii scholar from Iran who wrote on philosophy, history, and theology. He prepared an important commentary on the Qur'an called *Mafatihul Ghaib* (The Keys of the Unseen). *See* **Tafsir**.

**Ar Razzaaq** (Ar: razzāq) Theo. A name of God meaning "The Provider."

**Redha**. Spelling variant. *See* **Rela**.

**Redha, Muhammad Rasyid**. *See* **Rasyid Ridha**.

**Regen** (In.); Regenten (Dutch) Hist. Local aristocracy with various titles (e.g. pepatih) who ran the general administration of princely houses during the colonial period.

**Rela** (In.); redha; ridlo (Ar: riḍā'). Doct. Favor, goodwill, blessings.
*Usage*: *ke___an Allah, ke___an Tuhan*, favor of God; *mohon ampun ke___annya*, ask God's favor in pardoning (sin).

**Remaja Masjid** (In.) Assn. "The Mosque Youth Association," founded in the 1970s. It meets after regular worship, such as the morning (subuh) and Friday prayers, in order to indoctrinate youth and prepare them for leadership roles.

**Rencana Pembangunan Lima Tahun—Repelita** (In.) Pol. "Five Year Development Plan," a staple of Indonesian economic planning since the late 1960s. Religious development, such as building houses of worship and work with scripture are part of the plans. The dates of the plans are as follows: 1969-74 (Repelita I), 1974-79 (Repelita II), 1979-84 (Repelita III), 1984-89 (Repelita IV), and 1989-94 (Repelita V).

**Repangi, Ahmad** (In.) Biog. (d. 1875). Sufi shaykh from Central Java who wrote several tracts using Javanese in the Arabic script as his medium. He is illustrative of a group of Muslim adepts who used that language.

**Repelita**. *See* **Rencana Pembangunan Lima Tahun**.

**Resolusi Jihad** (In.) Hist. A resolution of the Nahdlatul Ulama on 22 October 1945 which stated that a holy war (jihad) existed for the Indonesians in defense of their homeland in pursuing the Indonesian revolution and that every Muslim must participate.

**Revolusi Indonesia** (In.) Pol. "Indonesian Revolution," used officially and popularly to refer to the events of 1945 to 1949 which followed the declaration of independence by Indonesian leaders. It is a key event in the history of the Indonesian republic and implies a struggle for proper national aspiration.

**Riayat Syah, Sultan Alauddin**. *See* **Aceh.**

**Riayat Syah, Sultan Ali**. *See* **Aceh.**

**Riba** (In.) (Ar: ribā) Juris. Usury; in general any unjustified increase of capital for which no compensation is given.
*Usage*: ___ *nasiah*, credit involving usury; ___ *qiradh*, borrowing involving usury; ___ *salaf*, lending involving usury.
*Hukum* ___, the law or principle of usury in Islam; *melarang* ___, to forbid usurious transactions; *membolehkan* ___, to permit usury; *mengharamkan* ___, to judge as usury (and disallow as permitted); *persoalan* ___, the issue of usury in Islam; *transaksi* ___, a usurious transaction; *tukang-tukang* ___, money lenders.

**Rida, Rashid.** *See* **Rasyid Ridha.**

**Ridlo.** Spelling variant. *See* **Rela.**

**Ridwan** (Ar: riḍwān) Doct. An angel who guards the portals of heaven.

**Rifa'iyah** (rifa'iyyah) Myst. A mystical order of Islam founded by Muhammad Ar Rifa'i (d 1183) in Asia Minor. Known for using sharp objects to pierce the body while in a mystical state.

**Rijksbestierder.** *See* **Pepatih Dalam.**

**Riqah** (Ar: raqīq) Juris. A freed or runaway slave without means of support who is eligible for funds from the distribution of the poor tax.

*Ar Risalah* (Ar: ar-rislāh fī usūl al-fiqh) Lit. title. "Introduction to the Principles of Jurisprudence," by Muhammad As Syafii (d.

820), regarded as one of the seminal works by the founder of the Syafii school of jurisprudence.

**Riwayat** (In.) (Ar: riwāyat) Trad. The transmitting or relating of the contents of a report concerning the words and behavior of the Prophet Muhammad. The major categories are: ___ **Ahli Bid'ah** (Ar: ahli bid'ah) A line of transmission which included people from suspect sects who had ideological motivation to fabricate or alter reports. Such reports are weak. ___ **Akakir 'Anish Shogo'ir** (al-akabir ani aṣ-aṣghā'ir) Two people adjacent to one another in a line of transmission in which the receiver is younger than the giver. ___ **Aqran** (Ar: al-aqrān) Two people adjacent to one another in a line of transmission who are close to the same age, which places doubts on the authenticity of the transmission. ___ **Ikhwan wal Akhawaati** (Ar: al-ikhwān wa al-akhawāt). Three people adjacent to one another in a line of transmission who were brothers. ___ **Mukh-talith** (Ar: al-mukhtaliṭ) A line of transmission which underwent change because of the deterioration of the memory or skills of one of the transmitters. Such reports are weak. ___ **Penolak** (In: tolak) A report rejected as faulty by one of the people in the line of transmission. Such reports are usually judged as weak. ___ **As Sabiq dan Al Lahiq** (Ar: as-sābiq wa-llāḥiq) A recognition that the lines of transmission differ in length because of the different lifespans of people in them. *Usage*: *di__kan*, to relate or recite a Tradition. *See* **Ilmu Riwayat Hadis**.

*Riyadhush Shalihin* (Ar: riyād aṣ-ṣāliḥīn) Lit. title. "Gardens of the Righteous," a jurisprudential text long popular in Indonesia, written by An Nawawi (d. 1278).

**Roh**. Spelling variant. *See* **Ruh**.

**Roh Suci** (In. fr. Ar: rūh and San: suci) Indonesian variant of Arabic Ruhul Qudus. *See* **Ruhul Qudus**.

**Rohani** (In.) (Ar: rūḥ) Doct. Spiritual.
*Usage*: *ke___an*, spirituality; *amalan-amalan* ___, spiritual attainments; *kebangkitan* ___, spiritual development; *kesehatan jasmani dan* ___,

physical and spiritual health; *rasa ___iyah*, spiritual sense.

**Rokh**. Spelling variant. *See* **Ruh**.

**Romadhan**. Spelling variant. *See* **Ramadan**.

**Ronkel, Philippus Samuel van** (Dutch) Biog. (d. 1954). Dutch scholar who served with the Dutch civil service in the Netherlands Indies. He was editor for the Batavia Society for Arts and Legal Studies (Bataviaasch Genootschap van Kunsten en Wetenschappen) and later, at Leiden, an editor for the Royal Institute of Linguistics and Anthropology (Koninklijk Institut voor Taal-, Land- en Volkenkunde).

**Rowi Hadis** (Ar: rāwī ḥadīth) Trad. A person among the first generations of Muslims who is mentioned as a transmitter of a report relating the words and behavior of the Prophet Muhammad.
*Usage*: ___ *genap lemah*, a transmitter regarded as weak; *para* ___, transmitters as a collective group; *seorang* ___, an individual transmitter.

**Rububiyah** (Ar: rubūbiyyah) 1. Juris. The basic principles of Islamic jurisprudence. 2. Theo. God-like qualities.
*Usage*: *sifat* ___, God-like characteristics.

**Ruh**, roh; rohi (In.); rohk (Ar: rūḥ) Theo. Spirit.
*Usage*: ___ *dan tubuh*; with soul and body involved; ___ *Islam*, Islamic spirit or essence.

*Ruhul Ma'ani* (Ar: rūḥ al-ma'ānī) Lit. title. Commentary on the Qur'an by Al Alusi (d. 1853)., which shows the influence of mysticism and interprets verses on the basis of their unexpressed meanings. *See* **Tafsir**.

**Ruhul Qudus** (In.) (Ar: rūḥ al-qudus) Doct. 1. The Holy Ghost to the Christians. 2. The angel Jibrail because he brings inspiration to prophets.

**Rujuk**; ruju' (In.) (Ar: rujū') Juris. Reconciliation in marriage. In Indonesia such matters are handled by the Islamic court.
*Usage*: *la* ___ *kepada isterinya*, he recalled his decision to divorce his wife.

**Rukun Iman** (In.) (Ar: rukn imān) Doct. The six basic beliefs of the Islamic religion: to God, to angels, to holy books, to prophets, to the Day of Judgment and to the complete power of God. *See* **Arkanul Iman.**

**Rukun Islam** (In.) (Ar: rukn islām) Doct. The five basic pillars of the Islamic religion: confession of the faith, prayer, fasting, pilgrimage, and alms to the poor. *See* **Arkanul Islam.**
*Usage*: *melaksanakan* ___-___ *Islam*, performing the five pillars of Islam; *pelaksanaan* ___-___ *Islam*, performance of the five pillars of Islam; ___-___ *yang lima*, the five pillars of Islam.

**Rukun Salat** (Ar: rukn ṣalāh) Doct. The essential elements of prescribed prayer and the order in which they are performed. *See* **Salat.**

**Ar Rum** (Ar: ar-rūm) Qur. The thirtieth chapter of the Qur'an, titled "The Romans." The chapter states that the Qur'an is compatible with human reason.

**Al Rumi, Muhammad Jalaluddin** (Ar: muḥammad jalāluddīn ar-rūmī) Biog. (d. 1273) A Persian poet from Central Asia who became the leading mystic of his age. His book, the voluminous *Masnawi*, is a classic for followers of mysticism, rivaling the Qur'an among them for inspiration.

**Ru'yah** (Ar: rū'yah) Juris. Sighting of the new moon to open or close the fasting month, as opposed to mathematically calculating the date.
*Usage*: *berdasarkan* ___, to base the decision to begin or end fasting on sighting the new moon; *masalah hisab dan* ___, the issue of determining the beginning or end of the fasting period by calculation or sighting.

# S

**Saba'**; Sabak (Ar: saba') Qur. "The People of Saba'," the thirty-fourth chapter of the Qur'an. It tells of punishments visited on the Sabaens for turning aside from Allah.

**Sa'ban**. Spelling variant. *See* **Syakban.**

**Sabang ke Merauke** (In.) Pol. A popular phrase indicating the extent of the Indonesian nation, from Sabang at the extreme tip of Sumatra to Merauke in Southeast Irian Jaya.

**Sabar** (In.) (Ar: ṣabr) Doct. Patience; not giving way to anger. In Islam such behavior is regarded as a virtue.

**Sabda** (In.) Trad. "Stated," used in the reciting or writing the Traditions of the Prophet to indicate Muhammad's pronouncement or comment on some matter.
*Usage*: *ber* ___, to recite the Tradition of the Prophet Muhammad.

**Sabdho Pandito Ratu** (Jav.) Title. Union of scholar and ruler, as occurred in the early days of the Demak kingdom in the fifteenth century.

**Sabil** (In.) (Ar: sabīl) Doct. Way, cause.
*Usage*: *ibnis* ___, wayfarer, who may be eligible for alms and the distribution of the poor tax; *orang perang* ___, the crusader, the person engaged in a war with a cause.

*Sabilul Muhtadin* (Ar: sabīl al-muhtadīn) Lit. title. "The Rightly Guided Path," a book on jurisprudence by Muhammad Arsyad Al Banjari (d. 1812), written in Melayu in Jawi script. It draws heavily on the works of well known Syafii legal scholars, i.e., Syarbini (d.

1570), Ramli (d. 1596) and Ibnu Hajar (d. 1567)

**Sabilillah** (In.) fi sabillah (Ar: fī sabīlullāh) "Fighting in the Way of God." 1. Doct. A person committed to a campaign for preserving or extending the standards of Islam on earth. Title often given to fighters for a holy cause. 2. Juris. The campaign itself.

**Sabilullah** (In.) Assn. "Fighting in the Way of God," an organization of youth organized as a paramilitary force during the Japanese occupation. They were later integrated with Indonesian forces during the revolution.

**Sab'iyah** (Ar: sab'iyyah) Doct. An important sect of Syiah Islam who believe that there were seven leaders (imams) of the true Muslim Community, i.e., Syiah, before the leadership became hidden. Syn: Ismailiyah.

**Sabt**. *See* **Yawmul Sabt**.

**Sadakah**. Spelling variant. *See* **Sedakah**.

**Sadakallahulazim**. (In.) (Ar: ṣadaq allāh al-'aẓīm) Expres. "The truth of God, Who is Almighty," a phrase said after reading from the Qur'an.

**Sadaqah**. Spelling variant. *See* **Sedakah**.

**Sadiliyyah** (Ar: shādhiliyyah) Myst. Name of a mystical order in Islam, founded by Abul Hassan Ali As Sadzili (d. 1256).

**Sa'dillah, Sultan**. *See* **Banjar**.

**Sadiq, Syekh Jakfar**. *See* **Kudus, Sunan**.

**Safar** (In.); Shafar (Ar: ṣafar) Cal. The second month, meaning "the month which is void."

**Sagar**. *See* **Neraka**.

**Sah** (In.) (Ar: ṣāḥ) Juris. Valid.

**Sahabat** (In.); shahabat (Ar: ṣaḥābah) Hist. The Companions of the Prophet, that is, any Muslim, who, as a Muslim, ever met the Prophet during his lifetime. The Companions are regarded as the proper interpreters of Islam because of that contact with Muhammad. Consequently they provided the

material about Muhammad which eventually came to be known as the "Way (sunnah)." Two groups are distinguished among them. The Muhajirinul Uwwal were those who accompanied Muhammad to Madinah from Makkah and the Anshar who were those from Madinah and elsewhere who joined his community after arrival in Madinah.
*Usage*: ___ *Isa*, the disciples of Isa (Jesus); ___ *nabi, para* ___ the Companions collectively.

**Sahih** (In.); shahih (Ar: ṣaḥīḥ) Trad. "Firm," a category indicating that transmissions or reports concerning the words and behavior of the Prophet Muhammad are considered authentic by the rules of analysis. ___ **Li Dzatihi** (Ar: li dhātih) All the reporters in a particular line of transmission are upright and not liable to falsehoods or even indeliberate change. ___ **Li Gharirihi** (Ar: li ghayrih). While some weak points exist in some lines of transmission, they are overcome with other lines of transmission that are undoubtedly accurate.

*As Sahih* (Ar: aṣ-ṣaḥīḥ) Lit. title. "Firm," a short title given to Tradition collections, referring to the use of Traditions in them judged to be authentic. The term is used to refer to collections by Al Bukhari (d. 870) and by Muslim (d. 873), together known as the *Shahiihaan*. *See* **'Ala Syar-thil Syaikhain**.

**Sa'i** (In.) (Ar: sa'y) Juris. Walking back and forth between the hills Safa and Marwah in Makkah as one of the rites of the pilgrimage.

**Sai Keirei** (Jap.) Hist. The deep bow toward Tokyo as a token of obeisance to the emperor which marked the commencement of every official Japanese function prior to the end of World War II. In Indonesia, this was part of a daily brief morning ceremony in all government offices during the Japanese occupation. The sai keirei was similar in form to the prostration (ruku') of Muslim ritual prayer and several 'ulama' objected to it on that basis. The Japanese maintained that the two prostrations were entirely different in purpose.

**Said, Joko**. *See* **Kalijaga, Sunan.**

**Said, Orang Muda Muhammad**. *See* **Kalijaga, Sunan**.

**Saidil Mursalin** (Ar: sayyid al-mursalīn) Title. "The Leader of All Apostles," a title assigned to the Prophet Muhammad.

**Saidina**; say'dani (In.); saiyidina, sayyidinah (Ar: sayyidīnah) Title. "Our leader." a title assigned to important personages in Muslim history, such as the Righteous Caliphs. *Usage*: *membaca* ___, to assign the title to someone.

**Saidina Panotogomo Kalipatullah** (Jav.) Title. Title of Javanese sultans asserting rule over Muslims and claiming to be representative of God on earth.

**Saifuddin Zuhri**. *See* **Zuhri, Saifuddin**.

**Sailan**. *See* **Samudera-Pasai**.

**Sains** (In.) Educ. Science, as related to modern scientific methodology and hypothesis. Most Indonesians regard science as an important tool to be used in modernization. Muslims favor its use, but believe Islamic standards must be used to give science direction fitting with God's purpose.

**Sa'ir**. *See* **Neraka**.

**Saiyidina**. Spelling variant. *See* **Saidina**.

**As Saajdah** (Ar: as-sajdah) Qur. "Prostration," the thirty-second chapter of the Qur'an. It deals with the Day of Judgment and God's punishment for disbelievers.

**Sakar** (In.); saqar (Ar: saqar) Doct. Hell. *See* **Neraka**.

**Salaf** (In.) (Ar: salaf) Hist. 1. Reference to the early community of Islam and its manner of belief and behavior. 2. Orthodox Sunni belief and behavior. Syn: ahlus sunnah wal jama'ah. *Usage*: *aliran* ___, *gerakan* ___, *golongan* ___*iyah*, groups following orthodox Sunni belief and behavior; *sunnah para* ___, the manner of religious practice among the early Muslim generations; *tafsir-tafsir* ___, the explanations about religion of the early Muslim generations.

**Salah** (In.) Juris. Wrong, false, or mistaken, often in the sense of involving sinful behavior or heretical beliefs. Ant: benar.
*Usage*: *ber___ melakukan dosa*, to be engaged in committing a sinful act.

**Salahuddin, Sultan.** *See* **Aceh.**

**Salam** (Ar: salām) 1. Expres. Peace, greetings. 2. Juris. A litany, which is pronounced from the minaret every Friday about half an hour before the call to the community prayer. This part of the liturgy is repeated inside the mosque before the beginning of the regular worship by several people with good voices.

**As Salaam**, As Salam (Ar: as-salām) Theo. A name of God meaning "The Peaceful."

**As Salam Alaykum**; as salamu 'alaikum. Spelling variants. *See* **Aszalamualaikum.**

**Salat** (In.); shalat (Ar: ṣalāh) Doct. Prayer. in the sense of formal, ritual prayer addressed to God required of every Muslim.
*Usage*: ___ *ashar*, afternoon prayer; ___ *gerhana bulan*, prayer at the eclipse of the moon; ___ *gerhana matahari*, prayer at the eclipse of the sun; ___ *'Id*, prayer held on the feast days of Idul Fithri and Idul Adha; ___ *'Id dilapangan*, the prayer held in an open area on the 'Id feast days; ___ *'Id di mesjid*, the prayer held in a mosque on the 'Id feast days; ___ *istisqa'*, prayer for rain; ___ *isya*, evening prayer; ___ jamaah, ___ *jum'ah*, Friday communal prayer; ___ *jama'ah*, prayer with an imam in front and others behind him; ___ *khusuf*, prayer at the eclipse of the moon; ___ *kusuf*, prayer at the eclipse of the sun; ___ *lima waktu*, the five daily prayer times; ___ *maghrib*, early evening prayer; ___ *maktubah*, the five daily prayer times; ___ *marid*, prayer for the sick; ___ *musafir*, prayer at the beginning and end of a journey; ___ *nawafil*, the five prayer times; ___ *rawatib*, optional prayer before or after regular prayer; ___ *subuh*, early morning prayer; ___ *sunnat*, optional prayer; ___ *tahajud*, optional prayer in the middle of the night; ___ *tarawih*, special night prayer often recited in the

evening during Ramadan; ___ *zuhur*, noonday prayer. *Mendirikan ___, melaksanakan ___, melakukan ___, mengerjakan ___, menusaikan ___, mengqada* ___, to perform ritual prayer at the prescribed times; *mengulang* ___, to continue praying; *rakaat* ___, a ritual prayer set; *waktu* ___, prayer time.

**Salat Id** (In.); Shalat Ied, Shalat Id (Ar: ṣalāt al-'id_) Doct. The prayer marking the festival of Idul Fitri, where the entire community is expected to come together in a open area for worship. In Indonesia many cities hold it in a central part of the city, although neighborhood gatherings also take place.

**Salat Janasah** (In.); shalat jenazah (Ar: ṣalāt al-janāzah) Juris. The prayer held at the funeral of a believing Muslim.

**Salawat**; selawat; shalawat (In.) (Ar: ṣalawāt) 1. Expres. Good wishes, salutations. 2. Expres. The Arabic expression (Ar: allāhumma ṣālli 'alā muḥammad wa 'alā āli muhammad) "Blessings on Muhammad and his family." 3. Pop. Islam. Blessings and mercy from God. Special prayers (doa) asking for good fortune generally or for certain events specifically. 4. Doct. The act of angels in carrying out God's forgiveness of sin.
*Usage*: *membaca* ___, pray to God for forgiveness.

**Saleh** (Ar: ṣāliḥ) Qur. Personal name of a prophet mentioned in the Qur'an. He was sent to the tribe of Thamud.

**Salib** (In.) (Ar: ṣālib) Relig. Cross, crucifix; usually pertaining to Christians and Christianity.

**Salih**. Spelling variant. *See* **Shalih**.

**Salik** (Ar: sālik) Myst. Traveler; the mystic seeking God, hence a Sufi adept.

**Salim, Haji Agus** (In.) Biog. (d. 1954). Indonesian political activist, diplomat, and writer on Islamic themes during the nationalist period and early years of Indonesian independence.

**Sallallahualaihiwasalam—s.a.w** (In.); Shallallahu 'Alaihim Wa Sallam—s.a.w (Ar: ṣallāhahu 'alaihi wa sallam) Expres. "The blessings of God be upon him and peace," a phrase pronounced or written after mention of the name of the Prophet Muhammad.

**Salman, Masjid.** *See* **Masjid Salman.**

**Sama** (Ar: samā‘) Trad. Transference of a report concerning the words and behavior of the Prophet Muhammad by the receiver hearing it and memorizing it.

**Samanhudi, Ki Haji** (In.) Biog. (d. 1956). Javanese founder of the Sarekat Dagang Islam, the forerunner of the Sarekat Islam and one of the initial Indonesian political movements.

**Samaniyah** (Ar: samāniyyah) Myst. Mystical order of some importance in early Muslim history of Indonesia. *See* **Abdus Samad Al Palimbani.**

**Sama'un.** *See Hikayat Sama'un.*

**Samedi** (Jav.) Myst. In Javanese religious practice meditation connected with mystical practice.

**As Samii'**, As Samie' (Ar: as-samī‘) Theo. Name of God meaning "The Hearer." Syn: Yang Maha Mendengar.

**Samin, Surantika** (In.) Biog. (d. 1914). West Javanese leader of a sect called Elmu Nabi Adam which had some rudimentary Islamic features but primarily exhibits pre-Islamic mystic features. The movement was against Dutch control and its members refused to pay taxes or do corvee labor. Samin was exiled to Palembang.

**Samman, Shaikh Muhammad.** *See Hikayat Shaikh Muhammad Samman.*

**Samudra-Pasai** (In.) Geog. Port on the northern tip of Aceh where the oldest known Islamic inscription on gravestones in Southeast Asia has been found. It was an important port for cross Indian Ocean trade from the twelfth to sixteenth centuries. It was absorbed eventually by Aceh. *See Hikayat Raja-Raja Pasai.* It primary rulers, using the title Al Malik were Shaleh (unk/1297), Zhahir I (1297-1326), (separate entry), Zhahir II (1326-48), Zainal Abidin (1348-ca. 1405), and Sailan (ca. 1405-unk).

**Sanad** (In.) (Ar: sanad) Trad. "Chain," or list of successive transmitters of reports concerning the actions and behavior of Muhammad. Scholars in early Islam set rules by which the transmitters could be judged for verity as real transmitters of such reports. The chain stands in opposition to the "substance" (matan) of a report.
*Usage*: *memeriksa* ___, examine the line of transmission; *nama-nama* ___, the names in the line of transmission; *permulaan* ___-___, *sampai akhir* ___-___, from the beginning of the lines of transmission to their ends.

**Sanga**. *See* **Institut Agama Islam Negara**.

**Santri** (In.) Anthro. An Indonesian social group which adheres to the tenets of classical Sunni Islam, as opposed to the abangan group whose practice is less devout.
*Usage*: ___ *kekotaan*, urban santris; ___ *pedesaan*, rural santris.
*Dikotomi* ___ *dan non* ___*/abangan*, the dichotomy between santris and abangan groups; *kalangan para* ___, *kelompok* ___, santris as a group; *lingkungan* ___, in the circle of santris; *para* ___, santris as a group.

**Santrisme** (In.) Anthro. The lifestyle of santris, consisting of emphasis on traditional learning and ritual of Islam and an attempt to place Islamic values in effect in society and everyday life.

**Sanusiyah** (Ar: sanūsiyyah) Myst. Mystical order founded by Muhammad Ali As Sanusi (d. 1859) in Libya. It rejects outside, i.e. non-Islamic, influence in political or religious matters.

**Sapta Darma** (Jav.) Sect. Javanese mystical sect.

**Saqar**. Spelling variant. *See* **Sakar**.

**Saqim**. *See* **Ilmu Mushthalah Hadis**.

**Sarekat Buruh Islam Indonesia—SBII** (In.) Assn. "The Indonesian Islamic Workers' Association," a labor organization founded by Masjumi to provide political support in the labor sector. In the 1960s it federated with the Gabungan Sarekat Buruh Islam

Indonesia and the union was called SBII/Gasbiindo.

**Sarekat Buruh Muslimin Indonesia—Sarbumusi** (In.) Assn. "The Indonesian Muslim Workers' Association," a labor organization affiliated with the Nahdlatul Ulama, founded in the 1950s as part of that movement's attempt to create mass organizations to compete politically.

**Sarekat Dagang Islam Indonesia** (In.) Assn. "The Indonesian Islamic Business Association," affiliated with the Masjumi political party in the 1950s. It was a loose organization of individual businessmen.

**Sarekat Islam; Sharikat Islam** (In.) Assn. "Islamic Association," the name taken by an Indonesian mass political association, founded in 1912, which was the first great vehicle for Indonesian nationalist activity. After its political decline, Indonesian Muslim writers idealized it into a political model for Indonesians to emulate.

**Sarekat Mahasiswa Muslimin Indonesia—SEMMI** (In.) Assn. "The Indonesian Muslim Students' Association," affiliated with the Partai Sarikat Islam Indonesia (PSII) in the 1950s.

**Sarekat Nelayan Islam Indonesia—SNII** (In.) Assn. "The Indonesian Islamic Fishers' Association," founded in the 1950s by Masjumi to organize that profession politically. It was strong in East Java and at Asahan in north Sumatra. It was a special member of Masjumi.

**Sarekat Pelajar Muslimin Indonesia—SPMI** (In.) Assn. "The Indonesian Muslim Students'Association," affiliated with the Partai Sarekat Islam Indonesia (PSII) in the 1950s.

**Sarekat Sarjana Muslimin Indonesia—SESMI** (In.) Assn. "The Indonesian Muslim Scholars' Association," affiliated with the Partai Sarekat Islam Indonesia (PSII) in the 1950s.

**Sarekat Tani Islam Indonesia—STII** (In.) Assn. "The Indonesian Islamic Farmers' Association," affiliated with Masjumi and founded at Masjumi's inception in 1945. It was active in North Sumatra in the 1940s, 1950s and 1960s.

**Saum** (In.) (Ar: ṣaum) Doct. Fasting. Syn: Puasa.

**S.a.w.** *See* **Sallallahualaihimwasallam.**

**Say** (In.); sayiah (Ar: sa'y) Juris. The seven-times walk between Shafa and Marwa on the pilgrimage.
*Usage*: *sunnah* ___, the basis for the pilgrimage walk as found in the behavior of the Prophet Muhammad.

**Say'dani**. Spelling variant. *See* **Saidina**.

**Sayid** (In.); sayyid (Ar: sayyid) Title. A title commonly taken by persons claiming descent from the Prophet Muhammad, particularly through his grandson Husayn.
*Usage*: *golongan* ___, the sayids as a collective group.

**As Sayuthi, Jalaluddin**; As Suyuthi (Ar: jalāluddīn as-sayūṭī) Biog. (d. 911H/1505). A renowned Arab scholar in Egypt during the middle period who wrote an important commentary of the Qur'an and prepared several important jurisprudential texts. *See Jamiiush Shagir; Ad Durrul Mantsur;* and **Tafsir.**

**Sayyidina.** Spelling variant. *See* **Saidina.**

**SBII.** *See* **Sarekat Buruh Islam Indonesia.**

**Schrieke, B. J. O.** (Dutch) Biog. (d. 1945) Dutch Indologist who wrote extensively about early Indonesia especially at the time of the arrival of Islam. His *Sociological Studies* are a trove of material on the Mataram era in particular.

**SDSB.** *See* **Sosial Dana Sumbangan Berhadiah.**

**Sedekah** (In.); sadakah; sadaqah; sedeqah (Ar: ṣadaqah) 1. Doct. Giving charity, alms and help to the less fortunate, whether through prescribed institutions, such as zakat, or free-will donations. 2. Pop. Islam. In the Indonesian context, sedakah retains its association with ritual meals where food is given to the poor, invited for this purpose. Such contributions are considered to be alms which redound to the religious merit of the giver of the

meal. Syn: kenduri, hajatan, selamatan.
*Usage*: *ber___*, giving alms and charity donations; ___ *jariah*, an endowment for assisting the poor, i.e., waqf.

**Sehat** (In.) Gen. vocab. Healthy, sound.
*Usage*: *ke___an jasmani dan rohani*, physical and spiritual health.

**Sekolah Menengah Atas—SMA** (In.) Educ. Senior high school.

**Sekolah Menengah Pertama—SMP** (In.) Educ. Junior high school.

**Sekolah Menengah Tengah Attas—SMTA** (In.) Educ. Middle school.

**Sekolah Tengah Pertama—STP** (In.) Educ. Middle school.

**Sekularisme** (In.) Pol. A philosophy which draws a distinction between religion and political matters and excludes the former from direct consideration in affairs of state.

**Selamatan** (In.); slametan (Jav.) Pop. Islam. A communal feast, popular among the nominal Muslim (abangan) population on Java, given to commemorate important events in an individual's life. The ceremony attached to the meal has an animistic and shamanistic flavor. Syn: kenduri, hajatan, sedaqah.

**Selawat.** Spelling variant. *See* **Salawat.**

**Semangat** (In.) Doct. Soul, spirit.
*Usage*: ___ *korban*, spirit of sacrifice; *membangkitkan* ___, development of the spiritual attribute of humans.

**Semangat Islam** (In.) Pol. "Essence of Islam," an expression used by President Sukarno to indicate his desire to move the Indonesian Muslim community into modern political and economic development.

**Sembah** (In.) Juris. Homage, tribute, respect.
*Usage*: *menizinkan menyembah kubur*, to be permitted to show respect at a tomb.

**Sembahyang** (In.) Juris. Worship, give honor and obeisance.
*Usage*: ___ *fardu*, obligatory worship; ___ *'Id*, the worship

ceremony performed on Idul Fithri and Idul Adha; ___ *jama'*, combining the noonday (zuhur) and afternoon (ashar) prayers or the sunset (maghreb) and evening (isya) prayers; ___ *jamaah*, communal prayer; ___ *jari*, the five daily prayers of Islam; ___ *Jum'at*, community prayer on Friday; *menjembahyangkan seorang mayat*, performing the prayer for the dead; ___ *orang sakit*, prayer for the sick; ___ *qasar*, intensification of prayer by increasing the number of prayer sets required; ___ *sunnat*, optional worship; ___ *sunnat ba'diyah*, an optional prayer done in parts (rather than all at once because of time constraints); __ *sunnat istisqa*, optional prayer for rain; ___ *sunnat qabliyah*, optional worship undertaken in preparation for the required prayer; ___ *sunnat rawatib*, optional prayer undertaken after completion of the obligatory prayer; ___ *sunnat tahiat*, ___ *tahiatul masjid*, the optional prayer after entering the mosque for regular prayer; ___ *tarawih*, optional prayer in the mosque in early evening during Ramadan; ___ *witir*, worship with an uneven number of prayer sets; ___ *yang lima waktu*, the five daily prayers of Islam. *Masalah kunut* ___ *subuh*, the issue concerning reading a special benediction during the performance of the morning prayer; *mengqada* ___, to be commanded to worship (by God).

**Seminar Pondok Pesantren Seluruh Indonesia** (In) Hist. "The All-Indonesia Seminar on Private Religious Education," which met in 1965 at Yogyakarta to assess the role and needs of the schools involved. It called for some standardization of curriculum, for a financial foundation (yayasan) at every site and recognized the schools as being an important promoter of the goals of the Indonesian Muslim community.

**SEMMI.** *See* **Sarekat Mahasiswa Muslimin Indonesia.**

**Sempurna, Yang Maha** (In.) Theo. Name of God meaning "The Most Perfect."

**Senopati** (Jav.) Biog. (d. 1601). Javanese founder of the Mataram empire of Central Java in the late fifteenth century.

**Sentot Prawirodirjo** (Jav.) Biog. (d. 1855) Javanese figure who, as a young man, commanded the forces of Prince Diponegoro in the Java War. Afterwards he retained command in the Sultan's army and was sent with his troops to west Sumatra to fight against the Paderi forces. When he became sympathetic with them, he was returned to Java.

**Seerah** (Ar: sīrah) Lang. Biography, particularly of the Prophet Muhammad. Genre in Muslim intellectual writing.

**Serambi Makkah** (In.) Expres. A nickname applied to Aceh because of its historical ties with the Islamic holy land, especially in the seventeenth and eighteenth centuries when pilgrims from Southeast Asia passed through Aceh.

**Serat** (Jav.). Lang. Word for book or compilation. *See* following word.

*Serat Centini* (Jav.) Lit. title. Book on Javanese mysticism ordered assembled by Sultan Pakubuwono V (d. 1823) of Surakarta. It discusses mystical union in terms similar to Buddhist Tantrism, while still purporting to be Islamic.

*Serat Kanda* (Jav.) Lit. title. "Book of Tales," a compilation of historical anecdotes centering on the Demak period of history of the fifteenth century. It is a primary historical source for that era.

*Serat Wirid Hidayat Jati*. (Jav.) Lit. title. "Book of the Rightly Guided Recitation of God's Names," written by Ronggowarsito (d. 1873), an important poet in mid-nineteenth century Surakarta. It describes Islamic mysticism and Javanese mysticism as compatible, but using different terminologies.

*Seruan Azhar* (In./Mal.) Lit. title. "The Voice of Al-Azhar," the periodical of Malayan and Indonesian students studying at Al-Azhar University in Cairo between 1925 and 1928.

**Sesajem** (Jav.) Anthro. In Javanese religious practice festivities (selamatan) that reflect Javanese calendrical celebrations.

**Sesat** (In.) Juris. To be in error, particularly religious error.

**SESMI.** *See* **Sarekat Sarjana Muslimin Indonesia.**

**Setan**; syaithan (In.); Syetan; Seton (Ar: shaiṭān) Doct. Beings arising either from humans or jinn who serve the forces of evil. They act as tempters and perpetrators of evil action. They fear the Qur'an and can be dispersed by reciting key passages from it.
*Usage*: *bahaya-bahaya* ___, the dangers of Satan; *sifat* ___*iyah*, Satan-like attributes or characteristics.

**Ash Shabuur** (Ar: aṣ-ṣabūr) Theo. Name of God mentioned in the Qur'an meaning "The Forbearing."

**Shaad**; Shad (Ar: ṣād) Qur. The thirty-eighth chapter of the Qur'an, named for the Arabic letter Shad. It states that the Qur'an is the revelation of God.

**Shadaqah.** Spelling variant. *See* **Sedakah.**

**Shafar.** Spelling variant. *See* **Safar.**

**Ash Shaff**; Ash Shaf (Ar: aṣ-ṣaff) Qur. "Array," the sixty-first chapter of the Qur'an. It states that Paradise can be attained through faith and by struggling with wealth and spirit.

**Ash Shaffaat**; Ash Shaffat (Ar: aṣ-ṣaffat) Qur. "Ranks," the thirty-seventh chapter of the Qur'an. It details the continuing conflict between good and evil, with references to the role of angels.

**Ash Shafuuh** (Ar: aṣ-ṣafūḥ) Theo. Name of God meaning "The Pardoner."

**Shahih.** Spelling variant. *See* **Sahih.**

**Shalat.** Spelling variant. *See* **Salat.**

**Shalat Ied**, Shalat Id. Spelling variants. *See* **Salat Id.**

**Shalat Janasah.** Spelling variant. *See* **Salat Jenazah.**

**Shalawat.** Spelling variant. *See* **Salawat.**

**Shaleh, Malik.** *See* **Samudera-Pasai.**

**Shalih**; salih (Ar: ṣāliḥ) Qur. Prophet mentioned in the

Qur'an as having been sent to the tribe of Tsamud.

**Shallallahu 'Alaihim Wa Sallam**. Spelling variant. *See* **Sallallahualaihiwasalam**.

**Ash Shamad** (Ar: aṣ-ṣamad) Theo. Name of God meaning "The Eternal."

**Shams Al Din Pasai** (In.) Biog. (d. 1630). Court scholar of Acehnese ruler Iskandar Muda (d. 1636) and an important member of the Wujudiyya movement of Hamzah Fansuri (1625). *See Mir'at Al Mu'min.*

**Shan'ani, Muhammad;** Shananij (Ar: muḥammad ibn ismā'īl ṣana'ānī) Biog. (d. 1768). Arab Syafii scholar of the late middle period whose works on Traditions have been popular study material in Indonesia during the last century. *See Subulus Salam.*

**Sharaf** (Ar: ilm aṣ-ṣaraf) Educ. The science of grammar in Arabic language study.

**Shariati, Ali**. *See* **Syari'ati, Ali**.

**Sharif**. *See* **Hadis**.

**Sharikat Islam**. *See* **Sarekat Islam**.

**Shattariya**. Spelling variant. *See* **Syattariya**.

**Shaum** (Ar: ṣawm) Doct. The fast. Syn: Puasa.

**Shiddiq**. *See* **Abu Shiddiq**.

**Ash Shiddieqy, T. M. Hasbi** (In.) Biog. (d. 1975) Noted Acehnese academic who compiled a large number of Indonesian texts on Qur'an and Traditions (hadis) which served as learning material for Muslim education in Indonesia in the 1960s and afterward. *See* **Fikih Mazhab Nasional**.

**Shiffin** (Ar: ṣiffīn) Geog. The site of a battle in 657 between the forces of Ali and Mu'awiyah both claiming the ealiphate. During the battle Mu'awiyah's forces placed pages of the Qur'an on their swords and lances which caused the forces of Ali great consternation and led to their failure to press the battle. Mu'awiyah's success allowed him to consolidate the Umawi kingdom over the early Muslim community.

**Shilaturrahim**. Spelling variant. *See* **Silaturrahim**.

**Shiyam**, Siyam (Ar:ṣiyām) 1. Juris. Fasting. *See* also **Puasa**. 2. Myst. In Javanese religious practice, refraining from food or pleasure in order to practice release from worldly enjoyment and prepare oneself for mystical practice.

**Shuffah** (Ar: aṣḥāb aṣ-ṣuffah) Hist. "People of the bench," poor Muslims who attended Muhammad at Madinah and accepted alms for sustenance. *Usage*: *ahlus* ___, the poor of the Prophet Muhammad's time.

**Shumubu** (Jap.) Pol. Department of Religion under Japanese Administration (1942 to 1945), headed by K. H. M. Hasyim Asyarie (d. 1953).

**Siak**. *See* **Kesultanan**.

**Siddiq, Achmad** (In.) Biog. (d. 1991). Religious scholar at the Pesantren Ash Shiddiqiyah in East Java and general chair of the Nahdlatul Ulama 1983-91. During his term of office the Nahdlatul Ulama accepted Pancasila as the sole basis of its organization.

**Sifat** (In.) Theo. Characteristic, attribute. *Usage*: ___ *bahimiyah*, animal-like attribute; ___ *rububiyah*, god-like attribute; ___ *subu'iyah*, savage-like attribute; ___ *syaitaniyah*, demon-like attribute.

*Sifat Dua Puluh* (In.) Lit. title. "The Twenty Attributes," the popular name of a text used in older Islamic schools to teach students basic Islamic beliefs. The book concentrated on the characteristics of God and the attributes it would be impossible for him to possess.

**Sihir** (In.) (Ar: siḥr) Pop. Islam. Black magic.

**Sila** (In.) Pol. Principle, statement. *See* **Pancasila**. *Usage*: *Panca* ___, the Five Principles (Indonesian national philosophical statement).

**Silaturrahim** (In.) Shilaturrahim (Ar: ṣilat ar-raḥīm) Doct. Good will, especially among Muslims applying God's great mercy toward humans as a model for relationship among humans.

**Silsilah** (In.) (Ar: silsilah) Hist. A line of transmission of knowledge, authority, or title, frequently used in Southeast Asian princely court records.

*Sinar Hindia* (In.) Lit. title. A newspaper in the 1920s expounding Communist Party views.

**Singkel, Abdul Rauf.** *See* **Abdul Rauf Al Singkil.**

**Singodimedjo, Kasman.** *See* **Kasman Singodimedjo.**

**Sinkretisme** (In.) synkretisme (Eng.) Relig. Mixing the religious beliefs and practices of one religion with those of another so that a blend exists which constitutes different religious forms than those existing previously. In Indonesia Javanese religion is frequently said to be syncretic of Old Javanese religions, Hindu-Buddhism, and Islam.

*As Siraji Munir* (Ar: as-sirāji al-munīr) Lit. title. "The Lighted Lamp," a commentary on the Qur'an by Khatib Asy Syarbini (d. 1570), historically important in Indonesia as a summary of the commentary of Baidhawi (d. 1291). Also known as *Tafsir Syarbini*. *See* **Tafsir.**

**SIS.** *See* **Studenten Islam Studie Club.**

**Siti;** sitti (Ar: sitt). Title of respect for a revered woman in Islam. *See* following word.

**Siti Jener, Syekh** (Jav.) Biog. (d. unk.) Sufi leader and one of the primary missionaries given credit for the conversion of Java to Islam in the late fourteenth century. He was sentenced to death by other religious scholars for his equation of God and creation, an idea which was considered heretical. Also known as (Syekh) Lemah Abang. *See* **Wali Songo.**

**Siyam.** Spelling variant. *See* **Shiyam.**

**Sjadzali, H. Munawir.** *See* **Menteri Agama.**

**Sjaltout.** Spelling variant. *See* **Syaltut, Syaikh Muhammad.**

**Slametan.** Spelling variant. *See* **Selamatan.**

**SMA.** *See* **Sekolah Menengah Atas.**

**SMP**. *See* **Sekolah Menengah Pertama.**

**SMTA.** *See* **Sekolah Menengah Tengah Attas.**

**SNII.** *See* **Sarikat Nelayan Islam Indonesia.**

**Snouck Hurgronje,** C. *See* **Hurgronje, Christiaan Snouck.**

*Sociological Studies. See* **Schrieke, J. B. O.**

**Soorkati, (Syekh) Ahmad** (In.) Biog. (d. 1943). Arabo-Indonesian founder of the Al Irsyad, a modernist Muslim organization for Arab-born Indonesians, in the early part of the twentieth century.

**Sopan** (In.) Anthro. Politeness, refinement, culture. A feature of the writing of some Muslim writers on Java in the nineteenth and twentieth centuries.

**Sorban** (In.) Hist. A turban. *Usage*: *agama* ___, old-fashioned religion, a pejorative reference to Islam made by the secular nationalists in the early part of the twentieth century.

**Sorga**. Spelling variant. *See* **Surga.**

**Sosial Dana Sumbangan Berhadiah—SDSB** (In.) Pol. "Social Contribution (with) Prize," a lottery-type operation in Indonesia very popular with poor people but generally disliked by pious Muslims and their leaders as contrary to Islamic ideals.

**Sosialisme** (In.) Pol. Political, economic, and social philosophy stressing equality of individuals, equal distribution of economic wealth, and, often, state ownership or regulation of the means of production. In Indonesia there has been an attempt by many different political groups to associate socialism with them, including Muslim groups.

**Sosialisme Islam** (In.) Pol. A term used by Islamic activists in the Sarekat Islam during World War I to describe the social message of Islam in response to communist and socialist propaganda.

**Spanyol** (In.) Pol. The Spanish, especially in a historical sense in the sixteenth to nineteenth centuries when Spanish colonialism was active in the Philippines and for a time in Eastern Indonesia.

*Spirit of Islam* (Eng.) Lit. title. An important work by Ameer Ali (d. 1928), a South Asian Syiah scholar, laying out the modernist Muslim position on Islam in the first quarter of the twentieth century.

**SPMI.** *See* **Sarekat Pelajar Muslimin Indonesia.**

**Sri Maharaja** (In.) Title. Title taken by the first Malakkan rulers in the fifteenth century reflecting Indian cultural identification.

**Srivijaya** (In.) Hist. A major kingdom of Southern Sumatra with overseas imperial influence (ca. 700 to ca. 1400) and a major political entity of the classical Hindu-Buddhist period. It is regarded as a predecessor state to the Indonesian Republic by nationalist historians. Modern Indonesian intellectuals regard it as a model for an entrepreneurial economic state undertaking foreign trade in contrast to the Majapahit model of a closed, agricultural state.

**STII.** *See* **Sarekat Tani Islam Indonesia.**

**Stoddard, Lothrop.** *See Dunia Baru Islam.*

**STP.** *See* **Sekolah Tengah Pertama.**

**Studenten Islam Studie Club—SIS** (In.) Assn. "The Islamic Students Study Club," a group founded in 1399 by Yusuf Wibisono for graduates of Indonesian-language schools for discussion of intellectual issues. Modeled on the Jong Islamieten Bond (JIB). A prototype for many later Indonesian student organizations.

**Sual-Jawab** (In.) (Ar: su'āl wa jawāb) Juris. Literally "question and answer." A device used by several writers in the twentieth century to expound their viewpoint, by asking a hypothetical question pertaining to some matter of Islamic belief, practice, or behavior and then answering it. It was popularized by Ahmad Hassan (d. 1958) of the Persatuan Islam in the 1930s and 1950s.

*Suara Muhammadiyah* (In.) Lit. title. "Voice of the

Muhammadiyah," a magazine published from 1920 to the present in Yogyakarta as the organ of the Muhammadiyah association.

**As Subbuuh** (Ar: subbūh) Theo. Name of God meaning "The Most Holy." Same as Yang Sangat Suci.

**Subchan, Z. E.** (In.) Biog. (d. 1973). Nahdlatul Ulama activist, trained as an economist in the United States, who led the youth wing during the Guided Democracy era, generally opposing communist and leftist attempts to mobilize society. He was later involved in a struggle for leadership of the Nahdlatul Ulama but lost the competition.

**Subhah** (Ar: subḥah) Myst. Muslim prayer beads, usually strung in a loop of eleven, thirty-three, or ninety-nine, with suitable marker beads to aid in progressing through ritual repetitions of "the most beautiful names," numbering ninety-nine, and other formulas.

**Subhanahu Wata'ala—S.w.t** (Ar: subḥānahu wa ta'āla) Expres. "Praise God Who is Most Exalted," a formula pronounced or written after mention of the name "Allah."

**Subhanallah** (In) (Ar: subḥān allāh) Pop. Islam. "Praise to God!"

**Subuh** (In.) (Ar: ṣalāt uṣ-ṣubḥ) Juris. The required early morning prayer.
*Usage*: *kada sunnat* ___, making up the required morning prayer at some other time; *kuliah-kuliah* ___, *kunut* ___, the lessons or exhortations after the early morning prayer.

**Subu'iyah** (Ar: sabu'iyyah) Myst. Savage.
*Usage*: *sifat* ___, the attribute of savagery, used as a pejorative reference by mystics.

*Subulus Salam* (Ar: subul as-salām) Lit. title. "The Contented Way," a standard book on Tradition criticism and usage by As Shan'ani (d. 1768) enjoying long usage in Indonesia by the traditionalist scholars and by some modernist groups as well.

**Suci** (In.) Relig. Holy.
*Usage*: *men*___*kan*, to undertake pious activities

connected with religion; *kitab-kitab* ___, holy books.

**Suci, Yang Maha**. Theo. A name of God meaning "The Most Holy One." Syn: As Subbuuh.

**Sudratil Muntaha** (Ar: sidrat al-muntahā) Doct. "The Lote tree of the Uttermost Limit," the last place before God Himself. It is beyond the Seventh Heaven and was visited by Muhammad on his Night Journey.

**Sufi** (In.) (Ar: ṣūfī) Myst. A mystic of Islam who strives to make contact with God through mystical practices. Mysticism was extremely important in Islam between the tenth and nineteenth centuries. With the rise of Islamic modernism and nationalism, its popularity and respect has waned appreciably.
*Usage*: *ahli* ___, Islamic mystics (sufis); *bahasa* ___, special terminology employed by mystics in their references to mystical practice; *gerakan-gerakan* ___, mystical orders; *kaum* ___, Islamic mystics.

**Sufisme** (In.) (Ar: taṣawwuf) Myst. Islamic mysticism. Syn: tasawuf.

**Sujud** (In.) (Ar: sujūd) Juris. Prostration during prayer, hence, to pray.
*Usage*: *ber*___, *menjalankan* ___, to undertake prayer; *tempat* ___, place of prayer.

**Sukarno (President)** (In.) Biog. (d. 1968). First president of Indonesia, 1945-68 and highly respected national hero for his efforts in winning independence. Nominally a Muslim, he campaigned for a national philosophy called Pancasila and against the installation of an Islamic state. His willingness to tolerate a communist presence in government in the 1960s created political instability that led to his isolation from political power and influence. *See Surat-Surat Islam Dari Endeh*.

**Sukarnoisme** (In.) Pol. Ideology of President Sukarno between the years 1961-65 which called for political unity of all factions behind a policy of leftist economic radicalism in Indonesia and a new international order favoring leftist "restructuring." Muslims were included so long as they cooperated, but many were imprisoned or banned from public life as unsuitable.

**Sukiman Wiryosanjoyo** (In.) Biog. (d. 1974). Prominent Javanese member of the Masjumi political association during the 1950s and head of its modernist wing. Prime Minister of Indonesia (1951-52). *See* **Madjelis Sjuro Muslimin Indonesia**.

**Suku** (In.) Anthro. Basic ethnic groups, particularly on Sumatra among the Bataks and the Minangkabau.

**Sukuran** (Jav.) Pop. Islam. Syn: selamatan, kenduri, pesta.

**Sulaiman** (Ar: sulaymān) Qur. Personal name of a prophet mentioned in the Qur'an, associated by scholars with the Old Testament Solomon. He was noted for his skill and wisdom and once took a census of birds and other animals.

**Sulaiman, Sultan**. *See* **Banjar**.

**Sultan** (In.); sulthan (Ar: sulṭān) Hist. Title originating in the Middle East and given to a high grade of Muslim ruler. This title in Southeast Asia was used in the fifteenth and sixteenth centuries by several prominent rulers and was intended to be superior to the title "raja," which preceded it in time. *Usage*: *ke___an Banten*, the Sultanate of Banten; ___-___ *Pasai*, the sultans of (the kingdom of) Pasai.

**Suluk** (In.) (Ar: sulūk) 1. Myst. Wayfarers, connoting adepts in mysticism searching for the means to approach God. 2. Educ. Name of a literary form. Syn: Primbon. *Usage*: *rumah* ___, a retreat for mystics

**Sumah, Abu**. *See Hikayat Abu Sumah*.

**Sumatra Utara**. *See* **Institut Agama Islam Negara**.

**Summa Bank**; Bank Summa (In.) Econ. A financial bank sponsored by the Nahdlatul Ulama in the 1980s which uses Islamic guidelines in providing financial services to investors so that interest on money is avoided.

**Sunah** (In.); sunnah; sunnat (Ar: sunnah) Juris. "Way of the Prophet," describing the style of life of the Prophet, especially his belief, his behavior and his observance of religious obligations. Traditions (hadis), are the individual records of the memories of Muhammad by his contemporaries. Sunah is the essence of the message in those memories. The various sunah are as follows: ___ **'Ain** (Ar: ʻayn) Behavior of the Prophet dealing with matters of worship, a category of principles in the Syafii school of jurisprudence. ___ **Allah** (Ar: allāh) The things general to God, such as His laws to humankind, a category of principles in the Syafii school of jurisprudence. ___ **Amaliyyah** (Ar: ʻamaliyyah). The actions of the Prophet concerning proper behavior, a category of principles in the Syafii school of jurisprudence. Syn: Sunnah Fa'liyyah. ___ **Goer Muakkadah** (Ar: mu'akkadah) The actions of the Prophet Muhammad which show the proper relationship of certain actions, such as the order of prayer. A category of principles found in the Syafii school of jurisprudence. ___ **Had-jin** (Ar: [?]) Juris. An action commanded in the Qur'an, without a procedure for performing the action being outlined. This principle is used for completion of certain actions of worship, such as the call to worship or the procedure for the Friday communal worship. A category of principles found in the Hanafi school of jurisprudence. ___ **Kifaayah** (Ar: kifāyah) Allowable behavior of the Prophet that deals with the ancillary matters of worship, such as the call to prayer. A category of principles found in the Syafii school of jurisprudence. ___ **Muakkadah** (Ar: mu'akkadah) All the allowable actions which were performed by the Prophet Muhammad. A category of principles found in the Syafii school of jurisprudence. ___ **Qauliyyah** (Ar: qawliyyah) In the Syafii school of jurisprudence a category of principles which are only valid when preceded by general (amaliyyah) principles. ___ **Taqririyyah** (Ar: taqrīriyyah) In the Syafii school of jurisprudence a category of behavior by the Prophet Muhammad which only can be interpreted in the context of general knowledge (ammiyah). ___ **Zaaidah** (Ar: zā'idah) Behavior of the Prophet Muhammad that had no connection with worship, such as eating and drinking. This is a category of principles used in the Hanafi school of jurisprudence.

*Usage*: *as ___ yang shahih*, the Sunnah as verified through the sciences of Islam; ___ *hasanah*, reports about Muhammad's behavior that prabably are authentic; ___ *para salaf*, the Sunnah as established by the orthodox writers of Islam; ___ *Rasulullah*, ___*tur rasul*, the "Way" of the prophet of God; *ahlus ___ wal jamaah*, the orthodox Sunni majority throughout history.

**Sunan** (In.) Title. "Eminence," designating sacredness of being, given to royalty and certain religious personages, such as the nine original propagators of Islam in Java. *See* following name.

*As Sunan* (Ar: as-sunan) Lit. title. "Good," a short name of Tradition collections, in reference to their use of Traditions judged as "probably authentic." Collections by Abu Dawud (d. 875), An Nasa'i (d. 915), At Turmuzi (d.892) and Ibnu Majah (d.886) are designated by that short title.

**Sunisme** (In.) Doct. The totality of Sunni beliefs, doctrines, and practices which constitute the Sunni system. *See* **Sunni**.

**Sunnah**. Spelling variant. *See* **Sunah**.

**Sunnat** (Ar: sunnah) Juris. 1. Recommended action, worthy of reward when performed, but not required. *See* **Sembahyang**. 2. *See* **Sunah**.

**Sunni** (In.) (Ar: sunnī) Doct. A major sect of Islam which has been a primary carrier of Islamic teachings, values, and histories. It dominates Indonesia as well as nearly all the Arabic world. *See* **Syiah**. *Usage*: *golongan ___, kaum ___*, both terms meaning the people associated with the doctrines and practices of the Sunni sect of Islam.

**Sura** (Ar: sūrah) Qur. A chapter of the Qur'an. There are 114 suras in the Qur'an, ranging from Al Nashr with three verses (ayat) to Al Baqarah with 286 verses.

**Sura Yaa Siin**. *See* **Yaa Siin**.

**Surakarta** (In.) Geog. City in Central Java which was the site of a kingdom headed by a ruler with the Javanese royal title of susuhunan and sometimes the title of sultan (1788-1945). The kingdom was a successor state to the Mataram empire and was carefully controlled by Dutch governor-generals during the colonial era. *See* **Pakubuwono** and **Hamengkurat.**

*Surat-Surat Islam Dari Endeh* (In.) Lit. title. "The Letters concerning Islam from Endeh," the title of Sukarno's (d. 1968) correspondence with A. Hassan (d. 1957) in the 1930s. Sukarno described a revitalized political Islam reacting to modern politics on the lines used by Mustafa Kemal Ataturk (d. 1935) in Turkey at the time.

**Surau** (In.) Educ. Rural schools, largely outside of Java, such as Aceh and Minangkabau. While traditions vary in part from the Javanese pondok-pesantren the tradition is much the same in these schools and they seem to have a common ancestry.

**Surga** (In.); Syurga; Sorga; Syorga (San: shurga) Doct. Paradise. Described in the Qur'an as a place of reward for proper believing Muslims who have led pious lives. It is a place of gardens, food, sexual gratification, and spiritual contentment. Syn: firdaus, na'im, 'adn, ma'wa and khulud.
*Usage*: *(me)masuk* ___, to be awarded paradise for a good Muslim life.

**Suriansyah, Sultan**. *See* **Banjar.**

**Susuhunan** (Jav.) Title. "The Venerated," a title assigned to Javanese royalty and to religious scholars. Variant of Sunan.

**Sutan Mansur**. *See* **Muhammadiyah.**

**As Suyuthi, Jamaluddin**. *See* **As Sayuthi, Jamaluddin.**

**S.w.t.** *See* **Subhanahu Wata'ala.**

**Sya'ban**. Spelling variant. *See* **Syakban.**

**Syabandar**; syahbandar (Mal.) Hist. Chief port official in the early Muslim ports of Southeast Asia, who maintained order, collected tariffs and cleared import and export of goods.

**Syadz**. *See* **Syu-dzudz.**

**Syafaat**; syafa'at (In.) (Ar: shafā'ah) Doct. Intercession of Muhammad on behalf of Muslims on Judgment Day.

**Syafii** (In.); Syafi'i (Ar: muḥammad ibn idris ash-shāfi'ī) 1. Biog. (d. 820). Arab scholar of Traditions who laid the basis for the Syafii school of jurisprudence. *See Kitab Al Umm* and *Risalah*. 2. (Ar: shāfi'ī) Juris. The Sunni school of jurisprudence which is generally prominent in Egypt, South Arabia, South India, and Southeast Asia. It is based on systematic analysis and steers a path between legalism and traditionalism. *Usage*: *bermazhab* ___, to follow the Syafiite school of jurisprudence; *faham* ___, Syafiite thinking or teachings.

**Syah, Sultan Alauddin Mansur**. *See* **Aceh**.

**Syah, Sultan Alauddin Riayat**. *See* **Aceh**.

**Syah, Sultan Ali Mugayat**. *See* **Aceh**.

**Syah, Sultan Ali Riayat**. *See* **Aceh**.

**Syah, Sultana Taj Al Alam Safiat Ad Din**. *See* **Aceh**.

**Syahadat** (In.) (Ar: shahādah) Doct. "Witnessing;" in the religious use of the word; the profession of faith, "There is no god but God; Muhammad is the Prophet of God." *Usage*: *kalimat* ___, the Profession of the Faith.

**Syahid** (In.) (Ar: shāhid) 1. Juris. "Witness for the faith," a term referring to martyrdom for Islam. Such martyrs are rewarded with Paradise. This includes dying while on the pilgrimage. *Usage*: *mati* ___, death of a martyr. 2. *See* **Ilmu Mushthalah Hadis**.

Asy **Syaahid**, Asy Syahiid (Ar: ash-shāhid) Theo. A name of God meaning "The Witness."

**Syaithan**. Spelling variant. *See* **Setan**.

**Syakban** (In.); sya'ban, sa'ban (Ar: sha'bān) Cal. The eighth month, meaning "the month of division." The night of the 15th is Lailatul Bara'ah, when, it is popularly believed, destinies of humans are fixed. Consequently, it is a night of intense prayer.

**Syakh**. Spelling variant. *See* **Syekh**.

**Syakib Arsylan, Amir.** *See* **Arsylan, Amer Syakib.**

**Asy Syakurr**; As Syakur; Asy Syukur (Ar: ash-shakūr) Theo. Name of God meaning "The Grateful."

**Syaltut, (Syaikh) Mahmud;** Sjaltout ... (Ar: maḥmūd ash-shaltūt) Biog. (d. 1964) An important Egyptian scholar in the mid-twentieth century and rector of Al-Azhar University. He was frequently quoted by Indonesian Muslim intellectuals in the 1980s.

**Asy Syams** (Ar: ash-shams) Qur. "The Sun," the ninety-first chapter of the Qur'an. The Tribe of Thamud is punished by God for its transgressions.

**Syamsuri, K. H. Bisri.** *See* **Nahdlatul Ulama.**

**Syara' Bersendi Adat** (Minang.) Juris. In Minangkabau, Islamic law based on Minangkabau custom.

**Syarbini, Khatib** (Ar: muḥammad ibn aḥmad khaṭib ash-sharbīnī) Biog. (d. 1570). Middle East and Syafii legal scholar who wrote a well-known commentary on the Qur'an and several works on jurisprudence that have enjoyed usage in Southeast Asia. Also known as Abu Shuja'. *See Mughni Muhtaj, Sirajul Munir; Al Iqna'*; and **Tafsir.**

**Syarekat Dagang Islam** (In.) Assn. "Muslim Trade Association," founded in 1909 to promote trade among Muslims in response to a similar trade association established by Chinese merchants. In 1911 it converted into the Sarekat Islam with a political agenda.

**Asy Syarh** (Ar: ash-sharh) Qur. "Phlegmatic," an alternate name for the ninety-fourth chapter of the Qur'an. The usual name is Alam Nasyrah and it is also known as Al Insyiraah.

**Syariat** (In.); syari'ah; syari'at (Ar: sharī'ah) 1. Juris. The holy law of God which Muslim conduct seeks to satisfy. Theoretically unattainable, it has inspired generations of legalists, who have sought to build a model syariat with rules of behavior based on Qur'an and Traditions. Traditionalists hold that existing jurisprudential canons (fikih) are sufficient, while modernists hold that such principles of law should be distilled from Islamic scriptures. 2. Educ. One of the major academic programs offered at the national Islamic Studies Institutes (IAIN) and other Islamic institutions of higher education in Indonesia in which stress is placed on jurisprudence.

**Asy Syari'ah** (Ar: ash-sharīʻah) Qur. An alternate name for the forty-fifth chapter of the Qur'an, titled "Sacred Law." The usual name of the chapter is Al Jaatsiyah.
*Usage*: ___ *Ilahi*, ___ Islam, the sacred law established by God; ___ *Nabi Musa*, the sacred law given to the Prophet Musa; ___ *Tuhan*, the sacred law established by God; *di__kan oleh Allah*, decreed as sacred law by God; *membawa* ___ *Islam*, to carry the sacred law of Islam (as the Qur'an does); *meninggalkan* ___, to forget the standards of sacred law; *menjalankan* ___, to apply the standards of the sacred law to life; *nilai* ___, the standards set by sacred law; *soal* ___, the issue of the sacred law; *Tuhan menjari'atkan*, decreed as sacred law by God.

**Syari'ah, Thoriqah, Ma'rifat Dan Haqiqah** (Ar: sharīʻah, ṭarīqah, maʻrīfah wa-ḥaqīqah) Myst. "Sacred law, mystical orders, mystical knowledge, and mystical truth," a slogan used among mystics to indicate the belief that the ways to an understanding of God and salvation rests on these four factors.

**Syari'ati, Ali** (Iran.) Biog. (d. 1977). Modern Iranian writer of the radical fundamentalist school whose writings on Islam and sociology were important contributions to the rise of Islamic thinking during the 1970s and 1980s.

**Syarif** (Ar: sharīf) 1. Title. A title commonly taken by persons claiming descent from the Prophet Muhammad, particularly through his grandson Hassan. 2. Trad. A category of traditions relaying on the utterances of the prophet himself.

**Syarif Qasim, Sultan.** *See* **Institut Agama Islam Negara.**

**Syarifuddin.** *See* **Darajat.**

**Syathibi, Abu Ishaq**; Syatibi ... (Ar: abū isḥāq shāṭibī) Biog. (d. 1388). An Arab scholar of the middle period who worked in Maliki jurisprudence. *See Al I'tishan.*

**Syaththariya** (Ar: shṭṭāriyyah) Myst. A Sufi order founded by Abdullah As Syattari (d. 1417), influential in the North Indian area since the sixteenth century.

**Asy Syaukani** (Ar: muḥammad ibn 'alī ash-shawkānī) Biog. (d. 1834). Zaidi school legalist from Yemen, who stepped aside from the practice of employing the decisions of his own school for a comparative approach to legalism. *See Nailul Authar.*

**Syawal** (In.); Syawwal; Syawal (Ar: ash-shawwāl) Cal. The tenth month meaning "the month of hunting." The 1st day is the feast of Idul Fitri, which celebrates the end of the fast of Ramadan.

**Syekh**; syakh (In. fr. Ar: shaykh) 1. Pol. A tribal leader in Arab society, selected on the basis of seniority and respect, who speaks for the tribe in political and social matters. 2. Pol. A guide assigned by the Arabian government to groups of tourists to assist them in the rites of the pilgrimage at Makkah. 3. Myst. The senior adept who helps the beginning and intermediate adepts master the techniques of mysticism and assists in interpretation of mystical experience. Many shaykhs have gained renown and some have been regarded as having special powers for casting spells, healing, and foretelling auspicious times and events.

**Syetan**. Spelling variant. *See* **Setan**.

**Syiah** (In.); Syi'ah; Syi'ah (Ar: shī'ah) Doct. A major sect of Islam, originally the group that followed Ali and the Family of the Prophet as the rightful rulers of the Muslim community in the early era of Islamic history. The sect is mostly associated with Iran where it took on certain cultural traditions that have differentiated it from Sunni Islam. Members of the Syiah sect are found in limited numbers in other locations of the Muslim world.

*Usage*: ___ *Isma'iliyah*, the Isma'ili sect; *aliran* ___, the Syiah Sect; *faham* ___, the thinking or teachings of the Syiahs; *firqah* ___, the Syiah Sect; *partai* ___, the Syiah Sect.

**Syifa** (Ar: shifah) Qur. A name of the Qur'an, indicating that it acts as a healing balm for the human spirit.

**Syiqoq** (In.) (Ar: shiqāq) Juris. Special third party committee that decides the case for contested divorce and the appropriate settlement.

**Syirazi, Abu Ishaq** (Ar: abū isḥāq ash-shīrāzī) Biog. (d. 1083). Shafii jurist from Iran. Famous as a teacher in Baghdad. *See Kitabul Muhadzdzab*.

**Syirik** (In.) (Ar: shirk) Juris. "Polytheism," the practice of worshiping more than one God, which is labeled as anti-Islam by the Qur'an. Practices or beliefs which recognize authority or power not subject to God's power are often cited as evidence of syirik by many Muslim writers. The term is usually translated as polytheism.

*Usage*: *dosa-dosa* ___, the sin of associating something with God; *menghukum* ___, judged as disbelief.

**Synkretisme**. Spelling variant. *See* **Sinkretisme**.

**Syorga**. Spelling variant. *See* **Surga**.

**Syu'aib** (Ar: shu'ayb) Qur. A prophet mentioned in the Qur'an, whom scholars associate with the Old Testament Jethro. He was sent to the Midyanites.

**Asy Syu'araa'**; Asy Syu'araak; Asy Syu'ara; Asy Syu'ara (Ar: ash- shu'arā) Qur. "The Poets," the twenty-sixth chapter of the Qur'an. It differentiates among the characteristics of pre-Islamic poets of the Makkan area and those of prophets, whose usage of language was similar.

**Syubhat** (In.) (Ar: shubhat) Juris. "Hesitation" or "doubt," a term used to indicate those matters in law which are not clear as to whether they are permitted or forbidden.

**Syu-dzudz**; syadz (Ar: shudhūdh) Trad. Strangeness

or foreignness, a term applied to a line of transmission of a report concerning the words and behavior of the Prophet Muhammad which conflicts with another line of transmission considered more reliable. *See* **Kiraat.**

**Syuhada** (In.) (Ar: shuhadā') Doct. Plural form of martyr. *See* **Syahid.**
*Usage*: *darah* ___, the blood of martyrs, a symbolic reference to effort put forth for the sake of Islam.

**Asy Syukur**. Spelling variant. *See* **Asy Syakuur**.

**Syura** (In.); syuro (Ar: shūrā) Pol. Discussion and consultation in general community matters. Contemporary writers on Islam nearly all acknowledge this aspect of Islamic teachings as applicable to elections, parliamentary action, and democratic processes in general.

**Asy Syuura**; Asy Syura (Ar: ash-shūrā) Qur. "The Council," the forty-second chapter of the Qur'an. It states that the basis of Islamic government is deliberation among community members.

**Syurga**. Spelling variant. *See* **Surga.**

**Szadz.** *See* **Ilmu Mushthalah Hadis.**

# T

**Ta Ha.** *See* **Thaha.**

**Ta'abbud** (Ar: ta'abbud) Juris. Special means of worship, utilizing a combination of formal worship, donations to the poor, fasting, the pilgrimage, recitation of the names of Allah, and free will prayer.

**Ta'addud** (Ar: ta'addud) Doct. Polytheism.

**Ta'alik.** Spelling variant. *See* **Ta'lik.**

**Ta'ashub**; tasub (Ar: ta'aṣṣub) Pol. Fanaticism; allegiance to a tribe or state. *See* **Ashabiyah.**

**Ta'awwudz**; ta'awudz (Ar: ta'awwudh) 1. Pop. Islam. An amulet, usually a metal charm worn on the breast that carries a holy inscription, encases a holy object or has been blessed. 2. Pop. Islam. The words a'ūdhu bi-Llāhi min ash-shayt.ani-r-rajīm, meaning "I seek refuge in God from the cursed Satan." Syn: Isti'azh.

**Tabaarak** (Ar: tabārak) Qur. "Most Holy," an alternative title for the sixty-seventh chapter of the Qur'an. A medium-length, lyrical chapter explaining the greatness of God and the duty of humans to worship Him.

**Tabari, Ibn Jarir.** *See* **Thabari, Abu Jafar ....**

**Tabi'at** (In.) (Ar: ṭabī'ah) Gen. vocab. Nature, character, disposition.

**Tabi'in** (In.); tabi'ien; tabi'in (Ar: tābi'īn) Hist. Name of a generation, meaning "The Followers," indicating the second generation of Islam, following the first generation, known as the Companions (shahabat). The tabi'in also include those of the generation of the Prophet who did

not know him personally but knew one of his Companions.
*Usage*: *para* ___, the Followers as a group.

**Tabi'it Tabi'in**; tabi'it tabi'in; tabi'iet tabi'ien (Ar: tābi'un at-tābi'un) Hist. "Followers of the Followers." In Muslim jurisprudence the third generation after Muhammad who related Traditions about the words and behavior of the Prophet.

**Tabligh** (In.) (Ar: tablīgh) Doct. Islamic concept concerning the deepening of understanding among Muslims concerning Islamic teachings through instruction. *See* **Dakwah**.
*Usage*: *ber*___, undertake activist efforts to propagandize Islam; ___ *agama*, Islamic propagation activities.

**Tabuk** (Minang.) Pop. Islam. Ceremony on the 10th day of the month of Muharram (Ashura), celebrated in Minangkabau, probably taken from early Shiite influence.

**Tadarusan** (Jav.) Qur. Recitation of the Qur'an, individually or collectively.

**Ta'diil dan Tajriih** (Ar: at-ta'dīl wa at-tajrīḥ) Trad. Characteristics demanded of transmitters of reports about Muhammad's words and behavior for confirmation of their veracity to be established. Such people must be "honorable" and "free of maliciousness."

**Tadwin** (Ar: tadwīn) Qur. Codification of the Qur'an for reference, reading, or other purposes.
*Usage*: *men*___, to undertake such codification.

*Tafshil Ayatil Quranul Hakim* (Ar: tafṣīl āyāt al-qur'ān al-ḥakīm) Lit. title. "Analysis of Qur'anic Verses," a compendium on the contents of the Qur'an by Jules La Beaume (d. 1878), which has been commonly used by modernist and postmodernist Muslim scholars in Indonesia.

**Tafsir** (In.) (Ar: tafsīr) Qur. A genre of religious literature that provides commentary on the structure, language, and usage of the Qur'an. A tafsir must be made according to practices which had their origins with the scholars of early Islam. In Indonesian Muslim practice a translation is frequently labeled a tafsir in order to acknowledge that the Qur'an only exists in

Arabic. Syn: takwil. The prominent Middle Eastern commentators of the Qur'an in Indonesian literary tradition are ___ **Abi Sa'ud** (d. 1574), also known as *Irsyadul 'Aqlissalim* (separate entries); ___ **Al Alusi** (d. 1853), also known as *Ruhul Ma'ani* (separate entries); ___ **Baghawi** (d. 1117), also known as *Ma'alimul Tanzil* (separate entries); ___ **Baidhawi** (d. 1291), also known as *Anwarut Tanzil* (separate entries); ___ **Ibnu 'Arabi** (d. 1240), *see Fatuhatul Makiyah* (separate entries); ___ **Ibnu Katsier** (d. 1773), also known as *Al Adzhiem* (separate entries); ___ **Al Jalalain** (by Al Mahalli [d. 1459] and As Suyuthi [d. 1505]) (separate entry); ___ **Khazin** (d. 1373), also known as *Lubabut Takwil* (separate entries); ___ **Al Manar** (by Muhammad Abduh [d. 1905] and Rasyid Ridha [d. 1935]) (separate entries); **Al Maraghi** (d. 1945); ___ **Nasafi** (d. 1245), also known as *Madarikut Tanzil* (separate entries); ___ **Nisaburi** (d. 1328H), also known as *Gharaibul Qur'an* (separate entries); ___ **Qasimi** (d. 1914), also known as *Mahasinut Takwil* (separate entries); ___ **Qurthubi** (d. 1273), also known as *Jami'ul Ahkam* (separate entries); ___ **Qutub** (d. 1966), also known as *Fi Zilalil Qur'an* (separate entries); ___ **Razi'** (d. 1209), also known as *Mafatihul Ghaibi* (separate entries); ___ **Sayuthi** (d. 1505), also known as *Durrul Mantsur* (separate entries); ___ **Syarbini** (d. 1570), also known as *Siraji Munir* (separate entries); ___ **Thabari** (d. 923), also known as *Jami'ul Bayan* (separate entries); ___ **Zamakhsyari** (d. 1144), also known as *Al Kas-syaf* (separate entries). *Usage*: *men___kan ayat-ayat suci*, to undertake commentary on the sacred verses of the Qur'an. ___ *menafsirkan*, to undertake commentary; ___-___ *khalaf*, commentaries by the later scholars of the classical era; ___-___ *salaf*, commentaries by the early scholars.
*Ahli* ___, classical and middle period Muslim scholars who made commentaries on the Qur'an; *kitab-kitab* ___, the major commentaries on the Qur'an.

*Tafsirul Jalalain* (Ar: tafsīr al-jalālayn) Lit. title. "Commentary of the Two Jalals," a popular name of commentaries on the Qur'an written by two scholars with the name Jalaluddin, notably Al Mahalli (d. 1389) and Al Sayuthi (d. 1505). This combined text has long been popular reading in Indonesian pesantren as a text on the Qur'an, its assembly, and its use. The book has remained important to the general community during the twentieth century. *See* **Tafsir**.

*Tafsirul Manar* (Ar: tafsīr al-qur'ān al-hakīm, also known as tafsīr al-manār) Lit. title."The 'Light' Commentary," by Muhammad Abduh (d. 1905) and Muhammad Rasyid Ridha (d. 1936), is a famous Qur'an commentary outlining a modernist Muslim approach. Consequently it has been widely used over the past seventy-five years by Indonesian modernists who proclaim it to be "the best" and "most outstanding" of all commentaries.

**At Taghaabun**, At Taghabun (Ar: at-taghābun) Qur. "Mutual Deceit," the sixty-fourth chapter of the Qur'an. It tells about the relationship of good and evil, now and in the Hereafter.

**Tahajud** (In.) (Ar: tahajjud) Juris. Night vigil; performing a voluntary prayer at night. *Usage*: *sembahyang sunat* ___, the voluntary night worship.

**Taharah** (In.); thaharah (Ar: ṭahārah) Juris. 1. Ceremonial purity. 2. Circumcision and its ceremonies.

**Tahiat**; tahiyat (In.) Ar: taḥiyyah) Juris. A recitation during worship honoring God, the Prophet Muhammad, and the Prophet's family. *Usage*: *sembahyang ___ul masjid*, honoring God, Muhammad, and the Prophet's family during prayer in the mosque.

**Tahlil** (In.) (Ar: tahlīl) Pop. Islam. Recitation of the phrase "la ilaaha illa 'llah," (there is no god but God!). It is believed by many Muslims that repetition of the tahlil will cleanse a person's sins and gain the reciter religious merit.

**Tahlilillah, Sultan**. *See* **Banjar**.

**Tahmid** (In.) (Ar: taḥmīd) Pop. Islam. The words "wa lill_hil ḥamd" meaning "all praise to Allah."

*Usage*: *membaca* ___, to recite "all praise to Allah!"

**Tahmiddillah, Sultan**. *See* **Banjar**.

**Tahrif** (Ar: taḥrīf) Qur. Falsification of the religious message, as Muslims claim was done by the followers of other monotheistic religions, which negated much of what God revealed to them.
*Usage*: *kaum* ___, the people who falsify their religion for their own gain or purposes.

**At Tahrim** (Ar: at-taḥrīm) Qur. "Prohibition," the sixty-sixth chapter of the Qur'an. It states that when God commands what is forbidden, no one can permit it.

**Tahu, Yang Maha** (In.) Theo. A name of God meaning "The All- Knowing."

**Tahun Jawa** (In.) Cal. A calendar instituted by Sultan Agung of Mataram with a base date of A.H. 78, still in use at princely houses on Java.

**Tajali** (In.); tajalli (Ar: tajallī) Myst. A concept central to Al Jili's (d. 1417) perception of mysticism in which creation is the outer aspect of real truth, manifested from the One God.

**Tajdid** (In.) (Ar: tajdīd) Doct. "Restorer of the Faith," a term given by admirers for actions undertaken by Ibnu Taimiyah (d. 1328), Ibnu Abdul Wahhab (d. 1205), and Al Afghani (d. 1897) considered to have revitalized Islam.

**Ta'jilan** (Ar: ta'jīl) Juris. Islamic ceremonial term for special services held in a mosque for those who were unable to complete the Fast during the month of Ramadan.

**Tajul Alam, Sultana** (Aceh.) Biog. (d. 1675). Sultana of Aceh (1641-75), succeeding her husband Iskandar Tsani (d. 1641) and father Iskandar Muda (d. 1636). First of a group of women rulers of Aceh, which saw authority move away from court to regional rulers. Aceh's overseas vassals also began to seek independence during this era. *See* **Aceh**.

**Tajwid** (In.) (Ar: tajwīd) Qur. The science of Qur'an recitation, with the meaning of "adornment" or "making beautiful." The science sets

down the rules for proper recitation of the vowels, consonants, and spacing of the words and sentences of the Qur'an.
*Usage*: *ber*___, to recite the Qur'an correctly; *kaidah* ___, the standards of reciting the Qur'an.

**Takabur** (In.); takabbur (Ar: takabbur) Gen. vocab. Pride, haughtiness, arrogance.

**Takafulul Ijtimak** (In.) Gen. vocab. Solidarity, common responsibility.

**At Takaatsur**; At Takatsur (Ar: at-takāthur) Qur. "Multiplying," the 102st chapter of the Qur'an. A short, lyrical chapter warning humans of the dangers of excessive wealth and comfortable living.

**Takbil** (Ar: taqbīl) Pop. Islam. A practice whereby a Muslim not descended from the Prophet Muhammad kneels and kisses the hand of those descended from the Prophet (sayyid or syarif). In considerable use in the Malay-Indonesian world in the nineteenth and early twentieth centuries, the practice was intended originally to show respect for the Prophet, but came to be the mark of Arabic superiority over non-Arab Muslims. Modernist Muslims generally opposed the practice.

**Takbir** (In.) (Ar: takbīr) Pop. Islam. The act of pronouncing the formula "Allahu akhbar" (God is Great!).
*Usage*: *membaca* ___, to recite the "God is Great" formula.

**Takdim** (In.); taqdim (Ar: taqdīm) Juris. Performing one required daily prayer immediately preceding the other at the same prayer time, such as the noontime prayer (zuhur) performed just before the afternoon prayer (ashar), followed by the afternoon prayer itself. This is done because the earlier prayer could not be performed at the normal time.

**Takdir** (In.); taqdir (Ar: taqdīr) Doct. Recognition that all matters of creation are determined by God, the Creator. In the eighteenth century the term often took the form of passive acceptance of whatever happened to an individual as what God willed to happen. Modernists

rejected such passivity for a less deterministic acceptance of the term.
*Usage*: ___ *Ilahi,* ___ *Tuhan*, the will or power of God; *Tuhan meng___kan*, God ordains all matters.

**Takhayul**; takhyul (Ar: takhayyul) Doct. "Superstition," a concept applied by some purist Indonesian Muslims to many folk practices in Indonesian life, such as a ritual meal (selamatan), the dynamism in certain blessed objects (keramat), and power of certain individuals (dukuns) to heal, cast spells, and foretell events.

**Taklid**; taqlid (Ar: taqlīd) Juris. Islamic legal term denoting strict adherence to the precepts set earlier by members of the same jurisprudential school. Such acceptance means dealing with new cases or with refinements of old decisions, only in the context of accepted teaching. Detractors refer to taklid as "blind obedience."
*Usage*: *ber___, men___*, to abide by the decisions of previous jurists on a matter of jurisprudence; ___ *buta*, to unquestioningly abide by the decisions of earlier jurists; *sikap* ___, the attitude of those who favor the doctrine of taklid.

**Takut** (In.) Doct. The general word for fear and, in a religious sense, it can mean fear of God. Syn: takwa.

**Takwa** (In.); taqwa (Ar: taqwā) Doct. Fear of God in the sense of realizing the power and majesty of God and knowing that an individual is completely subject to His will. The term also connotes fear of the retribution of God for human sins.
*Usage*: *ber___ (kepada Allah)*, to be fearful of God; *ke___an (kepada Allah)*, the state of fear toward God. ___ *kepada Allah,* ___*llah*, to be fearful of God. *sikap* ___, an attitude of fear of God; *soal* ___, the question of fear of God.

**Takwil** (In.); ta'wil (Ar: ta'wīl) Qur. Exposition of the subject matter of the Qur'an, particularly its allegorical interpretations. Syn: tafsir.
*Usage*: *men___kan*, to comment on the Qur'an and discuss the content, rather than the philological aspects, of the scripture.

**At Takwir** (Ar: at-takwīr) Qur. "The Folding Up," the eighty-first chapter of the Qur'an. A short, lyrical chapter announcing that on the Day of Judgment God will demand an accounting of all people for their actions.

**Takziah** (In.) takziyah; ta'ziyah (Ar: ta'ziyyah) Juris. Visitation by a member of one group to express condolences to another group whose leader has died. Generally practiced among Indonesian Muslims.

**Talak** (In.); thalaq; thalaaq (Ar: ṭalāq) Juris. Divorce and matters pertaining to dissolution of marriage. In Indonesia this matter is under jurisdiction of Islamic courts.
*Usage*: *menjatuhkan* ___, to repudiate a marriage; *soal* ___ *tiga sekaligus*, the issue of divorcing three times.

**Talfiq** (In.); talfik (Ar: talfīq) Juris. Following the regulations of a legalist school other than one usually followed. Traditionalist Muslims in Indonesia maintained that a Muslim should only follow consistently the regulations of a single school.
*Usage*: *at* ___ *fil madazib*, to choose parts from several schools of jurisprudence; *masalah* ___, the question of whether one might follow the dictates of more than one school of jurisprudence.

**Ta'lik**; ta'alik (In.) (Ar: ṭalīq) Juris. Divorce done through intervention of the court where the wife has filed grievances for the failings of the husband, or such matters as physical abuse or nonsupport.

**Talkin**; talqin (In.) (Ar: talqīn) Pop. Islam. A term used to denote an instruction given by a religious teacher, and generally denoting instruction given to the deceased at graveside at the close of the burial service, particularly concerning how to answer questions of faith that the angels Nakir and Munkar would ask. Modernists opposed the talkin as unwarranted innovation in religious matters.
*Usage*: *men*___*kan*, to recite the "instructions for the dead" at graveside; *hadis* ___, the purported sayings of the Prophet that justify the "instructions to the dead"; *membaca* ___, *menyatakan* *mayat*, to recite the "instruction to the dead" at graveside.

**Taman Siswa** (In.) (Jav. and Kawi) Educ. "Garden of Culture," a noted Indonesian educational association, famous in the first quarter of the twentieth century for its efforts in developing schools that combined traditional Javanese values with modern concepts of learning.

**Tamin Ad Dari**. *See Hikayat Tamin Ad Dari.*

**Tamjidillah, Sultan**. *See* **Banjar.**

**Tanah Air Kita** (In.) Pol. "Our Homeland," a national and nationalist expression for Indonesian nationhood. The term is used as imagery in patriotic speeches, writings, and songs.

**Tanah Suci** (In.) Pop. Islam. "Holy Land," the area in Arabia known as the Hijaz, which contains the holy cities of Makkah and Madinah, the shrines connected with the pilgrimage and the area where Muhammad was active during his lifetime.

**Tapabrata** (Jav.) Myst. Ascetic practice in preparation for mystical experience.

**Taqdim**. Spelling variant. *See* **Takdim.**

**Taqdir**. Spelling variant. *See* **Takdir.**

**Taqlid**. Spelling variant. *See* **Taklid.**

**Taqrir** (In. fr. Ar: taqrīr) Juris. Confirmation, proof, evidence.
*Usage*: ___ *nabi*, authentic story of the Prophet Muhammad's words and behavior.

**Taqririyyah**. *See* **Sunan.**

**Taqwa**. Spelling variant. *See* **Takwa.**

**Taqwallah**. *See* **Takwa.**

**Tarawih** (In.) (Ar: tarāwīḥ) Juris. Special prayer performed in the evening, usually in the month of Ramadan which is interspaced with Qur'an recitations and private prayer.
*Usage*: *masalah* ___, the issue of special prayers during Ramadan and their basis in scripture; *mengerjakan sembahyang* ___, to undertake or perform special tarawih prayers; *shalat* ___, *sembahyang* ___, special prayers.

**Tarbiah Islamiyah.** *See* **Persatuan Tarbiah Islamiyah.**

**Tarbiyah** (In.) (Ar: tarbiyah) Educ. A program of study offered at the national Islamic Studies institutes (IAINs) and other institutions of higher education in Indonesia in which stress is placed on teaching techniques for general Muslim education.

**Tarekat** (In.); thariqat; thariqah; thoriqat (Ar: ṭarīqah) Myst. An order of mystical practice. Tarekat were prominent in nineteenth century Indonesia, with the Naqsyabandiyah, the Qadariyah, and the Syathariyah, the major orders. They became less important with the rise of Islamic activity in the twentieth century emphasizing ritual regulated by jurisprudence and a stress on rational thinking.
*Usage*: *ahli-ahli* ___, people who follow the mystical way; *gerakan* ___, a mystical order of Islam; *orde-orde* ___, the mystical orders of Islam; ___ *Samaniyah*, the Samaniyah mystical order.

**Tarikh** (In.) (Ar: tarikh) Educ. History, usually limited to Muslim history.

*Tarjumanul Mustafid* (Ar: tarjumān al-mustafīd) Lit. title. "The Useful Interpretation," a commentary on the Qur'an in Arabic and Malay by Abdur Rauf Singkili (d. 1693), largely a rendering of *Tafsirul Jalalain* by Al Mahalli (d. 1389) and As Sayuthi (d. 1505). It is held to be the first commentary in Malay.

**Tartil** (Ar: tartīl) Qur. Slow, clear, rhythmic recitation of the Qur'an.

**Tasawuf** (In.); tashawwuf; tasauf; thasauf (Ar: taṣawwuf) Myst. Mystical practice itself, generally governed by the concepts of several leading Islamic mystics and regulated by specific orders or brotherhoods (*see* **Tarekat**). Because mysticism of other religious traditions preceded Islam to Indonesia, there are a large number of heterodox movements in the country which either fail to qualify as Islamic mystical orders or only qualify partially. Islamic mysticism remains strong in rural areas.

*Usage*: ___ *Islam*, Islamic mysticism; *ahli* ___, mystics; *amalan* ___, mystical practice; *firqah* ___, the mystical grouping; *hakikat* ___, the truth revealed through mysticism; *ilmu* ___, the science of Islamic mysticism; *mengamalkan ajaran* ___, *mengerjakan* ___, to practice mysticism; *pelajaran* ___, the teachings of mysticism; *pembangunan* ___, mystical development; *rumus-rumus* ___, mystical recitative formulas; *soal* ___, the issue of the place of mysticism in Islam; *unsur-unsur* ___, the basis of mysticism.

**Tasbih** (In.) (Ar: tasbīh) Pop. Islam. The act of repeating the formula "Subhan Allah," meaning "Praise God!"
*Usage*: *membaca* ___, to recite the phrase "Praise God!"

**Tasbis** (Ar: tasbīs[?]) Hist. Pantaloons. Derogatory term referring to old dress, insinuating that Muslims wear such costumes as evidence of their backwardness. A term used by secular nationalists in the 1930s.
*Usage*: *agama* ___, outmoded religion.

**Tasub**. Spelling variant. *See* **Ta'ashub**.

**Tashawwuf**. Spelling variant. *See* **Tasawuf**.

**Tashrif**. *See* **Ilmu Tashrif**.

**Taslim** (In.) (Ar: taslīm) Juris. The phrase "assalam alaikum wa rahmat Allah," (the peace and mercy of God be with you). This phrase is used as the benediction at the end of the obligatory prayer, uttered facing to either side.

**Tasyahud** (In.); tasyahhud (Ar: tashahhud) 1. Doct. Reciting the confession of faith, "Ashhadu al-lā ilāha illā-Llāh, wa ashha-du anna Muḥammadarrasūlu-Llāh," meaning "I bear witness that there is no god except Allah and that Muhammad is the Messenger of God." 2. Juris. Testimony to the Oneness of God and Muhammad as His messenger while in the sitting position in the ritual prayer (salat), with the index finger of the right hand extended as a physical symbol of the divine unity.
*Usage*: *waktu* ___, moment in prayer when the action is undertaken.

**Tasybih** (Ar: tashbīh) Relig. Anthropomorphism, especially characterizing God as possessing a human body and human attributes.

**Tasyhid** (In.) (Ar: tashhīd) Pop. Islam. Repetitious utterance of the confession of faith as an act of piety.

**Ta'thil** (Ar: ta'ṭīl) Doct. A concept whereby God is divested of all attributes.

**Taubah; taubat**. Spelling variations. *See* forms immediately below and **Tobat**.

**At Taubah** (Ar: at-tawbah) Qur. "Forgiving," the ninth chapter of the Qur'an. It discusses responses of Muslims toward unbelievers who do not keep their promises regarding political arrangements.

**Taubah, Yang Maha Penerima** (In.) Theo. A name of God meaning "The Great Receiver of Repentance."

**Taufik** (In.); taufiq (Ar: tawfīq) Juris. Piety, denoting proper belief and action, particularly in matters of worship.

**Tauhid** (In.); tawhid (Ar: tawhīd) 1. Doct. "The Unity of God," the nature of God as an all-inclusive being, which is the centerpiece of Islamic monotheism. The term is important to contemporary Muslims as a guide so that their own activities show a compatibility with God's purpose for humankind. 2. Qur. "Unity," the 112th chapter of the Qur'an. A very short, lyrical chapter declaring God to be a single unity.
*Usage*: *ke__an*, the "unity of God"; ___ *Islam*, the Islamic doctrine of "unity of God"; *jiwa* ___, the spirit of the "unity of God." recognizing the obligations of the principle; *membaca kalimah* ___, to recite the phrase meaning "unity of God"; *nafas ke__an*, revive a spirit of unity; *peranan* ___, the role of unity; *prinsip ke__an*, the principle of "God's unity" and what it entails for Muslims in their faith and behavior; *semangat* ___, the spirit of the "unity of God."

*Taurat* (In.); Tawrat (Ar: tawrāh) Qur. The Arabic form of Torah, referring to the books of Musa (Moses) which Muslims believe was originally a book of God

revealed at an earlier age, but has undergone change so that it now has serious differences with the original spripture.
*Usage*: ___ *diturunkan*, the Torah was revealed; *Kitab* ___, the Torah.

**Al Tauwab** (Ar: at-tawwāb) Theo. A name of God meaning "the Giver of Forgiveness."

**Tawadu** (In.); tawadhu; tawadlu' (Ar: tawaḍḍu') Juris. Washing before prayer to obtain ritual cleanness.
*Usage*: *konsep* ___, the concept of ritual cleanliness.

**Tawaduk** (In.); tawadluk (In.) (Ar: tawaḍḍu') Juris. Humility.
*Usage*: *khusyuk dan* ___ *kepada Tuhan*, proper humility to approach God; *mendoa dengan* ___, pray with proper humility; *sikap* ___, an attitude of humility.

**Tawaf**; thawaf (In.); thowaf (Ar: ṭawāf) Juris. Ceremony of circumambulating the holy shrine of Kabah seven times, three in quick step and four at the ordinary pace.
*Usage*: *ibadat* ___, circumambulating the Qur'an during the pilgrimage ritual; ___ *sunnat mengeliling Kabah Yang Mulia*, undertaking a voluntary circumambulation of the Holy Kabah.

**Tawajuk**; tawajjuh (In.) (Ar: tawajjuh) Myst. Turning one's face to God, particularly the mystic during esoteric exercises.

**Tawakal** (In.); tawakkal (Ar: tawakkul) Doct. Surrendering oneself to God's will in a matter after doing everything possible for a favorable outcome.
*Usage*: *ber*___, to surrender oneself to God.

**Tawaariichul Mutuun** (Ar: tawārīkh al-mutūn) Trad. A condition of examination of reports carrying information about the words and behavior of the Prophet Muhammad. This condition relates to the time and place the words were spoken or the action took place.

**Tawasul**; tawassul (Ar: tawassul) 1. Doct. Intercession, especially of Muhammad on behalf of Muslims. 2. Myst. Practice by which members of a mystic brotherhood remember their teachers before beginning the recitation of God's name(s).

*Usage*: *dengan ber___*, to pray asking for Muhammad's intercession; *masalah ___ dalam mendoa*, the issue of whether the request for Muhammad's intercession during prayer is proper or not; *mengerjakan doa ___*, to pray asking for Muhammad's intercession.

**Tawhid**. Spelling variant. *See* **Tauhid**.

**Ta'wil**. Spelling variant. *See* **Takwil**.

*Tawrah*. Spelling variant. *See* *Taurat*.

**At Tawwaab** (Ar: at-tawwāb) Theo. Name of God meaning "The Relenting."

**Tayamum**; tayammun (In.) (Ar: tayammum) Juris. Ritual ablution by means of clean earth (sand, dust) instead of water. Allowable only under emergency conditions where water is not available. *Usage*: *ber___*, to employ special ablution with clean earth.

**Ta'ziyah**. Spelling variant. *See* **Takziah**.

**Tazkiah** (In.) tazkiyah (Ar: taz'iyyah) Juris. In matters not regulated by God the community is bound by the principles of good motives and benefit of results achieved by certain behavior or actions.

**Tebuireng**. *See* **Pondok Pesantren Tebuireng**.

**Teknologi** (In.) Anthro. The application of advanced science to the work problems of society. Contemporary Western society is highly technological, while Third World nations, such as Indonesia, have policies to become more technological. *Usage*: *jiwa ___*, spirit of technology, a desire to use it; *perjalanan sains dan ___*, the path of science and technology.

**La Tenrittatia To Unru'**. *See* **Arung Palakka**.

**Teokratisme** (In.) Relig. Belief that politics can be operated on principles put forth by God, usually by religious officials.

**Termas Mahfuz** (In.) Biog. (d. 1338H). Well known religious Javanese scholar (kiai) in the early twentieth century, who operated the Pesantren Tremas in East

Java and was teacher of several well-known Indonesian scholars. He wrote commentaries on Syafii jurisprudence (fikih), such as the *Muhibah*, which was a study of the works of Ibnu Hajarul 'Asqalani (d. 1567).

**Ternate** (In.) Geog. An area in Eastern Indonesia which was the site of an important Islamic sultanate in the early sixteenth century involved in the clove trade. It cooperated initially with the Portuguese, later opposed them, and ultimately made an agreement with the Dutch. *See* **Kesultanan**. The prominent rulers in the fifteenth and sixteenth centuries were as follows: Zainal Abidin (1486-1500), Khairun (Hairun) (ca. 1558-70), Babullah (ca. 1570-83) (separate entry), Mandarsyah (ca. 1645-ca. 55).
*Usage*: *Kerajaan* ___, the Kingdom of Ternate.

**Terpuji, Yang Maha** (In.) Theo. A name of God meaning "The Most Praiseworthy." Syn: Al Hamid.

**Teuku** (Aceh.) Title. A title in Aceh given to officials who administer and preserve the customary law (adat).

**Teungku** (In.) (Aceh.) Title. Acehnese title given to religious scholars operating a religious school, such as a pesantren or surau. A Teungku Tjhik is a religious teacher whose fame has spread beyond his own locale.

**Teungku Kuala**. *See* **Abdur Rauf Al Singkili**.

**Thabaqaatur Ruwat** (Ar: ṭabaqāt ar-rūwāt) Trad. The ranking of importance of transmitters of reports concerning the words and behavior of the Prophet Muhammad in the early centuries of Islam. The ranking is done as a guide to the degree of accuracy of the various reports.

*Thabaqaatusy Syafi'iyyah* (Ar: ṭabaqāt ash-shāfi'iyyah) Lit. title. "Ranking of Syafii Legalists," a book on the teachings of the Syafii school of jurisprudence by Ar Rafi'i (d.1226).

**Thabari, Abu Ja'far bin Jarir**; At Tabari ... (Ar: abū ja'far muḥammad ibn jarīr aṭ-ṭabarī) Biog. (d. 923). Noted Arab scholar of the classical period whose writings encompassed the major fields of religious studies of the time. He is most famous for his histories but has a Qur'an commentary and works of jurisprudence that were extensively used. *See Jami'ul Bayan* and **Tafsir**.

**Thaha**; Tha-ha; Thaaha Ta Ha (Ar: ṭāhā) Qur. (The Arabic Letter) "Thaahaa," the twentieth chapter of the Qur'an. It relates the story of the Prophet Musa (Moses) receiving the revelation from God directly.

**Thaha, Sultan Saifuddin**. *See* **Institut Agama Islam Negara**.

**Thaharah**. Spelling variant. *See* **Taharah**.

**Thalaq**; thalaaq. Spelling variants. *See* **Talak**.

**Ath Thalaaq**; Ath Thalaq (Ar: ṭalāq) Qur. "Divorce," the sixty-fifth chapter of the Qur'an. It deals with the matter of divorce and its correct use among believers.

**Thalatha'**. *See* **Yawmul Tsulatsa'**.

**Thalib** (Ar: ṭalib) Educ. One who seeks. Usually a student aspiring to become a religious scholar.

**Ath Thaamah** (Ar: aṭ-ṭāmmah) Qur. "Misfortune," an alternate title for the seventy-ninth chapter of the Qur'an. A medium-length, lyrical chapter relating how God punished Pharaoh for his arrogance toward the Children of Israel. The usual title is Naazi'aat.

**Ath Thaariq**; Ath Thariq (Ar: aṭ-ṭāriq) Qur. "The Morning Star," the eighty-sixth chapter of the Qur'an. A short, lyrical chapter telling Muhammad to be patient for a time with the disbelievers.

**Thariqah**; thariqat. Spelling variant. *See* **Tarekat**.

**Thasauf**. Variant spelling. *See* **Tasawwuf**.

**Ath Thaul** (Ar: aṭ-ṭawl) Qur. "He Who has Compassion," an alternate title for the fortieth chapter of the Qur'an. The usual name of the chapter is Al Mu'min.

**Thawaf**. Spelling variant. *See* **Tawaf**.

**Thawalib**. *See* **Madrasah Thawalib.**

**Thawaf**; thowaf. Spelling variants. *See* **Tawaf.**

**Thoriqat**. Spelling variant. *See* **Tarekat.**

**Ath Thuur**; Ath Thur (Ar: aṭ-ṭūr) Qur. "The Mountain," the fifty-second chapter of the Qur'an. It is named for the mountain in Sinai where the Prophet Musa (Moses) received his revelation.

**Tidore** (In.) Geog. An area in Eastern Indonesia that was the site of an Islamic sultanate in the sixteenth century, heavily involved in the clove spice trade. It was a competitor of the Sultanate of Ternate and made an arrangement with the Spanish. In the seventeenth century it signed an agreement with the Dutch.

**Tijaniah** (In.); Tijaniyah (Ar: tijaniyyah) Myst. Mystical order founded by Abul Abbas ... al-Tijan (d. 1815) in Algeria. The movement has had some supporters in Indonesia.

**At Tiin**; At Tin (Ar: at-tīn) Qur. "The Fig," the ninety-fifth chapter of the Qur'an. A very short, lyrical chapter asserting that God will punish the transgressors and reward the faithful.

**Tinggi, Yang Maha** (In.) Theo. A name of God meaning "The Most High." Syn: Al Qahhaar.

**Tinja** (Bugi.) Pop. Islam. Vows made to a saint to prevent calamities, obtain wealth, or achieve happiness. Usually accompanied by a small offering.

**Tirakat** (In.) (Jav.) Pop. Islam. Taming passions by special acts, such as fasting.

**Tirmidzi**. *See* **Turmuzi.**

**Tiro, Cik de, (Teungku)** (Aceh.) Biog. (d. 1890) Influential religious scholar in Aceh who was a leader of the pro-war faction against the Dutch in the Aceh War (1873-1904).

**Tirtayasa, Abul Fath Abdul Fatah** (In.) Biog. (d. 1683). Ruler of Bantam (1651-83) as Sultan Ageng. He headed the faction which favored continuation of his kingdom's multilateral trading practices with European and Asian partners. He opposed the Dutch East India Company's attempts to limit Bantam's trade. War led to Dutch conquest and loss of sovereignty. Ageng died in Dutch control. He is regarded as an Islamic hero by modern Indonesian Muslim historians. *See* **Bantam.**

**Tobat** (In.); taubah; taubat (Ar: tawbah) 1. Doct. Repentance.
*Usage*: *ber___, ___ kepada Tuhan*, to undertake repentance (to God); *sikap* ___, an attitude of repentance.

**Tompolo** (Bugi.) Pop. Islam. Tonsure ceremony on the 7th or 40th day after birth. Syn: aqiqah.

**Tradisional** (In.) Anthro. Trait of identifying with the long-held beliefs and practices of Islam, especially as laid down in the schools of jurisprudence and particularly with the works of Syafii legalists. *See* **Kaum Tua.**
*Usage*: *golongan* ___, traditionalists; *para santri* ___, pious Muslims who are traditionalists.

**Transcendentalisme** (In.) Relig. The mystical understanding in which the essence of God is viewed as prior to, above, and having being apart from, the created universe.

**Trenggana, Sultan** (Jav.) Biog. (d. 1546) Ruler of Demak in the sixteenth century who conquered West Java and led the empire to its zenith in political and spiritual influence as an agent of Islamic conversion of the Javanese population. *See* **Demak.**

**Trunajaya, Raden** (Jav) Biog. (d. 1680). Madurese prince who led a rebellion, with strong Muslim overtones, against the Mataram ruler Amangkurat I. Dutch East India Company intervention defeated the rebellion but gave the Company greater control over Java. Modern Indonesian Muslim historians regard him as an early Indonesian Muslim hero.

**Tsamrah** (Ar: thamrah) Juris. The purpose of doing something. Used frequently in setting out religious exercises. Syn: faedah.

**Tsani, Sultan Iskandar**. *See* **Iskander Tsani** and **Aceh**.

**Tuanku** (Minangkabau fr. Mal: Tunku) Title. 1. A title of respect for a leader of a religious school in Minangkabau, usually a surau. 2. Local adat leaders in Minangkabau concerned with the application of customary law but who also administers Muslim law.

**Tuban** (In.) Geog. City on the north coast of Java noted as a center of early Islamization and for being a center of Muslim political activity in the fifteenth century.

**Tubuh** (In.) Doct. Body. *Usage: ruh dan* ___, soul and body.

*At Tufhaul Mursala* (Ar: at-tufḥah al-mursalah) Lit. title. "Gift Addressed to the Spirit of the Prophet," a work on mysticism by Al Burhanpuri (d. 1620). It outlined seven grades of being, which was a hallmark of early Indonesian mysticism. It was in wide use in seventeenth century Aceh, but was denounced by the reformist Ar Raniri (d. 1658).

**Tuhan** (In.) Relig. God, including Allah. *Usage*: *ber___ kepada*, to associate God with (something else); *ke___an*, divinity; ___ *Allah*, God; ___ *berfirman*, God commands; ___ *mensyariatkan*, God ordains; ___ *Sang Pencipta*, God, the Creator; ___ *Yang Kekal*, God, the Eternal; ___ *Yang Maha Esa*, God, the Only One; ___ *Yang Maha Kuasa*, God the Most Powerful; ___ *Yang Maha Mendengar*, God, the All-Hearing; ___ *Yang Maha Sempurna*, God the Most Perfect; *Bimbangan* ___, God's guidance; *ciptaan* ___, God's creation; *hubungan* ___ *dengan manusia*, God's relationship with humans; *iradat* ___, *izin* ___, God's permission; *kalimah* ___, the Word of God; *keampunan* ___, God's forgiveness; *Ke-Esaan* ___*(Yang Mutlak)*, (The Unconditional) Unity of God; *kodrat* ___, God's power; *lapangan ke___an*, metaphysics; *melihat* ___ to see God (mystically); *memperkenalkan* ___, to know and understand God (mystical); *mengaku* ___, to acknowledge God; *orang-orang yang anti-*___, people who are anti-God; *pengabdian kepada* ___, to serve God;

*perintah* ___, the command of God; *perwujudan* ___, unity with God in a mystical state; *rela* ___, *kereluan* ___, God's consent; *sifat* ___, attribute of God; *soal ke*___*an*, the question of God; *takdir* ___, God's power; *terserah kepada kebijaksanaan* ___, to surrender to the understanding of God; *wahyu* ___, God's revelation; *Zat* ___, God's essence.

**Tuhan Yang Maha Esa**. *See* **Ketahunan Yang Masa Esa**.

*Tuhfah* (Ar: tuḥfah) Lit. title. "The Gift," a leading Syafii treatise on Islamic jurisprudence by Ibnu Hajarul Haitami (d. 1567), which enjoyed wide circulation and use in Southeast Asia in the nineteenth and twentieth centuries.

**At Turmuzi**; At Turmudzi; At Tirmidzi (Ar: at-tirmidhī) 1. Biog. (d. 279H/892). Arab scholar and major compiler of Traditions (hadis), the sayings and actions of the Prophet Muhammad. 2. Trad. Reference to the books of Tradition collections assembled by At Turmuzi. *See Al Jamiush Shahih*.

# U

**Uhud** (Ar: uḥud) Geog. Hill near Madinah, where, in 625, the forces of Muhammad met the Makkans in battle. Near victory, the Muslim forces were beaten by a Makkan counterattack.

**Ujub, Takabur dan Riya** (In.) Juris. "Proud, vain and haughty," a pejorative term for the believer who is short of the behavior required of the pious.

**Ukhuwah Islamiah** (Ar: ukhwwah islāmiyyah) Pol. Islamic solidarity as a religion and as a community.

**Ukhrawi** (In.) (Ar: ukhrāwi) Doct. Orientation toward the life of the Hereafter.

**Ulama** (In.); 'Ulama, 'ulama (Ar: 'ulamā') 'alim; malim are the singular. Title. Scholars of religious sciences in Islam and generally acknowledged leaders of the community in matters of religion; a term of high respect.

*Usage*: ___ *khalaf ahli-ahli fikih*, the later classical scholars of jurisprudence; ___ *salaf*, the classical scholars of Sunni Islam; ___ *terdahulu*, earlier scholars; ___-___ *fikih*, the scholars involved in the development of Islamic jurisprudence; ___-___ *Islam*, Islamic religious scholars; ___-___ *kampung*, rural scholars (of Indonesia). *Fihak alim* ___, the classical and medieval scholars of Sunni Islam; *golongan* ___ *Hanafi*, the scholars of the Hanafi school of Muslim jurisprudence; *ijmak* ___, consensus of the scholars (a principle of Muslim jurisprudence); *institusi ke*___*an*, religious scholars as an institution of the Islamic religion; *kalangan alim* ___, the classical and medieval scholars of Sunni Islam; *kepimpinan* ___, leadership by the scholars; *Majelis* ___ *Indonesia*, the Indonesian Religious Scholars' Council; *musyawarah* ___, the discussion among scholars; *para* ___, *para alim* ___, the classical and medieval scholars of Sunni Islam.

**Uleuebalang** (Acehnese: ule'ue'balang) Pol. A group in Aceh for officials concerned with administering and defining customary law (hulubalang). They use the title Teuku.

**Ulil Amri** (In.) (Ar: 'ulu-l amr) Pol. Political leadership or authority.

**Umar, H. Muhammad Thaib** (In.) Biog. (d. 1920) Modernist Muslim advocate in early twentieth century Minangkabau, noted for reforming Islamic education to introduce new Islamic texts, use of new teaching techniques for language learning, and reordering the curriculum for clearer goals.

**Umar, Teuku** (Aceh.) Biog. (d. 1899) Leader of Acehnese forces during the middle years of the Aceh War (1882 to 1904). Killed in a Dutch ambush. Acknowledged by the Indonesian Republic as a preindependence hero of the Aceh area.

**Umar Bin Khaththab**, 'Umar bin Khaththab (Ar: 'umar bin khaṭṭāb) Biog. (d. 644) A close associate of the Prophet Muhammad and second ruler after Muhammad's death.

**Umat** (In.); ummat (Ar: ummah) Doct. "Community of believers," usually used for Muslims. It differentiates Muslims from others and promotes unity of purpose and brotherhood.
*Usage*: ___ *al 'ilm*, the community based on science; ___ *Budha*, the Buddhist religious community; ___ *Islam*, Islamic community of believers; ___ *Islam dunia*, the (worldwide) Islamic community of believers; ___ *Islam Indonesia*, the community of Muslim believers in Indonesia; ___ *Kristen*, the Christian religious community; ___ *manusia*, the human community. *Berkumpul* ___ *Islam*, to unify the Islamic community; *kalangan* ___ *Islam*, the Islamic community of believers; *kehidupan* ___, the life of the community; *kerjasama* ___ *Islam*, the common effort of the Islamic community; *masyarakat* ___ *Islam Indonesia*, the community of Muslim believers in Indonesia; *mempersatukan*

___ *Islam*, to unify the Islamic community; *pandangan* ___ *Islam*, the perspective of the Islamic community; *perjuangan* ___ *Islam*, the struggle of the Muslim community for survival and progress toward its aspirations.

**Umatul Ilm** (Ar: ummat-l 'ilm) Anthro. A term denoting that a particular group bases itself on scientific principle. A term used by Indonesian Muslim intellectuals in the 1980s.

**Umayyah** (Ar: ad-dawlah al-umawiyyah) Hist. The Arab kingdom that ruled the Islamic world from 661 to 750. The dynasty was noted for use of Arab forms of political rule while retaining much of Hellenistic culture in the Eastern Mediterranean. It survived in Spain until 1031. *See* **Khilafah.**
*Usage*: *bani* ___, the Umayyah dynasty.

**Al Umm.** *See Kitabul Umm.*

**Ummat.** Spelling variant. *See* **Umat.**

**Ummulmu'minin** (Ar: umm al-mu'minīn) Hist. "Mother of Believers," a term applied to the wives of the Prophet Muhammad, especially after his death.

**Umrah** (Ar: 'umrah) Juris. The lesser pilgrimage, entailing only the rites performed in the vicinity of the Kabah. This visitation may be performed at any time of the year, whereas the pilgrimage proper must be observed on the set days of the pilgrimage month.
*Usage*: *haji* ___, the lesser pilgrimage; *mengerjakan* ___, to perform the lesser pilgrimage.

**Undang Perkawinan** 1973 (In.) Pol. An enactment of Indonesian Parliament that placed restrictions on the number of wives a Muslim male could marry. The law was opposed by many Muslims as an unwarranted interference by the government in Muslim affairs, even while they agreed with the law's intent.

**Undang-Undang Peradilan Agama** (In.) Pol. A set of laws which govern marriage matters instituted by the Indonesian government beginning in 1946.

**Universitas** (In.) Educ. University.
*Usage*: ___ *Al Azhar*, an important Muslim university in Cairo, where many students from Southeast Asia have studied over the past two centuries.

**Urdu** (In.) (Urdu) Lang. A language of the Indian subcontinent similar to Hindi, but built on a script adopted from Persian. The primary influence on it during its development was Persian art, culture, and language.

**Usali** (In.); ushalli (Ar: uṣallī) Juris. The intention at the beginning of prayer given by some Muslims. *See* **Niat**.
*Usage*: *ber___, membaca* ___, to recite the intention at the beginning of prayer.

**Ushul Fikih**; ushul fiqh (In.); ushul fiqih; usul al-fiqh (Ar: uṣūl al-fiqh) Juris. The principles of Islamic jurisprudence, i.e., the major assumptions in the science of developing the codes of behavior by Muslim scholars. The four main principles are the lessons of the Qur'an, those from Traditions, the consensus of scholars (ijmak), and analogy (kias) of the other sources.

*Ushul 6(enam) Bis* (In.) Lit. title. "The Six Bismilliahhi Rahman Ar Rahims," a reference to a text by Samarkandi (d.xx) from the pesantren known to have been used as early as the Demak period (fifteenth century). It was a writing of six sections, each dealing with a different matter of religion.

**Ushuluddin** (Ar: uṣūl ad-dīn) 1. Doct. Principles of religion. *See* Aqidah. 2. Educ. A program of study offered at the national Islamic Studies institutes (IAIN's) and other Indonesian institutions of higher education in which stress is placed on matters of faith and practice in Islam.

**Usman, Faqih** (In.) Biog. (b. 1900). Muhammadiyah activist from Central Java and national chair from 1968 to 1971. *See* **Muhammadiyah** and **Menteri Agama**.

**Usmaniyah**. *See* **Khilafah**.

**Ustadz** (In.) (Ar: ustādh) Title. Title for a certain grade of Islamic scholar.
*Usage*: *para* ___, the Islamic scholars as a group.

**Uswatun Hasanah** (Ar: uswatun ḥasanah) Myst. A

fine example to follow, as the life of the Prophet Muhammad.

**Utsman Bin 'Affan** (Ar: uthmān ibn 'affān) Biog. (d. 656). The third ruler of the early Muslim community after the death of Muhammad. His assassination opened the way for the split between the Sunni and Syiah sects in Islam. The compilation of the Qur'an was completed in his reign.

# V

**Van Ronkel.** *See* **Ronkel, Philippus Samuel van.**

**Veerignde Oostindische Compagnie—VOC** (Dutch) Hist. The "United (Dutch) East India Company." The Company won control of Indonesia in the seventeenth century through negotiated and coerced agreements with local rulers and then, until the early nineteenth century, operated an economic system selling spices and other goods from the region in the European marketplace.

*Vijf Gesandschaps Reizen* (Dutch) Lit. title. Report by R. Van Goens (d. 1681), an official of the Dutch East India Company, about the royal court of the Mataram ruler and the organization of the realm in the seventeenth century.

**Vinsinck, A. J.** *See* **Wensinck, A. J.**

**VOC.** *See* **Vereenigde Oostindische Compagnie.**

**Volksraad** (Dutch) Hist. "People's Chamber," the legislative council established by the Dutch colonial administration in Indonesia in 1917. It consisted of both appointed officials and elected members. Since it had no power to legislate, but could only advise the governor-general, Indonesian nationalist groups used it as a sounding board but sometimes boycotted it. It was abolished at the beginning of the Japanese occupation in 1942.

# W

**Wahab, Ibn Abdul.** *See* **Abdul Wahab.**

**Wahab, K. H. Wahid.** *See* **Menteri Agama.**

**Wahab Hasbullah, K. H.** *See* **Nahdatul Ulama.**

**Al Waduud**; Al Wadud (Ar: al-wadūd) Theo. A name of God meaning "The Loving."

**Wahabi** (Ar: wahhābiyyah) Pol. 1. The puritanical reform movement founded in Arabia in the the eighteenth century by Ibn Abdul Wahab (d. 1787). Impressed with its ideas, some Indonesian pilgrims adopted the movement's outlook and militancy and founded the Paderi movement in Minangkabau. *See* **Paderi**. 2. "Fanatic," a term of approbation used by traditionalists to refer to the behavior and doctrines of the Muslim modernists which they consider excessive. *Usage*: *ajaran* ___, doctrines of the Wahabis; *golongan fundamentalis* ___, the Wahabi fundamentalist movement.

**Wahdatul Wujud** (In.) (Ar: wiḥdat ul-wujūd) Myst. Unity of being. The viewpoint of Ibnu Arabi (d. 1240) that God is refracted into all other beings, creatures, and objects and that, therefore, God is the hidden identity behind all things. The doctrine was later attacked by other Muslim scholars as pantheistic.

**Al Wahhaab**, Al Wahhab (Ar: al-wahhāb) Theo. Name of God meaning "The Most Generous." Syn: Yang Maha Pemberi.

**Al Waahid**; Al Wahid (Ar: al-wāḥid) Theo. Name of God meaning "The Unique." Syn: Al Ahad.

**Wahid, Abdurrahman** (In.) Biog. (b. 1940). Javanese Muslim educator and administrator trained at the University of Iraq. Managing chair (ketua) of the Nahdlatul Ulama in the 1980s who put forth numerous proposals for the practical Islamization of Indonesian society. *See* **Nahdatul Ulama.**

**Wahid Hasyim, K. H. A.** *See* **Hasyim, (Ki) Wahid** and **Menteri Agama**.

**Wahid Wahab, K. H.** *See* **Menteri Agama**.

**Wahyu** (In.) (Ar: waḥy) Doct. Revelation from God to humans. This is usually done in the form of books, such as the Qur'an, which give guidance to humans. Revelation (wahyu) differs from inspiration (ilham) in that the latter is given to an individual rather than to humans in general.
*Usage*: *me___kan*, to reveal. ___ *Allah*, inspiration from God for revelation of holy books; ___ *Ilahi*, inspiration from God for revelation of holy books; ___ *kecil*, inspiration from God not involving revelation; ___ *suci*, divine inspiration from God for revelation of holy books. *dalil* ___, proof or indicators of revelation; *menerima* ___ *dari Tuhan*, to receive revelation from God; *menghembuskan* ___, to reveal; *petunjuk* ___, indications of revelation; *turun* ___, to reveal.

**Wail.** *See* **Neraka**.

**Wajib** (In.) Juris. 1. Necessary, incumbent upon as a religious obligation. 2. A category of obligatory behavior and action in Muslim jurisprudence.
*Usage*: *bidah yang* ___, innovation that is incumbent; ___ *dikada*, decreed (by God) as obligatory.

**Al Wajid** (Ar: al-wājid) Theo. Name of God meaning "The Giver."

**Wakaf** (In.); waqf (Ar: waqf) Juris. Pious endowment given by Muslims for the support of religious activities. Usually property, there are complicated regulations in Muslim jurisprudence for tending such property and assuring that proceeds go for the donor's stated purpose. In Indonesia a similar form under national law is usually used, called "yayasan." *See* **Yayasan**.

*Usage*: *ber___, me___kan (tanah)*, to dedicate (land) for a pious endowment; ___ *gantung*, endowment contingent on a condition.

**Wakil** (In.) (Ar: wakīl) Doct. Deputy, substitute.
*Usage*: ___ *Nya di bumi*, God's steward on earth.

**Al-Wakiil**, Wakil (Ar: al-wākil) Theo. A name of God meaning "The Steward."

**Wali** (In.); waliyu (Ar: walī) 1. Doct. The steward of God on earth. Syn: khalifah. 2. Myst. Literally "near one," or "friend." Especially a friend of God, a title generally involving mystical practices and forms.
*Usage*: ___ *Allah*, God's agent; ___ *Songo*, the nine saints of Java.
*Para* ___, a group of walis; *para* ___ *penyiar dan penjebar* Islam di Nusantara, the saints who spread and converted Islam in the Indonesian archipelago.

**Wali Songo**; Wali Sangha; Wali Sanga (Jav) Hist. "The Nine Saints," a reference to the nine prominent missionaries who are popularly believed to have converted Java to Islam. Sometimes several others are attached to the list as important, especially Syekh Siti Jenar. The most common name is listed below, although each is known by a variety of names. *Original Nine*: Sunan Ampel (separate entry), Sunan Bonang (separate entry), Sunan Giri (separate entry), Sunan Darajat (separate entry), Sunan Gunung Jati (separate entry), Sunan Kalijaga (separate entry), Sunan Kudus (separate entry), Sunan Malik Ibrahim (separate entry), and Sunan Muria (separate entry). *Associated later*: Sitti Jenar, Syekh (separate entry); Raden Fattah (separate entry). *See Babad Tanah Jawa*.

**Waliyullah, Syekh Yusuf** (In.) Biog. (d. 1700). Javanese Muslim scholar who was instrumental in spreading Islam in South Kalimantan in the mid-seventeenth century. After anti-Dutch activity at Bantam in 1682 he was sent into exile to Sri Lanka and died later in South Africa.

**Al Waliyy**; Al Waliy (Ar: al-walī) Theo. Name of God meaning "The Patron."

**Waliyyul Amri Dlaruri Bisy Syaukat** (Ar: waliyu-l amri ḍarūrī bish-shawkah) Pol. "The Retainer of National Power," a title awarded President Sukarno by the Muslim Scholars Council (Konperensi Alim-Ulama) in 1954 with a resolution that obedience to him was not at odds with Muslim jurisprudence.

**Waqf.** Spelling variant. *See* **Wakaf.**

**Al Waaqi'ah**; Al Waqi'ah; Waqi'ah (Ar: al-wāqi'at) Qur. "The Inevitable Day," the fifty-sixth chapter of the Qur'an. It tells of God's division of humans into bad and good on the Final Day.

**Wara** (In.) Myst. Abstinence. *Usage*: *hidup* ___, life of abstinence.

**Waratsah** (Ar: warāthah) Juris. Law dealing with inheritance matters.

**Warid** (In.) Gen. vocab. Traditional.
*Usage*: *membaca* ___, to recite prayers in the traditional way.

**Al Warits** (Ar: al-wārith) Theo. Name of God meaning "The Inheritor of All Things."

**Washiyat.** Spelling variant. *See* **Wasiat.**

**Al Washliyah.** *See* **Jam'iyatul Washliyah.**

**Wasiat** (In.); washiyat (Ar: waṣiyyah) 1. Doct. Commandments given by God, such as the commandments given Musa (Moses). 2. Trad. Transmission of a report concerning the words and behavior of the Prophet Muhammad by a last minute exhortation or command to another to become the next transmitter.

**Al Waasil** (Ar: al-wāṣil) Theo. Name of God meaning "The Generous."

**Wasilah** (Ar: wasīlah) Qur. The highest station in Paradise which Muhammad hoped to obtain for himself. Muslims pray that this may happen. This prayer for intercession on behalf of the Prophet is often reversed so that the prayer becomes a call for the intercession of the Prophet for the person making the prayer.

**Al Waasi'un**; Al Wasie'; Al Wasi'i (Ar: al-wāsi') Theo. Name of God meaning "The Vast."

**Wawasan Nasional** (In.) Pol. "Archipelagic Principle," a declaration of the Indonesian national boundary adopted by the Indonesian government in 1957 and affirmed by International convention on the Law of the Sea in 1983. The principle includes a 200-mile exclusive economic zone and fixes a maritime boundary within which lie the islands and seas which make up Indonesia.

**Wayang** (In.) (San.) Anthro. A play or performance depicting legendary stories, of both Javanese and the Hindu Ramayana origin. The wayang kulit is a shadow play whose dialogue and action highlights moral and ethical lessons, given usually to celebrate important events in a village, city or person's life. The wayang orang is performed by human actors. Specialized forms exist as well and sometimes have been used specifically to promote Muslim values.

**Wensinck, A. J. Vensinck...** (French) Biog. (d. 1939) A French researcher on Islam who wrote on Muslim traditions, the creed, and general Islamic subjects. *See Miftah Kunuzis Sunnah*.

**Westernisme** (In.) Anthro. Attitude of some non-European peoples in the twentieth century who seek to emulate the West as a means of modernizing and obtaining economic improvement. This attitude is roundly condemned by most contemporary Indonesian Muslim writers, although an eclectic selection of traits, procedures, and methodologies is viewed as acceptable.

**Weton** (In.) (Jav.) Educ. Method of instruction by a religious scholar (kiai) at an Islamic boarding school (pesantren). Students sit in a circle in front of the scholar working on various texts. He calls on various ones to recite and clarify what they are reading. It is called bandungan (West Java) and halaqah (Sumatra).
*Usage*: ___ *methode*, the weton method of education.

**Wibisono, Jusuf** (In.) Biog. (b. 1909). Leader of the Indonesian Muslim Labor Alliance (Gasbiindo) and its representative in Parliament during the 1950s. He was imprisoned in the later years of the Sukarno era and was active in the early days of the New Order in support of the new government.

**Wijadah** (Ar: al-wijādah) Trad. The transmission of a report concerning the words and behavior of the Prophet Muhammad by inadvertent discovery, usually in written form left by an earlier transmitter.

**Wilde Schoolen** (Dutch) Educ. "Wild (unauthorized) Schools," a term for private schools not receiving government subsidy during the 1930s. In 1932 the government passed an ordinance calling for the registration of such schools, but the law was suspended after nearly universal Indonesian protest.

**Wiraja, Puspa**. *See Hikayat Baktiar.*

**Wirid** (In.) (Ar: wird) Pop. Islam. Repetition of God's names or other formulas used for the purpose of allowing the worshiper to express his devotion to God. Often recited in the morning and evening over a lengthy period of time. Syn: zikir.

*Wirid Hidayat Jati. See Serat Wirid Hidayat Jati.*

**Wiryosanjoyo, Sukiman**. *See* **Sukiman Wiryosanjoyo.**

**Withdatul Wujud**. Spelling variant. *See* **Wahdut ul Wujud.**

**Witir** (In.) (Ar: witr) Juris. Optional prayer with an uneven number of sets, performed between night prayer (isha) and dawn.

**Wudu** (In.); wudlu; wudlu'; wudhuk (Ar: wuḍū') Juris. The lesser ablution intended to take care of minor defilements occurring after a major ablution. Washing before prayer is wudu. *Usage*: *ber*___ to wash for purposes of ablution; *membatalkan* ___, to negate purification (by some unclean act); *rukun* ___, the rite of ritual washing.

**Al Wuhdan** (Ar: al-wuḥdān) Trad. Indicator that the line of transmission for a report concerning the words and behavior of the Prophet Muhammad is exclusively between a father and his son.

**Wujud** (In.) (Ar: wujūd) Myst. Essence, being.

**Al Wujudiyya** (In.) (Ar: wujūdiyyah). Myst. A system of worship and mystical practice followed at the Acehnese royal court by Hamzah Fansuri (d. 1625) drawn largely from the influence of Ibnu Arabi (d. 1240). It was later labeled "pantheistic" by Nuruddin Raniri (d. 1658) who had the works of the Wujudiyya writers burned as heretical.

**Wuruk, Hayam.** *See* **Hayam Wuruk.**

# Y

**Ya Rabbil Alimin** (Ar: yā rabb al-'alamīn) Expres. "O, Lord of the Worlds."

**Yaa Siin**; Yaasiin; Ya Sin (Ar: yā sīn) Qur. The Arabic alphabet letters "Ya" and "Sin," the thirty-sixth chapter of the Qur'an. It contains the doctrine of revelation and the concept of the Hereafter. A popular recitation in the late afternoons, on Thursday evenings in the mosques, at funerals, and at moments of fear or danger.
*Usage*: *membaca Surah* ___, to read or recite the Surah, usually as an act of piety.

**Yahudi** (In.) (Ar: al-yahūd) Relig. 1. The Jewish people in general. 2. In the Qur'an they are sometimes the Children of Israel. 3. In the Qur'an, they are sometimes the several tribes residing in Madinah, with whom Muhammad had difficulty, leading to expulsion of those tribes from Madinah.
*Usage*: ___ *agama*, Judaism; *beragama* ___, to practice Judaism; *kelompok* ___, *para* ___, the Jewish People; *suku-suku* ___, the Jewish tribes.

**Yahya** (Ar: yaḥyā) Qur. A prophet mentioned in the Qur'an, whom scholars have associated with the Biblical John the Baptist.

**Yakin** (In.) Doct. Belief.
*Usage*: *ke___an*, belief in Islam.

**Ya'kub**; Ya'qub (Ar: ya'qūb) Qur. A prophet mentioned in the Qur'an, whom scholars have associated with the Old Testament Jacob.

**Yang** (Mal./In.) Gen Vocab. Pronoun for "who." *See* following noun.

**Yatim** (In.) (Ar: yatīm) Juris. The orphan who, if needy, is eligible for alms and to share in the distribution of the poor tax.

*Usage*: *anak* ___, orphan.

**Yatsrib** (Ar: yathrib) Geog. The oasis town to which Muhammad and his fellow Makkan Muslims migrated in the Flight in 622. Also, and most particularly known thereafter, as Madinat An Nabi (The City of the Prophet).

**Yawmul Ahad** (Ar: yawm al-aḥad). Cal. The first day of the Muslim week, i.e. Sunday.

**Yawmul Akhir** (In.) (Ar: al-yawm al-ākhir). Doct. The Day of Judgment.

**Yawmul Arbi'a** (Ar: yawm al-arba'ā') Cal. Fourth day of the Muslim week, i.e., Wednesday.

**Yawmul Din** (Ar: yawm ad-dīn) Doct. The Day of Judgment.

**Yawmul Hisab** (Ar: yawm al-ḥisāb) Doct. The Day of Reckoning, i.e., the Day of Judgment.

**Yawmul Itsnain** (Ar: yawm al-ithnayn) Cal. Second day of the Muslim week, i.e. Tuesday.

**Yawmul Jaza** (In.) (Ar: yawm al-jazā') Doct. The Day of Judgment.

**Yawmul Jum'ah** (Ar: yawm al-jumu'ah) Cal. The sixth day of the Muslim week, i.e., Friday. It is the day of the communal prayer near the midday hour.

**Yawmul Khamis** (Ar: yawm al-khamis) Cal. The fifth day of the Muslim week, i.e., Thursday.

**Yawmul Kiamah** (In.) (Ar: yawm al-qiyamah) Doct. The Day of Judgment.

**Yawmul Mizan** (Ar: yawm al-mīzān) Doct. The Day of Judgment.

**Yawmul Sabt** (Ar: yawm as-sabt) Cal. The seventh day of the Muslim week, i.e., Saturday.

**Yawmul Tsulatsa'** (Ar: yawm ath-thulāthā') Cal. The third day of the Muslim week, i.e., Wednesday.

**Yayasan** (In.) Econ. A "foundation" under Indonesian civil law which can gather money and property for use of educational, social welfare, and religious activities. The Arabic term "waqf" is used only infrequently.

**Yayasan Amal Bhakti Muslimin Pancasila** (In.) Assn. "Foundation of Indonesian Muslim Pancasila," an endowment with close government ties which provide subsidies for the building of mosques and prayer houses.

**Yayasan Paramadinah** (In.) Assn. An endowed foundation, headed by Nurcholis Madjied (b. 1939), as a vehicle to promote post-modernist research and thinking as an approach to Islam's place in the contemporary world.

**Yayasan Perjalanan Haji Islam**. *See Kiblat.*

**Yogyakarta** (In.) Geog. 1. City of Central Java near outstanding pre-Islamic architectural wonders, such as Borobudur and Prambahanan. 2. The name of a kingdom which split off from the Surakarta kingdom in 1755. Rulers used both the titles of susuhunan and sultan. During the Dutch administration the court was controlled by the Dutch, but it championed the new Republic of Indonesia in 1945 and thereby retained its identity as a special district.

**Yunus** (Ar: yunūs) Qur. 1. A prophet mentioned in the Qur'an, associated by scholars with the Old Testament Jonah. He was swallowed by a large fish, but delivered up after acknowledging God. 2. The tenth chapter of the Qur'an, named after the Prophet Yunus. It contains the stories of Yunus and the whale and also the story of the Israelites in Egypt under Pharaoh.

**Yunus, Anis**. *See* **Muhammadiyah**.

**Yunus, Mahmud** (In.) Biog. (d. 1973) Minangkabau Muslim educator, trained in Egypt. He prepared a popular commentary on the Qur'an, a history of Muslim education in Indonesia, and other works on Islamic subjects.

**Yunus, Sultan**. *See* **Demak**.

**El Yunusi, Zainuddin Labai** (In.) Biog. (d. 1924) Educator in Minangkabau in the early part of the twentieth century.

**Yusuf**; Yusup (Ar: yūsuf) Qur. 1. A prophet mentioned in the Qur'an, associated by scholars with the Old Testament Joseph. 2. The twelfth chapter of the Qur'an, named after the Prophet Yusuf. It tells the story of the Prophet Yusuf and his miracles in Egypt, such as interpretation of dreams.

**Yusup, Maulana.** *See* **Bantam.**

# Z

**Zabaniyah, Zabaniah.** *See* **Malaikat.**

*Zabur* (In.) (Ar: zabūr) Qur. According to the Qur'an, a pre-Islamic scripture revealed by God to David, regarded as a reference to the Psalms of David.

*Zadul Ma'ad* (Ar: zād al-ma'ād) Lit. title. "Provisions for the Haven," by Ibnu Qayyim (d. 1350), is a biography of the Prophet Muhammad, used throughout the Muslim world.

**Al Zahir (Al Malik)** (In.) Biog. (d. 1326) Leading ruler of Samudera-Pasai in the mid-fourteenth century, when the Muslim traveler Ibnu Battutah (d. 1368) visited the area. The description tells of an Arab speaking court with a developed economic system and cultural accomplishments.

**Zaa'idah.** *See* **Sunan.**

**Zaidiyah** (Ar: zaydiyyah) Doct. A small Syiah sect, prominent in Yemen, quite close in outlook to Sunni Islam.

**Zainal Abidin, Sultan.** *See* **Samudera-Pasai.**

**Zainal Abidin.** *See* **Ternate.**

**Zainuddin al Malibari.** *See* **Al Malibari, Zainuddin.**

**Zakariya** (Ar: zakariyyā) Qur. A prophet mentioned in the Qur'an, associated by scholars with the Old Testament Zacharias, the father of John the Baptist.

**Zakat** (In.) (Ar: zakāh) Doct. The yearly religious tax required of all Muslims as part of their religious obligations. The tax is voluntary in Indonesia and is usually given to the poor through mosque committees. *Usage*: *harta yang di__kan*, assets to be assessed for the poor tax; *membayar* ___, *memberi(kan)* ___, to pay the poor tax; *mengeluarkan* ___, *menunaikan* ___, to give the poor tax; *pembayar* ___, payment of the poor tax; *perhitungan* ___, *ukuran* ___ *fitrah*, to calculate the amount of poor tax to be paid.

**Zalim** (In.); zhalim (Ar: z.ālim) Doct. Unjust, tyrannical.
*Usage*: *ke___an*, injustice, tyranny.

**Az Zalzalah** (Ar: az-zalzalah) Qur. "The Earthquake," the ninety-ninth chapter of the Qur'an. A very short, lyrical chapter foretelling a Day of Judgment when people's deeds will be judged. Also known as Az Zilzal.

**Zamakhsyari** (Ar: abū al-qāsim maḥmūd ibn 'umar az-zamakhshārī) Biog. (d. 1144). Persian scholar who was an authority on the Arabic language. His Qur'anic commentary maintains the Free Thinkers (Muktazalite) point of view and extols the beauty of the Qur'an. *See Al Kas-syaf* and **Tafsir**.

**Zamzam** (Ar: zamzam) Geog. A well near the Kabah in Makkah, considered sacred. The water from the well is considered by some to be especially holy, even containing magical powers.
*Usage*: *berwudlu air* ___, to purify oneself by bathing in water from the Zamzam well.

**Adz Zaariyaat**. Spelling variant. *See* **Adz Dzaariyaat**.

**Zarkasyi, Badaruddin** (Ar: muḥammad ibn bahādur az-zarkashī) Biog. (d. 1392). Syafii legalist from Egypt who wrote an important commentary and worked extensively with Traditions. *See Al Burhan fi 'Ulumil Qur'an*.

**Zat** (In.); dzaat (Ar:dhāt) Myst. Essence of God.
*Usage*: ___ *Allah*, ___ *Tuhan*, the essence of God; ___ *Yang Maha Kuasa*, the essence of God, the Most Powerful; ___ *Yang Satu*, the essence of God, the Only One.

**Zawiyah** (Ar: zāwiyah) Myst. Religious retreat especially for mystics, for prayer and invocation of the names of God (zikir), and other pious formulas. Syn: khanaqah.

**Zending** (Dutch) Relig. The Dutch term for mission activities, particularly those operated during the nineteenth and twentieth centuries in the Netherlands Indies. Muslim groups insisted that the presence of missionaries, well financed from Europe, were given special consideration and that even-handed treatment was not given Muslim activities. Syn: missi.

**Az Zhaahir; Az Zhahir** (Ar: aẓ-ẓāhir) Theo. Name of God meaning "The Outer."

**Zhahir, Sultan**. *See* **Samudera-Pasai.**

**Zhalim**. Spelling variant. *See* **Zalim.**

**Zhilailul Qur'an**. *See Fi Zhilailul Qur'an.*

**Ziarah** (In.) (Ar: ziyārah) Pop. Islam. Visitation to a shrine, grave or other object considered sacred. It is applied first and foremost to the Kabah in Makkah but can also mean visitation of saints' graves for the blessing that such visits are believed to bestow in popular Islam. *Usage*: *ber__kan kubur, men__i*, to visit a grave often for the purpose of gaining supernatural powers; ___ *ke makam nabi*, to visit the tomb of the Prophet (in Madinah); *pen__kan*, the act of visiting a tomb to gain supernatural powers.

**Zikir** (In.) dzikir (Ar: dhikr) Myst and Pop. Islam. Repetition of the names of Allah and certain religious formulae as a means of demonstrating piety or, in the case of mystics, also to induce a mystical trance. In zikir jahar, the repetition is spoken aloud, while in zikir khafi, the repetition is done silently. The most frequent formula used are as follows: ___ *La ilaaha illal Lah* (there is no god but God), ___ *Allahu Akbar* (God is Great!), ___ *Alhamdulillah* (All Praise to God!), and ___ *Subhanallah* (God is Holy!). *Usage*: *ber___ (kepada Allah)*, to recite the zikir formula; ___ *dengan hati*, silent recitation of the zikir formula. *ayat-ayat* ___ Qur'anic, verses referring to the repetition of God's name; *masalah* ___, the question of reciting the name of God and its place in proper religious observance; *membaca* ___, to recite the zikir formula (to God); *memperbanyak* ___, to increase the recitation of the zikir formula; *soal* ___, the issue of reciting the name of

God and its place in proper religious observance.

**Al Zikir**; Al Zikr (Ar: dhikr) Qur. A name of the Qur'an indicating that it has remembrance for humans and news for them.

**Az Zilzaal**; Az Zilzal (Ar: az-zilzāl) Qur. "The Earthquake," an alternate title for the ninety-ninth chapter of the Qur'an. Its usual name is Az Zalzalah.

**Zimmi**; dzimmi (Ar: dhimmī) Doct. A non-Muslim who is a member of a religion which was founded by a prophet with revelation from God, such as a Christian or a Jew.

**Zina** (In.); zinah (Ar: zinā) Juris. Fornication or any sexual intercourse between persons who are not in a state of legal matrimony or concubinage.
*Usage*: *ber___*, to be engaged in fornication.
*Anak* ___, bastard, child born out of wedlock; *dekati perbuatan* ___, to undertake fornication; *dosa* ___, the sin of fornication; *hukum per___an*, the laws concerning unauthorized sexual activity; *mendekati* ___, to undertake fornication; *per___an*, the act of fornication.

**Zindik** (In.); zindiq (Ar: zindīq fr. Persian zand) Doct. "Free interpretation," hence heresy, originally applied to the Dualists (Manicheans) who believed in good and evil, light and darkness. Now a general term for heresy.
*Usage*: *kafir-* ___, disbelief in Islam; *orang-orang* ___, people in history who believed in doctrines found in gross error by the Sunni community.

**Zuama** (In.); zu'ama' (Ar: zu'amā') Pol. Societal or governmental leader.

*Zuhratul Murid* (Ar: ẓuhrat al-murīd) Lit. title. "Guide for the Student," a treatise on God's unity (tauhid) by Abdus Samad Al Palimbani (d. 1828), which enjoyed some popularity in Southeast Asia in the early nineteenth century.

**Zuhri, Saifuddin** (In.) Biog. (b. 1919) Journalist, educator and political figure associated with the Nahdlatul Ulama. Minister of Religion 1962 to 1967. *See* **Menteri Agama**.

**Zuhud** (In.) (Ar: zuhd) Doct. Abstinence, religious life. Exercising oneself in the service of God, especially being abstinent in respect to eating and subduing the passions.
*Usage*: *hidup* ___, a life of abstinence; *orang* ___, an ascetic; *sikap* ___, an attitude of abstinence.

**Zuhur**; dhuhur; lohor (Ar: ẓuhr) Juris. The name of the required prayer performed at midday. Syn: lohor.
*Usage*: *sembahyang sunnat ba'diyah* ___, doing the midday prayer in parts at intervals of time because of circumstances; *sembahyang sunnat qabliyah* ___, extra, optional prayer undertaken at midday to earn merit.

**Az Zukhruf** (Ar: az-zukhruf) Qur. "The Armaments," the forty-third chapter of the Qur'an. It contrasts the wealth of the rich with the worship of real believers.

**Zulhijah** (In.); zulhijjah; dzulhijjah (Ar: dhu al-ḥijjah) Cal. The twelfth month of the Islamic calendar, with the meaning "the month of pilgrimage." On the 8th, 9th, and 10th the rites of the pilgrimage take place at Makkah. On the 10th is Idul Adha, the feast of sacrifice, when all financially able Muslim families normally sacrifice an animal.

**Zulkaidah** (In.); zulqaidah; dzulqaidah (dhu l-qa'dah) Cal. The 11th month of the Islamic calendar, meaning "the month of rest."

**Zulkifli** (Ar: dhul-kifl) Qur. A prophet mentioned in the Qur'an.

**Az Zumar** (Ar: az-zumar) Qur. "The Troops," the thirty-ninth chapter of the Qur'an. It relates how God has established all creation in categories and on Judgment Day there will be a final sorting of humans for heaven and hell.

**Monographs in International Studies**
**Titles Available from Ohio University Press**
**1995**

**Southeast Asia Series**

**No. 56 Duiker, William J.** Vietnam Since the Fall of Saigon. 1989. Updated ed. 401 pp. Paper 0-89680-162-4 $20.00.

**No. 64 Dardjowidjojo, Soenjono.** Vocabulary Building in Indone–sian: An Advanced Reader. 1984. 664 pp. Paper 0- 89680-118-7 $26.00.

**No. 65 Errington, J. Joseph.** Language and Social Change in Java: Linguistic Reflexes of Modernization in a Traditional Royal Polity. 1985. 210 pp. Paper 0-89680-120-9 $20.00.

**No. 66 Tran, Tu Binh.** The Red Earth: A Vietnamese Memoir of Life on a Colonial Rubber Plantation. Tr. by John Spragens. 1984. 102 pp. (SEAT*, V. 5) Paper 0-89680-119-5 $11.00.

**No. 68 Syukri, Ibrahim.** History of the Malay Kingdom of Patani. 1985. 135 pp. Paper 0-89680-123-3 $12.00.

**No. 69 Keeler, Ward.** Javanese: A Cultural Approach. 1984. 559 pp. Paper 0-89680-121-7 $25.00.

**No. 70 Wilson, Constance M. and Lucien M. Hanks.** Burma-Thai land Frontier Over Sixteen Decades: Three Descriptive Docu ments. 1985. 128 pp. Paper 0-89680-124-1 $11.00.

**No. 71 Thomas, Lynn L. and Franz von Benda-Beckmann,** eds. Change and Continuity in Minangkabau: Local, Regional, and Historical Perspectives on West Sumatra. 1985. 353 pp. Paper 0-89680-127-6 $16.00.

*SEAT= Southeast Asia Translation Project Group

**No. 72 Reid, Anthony and Oki Akira,** eds. The Japanese Experience in Indonesia: Selected Memoirs of 1942-1945. 1986. 424 pp., 20 illus. (SEAT, V. 6) Paper 0-89680-132-2 $20.00.

**No. 73 Smirenskaia, Ahanna D.** Peasants in Asia: Social Conscious ness and Social Struggle. Tr. by Michael J. Buckley. 1987. 239 pp. Paper 0-89680-134-9 $14.00.

**No. 74 McArthur M. S. H.** Report on Brunei in 1904. Introduced and Annotated by A.V.M. Horton. 1987. 297 pp. Paper 0-89680-135-7 $15.00.

**No. 75 Lockard, Craig A.** From Kampung to City: A Social History of Kuching, Malaysia,1820-1970. 1987. 325 pp. Paper 0-89680-136-5 $16.00.

**No. 76 McGinn, Richard,** ed. Studies in Austronesian Linguistic 1986. 516 pp. Paper 0-89680-137-3 $20.00.

**No. 77 Muego, Benjamin N.** Spectator Society: The Philippines Under Martial Rule. 1986. 232 pp. Paper 0-89680-138-1 $15.00.

**No. 79 Walton, Susan Pratt.** Mode in Javanese Music. 1987. 278 pp. Paper 0-89680-144-6 $15.00.

**No. 80 Nguyen Anh Tuan.** South Vietnam: Trial and Experience. 1987. 477 pp., tables. Paper 0-89680-141-1 $18.00.

**No. 82 Spores, John C.** Running Amok: An Historical Inquiry. 1988. 190 pp. Paper 0-89680-140-3 $13.00.

**No. 83 Malaka, Tan.** From Jail to Jail. Tr. by Helen Jarvis. 1991. 1209 pp., three volumes. (SEAT V. 8) Paper 0-89680-150-0 $55.00.

**No. 84 Devas, Nick, with Brian Binder, Anne Booth, Kenneth Davey, and Roy Kelly.** Financing Local Government in Indonesia. 1989. 360 pp.Paper 0-89680-153-5 $20.00.

**No. 85 Suryadinata, Leo.** Military Ascendancy and Political Culture: A Study of Indonesia's Golkar. 1989. 235 pp., illus., glossary, append., index, bibliog. Paper 0-89680-154-3 $18.00.

**No. 86 Williams, Michael.** Communism, Religion, and Revolt in Banten in the Early Twentieth Century. 1990. 390 pp. Paper 0-89680-155-1 $14.00.

**No. 87 Hudak, Thomas.** The Indigenization of Pali Meters in Thai Poetry. 1990. 247 pp. Paper 0-89680-159-4 $15.00.

**No. 88 Lay, Ma Ma.** Not Out of Hate: A Novel of Burma. Tr. by Margaret Aung-Thwin. Ed. by William Frederick. 1991. 260 pp. (SEAT V. 9) Paper 0-89680-167-5 $20.00.

**No. 89 Anwar, Chairil.** The Voice of the Night: Complete Poetry and Prose of Chairil Anwar . 1992. Revised Edition. Tr. by Burton Raffel. 196 pp. Paper 0-89680-170-5 $17.00.

**No. 90 Hudak, Thomas John,** tr., The Tale of Prince Samuttakote: A Buddhist Epic from Thailand. 1993. 230 pp. Paper 0-89680-174-8 $20.00.

**No. 91 Roskies, D.M.,** ed. Text/Politics in Island Southeast Asia: Essays in Interpretation. 1993. 330 pp. Paper 0-89680-175-6 $25.00.

**No. 92 Schenkhuizen, Marguérite, translated by Lizelot Stout van Balgooy.** Memoirs of an Indo Woman: Twentieth-Century Life in the East Indies and Abroad. 1993. 312pp. Paper 0-89680-178-0 $23.00

**No. 93 Salleh, Muhammad Haji.** Beyond the Archipelago: Selected Poems. 1995. 247pp. Paper 0-89680-181-0 $20.00.

**No. 94 Federspiel, Howard M.** A Dictionary of Indonesian Islam. 1995. 327 pp. Paper 0-89680-182-9 $25.00.

## Africa Series

**No. 43 Harik, Elsa M. and Donald G. Schilling.** The Politics of Educa tion in Colonial Algeria and Kenya. 1984. 102 pp. Paper 0-89680-117-9 $12.50.

**No. 44 Smith, Daniel R.** The Influence of the Fabian Colonial Bureau on the Independence Movement in Tanganyika. 1985. 99 pp. Paper 0-89680-125-X $11.00.

**No. 45 Keto, C. Tsehloane.** American-South African Relations 1784-1980: Review and Select Bibliography. 1985. 169 pp. Paper 0-89680-128-4 $11.00.

**No. 46 Burness, Don,** ed. Wanasema: Conversations with African Writers. 1985. 103 pp. Paper 0-89680-129-2 $11.00.

**No. 47 Switzer, Les.** Media and Dependency in South Africa: A Case Study of the Press and the Ciskei "Homeland". 1985. 97 pp. Paper 0-89680-130-6 $10.00.

**No. 49 Hart, Ursula Kingsmill.** Two Ladies of Colonial Algeria: The Lives and Times of Aurelie Picard and Isabelle Eberhardt. 1987. 153 pp. Paper 0-89680-143-8 $11.00.

**No. 51 Clayton, Anthony and David Killingray.** Khaki and Blue: Military and Police in British Colonial Africa. 1989. 347 pp. Paper 0-89680-147-0 $18.00.

**No. 52 Northrup, David.** Beyond the Bend in the River: African Labor in Eastern Zaire, 1864-1940. 1988. 282 pp. Paper 0-89680-151-9 $15.00.

**No. 53 Makinde, M. Akin.** African Philosophy, Culture, and Traditional Medicine. 1988. 172 pp. Paper 0-89680-152-7 $16.00.

**No. 54 Parson, Jack,** ed. Succession to High Office in Botswana: Three Case Studies. 1990. 455 pp. Paper 0-89680-157-8 $20.00.

**No.56 Staudinger, Paul.** In the Heart of the Hausa States. Tr. by Johanna E. Moody. Foreword by Paul Lovejoy. 1990. In two volumes. 469 + 224 pp.,maps, apps. Paper 0-89680-160-8 (2 vols.) $35.00.

**No. 57 Sikainga, Ahmad Alawad.** The Western Bahr Al-Ghazal under British Rule, 1898-956. 1991. 195 pp.

**No. 58 Wilson, Louis E.** The Krobo People of Ghana to 1892: A Political and Social History. 1991. 285 pp. Paper 0-89680-164-0 $20.00.

**No. 59 du Toit, Brian M.** Cannabis, Alcohol, and the South African Student: Adolescent Drug Use, 1974-1985. 1991. 176 pp., notes, tables. Paper 0-89680-166-7 $17.00.

**No. 60 Falola, Toyin and Dennis Itavyar,** eds. The Political Economy of Health in Africa. 1992. 258 pp., notes. Paper 0-89680-168-3 $17.00.

**No. 61 Kiros, Tedros.** Moral Philosophy and Development: The Human Condition in Africa.1992. 199 pp., notes. Paper. 0-89680-171-3 $18.00.

**No. 62 Burness, Don.** Echoes of the Sunbird: An Anthology of Contemporary African Poetry. 1993. 198pp. Paper 0-89680-173-X $17.00.

**No. 63 Glew, Robert S. and Chaibon Babalé.** Hausa Folktales from Niger. 1993. 100pp. Paper 0-89680-176-4 $15.00.

**No. 64 Nelson, Samuel H.** Colonialism in the Congo Basin 1880-1940. 1993. 248 pp. Paper 089680-180-2 $20.00.

## Latin America Series

**No. 9 Tata, Robert J.** Structural Changes in Puerto Rico's Economy: 1947-1976. 1981. 118 pp. Paper 0-89680-107-1 $12.00.

**No. 12 Wallace, Brian F.** Ownership and Development: A Comparison of Domestic and Foreign Firms in Colombian Manufacturing. 1987. 185 pp. Paper 0-89680-145-4 $10.00.

**No. 13 Henderson, James D.** Conservative Thought in Latin America The Ideas of Laureo Gomez. 1988. 229 pp. Paper 0-89680-148-9 $13.00.

**No. 16 Alexander, Robert J.** Juscelino Kubitschek and the Development of Brazil. 1991. 500 pp., notes, bibliog. Paper 0-89680-163-2 $25.00.

**No. 17 Mijeski, Kenneth J.**, ed. The Nicaraguan Constitution of 1987: English Translation and Commentary. 1991. 355 pp. Paper 0-89680-165-9 $25.00.

**No. 18 Finnegan, Pamela.** The Tension of Paradox: Jose Donoso's *The Obscene Bird of Night* as Spiritual Exercises. 1992. 204 pp. Paper 0-89680-169-1 $15.00.

**No. 19 Kim, Sung Ho and Thomas W. Walker,** eds. Perspectives on War and Peace in Central America. 1992. 155 pp., notes, bibliog. Paper 0-89680-172-1 $14.00.

**No. 20 Becker, Marc.** Mariategui and Latin American Marxist Theory. 1993. 239 pp. Paper 0-89680-177-2 $18.00.

**No. 21 Boschetto-Sandoval, Sandra M. and Marcia Phillips McGowan,** eds. Claribel Alegria and Central American Literature. 1994. 263 pp., illus. Paper 0-89680-179-9 $20.00.

**No. 22 Zimmerman, Marc.** Literature and Resistance in Guatemala: Textual Modes and Cultural Politics from El Señor Presidente to Rigoberta Menchú. 1995. 2 volume set 320 + 370 pp., notes, bibliog. Paper 0-89680-183-7 $40.00.

## ORDERING INFORMATION

Individuals are encouraged to patronize local bookstores wherever possible. Orders for titles in the Monographs in International Studies may be placed directly through the Ohio University Press, Scott Quadrangle, Athens, Ohio 45701-2979. Individuals should remit payment by check, VISA, or MasterCard. * Those ordering from the United Kingdom, Continental Europe, the Middle East, and Africa should order through Academic and University Publishers Group, 1 Gower Street, London WC1E, England. Orders from the Pacific Region, Asia, Australia, and New Zealand should be sent to East-West Export Books, c/o the University of Hawaii Press, 2840 Kolowalu Street, Honolulu, Hawaii 96822, USA.

Individuals ordering from ouside of the U.S. should remit in U.S. funds to Ohio University Press either by International Money Order or by a check drawn on a U.S. bank.** Most out-of-print titles may be ordered from University Microfilms, Inc., 300 North Zeeb Road, Ann Arbor, Michigan 48106, USA.

Prices are subject to change without notice.

* Please add $3.50 for the first book and $.75 for each additional book for shipping and handling.

** Outside the U.S please add $4.50 for the first book and $.75 for each additional book.

www.ingramcontent.com/pod-product-compliance
Ingram Content Group UK Ltd.
Pitfield, Milton Keynes, MK11 3LW, UK
UKHW031843110225
454967UK00001B/20

9 780896 801820